PLANK ON FRAME

PLANK ON FRAME

The Who, What and Where of 150 Boatbuilders

PAUL LIPKE

INTERNATIONAL MARINE PUBLISHING COMPANY
CAMDEN, MAINE

To John Gardner
Advocate, boatbuilder, scholar, teacher, and friend

Library of Congress Catalog Card Number 80-80779
International Standard Book Number 0-87742-121-8
Typeset by A & B Typesetters, Inc., Concord, New Hampshire
Printed and bound by Halliday Lithograph, North Quincy, Massachusetts

Published by International Marine Publishing Company
21 Elm Street, Camden, Maine 04843

Contents

Preface

This book is the direct result of an independently funded survey of the professionally active, plank-on-frame, wooden boatbuilders of the United States. For a year, on foot and by automobile, I traveled over 40,000 miles, encompassing the Gulf, the Great Lakes, and the East and West Coasts. The survey is an overview of the traditional boatbuilding scene, accompanied by interviews with professional builders and sources. These interviews constitute the core of the survey and are based upon a questionnaire covering a broad spectrum, from opinions on the future availability of lumber and hardware to questions of function versus form.

Despite the survey format, this is a subjective book, so I wish to clarify some of my background and the sources of inspiration for this project.

Five years ago I wanted to learn how to build wooden boats, but I had rarely been aboard one. In fact, the bulk of my experience on the water consisted of ferry trips and daysailing a 15-foot fiberglass sloop. I had not grown up around boatyards, worked on wooden boats, or known any wooden boat devotees. However, I had sailed a gaff-rigged wooden sloop once or twice and was determined to find out how she was put together.

I knew nothing of the field. I had never heard of the various trade journals, or the work of John Gardner. I didn't know Whitehall was anything more than a street name, or that they built a lot of boats in Maine. With determination as my only guide, I pursued my interest in rather unorthodox ways.

At the Massachusetts Institute of Technology Library I looked into the trade listings and wrote down the address of each yard that had "wood" printed next to its name. I wrote 186 letters of application to boatyards located everywhere from New Zealand to the Isle of Wight. Of the three responses I received, only one (from England) was positive. Though the British labor board refused to grant me working papers, I was encouraged by the breakthrough and kept trying. Eventually, someone introduced me to John Gardner, *National Fisherman*, and the Maine coast; I began to make real progress. In time I found work with a fine builder in midcoast Maine, learning more in my first two hours on the job than I had in the previous year of reading and studying about boats.

During the next two years I had a hand in building several traditional boats: a peapod, a 14-foot Whitehall, and a 22-foot Friendship sloop. I spent a few weekends helping friends rebuild a 65-ton schooner. Then I began preparing for a six-month vagabonding tour of the United States—not in order to see *more* boats, but to take an extended vacation from them. As the planning phase drew to a close and the departure date drew closer, my feelings moderated. While I still expected to spend most of my time away from boats, I could not resist the opportunity to visit the famous yards of other regions. At about this time I saw John Gardner's comment in *National Fisherman* on the need for a survey of the various boatbuilding schools and wondered, "Why not survey boatbuilders?"

This was the first of a series of crucial turning points in my planning. As the weeks went by, the idea of an informal survey became more and more appealing. Those 186 letters gave me great sympathy for others struggling to get information on wooden boatbuilding. Question One: How does one get information, not "how to" data, but information on who is doing what? From working in boat shops I'd gained a professional builder's perspective and a serious interest in meeting their needs. What are those needs? Labor and materials mostly. Question Two: How do boatbuilders see the labor and material situations developing over the near, and not so near, future? Last, conflicting reports in the trade journals as to what was going on aroused my curiosity about the industry as a whole, regional differences, why discrepancies occurred, and so forth. Question Three: Is there a cohesiveness among wooden boatbuilders? Is there really a wooden boat revival?

Excited by the prospect of getting answers to these questions, I brainstormed further. Out of a list of just over a hundred questions, I chose 23, edited them, and typed up a questionnaire. I had a few extra copies made so I could use one at each yard, but I was still doing it just for myself. It was an "excuse" for interrupting boatbuilders. At that point I never even considered doing a proper survey with controlled variables and provable statistics. I just wanted to have a good time, not bother the builders too much, and continue to vagabond. I wrote, without success, to various periodicals and editors asking for lists of wooden boat builders. So I decided to go directly to Port Townsend, Washington, for the First Annual Wooden Boat Festival to kick off the vagabonding with a bang and get a lot of information about builders at the same time.

From that point on, my involvement escalated haphazardly, but rapidly. Even after the tremendous response to the idea at Port Townsend, I refused to commit myself. To those who asked, I'd say that *after* sightseeing, I was going to visit as many yards as I felt like visiting, but I couldn't say whether that would be 10 or a thousand. One contributing factor to my dilettantish attitude was my feeling about writing. Coming from a long line of innovative, persevering overachievers, I had reacted strongly and negatively to pre-departure suggestions from family and friends that I write up my experiences on the road and/or with the survey. It was important to me that I break away from the family habit and learn to do *nothing*; that I go on a trip of indeterminate length with no particular purpose, to no particular place, and do nothing particular with that experience except enjoy it. I had gone so far as to swear that I wouldn't write about the trip, because I wanted that promise to help me stay straight on the path of uselessness. Though I wavered at times, I held to my vow for the first few months.

Then, late one night in Oregon, while discussing the difficulties of keeping up with what is going on in the maritime world, author Terry Lesh and I came up with an unusual and seemingly foolproof solution. It was such a brainstorm that I broke all my promises. The idea was to use professional builders as the core of a loosely formalized grapevine of communication. That answered my first question about getting information. Port Townsend's Festival, visits to Dick Wagner's Old Boathouse, and Land Washburn's plans for the Wooden Boat Shop had already answered my question on the reality of the revival. As for the question (regarding labor and materials) I thought that at least the questionnaire would give some indication as to how concerned builders are about them. So what had begun as a six-month vacation ended as a two-year project.

As a result of this unsystematic development and my onetime questionable commitment, there are holes in this work. I have written only what I felt qualified to say, and only when I thought it would be of significant interest. If there is a general shortage of hard comparisons and statistics, it is due to my distrust of them, since they can be made to prove anything. It is important to remember that controlling all the variables in order to produce meaningful statistical tables would be a task of herculean dimensions far beyond what is appropriate to wooden boatbuilding at the present time. Nor is it something one man and $5,000 could accomplish. This project is based on that uncommon commodity called "common sense" and the most unscientific source imaginable, the grapevine. It is more concerned with the people of wooden boatbuilding than with the boats themselves. I may have given extra weight to a concern only one builder expressed on the basis of his tone, or the look in his eyes. If the information seems to point in different directions from those I take, please disagree with me, but keep the context in mind. If while writing of boatbuilding on the Gulf I speak positively of planking without shape or taper, I am not recommending it for all regions or conditions. Each individual, town, or region must develop its own programs and solutions, borrowing from and sharing with others only what is productive in the best sense of the word. There is certainly room for everyone. The heart and soul of traditional watercraft lie in individuality and the integrity of personal values.

Acknowledgments

I cannot begin to thank all the people who contributed to this book. The list goes far beyond those mentioned, and I am grateful to all who had a hand in what follows.

Special thanks go to all the members of my family, friends, and strangers who recognized the particular challenges of truly independent research/traveling, and who did their best to send me on my way with love and understanding.

John Gardner's unflagging encouragement has been a constant source of joy and inspiration. I am sure that at times he thought I was crazy, but he never let me down. Land Washburn and the Rabinowitz family of Seattle gave unstintingly of every kind of help, far beyond the call of friendship. Dick Jagels, now of Winterthur, Delaware, provided a jumping-off point for my forays into the Louisiana bayous and an invaluable perspective on wood utilization. Staff members of both *WoodenBoat* and *National Fisherman,* especially Jon Wilson, Maynard Bray, and Dave Getchell, have been most generous with their time, print space, and moral support.

Last, but never least, my thanks to my parents and to my wife, Marcelle, a lady of great courage, honesty, and endurance.

Introduction

This book is not intended as an in-depth study of wooden boatbuilding; it is an attempt to stimulate, inform, and serve many, at the risk of missing the mark completely. Some may want to read it cover to cover, others will skim according to their interests. It can help with needed repairs, enliven a dull evening, and/or encourage the pursuit of more detailed information on many related topics.

The resurgence of interest in traditional watercraft has created a tremendous demand among amateurs and professionals for pertinent information. Where can they find a thousand board feet of cedar? Is there an experienced finish man available? What's happening in traditional boatbuilding in other areas?

The central vehicle for this information is the grapevine, a web of people, projects, and places that runs through every aspect of the field. As a means of problem solving and information gathering, the grapevine has an ability to grow that is as interconnected and diverse as the field itself. It can thus be an increasingly useful tool for the person who is willing to invest his time and energy in making it work. In the wooden boatbuilding field, the key to successful use of the grapevine is found in active professional builders.

As a group, these builders are most knowledgeable: more than the amateur builders, traditional watercraft enthusiasts, fishermen, harbormasters, sailmakers, marina foremen, anyone, they know what's going on in their area, who's doing it, where to get X material, or how to solve a problem. If a builder doesn't know the answer, he knows someone who does, or at the very least, someone who can steer him in the right direction. The builders themselves are the heaviest users of the grapevine, constantly tapping it to keep in touch with their field. By tapping into *them*, the reader taps into the heart of the grapevine. However, I wanted the survey to do more than provide the reader with this point of access. It should also do something for the builders.

Much has been written about the boats themselves; how to build, maintain, design, sail, or power them; why we love them; discussions of particular designs; the historical significance of a classic type; the great yards, voyages, and/or boats of yesteryear. Not much has been written about the men and women who build them. What of their lives, interests, concerns, and views of the future? The survey gives builders the opportunity to speak out on questions that reflect their concerns, and, in addition, share the benefits of:

- A more extensive grapevine
- Increased business opportunities
- A basis for either formal or informal organization among themselves on a national, regional, or local scale
- Compensation, where appropriate, for the thousands of hours they spend consulting would-be clients and enthusiasts
- Greater recognition from the boating public of who they are, what they do, and why.

If this book is free of the idolatry that mars much of what little has been written about wooden boatbuilders, so much the better. What is really needed is plain knowledge, access, appreciation, and some sense of perspective. The entire field is not encompassed in this book, but hopefully the flavor, the essence, and a sense of balance are distilled into it.

Finally, a note about perspective. In a sense, this is not a book strictly about wooden boats, but rather one about quality. While it is impossible to say whether the boom in boating would have occurred without fiberglass and the attendant advertising, new levels in waterborne recreation are here, and the whole field has been opened to other mediums, from ferrocement to cold-molding and Airex foam. Wood can only take its fair share. Among serious enthusiasts, there is decreasing support for the purist who argues ceaselessly and vehemently with those who advocate the use of some other material. People who do this are simply insecure in themselves. An aware person presents his view as an alternative—no more, no less—and would not put down a fellow quality buff because his boat isn't built of wood. Fiberglass isn't inherently bad; it is what the industry so often does with it that turns off the traditional boat enthusiast. Few people complain about fiberglass Friendship sloops; they do complain about "glitter-decked, gizmo-encrusted, chrome-plated, badly designed and put together illusions of boats." Plastic, like much we make, can be beautiful. It is the application of a philosophy of "quality" to their view of the entire world that accounts for the enthusiasts' vehement feelings. Indeed, it is this that makes it all worthwhile.

Amidst the heavy timbers and vertical grain fir,
While walking among sharp, bright old tools
And even sharper, brighter minds,
Talking of bronze and galvanization
With a sixth-generation shipwright or first-generation skiff builder,
There is inspiration;
Unequaled demands for excellence within intended purpose.

I.
A National Perspective

LET'S HEAR IT FOR TEREDOS

The vagabond takes his time. It is, after all, the only thing he has a lot of. But that first morning was different. I had to cross the continent to reach the First Annual Port Townsend (Washington) Wooden Boat Festival. I had planned this vacation for years; I wanted to get on with it. My rider/driver, Nick, loaded his duffel and concurred, "Let's make tracks!"

We did, all of 30 miles, until I realized that my "friendly" mechanic had sabotaged the engine. We'd hardly made it off the highway before the lack of power degenerated into severe overheating and strange noises. We'd gotten all the way to Worcester, Massachusetts. I wondered aloud, "Maybe I can find a freelance mechanic."

Nick stared at me, "In Worcester? In August? On a Sunday? At nine o'clock? Are you nuts?"

We coughed and sputtered our way around the somnolent town until we found a coffee shop. Within 15 minutes, the young couple behind the counter had located and called a friend of a friend, named Al. He lived 17 miles away, but he said he'd be there in 30 minutes. The car was fixed in 50.

"Were the points okay?"

"Well, my 'friend' replaced them last week . . . but now that you've asked, the dwellmeter was a little jumpy just now."

He looked into the distributor, "He put in the wrong set of points." Al put in another set from his tool box and adjusted them. "Drive it 'round the block."

I came back, beaming. "You're a genius!"

"No, just a middle-aged man who's been around. Guys will do that just to get you to bring the car back for more work. Send me a postcard from Seattle. Ten dollars."

"Thirty-five miles of driving, the parts and labor, for 10 bucks!" Nick exclaimed as we hit Route 90 again. "I didn't think they made people like that anymore."

I was to find that a lot of wooden boatbuilders were "like that"; this theme was to recur (with variations) for the rest of my journey.

From that slow start, we gathered momentum. There is an unnamed force to be felt in a fast cross-continental drive. It derives from the rapid changes in the land; predawn cruises through empty city streets; the sudden engulfing night of the prairie beyond. We were in the grip of that momentum through Buffalo, Chicago, Sheridan—until Nick and I parted company on a Seattle entrance ramp. From there on, I traveled alone.

I had built a bed where the back seat and storage compartment used to be, and with the top down, I stretched out under the trees of Vashon Island, musing upon the future in the light of the past.

Man had always built boats and taken to the water with an awareness that he was doing something special. The sea is a unique force. The difficulties of both boat construction and boat handling gave added meaning to the vessels, large and small, that made life and commerce on the water possible. Real life at sea was hardly the stuff of children's tales. Boats leaked, food was awful, discipline severe, and boredom worse. A sailor's relationship with his craft was a matter of love and hate, especially in bad weather. The better built the boat, the more love and the less hate. Good craft earned their builders reputations to match.

A boatyard's existence was often precarious. Shipbuilders and boatbuilders had to go farther and farther afield for lumber. The market fluctuated with the weather, the erratic fishing industry, and politics. In the last century, new construction (as opposed to repair) was a way for yards to keep their best craftsmen busy during the slow periods.

Through social, political, and scientific upheavals, the wooden link of boatbuilding remained unbroken—from the first hollowed-out log through the Vikings to the present century. Except for a few very specialized exceptions, wood was basically unchallenged as the material for boatbuilding. Then plywood, aluminum, plywood-covered-with-fiberglass, and finally fiberglass-reinforced plastic made their way onto the scene. In a few quickly passing decades, boating values seemed to shift away from seaworthiness and durability, to styling and "sellability."

Fiberglass was a businessman's dream come true. Mass production and unskilled to semiskilled labor could lay up inexpensive, first-rate hulls that looked like a million dollars. The cartoon shown here appeared in 1948.

But the advantages of fiberglass were too many and too far reaching to be ignored or passed off with cynicism. Experimental projects became common. While the boats improved during the late Forties and Fifties, the risks became

apparent. There were fortunes to be made, with the recreational boating world at stake.

Between 1946 and 1953, approximately 4,000 small boats were produced annually in fiberglass. In 1954 that figure jumped to 16,000 units; by 1957 it was 55,000. The material begged for misuse because the high-gloss finish could hide bad layup, improper curing, even unfair hulls, from the untrained eyes of the public. Trade articles from this period suggested that sales tactics be geared more toward styling and convenience than utility. It was at about this time that the use of high-visibility showrooms for boats flourished.

The fine nature of the material, the way it lent itself to shoddy work and intense advertising, many good boats, and the acceptance of poor ones, combined with the public's increasing mobility and leisure time to bring unprecedented numbers of people to the fiberglass market. By 1960, the cartoons were more like the one shown on the next page.

The result was a crash within the wooden boat industry. Through the late Fifties, Sixties, and early Seventies, wood yards went bankrupt; switched over to fiberglass; evolved into repair, hauling, and storage facilities; became chandleries, boat dealerships, souvenir shops—or were simply sold out. The devastation was such that by the mid-Sixties, each of the few remaining wood fanatics (as others were wont to call them) felt almost alone in his dedication.

Yet in the late Sixties, even as the decline continued, there was a change. There were those who came to wooden boats as part of their rejection of a society that they found fraught with plastic—plastic food, plastic bombs, plastic morality. The few diehards who had stayed in touch brought together the disparate individuals. Some had published vital articles and books, while others had helped establish the expanding maritime museums. In 1965 at Clayton, New York, and in 1970 at Mystic Seaport, Connecticut, there were gatherings of traditionalists that were bellwethers of this shift. The Antique Boat Show at Clayton and the Rowing Workshop at Mystic were meant to slow

(WARNING! Yacht builders or show exhibitors adopting any of the above ideas do so at their own risk. Neither the artist nor the publishers are responsible people.—Ed.)

a desperate decline rather than spearhead a resurgence. Traditional boating was so close to disappearing that not even the organizers believed it could be revived. But relatively quickly, to their surprise, such gatherings increased. However, the decline had not been stopped; rather, the few wooden boat devotees had coalesced eagerly.

In 1974, ex-boatbuilder Jon Wilson published a magazine called *WoodenBoat* from a cabin in Maine. Circulation hit 30,000 in three years. The magazine reported on and carried advertisements from an increasing number and variety of boat shops. There was much talk of a *flourishing* interest in wooden boats. But new levels of interest did not necessarily guarantee business for the surviving professional builders, let alone the bumper crop of new, unproven ones. No one knew whether the builders were actually making a living entirely from new construction.

I wanted to know about the revival: what it was; what forces were behind it; where it was going. It made sense to go to those who were most heavily involved, those who had committed their lives and livelihoods to building wooden boats. My experience building boats in Maine had left me insatiably curious. Although at first the Port Townsend Wooden Boat Festival was only the starting point for my vagabonding, circumstances and my curiosity were to make it the starting point for a survey of professional wooden boatbuilders on the West, East, and Gulf Coasts, and the Great Lakes. The few professional builders I'd known were remarkable men. They were woodworkers, marine designers, and sometimes plumbers, electricians, and red-tape cutters all rolled into one. Yet most took home a wage far below what was commensurate with their skills. What motivated them? The amateur builders and enthusiasts I knew were largely moved by romance: love of the sea, the desire to work with their hands and natural materials, dreams of a return to an earlier, simpler age. The professionals were scornful of romance. They were practical men who fiercely maintained that it was "just a job like any other." Their fierceness belied their words. I wanted to find out why. One thing led to another, and eventually led to that spot under the trees on Vashon Island.

Port Townsend lies in the crook of the elbow of Puget Sound, and in the rain shadow of the Olympic Mountains, so it receives only a fraction of the Olympic Peninsula's 140 inches of annual rainfall. It has been called the Martha's Vineyard of the West Coast. Like the Vineyard, PT (as it is called by the locals) has a milder climate than the surrounding area, historic period architecture, easy access to major cities, craft shops, skyrocketing real estate, and tourists galore. This first of the Port Townsend Wooden Boat Festivals, in September 1977, astounded organizers and visitors alike. Three to five thousand devotees and more than a hundred wooden boats crammed the town and harbor for three days of nonstop boat talk, lectures, demonstrations, and races. There was bronze casting and toolmaking. Spike Africa, self-appointed "President of the Pacific Ocean," regaled crowds with tall tales and lessons in, "How not to dress like a landlubber." In the evenings, there was folk dancing, eating, drinking, and more gabbing. The participants overflowed the local bars, where the regulars grew so full of wooden boat talk that by the second evening there were shouts of, "I love dry rot. LET'S HEAR IT FOR TEREDOS!" Other wooden boat gatherings over the previous 10 years had laid the groundwork, but none had approached PT's size, duration, or energy. Wooden boat buffs had pulled out all the stops and the dark days were over.

Clayton, New York; Mystic, Connecticut; Christmas Cove, Maine; Cape

A wall of masts rises from Point Hudson, a perfect setting for the Port Townsend Wooden Boat Festival. Formerly a Coast Guard base, the narrow, U-shaped harbor had more traditional small craft displayed along its banks than were in the water.

Spike Africa hams it up for the author. With his nimble hands, he is wrapping a bottle in exquisite rope work. (He avoids the term "macrame.") In the background, boatbuilder Bob Coe looks over the Festival's schedule after arriving from Waldron Island in his Whitehall—a 40-mile row/sail.

Cod, Massachusetts; Santa Cruz, San Diego, and San Francisco, California; Seattle and Port Townsend, Washington, have all hosted significant gatherings of traditional watercraft enthusiasts. The Traditional Small Craft Association (TSCA) is developing and expanding a system of local chapters. There are boat shows, festivals, boat meets, and celebrations, each with their own style and approach. Some are primarily educational, others are for the pure fun of it. Weekend workshops and symposiums have grown in number, along with boatbuilding schools and apprenticeship programs. The circulations of the traditional watercraft periodicals continue to grow healthily. A random sampling of the builders listed shows an impressive number and variety of boats under construction:

36′ W. Garden schooner .... Shelton, WA
32′ and 38′ J. McGlasson sloops .... Newport, OR
42′ G. Vik gaff schooner .... Cathlamet, WA
34′ and 38′ W. Holland workboats .... Biloxi, MS
21′ tug and 31′ bay shrimper .... Bacliff, TX

73′ shrimpers by the score . . . . St. Augustine, FL
26′ Presto-style cat ketch . . . . Gloucester, NC
25′ deadrise sportfisherman . . . . White Stone, VA
36′ L. F. Herreshoff *Diddikai* . . . . Solomons, MD
37′ T. Gillmer ketch . . . . Boothbay, ME
26′ and 28′ A. Day lobsterboats . . . . Deer Isle, ME
35′ C. Hankins twin-screw sea skiff . . . . Lavallette, NJ
32′ soft-chine powerboat . . . . E. Boothbay, ME

In small craft, there are Whitehalls, wherries, Norwegian faerings, Swampscott dories, Sid skiffs, punts, peapods, and pulling boats of all kinds under construction. There are, by my guess, between 10,000 and 15,000 traditional wooden boats being built in the United States today. This includes the entire range from eight-foot prams to 80-foot shrimpboats. There are plain workboats and fancy little "toys" almost too precious to use. Amateurs are building and restoring every type of boat imaginable, and some that aren't. The same is true of the professional builders, whom I estimate number about 1,500. (I know of only half a dozen woman boatbuilders, none of whom run shops on their own. Because this book deals with things as they are, I have referred to builders as "he." I hope these women, and others in the future, will make this one-sided view inaccurate.)

The professional building activity is defined according to two major variables: whether a builder is geared toward commercial or recreational boats; and in the latter case, whether he is building traditional small craft,

Philip Bolger's three-piece collapsible ketch Triad *just after her launching in June 1978. The joint between her fore and mid-section is clearly discernible below the stainless steel bracket at the forward corner of the cabin trunk. (John Wisner photo)*

Above left: *A handsome spit-polished double-ender awaits launching at Jensen's Boat Works, Friday Harbor, Washington. Even from this perspective, the quality of her joinerwork is evident.* Above right: *Perhaps the most frequently built traditional small craft today, the 14' 3" Whitehall, detailed in Howard Chapelle's* American Small Sailing Craft. *This boat was the author's first solo building project, launched just a month or so before his departure for his cross-country survey of wooden boatbuilders.*

These Pacific dories are launched through the surf by the dozens in Pacific City, Oregon. Two 40-h.p. outboards provide power once the bar is cleared. Many of these dories are brightly painted—the lobster on the bow of the boat at left is one of the tamer examples.

custom cruising sail or powerboats, or special-purpose boats, such as river runners.

Traditional Small Craft

Boats have always been an accepted means for rich and poor alike to "get away from it all," as well as a way for some to make a living. But the advent of the cheap, practical "safety bicycle" in the last quarter of the 19th century, and later the development of engine-powered, land-based vehicles, diminished the importance of recreational small watercraft. Placing engines in boats had a great effect on recreational boating, not the least of which was a temporary (but far-reaching) decline in the quality of boat design. Any shape could be pushed along to some degree. John Gardner, who coined the phrase, defines "traditional small craft" as those boats designed in the late 19th century at the peak in development of waterborne transportation. They evolved from that century's great technological advances, but prior to the advent of the gasoline engine. Industrial innovations made possible the near-perfection of a large variety of sail- and human-powered small craft. For example, the types of short tacks essential to the construction of the Adirondack guide-boat were not invented or produced until about 1840. (See photo, page 331.) Today, traditional small craft can be of recent design if they conform to the same high standards of that earlier period. This does not mean yacht finish, but rather the highest possible attention to, and respect for, the boat's intended purpose. It is a measure of innate design quality, not simply of a style or period.

In recent years, traditional small craft have gained in popularity by leaps and bounds on the East and West Coasts. Fifty-five of the builders listed have recently and/or regularly built such boats. Twenty-five of these builders were on the West Coast, the rest on the Atlantic seaboard. Puget Sound, with its light airs and protected water, has become a focal point, and the Seattle-based Traditional Wooden Boat Society has a strong tendency toward traditional small craft.

Cruising boats, with the bunks, galleys, etc., the public has come to expect, are rapidly becoming too expensive for the middle class. The present popularity of traditional small craft stems partially from this, and partially from the return to integrity of product. Wooden boats are representative of that set of values, but traditional small craft are their embodiment. A boat that can be trailered and stored easily, maintained by the owner himself for little expenditure in time or money, is pollution-free, easily handled by children, and classy, is hard to beat. For something over a hundred dollars a foot (on the East Coast, at least), the boat can be of varnished mahogany and yellow metals. This is well within reasonable means. The increasing availability of excellent, detailed plans and/or directions on "how to" has given many enthusiasts the courage to build their own boats. A 15-foot Whitehall is certainly a more approachable do-it-yourself project than a 30-foot sloop. Many feel that these

Clean lines—the true signs of craftsmanship are as much in what is left out as in what goes in. The centerboard trunk in Pete Culler's Good Little Skiff shows just how simple simple can be.

small boats are the wave of the future in other materials as well. The rising cost of fuel and the shortage of docking and mooring facilities for larger boats add to their attractiveness.

Custom Cruising Sail and Power

Webster defines "custom" as, "made or done to order, or *sometimes* [emphasis mine—P.L.] made extra fine. . . ." A custom builder is one who builds specifically for, and in close cooperation with, the owner-to-be. I grouped "custom" with cruising sail and power because so few boatbuilders in this category, perhaps two percent of those listed here, build on speculation. For example, Paul Schweiss of Clinker Boatworks, Tacoma, Washington, is a custom builder with a strong "specialty" in "ancient Norwegian skiffs, traditional Scandinavian rowing, sailing, and power vessels. . . ."

The custom builder of cruising boats is in a difficult position. His labor and material requirements are the toughest in the field. His boats, foot for foot, are the most expensive. His clientele is limited and very discerning. Most potential buyers know of one or two older boatbuilders, at best, and they often assume that these are the last alive or active. This is an effect of the wooden-boat-building-is-a-dead-or-dying-art syndrome. The shortage of middle-aged builders leaves a large gap as older men retire. Since buyers are understandably reluctant to invest thousands of dollars (or even hundreds of thousands) in young, relatively unknown builders, established men like Joe McGlasson of Newport, Oregon, and Ferdinand Nimphius of Neshkoro, Wisconsin, have a great deal of work, while all but the exceptional newcomers are having a tough time breaking into the custom market.

There are two divergent trends within this market. The very fancy, larger boats are getting larger and fancier. These clients are in the cost-is-no-object, let's-have-a-trash-compacter-in-the-galley category. Moving in the other direction, there are those following the trend toward traditional small craft, simpler boats that put-me-in-touch-with-the-sea-and-nature.

Forty-seven percent of the recreational builders responding to my survey had more experience with sailboats than power craft, 27 percent had more with power, 26 percent split it down the middle. The market in custom wood boats, sail or power, is *slowly* gathering momentum. The resurgence was so unexpected, the response to traditional gatherings and magazines so supportive, that many builders quickly came to feel unequivocally positive in their view of the future. They are probably jumping the gun. Certainly amateur activity has taken off. I consider my estimates to be conservative, none more so than the guess at 15,000 traditional wooden boats under construction. Most professional shops, however, do not have enough work in new construction. While there is no question that the market is improving, it is far from booming.

Commercial Craft

Commercial builders build boats designed to be money-makers. These can be anything from clamming skiffs to lobsterboats. Unlike many recreational

There is elegance and efficiency in this finely bowed, easily driven double-ender slipping out of Point Hudson after the Port Townsend Festival. The opportunity to build something like this classic keeps custom builders' noses to the grindstone.

buyers, the fisherman knows exactly what he wants in a boat. He knows the equipment and costs involved, and as a rule, he knows what he's getting into when he commits his capital.

While professional wooden boatbuilding on the East and West Coasts is primarily recreational, the Gulf Coast building is almost exclusively commercial. Gulf Coast builders face the most difficult climate for wooden boats in the United States—and the teredos, those worms of legendary appetite. Only the specific advantages of wooden boats for commercial fishing (repairability, quietness, etc.) keep them in significant demand. To date, there has not been the interest, free time, or money to support a wooden boat "revival" like that seen on the East and West Coasts. It is not surprising that the only recreationally oriented southern wooden boating group, the Great Wooden Boat Cooperative of Seabrook, Texas, was in the prosperous Houston-Galveston area.

Southern builders are isolated by a lack of journalistic coverage. The relevant periodicals are anxious to cover activity there, but they have been unable to establish regular contacts. My pre-departure research uncovered only one contact (in Mobile, Alabama) for the entire coastline from Brownsville, Texas, to Tarpon Springs, Florida.

Commercial wooden boatbuilding is at its height in the Louisiana Bayous, St. Augustine, Florida, and the Carolina Banks. In Louisiana, there are numerous builders snowed under with work because of the Gulf's shrimping boom of the last two years. There are four mass-producers of shrimpboats in St. Augustine, two of which are completing boats as fast as one every four days! These are mostly 60-foot to 80-foot vessels, assembly-line-built from keel to electronics, for delivery to the Gulf, West, or East Coast, or to South America. Along the southeastern Atlantic seaboard, however, where white shrimp have been under federal protection due to extraordinarily low stocks, commercial builders are up against a wall.

Nevertheless, southern builders in general, with the cheapest labor in the nation, are giving northern builders a run for the money. I was able to find only one yard on the California coast that was still producing wooden commercial fishing boats. Oregon and Washington each have a couple of yards with the *capability*, but these are having difficulty keeping busy. Commercial New England and the Chesapeake Bay are holding their own against southern labor, if not against pollution and regulation.

Why All the Fuss?

If you study any subject long enough, it will grow accordingly intricate and inspiring. Collectors of barbed wire draw references to the taming of the American West, environmental issues, and man's quest for new territories. Wood boat aficionados are an equally rhetorical, fanatical breed. On the surface, it is insanity to devote one's precious energy to the enjoyment of a wooden boat. To do so is a contradiction in terms, since the boat will always

The simplest and the most complicated boats at Port Townsend. In the foreground is Paul Glassen's pine-planked, linseed oil and turpentine finished, five-day building project, Iconoclast. *Beyond the float is the Jay Benford-designed 34'* Sunrise, *built of red and yellow cedar, fir, teak, gumwood, ironbark, oak, and mahogany.*

find some new, more capricious, and baffling way to go to pieces. What outsiders fail to realize is that our throwaway, me-first society has bred strong individuals who value the care and attention that wooden boats require.

A simplistic traditionalist might describe his/her value system like this:

Traditional—that produced, designed, and used to an exacting standard of quality in all aspects.

Modern—that produced, designed, and used to an exacting standard of profit, salability, fashion, and status-consciousness.

The wooden boat must survive in an environment that is basically hostile to the material. It requires commitment to maintain and significant skill to handle. Few disciplines can equal traditional boating in its demands for excellence on such a broad scale. To many aficionados, wooden boatbuilding is the ultimate craft.

At Port Townsend there were hundreds of wooden boats—some simple, some fancy, all inspiring. Many discussions bespoke concern for more than just traditional watercraft. There are implications about our whole society if these boats are allowed to fade into obscurity. The grace of any good vessel underway, the integrity of her design and construction within her intended purpose symbolize for devotees a culture-wide return to crafts and values. The aesthetic qualities of wood, both as a boatbuilding material and in light of environmental and energy concerns, only serve to underline this appeal. To care about these boats is to say you care in general; apathy is unacceptable. This is all the more true (and intense) in the professional boat shops, but with some essential differences.

There is a mystique about a boat shop. It is hard not to be caught up in the seemingly ancient tools, the scent of cedar, all the things that speak of another era. A different set of values is in operation here, another world not quite so hectic, unfeeling and inhumane. To the professional, finding the right work space is often a life search. Often the shop is located a little off the beaten track. Four-fifths of the shops surveyed are in rural, small town settings (under 5,000 population). Those in the cities tend to be older shops established before real estate prices skyrocketed. Low overhead is essential.

With time, I developed an ability to smell out boat shops. The look of the street, the size of the town, perhaps an unusually high number of fancy wooden signs—the giveaways are endless, and yet hard to define.

As I drive down the street, I see a good-size (the average shop can handle a 47-foot boat) weathered barn or shed. It looks far from deserted. The gravel road is well worn with fresh tire marks, firewood is stacked beside big sliding doors, and a pile of lumber sits under a sheltering wall. Inside, the shop looks like a combination woodworking shop, junkyard, and, of all things, temple. Power tools of goodly proportions and equal antiquity are scattered around. The benches and worn wood floor are strewn with the hand tools used in recent days, and a barrel's worth of shavings and scrap lumber. More scrap is piled under the bench, in a corner, or at best sorted into bins. Perhaps it has never been quite decided whether to sort by size and shape, or by species. More confusion. Arranged in every nook or spare bit of shelf space are boxes of fastenings, preservatives, paints, bits of machinery, marine hardware, rarely used tools, and much other paraphernalia whose purposes and origins are unclear. Everything is covered with a layer of sawdust—the usefulness of the tool or material decreasing in direct proportion to the depth of its layer of dust. The scattered glint of steel and bronze reflects the light from a string of bare bulbs. The sweat-polished handle of a cherished plane or spokeshave may catch the eye. But the vessel itself fills the mind and rivets the attention.

The boat is the center of the builder's efforts, and as such is both icon and iconoclastic. The most-needed tools and materials are gathered in and around the hull like sacrifices to an idol. Yet the boat is often the cause of frustration, anger, and fatigue. The shop is simultaneously a sanctuary and a self-made challenge. Each boat begins as a serene white cloud in an otherwise blue sky and ends as an obliterating thunderhead. To escape from under it, the builder must see the project launched. There is brief respite in this joyful event, and then the cycle begins anew. There is only one thing worse than a head crammed full of boat-shaped difficulties, and that is an empty shop.

Boatbuilders are often described as eccentrics, men slightly out of step with the rest of the world who build boats as articles of faith. In fact, the harsh realities of their vocation make them the least romantic of all the boating

A Robert Rich-designed lobsterboat appears to be dwarfed in his Bernard, Maine, shop, partly because of the camera's wide-angle lens.

types. They are working to achieve an almost unobtainable balance among profit, speed, and the more elusive qualities of integrity and beauty.

Examples of people who gave up the rat race (or never entered it) in order to live and work as they wish are common enough, particularly in the light of the 1960s. Boatbuilders don't quite fit that category. As later chapters will show, there are many hours spent chasing down lumber deals, compared with minutes spent tapering a sternpost under the swing of an adze.

> Let there be no mistake; if you want to build . . . you have got to be a strong swimmer. You will be swimming against the mainstream of a ready-made, showroom-bred society all day, every day. . . . Most boats on the water today are built with little or no recognition of common sense or good taste. These only look like real boats in a picture or at a boat show. Imitations or illusions of boats are what are hot today with those who find the truth too much work and trouble. This is not exclusive of other materials; very occasionally we see a truthful plastic boat.
>
> *Art Brendze*

It is the search for truthful boats, often extending beyond logic or sense, that drives builders to slug it out with today's society.

> Don't ask me why I possess these feelings, it's probably for the same reasons I get excited about the Declaration of Independence and the salmon swimming upstream to spawn. Some of us are just plain addicted, and must pursue the truths of well-built boats. Such is apparently my fate.
>
> *Art Brendze*

As a house guest, I have heard from builders' wives accusations of imminent bankruptcy and/or insanity that are only partially intended to be humorous. Yet, for all the teasing, the troubles, the sour comments, the gloomy forecasts (in the interviews), builders are a cheerful lot. (I've often heard it said that wooden boat people in general are unusually personable and sensitive.) Builders don't dwell on their problems and always make the best of their situations. They are fully conscious of having made a choice, and they will live with that. The personal pride they exhibit in the interviews is genuine. They command respect within their communities for their skills, perseverance, and ability to do a lot with a little. I have rarely met a builder who didn't seem well above average in intelligence.

Clark Mills of Sarasota, Florida, may be the archetype. We are sitting in his backyard, overlooking his boatyard. Though now limited by his age to projects that don't require a great deal of climbing, he remains active. Reflecting on so many years in the business, he remarks gruffly, but with humor,

> The boatbuilding business doesn't make you a lot of money. The margin of profit is slim. If you want to go into the boat business, you'd better be able to laugh at yourself. But I'll tell you, I've had more fun with my trouble, and trouble with my fun, than anybody you know.

With easygoing attitudes like that, it's no wonder that builders tend toward longevity. I know of none with ulcers. Marvel Blix of Cathlamet, Washington, told me that he and his brother, Sonkey, refuse to allow their father to work in their shops. When I inquired why, Marvel (in his seventies himself) said, "He rushes me! Though he's well past 90, by the time I've bent over to pick up a timber, he's lifted his end and gone off with it across the shop floor."

Boatbuilders can be roughly classified by age, but their political philosophies and attitudes cannot be. It is only minimally true that younger builders are left-alternativist and the older builders more conventional. I know younger men who believe the 16-hour workday and traditional materials are inviolable institutions, and older men who say the purpose of boatbuilding is to evolve and enjoy yourself. Categorization is never a pleasant prospect in our computerized, polarized society. But the following characterization would apply to many builders I met.

The man coming down the scaffolding as I enter the boat shop might be in his late forties, but it's hard to tell. Almost without exception, builders are in pretty good shape—very rarely overweight. His clothing is a trademark—old sportshirt, tan chino pants, and an old cap.

"I'll be right with you. Hey, Smitty, is that cap flanged inside or out?"

There is a disembodied grunt from above—"Out." The first man grabs a large backing dolly from the cluttered workbench, and with a warning whistle, lobs it over the side. Smitty is either on the ball or knocked unconscious. I never hear it land.

"Now, what can I do for you?" The handshake is firm, testing; the voice is interested, alive, and bright.

First in knowledge, skill, experience, and reliability are the older men, whom I call affectionately, the "old-timers." One need not be old to be an old-timer, only trained under the old school and familiar with the era before the wooden-boat crash. Their skills have been verified by a long-lived generation of boats. They may be businesslike in manner but are rarely so in practice. Bookkeeping may be haphazard at best. They can be highly innovative, but it is innovation as the direct product of their accumulated experience. Through their long-standing reputations they have developed an excellent clientele; they needn't hype themselves or their shops. They are in a position to choose between the most profitable and the most interesting projects and may even alternate one after the other. Older builders who have run larger operations may cut back in order to be free to do more of the actual woodworking themselves. These are indeed the golden years of boatbuilding. The myth that they are tight-lipped codgers, wary of strangers, misses the point—their boat-related experiences and anecdotes could fill volumes.

The older men are pros at spotting fakers, or those who won't take to heart what they have to say. This is not to say you have to agree with them on everything. Old-timers like nothing more than a youngster with spunk, but he must show himself to be a thinking creature with a sense of perspective. There is nothing wrong with admitting ignorance; it is the pretense to the contrary that invites their silent scorn.

Pretense is an important word in considering builders' lives and personalities, young and old alike. They have neither the time nor the energy for deceptive appearances—either in their dealings with others or in the finish of their work. If you have a deal to offer, state it. If a boat is rough, don't try to spruce it up with the finish. All that matters is that things be honest, up front. They work and live simply. Even in their possessions this is true, not just by force of economics, but by preference. Their homes are modest, their vehicles utilitarian. The image of a builder in a $10,000 car is incongruous, if not downright laughable.

The number of older builders dwindles each year, even by percentage. This is due to the age gap that exists in all but the commercially oriented areas. Middle-aged builders are rare. Many men in this age range who would be building today were caught between the Great Depression and several wars. Those who survived were not anxious to return to a risky business such as wooden boatbuilding.

Those few who *did* choose the wood field take a more conformist course than their elders and juniors. They have less eccentric personalities and business habits. They keep accurate books(!), either out of personal preference or increasing legal necessity. Their good health and high level of experience combine with the above to make an unbeatable combination. These are by far the busiest of the builders, the ones often working on more than one boat at a time. Yards with high overhead and more than five employees are run by builders of middle years at a rate of 18-to-1, or 94.7 percent. Like the old-timers and youngsters, they can be innovative, but a change must have easily foreseeable, even provable, financial benefits before it is attempted. Having accepted the risks inherent in boatbuilding, they are not about to irrationally increase the odds against themselves. At the same time, they will calculate the risks, explore the problems, and do the paperwork for an unusual project when others wouldn't bother. In a nutshell, their personalities are like their shops: active, versatile, and accessible. They exude competence.

Last, but perhaps largest in numbers, are the youngsters, with from three to 15 years' experience. From middle-class, college-educated families, most of these have some college experience. They have emerged out of the political mayhem of the Sixties, carrying Howard I. Chapelle's *American Small Sailing Craft*. In many ways, they are a tangent to the back-to-nature movement, deeply committed to an alternative lifestyle, a sane, more coherent, more humane way of living. Human-energy-intensive systems, integrity of workmanship, quality, and flexibility are all part of this movement. Another significant aspect is mobility. They may relocate, commute long distances, even cut their

On a beach along Puget Sound, a well-designed steam box typifies the ingenuity often shown by alternativists in recycling the Establishment's throwaways.

Two designs by Bud McIntosh take shape in Jeff Fogman's shop in Barrington, New Hampshire. The rakish tilt of the bandsaw indicates that a difficult corner below decks is receiving attention.

rates in order to work on a particularly inspiring job. (The Stimson brothers, for example, have a shop that fits on the back of their flatbed truck.) If they lack long-term involvement with a particular aspect of boatbuilding, it is usually offset by the diversity of their experience. They are less concerned with solidity and security than with the quality of day-to-day living. Still, the desire (and need) to build a reputation overshadows much that they do. Since staying busy (and eating) is in large part dependent on distinction rather than advertising, this is understandable. Some have intentionally underpriced their work in order to build reputations more quickly.

Whatever the age, strip away the different politics and you will find much the same roots: individualism, independence, awareness. It is almost impossible to be a boatbuilder without these qualities, because they are a necessary part of a personal acceptance of boatbuilding as one's "fate." Difficult as it is, the craft is the key to the builder's happiness. Social acceptance, logic, and "insurance salesman economics" are all contrary to the profession. Even builders who began careers before the crash had to resist the switch to fiberglass. All types of builders had (and have) to make conscious decisions to stand firm against the hardships of boatbuilding and certain establishmentarian pressures. I've heard them say, "I'm too busy to be politically active," but in fact the way they live and work is a considerable catalyst for change. One cannot visit an active boat shop or meet a boatbuilder and come away unaffected by the statement they make.

Builders and enthusiasts alike are possessed by an ideal, an interest in the

This derelict set in concrete somewhere along the Gulf Coast epitomizes the idea of practical uses for old rotters. It has been painted brightly and is now part of the local playground.

return to crafts, and romanticism, but the builder tends toward a more practical involvement. When a starry-eyed traditionalist brings a marginal hulk into his yard, bubbling over with dreams of spit-and-polish restoration, the builder is probably thinking, "Let's burn her for scrap! I know that once we get into her we'll find more rot than good wood." The irony and absurdity of professional wooden boatbuilding is lost on few. Jim Prier said that he got started in a moment of "temporary insanity."

While there are a few successful builders who have steadfastly refused to build anything but varnished hulls with bright decks, most are more opportunistic and pragmatic. Fifty-nine percent said they would work in nontraditional modes, such as glued-strip and cold-molding. Twenty-seven percent of those who refused to do so, refused on the basis of experience with those modes. Forty-three and three tenths percent said they use a combination of traditional and modern paints and glues, according to what is best and/or available. Thirty-three and nine tenths percent preferred the traditional "proven" materials, 22.8 percent the modern ones.

For the most part, they have worked with what has come along and made the best of it. But this flexibility does not mean that they will arbitrarily cut corners, at least not where structural integrity is concerned.

> I can remember being four or five years old, seated in the bottom of a leaky skiff, bailing just as fast as I could. My arms got tired because I had to reach up as high as I could just to dump the water over the side! . . . A boat is made of thousands of interlocking parts. Anything but the finest fit weakens the whole. It sometimes goes beyond practicality to fanaticism. Like not shining the back of

Beautiful fits highlight the sternpost, transom, and rudder of James Blaiklock's version of Thomas Gillmer's Blue Moon. *On the opposite page, Blaiklock reminisces about the origins of his devotion to tight joints.*

your belt buckle; perhaps nobody will know, but it's not the same as if the job is done right. It isn't necessarily logical, but it *is* right boatwise and spiritually.

If a person is a boatbuilder, he will build boats in the face of all that is against him. Lack of knowledge, tools, money, materials, and markets will always plague him. If you are a boatbuilder, then *be* one. Build a boat; it's worth it.

James Blaiklock

One must realize that no boat is perfect, and the so-called perfectionist is doomed to a long life of drawn-out failures. There is a fine line between prudence and sloppiness, so one must do the best fit he can do in a reasonable length of time, and move on to the next step.

New construction is what all builders favor, but like everyone else, we must eat and pay taxes. Repair work then enters our lives, but it's not all bad, since this has its interesting points also.

Billy Perry

. . . It's a competitive thing. You've got to expedite a boat to keep in the market, while also pleasing the customer. A boat has to be well made, regardless. I get satisfaction out of producing a nice boat. It will have character and live on after I'm gone. Boatbuilding also promotes an integral part of our heritage. Our nation was built on, and remains, a maritime nation.

Maynard Lowery

THE QUESTIONNAIRE

In late August 1977, I left Martha's Vineyard, Massachusetts, for the Port Townsend Festival. I planned to head down the West Coast as the fall progressed, work the Gulf Coast in mid-winter, and wind up along the East Coast in the spring. If time and money allowed, I would loop through the Canadian Maritimes and the American Great Lakes as well. As I said before, I was not yet convinced of the survey's feasibility, or of my own long-term interest in so large a task. I was still inclined to be a vagabond, traveling purely for pleasure.

The precise structure the survey would take was still developing. Out of a list of 100 questions I picked 20 that I thought would capture the character and perspective of each builder. I had a certain kind of boat shop in mind, and a sample questionnaire. At Port Townsend I requested and received a lot of feedback. I was asked again and again, "Have you got so-and-so on your list? Good luck trying to get *him* to say more than 'Get out of here!'."

"Thanks," I'd say, and next to so-and-so's name, I'd note, "AWC" (Approach With Caution).

"Why not include cold-molding builders or retired masters?" "Why don't you ask such-and-such?" "How do you intend to compile the information?" "You don't expect builders to fill out this questionnaire, do you?"

My attitude, questions, background, and motivation all came under scrutiny. Through three days of explaining my interests and goals, and listening to others' thoughts on the difficulties they foresaw, the survey took shape. Two weeks later, I modified the questionnaire and had it reprinted.

*Name of builder
Name and address of shop or yard

Number of builders (employees or subcontractors)
Capacity (boats to ______ feet)
Specialties (particular designs, classes, custom cruising sail or power, workboats, traditional small craft)

Do you have: Design or drafting capabilities?
Lumber storage facilities? (How many board feet do you try to keep on hand?)
Metal casting or fabricating facilities? (Pattern making only?)

---

*NOTE: Answers considered too private for public consumption may be noted, "NFP" (Not For Public). All material marked as such will be kept in strictest confidence. If necessary, leave the question blank, but by all means complete the rest. Express yourself clearly; I'll print what you write! The better you say it, the better you will come across.

Will you work in modes other than traditional (glued-strip, cold-molding)? Do you have experience with these?

Are you more inclined toward traditional or modern paints, glues, etc. (e.g., oil- vs. epoxy-based paints)?

Are you more experienced with sail or power? (Percentage?)

Are you able to study your boats under use over the long term, in order to learn what is happening to them structurally?

History: When and how did you become interested in boatbuilding?
Where and how did you receive your training?
Why did you set up in this region or town?
How did you finance the shop?

Recent projects (Length, beam, design, materials, etc., of your last three or four boats)

Projects or goals in store (What do you have lined up?)

Unusual shop-made jigs, tools, or methods (Hand tools reground for a particular job, etc.? If possible, trace or rough-sketch it on reverse side.)

The market (Who is buying and why?)

Suppliers of lumber and hardware (Names and addresses if available, including small local mills, dealers, etc.)

Other wooden boatbuilders that you know of

Your opinions on:

1)The present and future quality and availability of lumber and hardware

2)Shop cooperatives and/or lumber-buying coops (For professionals? For amateurs?)

3)The market's future (Where are we going from here?)

4)The labor situation (Quantity and quality)

5)Modern and traditional design (Do you have a preference? If so, why?)

6)Vocational training (Boatbuilding schools, their products. Are they doing a good job?)

7)Restorations vs. replicas (Which should have higher priority, skills preservation or boat preservation?)

**8)Time vs. finish (Where does structural integrity end in your shop and "extra" work begin? Do the owner-to-be's preferences dictate this, provided he can afford it, or do you set *a* standard and if the person can't afford it they just have to find another builder? In short, is there a point where a dead fit, finish, etc., is a waste of your time and the owner's money?)

An open statement (A sentence or two expressing yourself on *any* area; for example, about your shop and what you try to do there.)

** AUTHOR'S NOTE: This question was usually rephrased during the interview as follows. Suppose there are three builders of equal longevity and reputation. Builder A says, "The only way to build and sell wooden boats for a living is with the finest fits throughout—limited only by the builder's skill." Builder B says, "Beyond structural integrity, going for a dead fit is a waste of the builder's time and the owner's money." Builder C says, "If it's glued, screwed, and bolted, and you don't claim it's any better than it is. . . ." Where do you place yourself along that spectrum? Do you have a fixed standard?

* * * *

After Port Townsend, I defined the builders I intended to interview as those who were "currently professionally active in plank-on-frame construction, and who are likely to remain so for the foreseeable future." Unless specifically stated otherwise, the terms "boatbuilder" and "builder" apply to this principal group only. They do *not* include :

1. Amateur builders: Those who build boats purely for their own recreation.
2. Semiprofessional builders: Those who build boats unofficially, as far as strangers, the Internal Revenue Service, insurance salesmen, etc., are concerned. If asked, they always say they are building this one for themselves.
3. Fishermen builders: Those who build boats in the slack of their fishing season, perhaps using the boat for a season before selling it.
4. Itinerant builders: Those who build boats out of a truck and scrounged lodging, often with access to a bandsaw and other shop-size equipment.
5. Apprentice builders: Apprentices, yard hands, students, or would-be professionals.
6. Repairers: Those who *rebuild* boats, going into new construction sporadically if at all.
7. Retired builders: These men may have built hundreds of boats in their lifetimes, but either by choice or by force of their years, they are no longer actively building.
8. Cold-molding builders: Those who build boats of veneers or plywood in

laminations over a mold, commonly known as cold-molding. The growth in this technique is too volatile to be suited to the purposes of the survey.

These definitions were the fairest criteria I could devise for screening the thousands of names that were suggested to me over the course of the project. Yet classification could be a two-edged sword. While it kept my traveling down (to a mere 40,000 miles), strict adherence to these guidelines could have excluded a number of excellent organizations and people without whom the project would be incomplete. Also, there were geographical areas where coverage was severely limited. In these few areas, I bent my rule in proportion to the scarcity of builders. For example, I'd include repairers and fishermen/builders when the rate and consistency with which they built boats coincided with a willingness to go public.

Builders are extraordinarily sensitive on the subject of what defines a qualified boatbuilder. My definitions had me walking on very thin ice. During one two-day period, I was accused of both "homogenization" and "elitism." There was always the risk of alienating borderline cases who were excluded. I tried to make my reasoning clear: (1) Plank-on-frame builders were a small group that I could afford to cover in terms of financing, time, and energy. (2) They were of particular interest to me after my experience building boats in Maine. (3) Their perspective, knowledge, and involvement with the grapevine was custom-tailored to my central purpose, which was to provide a point of access to everyone within the field.

The 141 builders listed do not by any means constitute the total number of shops I visited. Depending on the region, I might have looked into as many as eight boatyards for each builder I interviewed.

Allowing for the shops I missed completely, all the fresh-water builders outside the Great Lakes that I didn't even attempt to catalog, the borderline cases, and the rise in new, unproven shops, I would guess that there are 1,500 wooden boatbuilders nationwide. The listed builders represent approximately a nine percent sampling of the field.

Some well-known builders are conspicuous by their absence from the survey. The most common concerns were that tourists, the IRS, OSHA, or the Coast Guard would suddenly "discover" their shops, and the ensuing hassles and red tape would never end. In many cases, an overabundance of work, planned retirement, suspicion of a stranger (with out-of-state license plates), or just an unwillingness to work with others were reasons for not taking part in the survey. Because I was sensitive to their situations, even those who had personal reasons for staying unlisted were always willing to hear me out, suggest other builders, and support the survey in other ways.

There are a few builders listed whom I have never met and/or whose workmanship I have never seen. I may have seen their shops when they were boatless, or they may have filled out the form by mail.

Near the Florida-Alabama border, the author took these photographs in the shed of a builder who turned aside every question. This is a fine example of how much interesting information remains unknown. Is it going to be a twin screw? If so, why the dead-center engine bed? If not, why two engines? Does he work alone? Etc.

Getting the builders to fill out the questionnaire was a serious problem in itself. Boatbuilders seem to have a built-in resistance to putting pen to paper, let alone filling out forms. In any case, they were often too busy to stop working in order to do so. I entered a yard as a complete stranger, or worse, "another wooden boat nut who thinks I have nothing better to do than gab with him." To get them to sound off at all was difficult, to do so onto a form or in front of a tape recorder was close to impossible. I put the questions to them and paraphrased their answers. A simple question often would be answered by either a monosyllabic grunt or a 10-minute discourse on topics more or less related to the matter at hand. I quoted directly when they spoke directly. Otherwise I worked passages into short, clear, concise thoughts and when in doubt, read it back for their approval. I followed them around in their shops, firing questions at them and scrawling their answers as they worked. In this way, I was able to get a good perspective on how the yard operated and the relationship of the builder to his crew.

The Answers

On any given question, it is possible to find a case in point to support or discredit any opinion. Builders in the same area with similar interests are as likely to be at opposite ends of the spectrum as workboat and yacht builders 3,000 miles apart. Here, for example, are excerpts from interviews with two builders in the Northwest.

> Very few people want to work a 10-hour day in less than ideal conditions for any amount of pay. . . . I think the recent blowup on wooden boats is probably the kiss of death. Boatbuilders . . . are now being exploited far beyond their capabilities. Wood boats are really, or should be, the poor man's boat. . . . I'm not interested in putting a shiny new epoxy-saturated boat in every backyard. Most people should not own a wood boat—they are not prepared to deal with it. . . . I've seen five-to-10-year-old boats destroyed by neglect in the hands of wealthy boating people. . . .
>
> *David Clarke*

> I'd like to build a bunch of cheap, practical sharpies and the like, so more ordinary fishing and boating folks could take to the water without it being such a big deal [read expensive], and alienating [read complicated motors and unworkable synthetic materials]. . . . All these fine young boatbuilders coming along are going to produce a bumper crop of beautiful watercraft that will reeducate the tastes of the boating public.
>
> *Paul Glassen*

While David and Paul are moving in the same general direction, their reasons and attitudes are rather different. It is not just optimism vs. pessimism; it is the way in which each has come to grips with that romantic/pragmatic dichotomy of boatbuilding and present society. Here are some other Northwesterners:

> . . . the romance of boatbuilding fascinates me. . . . I build boats for fun and to keep body and soul together. I enjoy the challenge of doing the impossible and making a living at it. . . . I find working with and teaching students highly rewarding. There is great satisfaction in passing on knowledge. . . .
>
> *Carl Brownstein*

> Traditional wooden boatbuilding needs to be seen more as an occupation and less as a romantic endeavor . . . too many amateurs muddying the water.
>
> *Jim Prier*

In coming up with "statistics" based on builders' diverse opinions, I used a very unscientific method. Tone, as well as word, was considered in judging an individual's stand.

Not surprisingly, not all the questions were successful enough to be tabulated. Some went unanswered, others received the shortest treatment possible. Happily, there are things to be learned from the failures as well as the successes.

The question on financing went largely unanswered because of the obvious sensitivity of such information, and because a good many builders simply "wing it." Money is a matter of using it as you can get it. The average shop is a hodgepodge of projects; the cash flow is a web of complications. Most builders keep the simplest of books but go no further. Cost analysis is not used. I recall being surprised when one builder knew (off the top of his head) exactly what percentage of cost his 30-man crew represented.

One question I asked was, "Are you able to study your boats under use, over the long term, in order to learn what is happening to them structurally?" This is in fact a two-pronged question: "Do you keep track?"; and "Do you find problems occurring with your boats?" It was too easy to say yes to the first part, and not take the trouble to answer the second. What I was looking for was an openness. Were they willing to learn? Were they honest about their mistakes? In many cases, though, builders do keep track of their boats, and how they fare. Many service those they build. It is purely my opinion that most *are* open about their mistakes. It would not be consistent with their characters to be otherwise.

"Why did you set up in this region or town?" Ninety percent of the builders simply said,"I'm from here."

"The market: who is buying and why?" As one builder put it, "If I knew the answer to that one, I'd be rich." Or, "No particular kind. Some are millionaires, some are young, broke, and want to retire to Tahiti tomorrow. They're all just wooden boat nuts . . . people as crazy as I am." With these last two questions I was looking for trends, a person and/or place that was particularly infected with, or susceptible to, the boat bug. I wanted information that might help builders decide where to locate a shop, to whom they might gear their promotion, etc. It was a haphazard attempt at a marketing survey. (When I designed the survey, I was considering opening a shop myself. It is some measure of "the more you study, the less you think you know" that by the halfway mark, I had virtually dropped this plan for the foreseeable future.)

The query about "shop-made tools and methods not commonly known" was not a failure. Builders did respond when they could, but the nature of boatbuilding is to make do—to adapt to some situation that requires an approach that is original, at least in part. The tight spot that a regular tool will not reach and the truly impossible situations are usually handled by regrinding a common tool for a once-in-a-lifetime, soon-forgotten application. Occasionally, the true brainstorm strikes. George Luzier's "Mark I/4 Flintstone Sander" is perhaps the best example. If a workman can survive operating this little monster, he can fair and sand a 50-footer in short order. Don't laugh too hard; it does quite a job.

"Suppliers of lumber and hardware." As I will make clear later on, getting materials is a large part of a builder's daily trials. Good sources for boat lumber are hard to find and cultivate. For this reason, and sometimes because of stiff competition, builders tend to be secretive about them. The list at the end of this book is by no means complete, or even representative. I present it as what I was able to pry from the builders.

"Restorations and replicas." There are two angles on this subject. The first, which I did not pursue for reasons that will be obvious, is best described by John Gardner of Mystic Seaport Museum:

> In the past, irreparable damage was frequently done to a unique surviving example of an historic craft in the attempt to restore it to something approaching a new boat. Now, it is generally conceded that such extensive rebuilding and refinishing was a mistake. The old boat is recognized for what it is—an historic document—and for the purposes of exhibit, we build a replica.

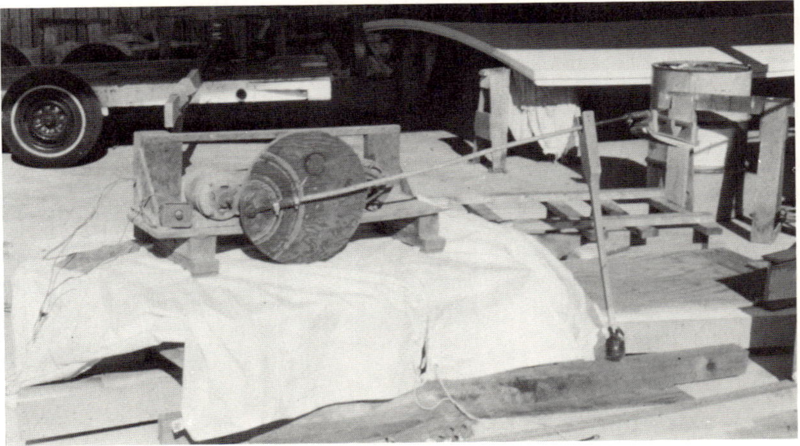

The Mark I/4 flintstone sander used by George Luzier in Sarasota, Florida.

Lance Lee of the Maine Maritime Museum Apprenticeshop put it this way: "A mistaken sense of responsibility has led some to feel they owe the public a restored, varnished boat."

The question also has political overtones and involves the direction that museums, foundations, and trusts should take in the allocation of funds. Restoration (however mistakenly) has generally been associated with large vessels, and replication with smaller craft. In the past, much of the money available went to the preservation (or attempted preservation) of large, visually more impressive ships, such as the *Constellation,* the *Star of India,* river steamboats, the *Charles W. Morgan,* etc. The public could then tour through them and marvel at the great works of man. Lance Lee and others have advocated increased emphasis on participatory programs, such as the building of historically accurate, traditional small craft. Such a program, they argue, teaches once in construction, again when on display, and continuously as long as people actually *use* the vessel. Neither cause denies the validity of the other, or wishes to deny the other financing. Unfortunately, they compete for the same limited funds.

Just prior to my departure for Port Townsend, this controversy was given considerable attention by the first annual meeting of the Maritime Division of the National Trust for Historic Preservation. Lance spoke eloquently for the skills preservationists on the value of small craft replication as offering more for the money than the restoration of large vessels. "I have watched intelligent people put graving pieces into rotten timbers in the side of large vessels."

I was interested in how professional builders viewed these arguments. They were outside the whole government grant, foundation, museum system and might have some insight as to how this money might best be spent. On the road I found that most builders viewed that system as so foreign, so removed from "earn a living" reality, that they had never given the question much thought. Those few who had, and those to whom I explained the issue, came up 88 percent as skills preservationists. This is hardly surprising. New construction of usable replicas, getting individuals out on the water, etc., is sure to appeal to builders—whereas putting back together a "$#!% hulk" does not. They feel that the replicas are more effective for showing what traditional boats and our maritime heritage are all about.

> They have to follow the model set forth by that prodigious genius of the field, John Gardner. Skills, value, and taste are what need preservation. Relics serve a very limited function in this.
>
> *Paul Glassen*

Below are 10 questions that, while not on the questionnaire, were actively under discussion throughout the survey.

1. Is there in fact a boom in wooden boatbuilding, or is this just the old

An exception to the rule of it-can't-be-done projects: the total restoration of the thoroughbred Wanderbird *under the guiding hand of Harold Sommer. She has been almost totally rebuilt, from copper sheathing and Irish felt-lined timbers to new spars.*

diehards (and their children) coming out of the woodwork? Is this new, or *renewed,* interest?

2. Why are there so few women in the field? Will the younger, less sexist builders make them welcome?

3. Where does the professional waterman fit in with the traditional water-craft enthusiast, and vice versa? How do we coordinate their interests?

4. What makes a boat last? Which practices are right for a given set of conditions?

5. Can a yacht builder afford to build a plain cruiser or workboat? Can his reputation for fine work withstand this?

6. Is there a place for specialized work crews? Could museums, for instance, jointly sponsor a replanking gang to be used by each on a rotating basis? Could Puget Sound or Maine support a full-time traveling rigging crew?

7. What precisely has happened to the general boating public's consciousness regarding alternative materials? What has been the evolution from the pre-crash era?

8. Can amateur and itinerant builders fill some of the seasonal needs of boat owners and repair facilities?

9. Why is there such vehement purism among some traditionalists? Does this serve as legitimate protection of historical types, or is it snobbery?

10. How are builders and enthusiasts going to deal with escalating regulations for boats and boat shops?

I will cover some of these questions later, but I present them here as questions for the reader to keep in mind.

The Market

> I'm surprised *anybody* is able to build in wood and make it financially.
>
> *Ahoi Mench*

> About the time the lumber runs out, so will the builders. If you can ever get the materials and know-how to build a wooden boat, you'll be able to sell it. There's a small, steady market, but it will never be like it was. The market simply won't support the numbers.
>
> *James Steele*

The boom in recreational boating as a whole, and the crash in wooden boating specifically, changed the wooden boatbuilder's market fundamentally. The boat user became less and less knowledgeable about construction and maintenance problems, particularly as a result of the mass-produced fiberglass boat and its "maintenance free" reputation. Today, the average boat consumer has almost no understanding of traditional boatbuilding. If he thinks of it at all, it is as a lost or dying art. Yet, like the car owner, he may face planned obsolescence and perhaps a feeling that something's just not right with his own boat. Here's Fritz Seyfarth in *The Telltale Compass* (Volume 9, Number 11):

> One of the other guests aboard *Webfoot* that evening was the owner of a new, 42′ ketch, one of the current fiberglass production models featuring a high, slab-sided, formless hull, center cockpit, aft cabin, an interior arrangement of color-coordinated plastics and cute gadgets and a dozen tiny bunks, with a few pieces of stick-on teak trim here and there to break the sterile monotony.
>
> The next day, I discreetly asked this owner what he thought of funny old wooden *Webfoot*. Surprisingly, he was quite glowing in his praise. "What a fine boat!" he enthusiastically replied. "I felt I was on a real and honest vessel. She smells so good, and just breathes warmth and personality and seaworthiness. What amazes me is that someone hasn't made a mold of her and produced her in fiberglass."

The relative merits of different designs, materials, construction methods, and maintenance arrangements are not only misunderstood for the most part, they often go unconsidered. At a boat show, the sections below the waterline are hidden behind crepe drapes, and the prospective buyer is carefully channeled into the cabin to look at the decorative color scheme.

> There's a certain person who should have a wooden boat, and some who should have a plastic one. The latter are for those who want boats like cars are supposed to be, turn the key and go. Wood is for those who enjoy the ownership and believe in maintenance.
>
> *John Swain*

Custom ordering and quality without chrome and razzle-dazzle have long since become contrary to public expectation, understanding, and experience.

> Downhill. There'll be less and less of a market, primarily because of labor costs for a well-constructed wooden boat. The disposable society has boat buffs looking elsewhere; to plastic and other non-quality materials that they think don't need care to maintain.
>
> *Don Johnson*

> I think you'll see wooden boats come back again due to a fallout effect from glass. People are starting with the cheaper, glass production boats. But once they learn what they want, they switch over to a custom wood boat.
>
> *Sonny Hodgdon*

The crux of this disagreement may well be the question of new and renewed interest. If much of the current interest in traditional watercraft is from people whose involvement is returning to a previous level, then Don Johnson's outlook is not without weight. Optimistic enthusiasts may be suffering under delusions of grandeur. Perhaps the field *is* simply regaining a stable population, and no real advances beyond previous levels are to be made. If we have sparked *new* interest, then Sonny Hodgdon's comments and the beliefs of many traditionalists are more valid. Since I believe that traditional watercraft are catalysts for social change, I obviously take the more optimistic view. I have been

Oh, I don't know, things have been slow; maybe we ought to save him.

Ken Mobert

impressed with how readily non-boat persons took to wooden boats and the traditional boat concept, and how far-reaching they found these concepts within the context of their own lives.

Let us assume that a boat buff is disturbed enough by what he sees in the showrooms and slick magazines to make a decision to depart from that sphere. There is no channel, no simple way to go about exploring the alternatives. His contacts at the boat dealer, broker, or chandlery may be as much in the dark as he is about *quality* fiberglass, ferrocement, foam, or wood watercraft. In wood, many of the most well-informed enthusiasts are still convinced that any boatbuilders they might know of are the last. In many areas of the country, the silent void of the Sixties has yet to be broken. Not too many years ago, Walter Simmons of Lincolnville Beach, Maine, had a customer come from Texas to pick up a 15-foot boat. This helps explain why 92 percent of the better-known, proven builders of the pre-crash era (those with long reputations) have all the work they can handle, and more.

> . . . a lack of communication has a lot of us thinking we are one of a few. I think the Traditional Small Craft Association and active listings like this book can go a long way toward dealing with this.
>
> *Walter Simmons*

> . . . yet we cannot reeducate a prospective customer in a letter, phone call, or afternoon's visit. We must help (not force) him/her to realign their thinking. *This* is a long-term commitment.
>
> *Anonymous*

Clearly, boatbuilders, small craft associations, and traditionalists in general feel that they have their work cut out for them. Information about, and support for, alternatives are the great justifiers of gatherings, boatyard chatter, and plain old advertising.

Once the boat consumer enters the wood market, the builders are concerned about the buyer's responsibility to them. Chief among the builders' concerns (after obtaining materials and labor) was the likelihood of "getting burned." Months and even years in contact with an interested, well-informed, wood-oriented buyer frequently comes to naught when the latter finally admits the project is beyond his finances or his true intent. The builder may well have spent over a hundred hours in reworking plans and discussing options with no chance to recoup his losses. Worse yet are those buyers who run out of money halfway through construction. Fortunately, the above types are counterbalanced by the occasional stranger who walks into a shop, takes a long hard look around, asks a few pertinent questions, and turns up a week later with a check in hand. If the builder says that he's sorry but he can't start on the project for eight months, this customer waves his hand and says, "That's okay, I've waited and saved for years, a few more months won't bother me at all."

The need for individualism in the boatbuyers' world is, happily, asserting itself. No longer are people satisfied with one in 10,000. This should lead to more opportunity for small, one-off builders.

Billy Perry

The professional builder's market lies in a select few: a person capable of appreciating a wooden boat for what it is; capable of paying for it; yet not so capable that they can find the time, interest, and skill to build their own. High levels of wooden-boat-related activity and interest alone do not translate readily into lots of work for all builders.

Most builders have experienced an increase in inquiries of about 30 percent during the last couple of years. A magazine article or boat-show presentation has been known to trigger a good response, but more often than not, inquiries are the result of praise from the satisfied customer. One boat of the right design, sold to the right person, in the right circle, has often resulted in a half-dozen sizable projects for the builder. As the revival grows stronger, there are more and more interested parties for the satisfied customer to influence. The geographical pockets where the revival is unknown are growing smaller, if very slowly. The Gulf and Great Lakes regions show varying degrees of awareness, indicating that things may improve there in the next eight to 10 years.

Within the active market, price variations are tremendous. How busy builders are, what's selling, even price per foot varies widely for infinite reasons. In addition to the builder's longevity and reputation, the variables are cost of materials, labor, overhead, location, complexity of boat, degree of finish, level of workmanship, how hungry the builder is, and how familiar he is with the particular design. In discussing materials, labor, and each region, significant factors, such as the high cost of lumber in the Northwest, are considered.

As a rule, however, the variations are simply too great to cover here in any meaningful way. As anyone who has taken a set of plans to a half-dozen builders can tell you, the differences in price and completion dates are simply incredible. The top figure can be as much as three times the bottom, both in price and in waiting period. Value, dollar for dollar, is as varied as the number of builders, their situations, and the variety of uses to which the boats are put by their clients. Two copies of a single design, produced by the same shop, may differ in cost and finish if one particularly adept employee works on one and not the other. However, farfetched and/or simplistic such a hypothetical situation may sound, it is precisely this kind of variable that is most often involved.

Following are the builders' responses to the question, "Where are we going from here?"

Numbers of Builders by Region

	North-west	Cali-fornia	Gulf Coast	South-east	Chesa-peake	North-east	Great Lakes	National
Up, seemingly unlimited	12	4	3	3	2	7		31
Small but stable market	9	5	9	13	7	34	3	80
No change	1				1			2
Declining	1		2	1	3	4		11
I don't know	3		1	2		3		9
Total								133

There may be more to be learned by looking at the regional breakdown of the top two opinion categories by percentage.

	North-west	Cali-fornia	Gulf Coast	South-east	Chesa-peake	North-east	Great Lakes	National
Up, seemingly unlimited	46	44	15	19	15	14	N.A.	23
Small but stable market	34	55	69	61	53	70	100	60

Only the booming Northwest had a majority of opinions on the unlimited side. From the Gulf eastward, builders were much more skeptical. Nationally, builders took the "small but stable" view over the bullish, 60 percent to 23 percent. One hundred eleven builders of the 133 who responded were certain that the direction would continue upward, but 80 of those had some serious reservations as to how big the market would be, and/or how lucrative. Only 11 were outspokenly negative, nine were noncommittal. The "small but stable" category includes the builders who said, "We'll do okay if the — — problem gets dealt with." The "ifs" related to concerns over materials and labor, skepticism as to the actual strength (and potential strength) of public interest, and the general uncertainty surrounding the economy of the United States. On the plus side for wood were the cost and ecological ramifications of steel and fiberglass, the spillover of people to wood from fiberglass, wood as a renewable resource, improved wood preservatives, and optimism about the revival of crafts and quality consciousness.

> There is a groundswell of demand for quality and integrity in all products. Traditional wood boats will be in increasing demand.
>
> *Dick Wagner*

Expanding. As the world runs out of petroleum and energy-intensive materials in general, wood will be more and more viable, perhaps even as a medium for mass production.

Bob Baker

There'll always be a market for good wooden boats, relatively stable and consistent. We'll see a return to more workboats, sail included, due to costs of gas and oil.

Jim Richardson

The future is with the freelancers. The alternativist lifestyle is the only way people will be able to build new boats for a living.

Myron Spaulding

As long as the there is somebody dumb enough to build a wooden boat, there'll be somebody dumb enough to buy one. [Said with care and humor—P.L.] Decent labor is a major problem nationwide—not just in boatbuilding. A man can make better money elsewhere. People are watching television and riding mopeds instead of rowing or what-have-you. And who can blame them for not wanting to work in a yard where conditions are often rough and the work hard?

Fred Ajootian

When all the comments were in, and had been floating around in my head for awhile, I came to the conclusion that the market for wood boats is not in doubt. The availability of materials and labor will indicate success or failure for the revival.

Materials

Lumber quality is poor, and there's a 10 percent increase annually in the price. Buy your boat now, tomorrow may be too late.

Victor Baggott

Let's not forget about the quality of lumber as a renewable resource. Builders have to be concerned with a balance between conservation and use.

Albert Sidl

We have a small shop, and we've built over 70 Seaford skiffs. Lumber is very difficult to get. I doubt I will build any more boats. We launched the last Seaford skiff today.

Paul Ketcham

Boats must be able to support human life in a constantly changing and often adverse environment. This is no small responsibility, but builders do not shirk it. "That boat is me, is Ken's Boat Shop. . . ." No matter how old or ordinary, the first questions asked about a boat are by whom and of what materials was she built. The best fits in the world won't save rot-prone wood or corrosion-prone metal.

The requirements for boat lumber—long lengths, careful drying, resistance

A "retired" builder in North Carolina had acquired a substantial supply of longleaf yellow pine timbers from old barns, torn-up wharfs, and so forth. This is only part of his stash, the biggest timber of which measured 26′ x 20″ x 18″!

to rot, strength and stability—vary according to use in the structure, the use to which the boat will be put, and the climate(s) in which she will operate. Similarly, the choice of metals—galvanized vs. bronze vs. copper vs. stainless steel—is made in relation to electrolysis, vibration, and so forth. The importance builders place on the materials with which they work cannot be understated. Regardless of whom I asked about the availability and quality of lumber, I invariably got answers filled with personal energy. Even if the answer consisted of a grunted, "Lousy," there was never any doubt as to the depth of the sentiment.

> Piss poor, and getting worse. Standards are dropping. You go up to the yards and pick through a whole pile for one clear board, and all the time you're at it you can hear the cash register going.
>
> *Ralph Morrow*

The builders' devotion to wood is sometimes stronger than their devotion to boats. "If I can't get decent materials, I won't build a boat," was an oft-heard refrain. If pressed, some said they would rather switch to some other form of high woodworking (cabinetmaking) given unacceptable boatbuilding materials. Wood is their element. Its versatility, appearance, and texture are only part of this fascination. The product of each log is different. This challenges the builder to use his skill, tools, and brains to produce a boat as quickly, efficiently, simply, and beautifully as is humanly possible.

In assessing the materials situation, we face not only the individual builder's varying standards, but regional differences as well. In the Northwest, planking stock is knot-free by definition, whereas in the Northeast and Southeast, solid knots are considered perfectly acceptable, especially in cedar. Whether this constitutes a lowering of standards depends on where your loyalties lie.

Each builder, consciously or otherwise, has an equation he applies to a given lumber deal. The factors are cost per thousand board feet (A); plus the length, clearness, and quality of the grain (B); plus the energy (as in dollars or calories) necessary to get it to the shop, stacked, dried, and ready for use (C). If the deal is to go through, A + B + C must equal "reasonable." If builder X cuts his own lumber, he has different requirements than builder Y, who is used to having it delivered milled to his door. The only industry-wide standards are to strive for the best you can get.

> It all depends on how much freight you're willing to pay. We don't foresee a problem for at least 10 years.
>
> *Desco Marine*

> It's there if you want to be patient and pay the price.
>
> *Clark Mills*

Of cutting your own, buying logs, buying from the mill, dealer, or lumberyard, buying from the independent mill is by far the preferred method. In the Northwest, builders are paying from $750 to $900 per thousand board feet at the mill for first-quality fir. Nationally, other plank stock of similar dimensions runs about $550 to $850 at the mill for cedar, depending on location, etc. At the lumberyard or dealer, the same materials run from $1,100 to $1,600 per thousand board feet in the Northwest, and $900 to $1,200 nationally.

In working with the independent mill, the procedures are basically the same everywhere. The builder keeps an eye open and an ear to the ground for good deals. The mill and/or loggers are made aware of the shop's needs, and whenever a good stand or log becomes available, the builder hops into the truck to go take a look.

It can take years for a builder to cultivate a good relationship with a supplier. (In one place I worked, we used to make sure we took the Dodge pickup, not the Toyota, on runs to the mill, since the sawyer was an arch-America-Firster.) If a point can be reached where the logger calls the builder, or the mill simply says, "Come and get it," the builder is way ahead. To achieve this goal may require buying an occasional round of drinks, praising the good stuff loudly in public, and quietly discussing the not-so-good batches just between the two of them.

The average yard stocks between 3,000 and 4,000 board feet at any given time; a few keep as much as 30,000 on hand. One such builder said, "It's better than money in the bank. I've always been able to sell it at a profit, but with inflation, it's an exceptional cushion."

Up until now I have only implied that the builders consider lumber a concern. The figures are on the next page.

Numbers of Builders by Region

(The situation is:)	North-west	Cali-fornia	Gulf Coast	South-east	Chesa-peake	North-east	Great Lakes	National
Good and getting better		1						1
Good and holding	15	2	2	5	3	19		46
Good but declining	4				3			7
Bad and getting better		3	1			2		6
Bad and holding			1	1		5		7
Bad and getting worse	8	1	9	7	6	17	3	51
We have availability/price problems	10	3	5	7	6	26	1	58

Or, by percentage:

	North-west	Cali-fornia	Gulf Coast	South-east	Chesa-peake	North-east	Great Lakes	National
Declining or bad with no reversal	44	14	83	57	75	51	100	58
Improving or good with no reversal	56	86	17	43	25	49		42

As with the market, Northwesterners were upbeat. This time, however, they were almost joined by the Northeasterners.

> No problem. There are so many trees growing, to worry about it is like worrying about a shortage of potatoes. The only hitch is as to what suppliers are willing to cut. I'm planning a portable combination sawmill for logs, resawing, and heavy timber. . . .
>
> *Nick Roth*

The national figures of 58 percent declining against 42 percent improving hide a very important split between the commercial and recreationally oriented areas. Seventy-one percent of the former thought the situation was declining; 53 percent of the latter were optimistic in their outlook. I believe that this last figure is misleadingly high. A separate tally on "availability and price" found that in both the Northwest and the Northeast, very high percentages of builders cited concerns about quantity, quality, and price, even as they said they were optimistic. In the Northeast, 22 said that the situation was declining or poor with no foreseeable reversal, 21 said it was good and/or improving. But, 16 of that 21 by the separate tally expressed worry over price and/or quality. If we add those 16 to the pessimistic side, 88 percent of the Northeastern builders come up negative!

True, builders of a hundred years ago complained about the poor quality of lumber. But as a final, close-the-subject answer, this is too pat. The situation today is much more complex. The technologies developed can make or break a forest in much less time. Consumption of timber in the United States in 1974 (exclusive of imports) was about 12 billion board feet. When the U.S.D.A. recommended an 86-million-board-foot annual limit for Washington and Oregon, one commentary called that figure "modest."

> Lumber is of a lower and lower grade. Good lumber is being shipped off the Olympic Peninsula to Japan in tremendous volume.
>
> *David Clarke*

> Japan will sell it back to us when we are hard up for wood. In general, standards will drop off to meet supply, as they have in the Northeast.
>
> *Carl Brownstein*

> With the stupidity and selfishness of the government, and shipping to Japan, we have to stay two years ahead. Our only hope is in a change in government —reseeding should be mandatory.
>
> *Orville Wike*

> Reforestation is the key to the future of wood construction. We are not reforesting boatbuilding woods. . . . The paper companies cut all the timber and reforest (when they do reforest) only fast pines. We must start new trees, especially juniper.
>
> *George Stevenson*

> The oil crunch will raise Cain with the wood market since good-quality timber is being cut for firewood. The cutting is now indiscriminate.
>
> *Gordon Swift*

> Demand for [wood] in other industries (like furniture) is using up local sources. It's easier for mills to use and handle short logs than big stuff, so their labor is easier to get, too.
>
> *Virgil Miller*

> I've seen 12-foot sheets of plywood with two scarfs in them!
>
> *Valcour Rodrigue*

> Cost will go up if we have to laminate. . . .
>
> *John Wisner*

According to a 1973 Sierra Club bulletin, United States exports to Japan totaled about 14 percent of our total annual harvest of wood suitable for lumber production in 1970. While this may be a slightly inflated figure, it points up the severity of the problem. Hand in hand with this goes the boom in the pulp industry. According to the August 1, 1976, *Paper Trade Journal*, paper and fiberboard demand is so great that this industry will have a shortfall of 44 million tons by 1985. With exports and pulp so profitable, high-quality, long-length lumber needs are not likely to receive the priority rating that wood buffs would like to see. It is almost ludicrous to compare the needs of the wooden boat "industry" to those of the forest industry as a whole. My estimates of wooden boat users' needs compared with data in *Forest Industries* of April 1979 indicate that one fair-size mill in the Pacific Northwest cuts more timber (for plywood) than wooden boatbuilders (professional and amateur) could use in a year. Anacortes, Washington, mills are rated at an annual capacity of 174 million square feet of ⅜-inch plywood. Even with a large industry to back them up, those building plywood boats are having trouble obtaining ply of acceptable quality. Builders of virtually every region, and suppliers in Washington and Louisiana, noted this problem.

The import situation is no better. In Louisiana, where native cypress had been the preferred stock for decades, poor quality and availability have forced many builders to use Brazilian Spanish cedar at $1,300 per thousand board feet. Philippine mahogany is in use throughout the country, and in some areas can compete with native woods in price. Since, as a rule, only the top grades are imported, and since there is a certain amount of selling power in "exotic" woods, dollar for dollar, defect for defect, imports look better and better to some U.S. boatbuilders. But:

> It depends on what happens in Africa. Worldwide instability makes predictions difficult.
>
> *George Patten*

> At a gut level, lumber I don't supply myself is basically a source of uneasiness.
>
> *Chip Stulen*

Melbourne Smith cuts and ships his own lumber from Central America for projects like the *Pride of Baltimore:*

> We are running out of hardwood in Central America even. As regards large vessels, there is no decent lumber left in the U.S.

A recent article in the *Boston Globe* presented devastating evidence of the rape of the Amazon jungle. It explained that the region would not naturally be rich in lumber by nature of its soil, but rather that the forest is there because undisturbed millenniums allowed the build-up of a conducive, shallow surface layer. Once logged, this area will not readily generate new timber. Approximately the same thing happened on portions of the Oregon Coast. As I understand it, without trees to hold warm ground air until it mixed with sea air to produce fog, there was insufficient moisture to successfully replant harvestable trees. By one account, there were studies predicting this problem long before those forests were stripped.

The scarcity and cost of petroleum and its by-products are putting increased pressure on wood resources. This is a double-edged sword. While improvements in forest management are getting increased support, the demand for

The clipper replica Pride of Baltimore. *It has been said that the value of restoring and replicating large vessels will only be understood when we have to return to working sail in a fuel-short economy. (Bob Dollard photo)*

wood is outstripping even the best of efforts. More and more small operations are logging themselves out of existence, or are forced under by safety and environmental regulations with which they are unwilling or unable to comply. Other small operations are bought out by larger companies or work for them under contract, diminishing still further the already small segment of the industry geared toward the low-volume purchaser. It is less and less profitable to take the trouble to saw boat lumber. Milling eight-foot cedar fence posts or shingling is less work and less trouble. The clear logs can get cut up with the knotty ones; it's all the same.

> Retailers want to do everything by forklift, convenience, not work with their hands and brains. The average sawyer doesn't know much about what a stem is, or how to cut one to suit a builder. Fewer still are interested in slowing down production long enough to do so.
>
> *Arno Day*

Conservation measures have also taken their toll. To oversimplify it, the builders are left in the middle of two factions: the conservationists to whom the cutting of a tree is a crime, and the loggers with families to feed and a growing demand to meet. (It is interesting to note that not too long ago, "conservation" and "forest utilization" for recreational *and* timber uses were synonymous.)

If the larger picture is bad, and builders who rely almost entirely on small-scale operations say that *that* supply is declining, the future looks pretty grim. The search for a good batch of cedar gets tougher each year, and will continue to do so unless. . . . "Unless" is for a later section.

Traditional hardware has almost disappeared. The crash, inventory taxes, soaring shipping charges, and high advertising costs were too much for small, "antiquated," family-size manufacturers. Those that survived were bought up by conglomerates who thought they could expand the lines, "modernize," and make the same profit margin on a much larger scale. When they realized the older lines weren't suited to mass-market appeals based on the lowest common denominator, these were simply discontinued. (I know, my prejudices are showing. . . .) Regardless of the causes, most hardware today is "chrome-plated, neoprene-cushioned, nylon snap shackles, and nautical cocktail service."

I have a catalog from 1927 that I take out whenever I want to have a good cry.

Anonymous

Can you image restoring Wanderbird *(page 31) and simultaneously maintaining in mint condition a good-sized sloop? This is the foredeck of Harold Sommer's* Freda, *complete with a handsome winch that harks back to the days when such gear was readily available.*

It's getting almost impossible to find some items. Apparently the big companies are getting out of small, slow-moving items, and turning to plastic, quick-sell. I think the unions are one of the big causes of high cost and delay.

Robert Rich

My biggest problem is hardware. Distributors don't carry stock, and when they do, they are unreliable in delivery.

Fred Ajootian

You run in cycles; sometimes it's the end of the world, sometimes it's rosy. I'm inclined to be optimistic. Prices aren't too bad; you just have to work at least two months ahead.

Paul Rollins

There are more support industries springing up: Flounder Bay Lumber Sales, Skookum Fastenings, Grant Sarver's toolmaking business.

David Jackson

You know how it is, any item that has "marine" printed on it doubles in price automatically.

Bryan Blake

Traditional hardware is hard to get, but since new people seem to be getting into producing it (on a small scale at least), things may improve slightly.

Tom Tucker

Fifty-two percent of the builders were negative about the present *and* future of traditional hardware; the other 48 percent saw the solution in new small-scale companies and/or in builders' developing their own casting blanks for mail order sales to amateurs. Ken Steinmetz of Seaford, New York, did this with some oversize oarlocks in 1978, with good results. By separate tally, 84 percent of the builders felt that hardware prices were inflated way beyond the expected 10 percent annual increase. Many remarked that certain items were doubling in price at least every four years.

The tool situation can be included in this assessment. A builder's tools are an extension of his self. Once a chisel or mallet has proven its ability to hold an edge or balance in the hand, it becomes a favorite. The casualness with which tools are often strewn around boat shops is deceptive. The unavailability of quality replacements at affordable prices invariably elicits sad remarks about cheap steel, badly balanced pieces, and disintegrating plastic handles. Except for buying from custom tool makers like Seattle's Grant Sarver, scrounging seems to be the only immediate solution.

I see the problem of lumber, tools, and hardware as one that mass purchasing and cooperatives can help solve. Organized purchasing power can enable builders to obtain materials either currently out of production or prohibitively expensive.

Dennis Hough

Cooperatives have been seen as the answer by a few. The advantages of coops are well known, as are their pitfalls. The principal applications to wooden boatbuilding would seem to be material cooperatives and/or boats built on a cooperative basis. Fifty-one percent of the builders liked the idea of cooperatives for buying materials, even if they expressed reservations about the independent nature of builders, fighting over who got the best of a shipment, and shortage of working capital upon which to begin such an effort.

> I can foresee a group of builders getting together to support a foundry, not so much the old-timers but rather their proteges who are more open to change.
>
> *Gardner Grice*

> We have already tried it, and still use it on certain parts of the boats now. We have bought screws in lots as large as 15,000. We are "into" cooperation with others.
>
> *Don Hill*

> Buying lumber has possibilities, although . . . no one is really cooperating these days. . . .
>
> *Ken Mobert*

> One day it may come to buying carloads, and that's too much money for one concern.
>
> *Joseph Landry*

> It has been tried here. There are not enough builders, and organization takes too much time.
>
> *Bruce Farrin*

Shops run on a cooperative basis were often dismissed out of hand as unworkable. "Too many builders only have their own way of doing things . . . too independent . . . there has to be someone to delegate responsibility." This was an oft-heard refrain. For amateurs, however, many felt a pooling of resources could be most satisfactory. The Gate Three Cooperative in Sausalito, California, has been in operation for years now. Numerous small projects and two versions of Slocum's *Spray* (one of them lapstrake) have been built there. (See *WoodenBoat,* No. 17.) For several years, a fine cooperative boatyard in the Southeast specialized in repair and restoration of classic sailing vessels. That this and the Seabrook, Texas, Coop were short lived should *not* lead to an overall dismissal of the concept. Their circumstances were unique, and not representative.

Many builders commonly split a truckload with one or perhaps two other builders, or exchange help with labor-intensive projects. I remember jumping into a pickup with one builder to go help another some 15 miles away. While there, he traded a used propeller shaft for another of a different diameter. Since there was a foot's difference in length, he threw in a nice chunk of lignumvitae to make the deal square. This cooperative barter system can go much further, as builders and amateurs recognize its full potential. The time and situation would appear to be ripe for its expansion.

Indian Haulover, shown here before it closed, was the name of the southeastern boat-builders' cooperative. Farther up the canal was a large power plant that used the canal water as part of its cooling system. Water temperatures fluctuated so widely that the canal was free of teredos! A better location for restoring old wooden boats would be hard to imagine.

Labor

If you take the trouble to watch people who excel at what they do, and to listen to them carefully, you soon discover that they all have developed the same basic disciplines. The proper construction of a wooden vessel requires a formidable blend of disciplines: concentration, singleness of purpose, sense of balance, steadiness of hand and eye, sensitivity to material, coordination, inner strength, dexterity, creativity, confidence, experience, awareness, tenacity, endurance, sacrifice, forbearance, patience, judgment, maturity, and wisdom. Thorough knowledge of, and competency with, the incredible varieties of wood, metals, and hardware, and the difficulties of acquiring them, are fundamental.

A builder may bore a shaft log and help install an auxiliary engine in a ketch one week, make blocks and rig her a few weeks later, and then turn out a tender for her to polish off the job. The ability to visualize and analyze complex, three-dimensional shapes is vital. The stress loads on a vessel (power, oar, or sail) are considerable; so an awesome complexity of variables must be considered in deciding the best construction method for a particular part of a particular vessel, in the light of its particular owner and particular use. Marine design and drafting are common additions to the builder's repertoire. Sixty-one percent of the builders surveyed could (and did) do some designing, 21 percent had limited design capabilities. Eighteen percent did not and could not. Most have at least a minimal familiarity with, if not mastery of, diesel mechanics, plumbing, governmental safety regulations, and insurance requirements. I saw very few shops with secretaries. The builder must keep all the records straight (both written and photographic) and do his own books. More realistically, he cons his wife into doing the books, and the Coast Guard into believing, "I'm only building this one for myself." The image is precisely that of W.C. Fields as a tightrope walker, working without a net on a windy day. Although it is understandably rare for all these attributes to come together in one man, it happens far more often than one would expect. It is quite common to find them in two men working side by side. It should not be a surprise that the search for materials is often matched in intensity and duration by the pursuit of a good working partner.

> Boatbuilding takes different disciplines for different kinds of work.
>
> *Jim Peacock*

> By the nature of the beast, boatbuilding doesn't hold dilettantes. The work is too demanding. . . . Yet the people this business attracts are not into a nine-to-five routine. And seeing that my routine is eight-to-six, I find myself alone for the most part. It takes a special fiend to roll this boulder uphill; my hope is that I will soon find another fiend, since it takes two to make a truly efficient shop.
>
> *Ray Speck*

Successful combinations are understandably tightly knit, each person having certain skills and attributes that mesh with those of the other members to form a productive whole. Even in good yards, however, turnover can be substantial. Such turnover is not out of a lack of effort to keep good men on but results from the employee's new mobility and the seasonal fluctuations in the business.

The almost never-ending arguments and discussions as to just who is and what defines a "boatbuilder" stem from this tightness and the complexity of skills required. The successful builder who has mastered most of these skills is irate if a newcomer who specializes in building 12-foot dinghies is called a boatbuilder. He feels that his 15 years of full-time, concentrated effort in learning all the necessary boatbuilding skills is thereby made farcical. There are so many different levels at which builders operate that this kind of debate becomes meaningless. In addition to all the itinerants, part-timers, repairers, etc., there are endless variations within the realm of the professional. To some, a shop producing one large boat a year isn't worthy of the name. To others, four or five is a meaningful figure. As for employees, some would call experienced boat mechanics "boatbuilders," while others consider only the head man able to hold the title.

To simplify matters, I interviewed only one man per yard. In the case of partners, I would interview them as a team, or one would be delegated as spokesman while the other went back to work. The average shop had 3.86 workers, with a high of 60. In this average, the two largest manufacturers of shrimpers, Desco and St. Augustine Trawlers, have been left out; their crews of 350 and 260, respectively, are unique situations. There were clusters in the average shop size: 50 one-man operations; 18 with two men. Shops specializing in traditional small craft averaged 1.3 men; the 48 shops in custom cruising boats averaged 3.75 men; and the 36 commercial businesses (excluding Desco and St. Augustine) averaged 6.08 men.

The pay these men received varied among different kinds of shops and different regions. Not surprisingly, California ranked highest, followed in descending order by the Northwest, Great Lakes, Northeast, Southeast (not including Florida), and the Gulf Coast. The variations were so extensive, and the reasons for them so idiosyncratic, that a separate study would have been necessary to determine all the variables and draw meaningful conclusions from them.

For example, in dealing with alternativist one-man shops or itinerants, it is almost impossible to know just how much of the hourly rate is labor and how much is overhead. The builder himself may not know, or the percentage may vary drastically from job to job. The hourly rate charged by the business is a separate category. An informal random check during the spring of 1979 revealed the following rates for top finish men.

Dollars per Hour

	California	Northwest	Great Lakes	Northeast	Southeast/ Chesapeake	Gulf Coast
Employees	$10-12	$ 8-10	$ 5-7	$4-8.50	$4-6	$3-8.50
Itinerants	$12-15	$10-14		$8-12	$6-8	
Shop charges	$18-20	$12-17	$12-15	$11-15	$10-12	$10-12
Union shops	$26	$25			$20	

Some readers may be shocked at how low the pay scales are. In general, the boat mechanic is earning considerably less than the house carpenter working up the street. Ironically, the boatbuilder needs a good many more skills. Boats require so much custom work that the builder is caught between the need to keep costs down to a marketable level and the need to take home a decent paycheck. State taxes on inventory, workmen's compensation, social security, and insurance rates—not to mention material and space costs—are rising faster than selling prices.

It is an eye-opener to figure the cost of a small, open boat at the hourly rates charged by one's local garage mechanic, dentist, or psychiatrist. Yet a first-class custom builder's "education" takes longer to complete than medical school. Building a 17-footer, perhaps a 300-hour project, figured at shop charges of $10, $15, $25, and $40 an hour, runs into figures that seem truly unreasonable. Even at $10 an hour, it would be a $3,000 boat. It is some measure of the squeeze that to the buying public this seems astronomical, while the builder may be realizing only $4.50 an hour on his labor.

In a small shop, quality control is as effective as the builder cares to make it, and despite the financial limitations, he usually cares a great deal. The builders I met talked repeatedly of doing it right or not doing it at all, and never mind the lack of money.

John Gardner, in the Traditional Small Craft Association newsletter, *Ash Breeze,* commented on the origins of today's labor situation in American boatbuilding:

> None of the old-time boatbuilders in this country ever went to school to learn their trade, and there was little apprenticing in boatbuilding in the United States from the 19th century on. There was more in shipbuilding, which is quite different from boatbuilding, being more specialized and on a much larger scale. It is not something that an individual can do by himself alone. Indeed, that was what distinguished shipbuilding from boatbuilding for Howard Chapelle.
>
> The apprentice system, brought to this country from the old world, at the beginning was a restrictive system that tended to die out as economic and social barriers were broken down, particularly following the American Revolution. Sometimes the boatbuilding trade was passed on in the family from father to son, but more often, the young would-be boatbuilder picked up his trade by himself, and often with difficulty. Established builders tended to be secretive about the fine points of the trade.

The Depression and then World War II radically upset the labor pool. Men with building experience went to work in large plants, and when the war ended, went back to the small, local boatyards just in time to catch the beginnings of the wooden boatbuilding crash. With the heavy shakeout of the next 10 to 15 years, there was little incentive for newcomers to enter the shop. The new priority on secure income and the ever-tighter grasp with which settled men held on to their jobs and knowledge had their effects.

Professional boatbuilding had always required dedication, pride, and an unromantic and unglorified view of the business. More recently, you could add to those the belief that quality of life comes before money. With the crash, it became obvious that it would be years before wooden boatbuilding became economically viable—if it ever would.

It is ironic and yet fitting that the salvation of a tradition as old as wooden boatbuilding grew in large part out of the chaos of the Sixties. A period marked by the upset of many "traditional" values helped mold individuals who saw the importance of wooden boats not only as a heritage but on their own merits as well. These same people were motivated enough to reshape the training system in order to keep that heritage alive. In the late Sixties/early Seventies, there were very real demands for good labor going unmet. The vocational training schools were not yet in operation, with the exception of two long-established institutions in the Northwest. In the Northeast, some of the better-known yards experienced a curious phenomenon. College-educated, urbanized, young men were asking for work. The youths often had limited experience with woodworking or boats, and much of their education (if not all of it) was in unrelated fields. Still, they'd decided they wanted to learn how to build wooden boats. Builders were caught in a bind. Digging their way out of the crash, they needed men who could step right into the job and do the work *quickly*. But experienced men were not out looking for work. With the escalating minimum wage, taxes, and insurance, bringing a man through the ropes from scratch was often beyond a yard's financial capabilities. Yet many young men offered service without pay, for at least a trial period, in exchange for the opportunity to learn. In light of the crisis at hand, it couldn't hurt to try them out.

The seasonal rotation of spring outfitting, summer repairs and service, fall storage, and new construction in winter (when the yard could get it) required a willingness to work hard at jobs that were unpleasant (scraping paint and cleaning bilges) and not apparently related to boat*building* as far as the newcomer was concerned. (That same cycle tended to deceive those still looking for work, since a yard might be short of work one week and have a 50-footer to build the next. It was mostly a matter of saying the right thing at the right time, in the right place.) Modern apprentices often found that the romance and inspiration of wooden boatbuilding eluded them, amid the sanding and clean-up that is an integral part of a boat shop—even for finish men. Many youngsters had literally talked their way in. When they appeared unhappy about the less pleasant aspects of the vocation, the builder felt a certain frustration. If this kind of experience was repeated with a number of apprentices, the builder became very wary of these "dreamers."

> We have to train our own men. Ten percent of all the applicants are any good. They are doers and leaders, not watchers and sheep. When an "apprentice" is helping me at the planer, and he doesn't move around to the other side without being asked, I know he's not thinking for himself. *That's* what I mean.
>
> *Orville Wike*

> You don't know until new help has been in the shop for a couple of months . . . two out of a hundred are worth keeping on. Mostly the glamour wears off, so they don't stay.
>
> *George Luzier*

> It takes a good many years to acquire the diversity needed, and then the good men tend to go off on their own. We have tried to stabilize things with a profit-sharing plan and other inducements.
>
> *G. C. Whiticar*

> There are *some* good men, both young and old. You've got to love boats and be someone who can be content with good work. You can't come to work thinking about your lunch box. There'll be a greater problem here with molded materials. Men will come to work hating every moment of the job, like on an assembly line. I never did know a man who liked assembly line work.
>
> *Virgil Miller*

On the apprentice's part, there were mixed experiences as well. Builders can only allow so much time for a given job, and some were only too willing to press this cheap labor for all they could get. In some shops, the apprentice was expected to run errands and sweep floors for six months, as apprentices always had in the past. To a product of the Sixties, this was unacceptable. If he was working for nothing (or close to it), he wanted to learn. The training in boatbuilding they were to receive in return for the sweat of their brow was often second-rate, or sometimes never materialized at all.

To all outward appearances, these apprenticeships were not all that different from those of generations before. But in fact, the tone (if not always the terms) of these modern relationships was very different. Disagreements may have stemmed from different standards as to what constituted an apprenticeship. The college-trained mind expected to be a student (to be taught, but treated as an equal), and the old-school builder expected an apprentice who picked up knowledge on his own (aggressively showing what he was made of), while at the same time behaving as a proper underling. If the present-day apprentice didn't like what he found, and change seemed unlikely, he simply left. The constraints of being from the same town, of having personal ties with the community and/or the shop no longer existed. Also, as a child of middle-class America, and a potential recipient of unemployment benefits, the modern apprentice was not faced with financial limitations.

There were, however, many successful arrangements. An apprentice who was on the ball might offer to work extra hours on a given project in return for the opportunity to loft the next tender. Builders were helpful and supportive when someone with little related experience showed exceptional aptitude for boatbuilding and an ability to get along with others in the yard, no matter how far apart they might be in background.

Today, this situation is only slightly changed. Because of the availability of trade journals and vocational training programs, the would-be boatbuilder is better informed. Builders either have decided not to take on strangers of uncertain talent, or have become better, more patient judges of who will and who won't be satisfactory. The majority of successful builders and trainees (86 percent) have been involved with wooden boats all their lives, and I would guess 95 percent of those "could not remember when [they] first began to use woodworking tools and to work around boats."

One of my original reasons for considering this project was a suggestion that the boatbuilding schools needed to be examined closely. Concrete charges of publishing misleading promotional copy and financial underhandedness on the part of administrators and teachers were leveled against one school in particular. That school is no longer in existence. Still, with the speed at which rumor and innuendo circulate in this tightly knit field, legitimacy remains a concern. There are personal growth programs of all kinds that essentially cover

The first major project of one group of Carteret's students shows strong lines. Note the upward pitch of the planking along the skeg behind the shaft log. This creates a "tunnel" or hollow that allows the prop to sit much closer to the hull, thus drawing less water.

techniques of wooden boatbuilding. The distinction between this type of program and a school designed to train professional builders is an important one that has not often been clarified, and as a consequence has caused a number of misunderstandings.

The former are small, local, often inconstant programs, commonly operating on the energy of a single individual. News of these rarely reaches the trade journals. In Texas, the Sea Scouts have a program. Salvageable small boats are hauled in off shoal water or marshland and rebuilt by the Scouts under the guidance of a retired builder. In Port Aransas, Texas, Doyle Marek teaches skiff building as part of the local public school elective curriculum. Carteret Technical Institute in Morehead City, North Carolina, is running a program on construction of Harkers Island boats. The Institute teaches the same techniques as the professionals on Harkers use, i.e., building by eye. There are the Evergreen State College Marine Studies Program, Daybreak Boatshop's Traditional Boat Center's classes, etc. There are intensive weekend or week-long symposiums, such as those given at Mystic Seaport and Port Townsend, in which curriculum is geared toward personal interest and home building, not professionalism. While these have an important effect on increasing the general boating public's awareness of what boatbuilding is all about, they are not likely to have any real effect on the labor pool.

At the other end of the spectrum, there are precisely six places offering a basis for a career in boatbuilding through well-conceived one- or two-year programs. Two of the six are only a year old, and as such are unproven. They are listed here because they have shown sufficient backing, integrity, and planning. In all fairness, it takes anywhere from five to 10 years for any school to lay a solid foundation. In order of longevity, then, they are:

Bates Vocational Technical Institute of Tacoma
Tacoma, Washington . . . . 30 years, 20 students

Seattle Central Community College
Seattle, Washington . . . . 19 years, 40 students

The Apprenticeshop and Restorationshop
Bath, Maine . . . . 7 years, 16 students

Washington County Vocational Technical Institute, Marine Center
Eastport, Maine . . . . 7 years, 42 students

Norfolk School of Boatbuilding
Norfolk, Virginia . . . . 1 year, up to 60 students

The Landing Boatshop
Kennebunkport, Maine . . . . 1 year, 9 students

All the schools get many more applications than they have slots to fill. Some have waiting lists with several hundred names! Five of the schools are discussed in the back of the regional section corresponding to their locations. Each has a different approach, attitude, and curriculum. For now, it will be sufficient to spotlight two of the more differentiated programs, The Apprenticeshop in Bath, Maine, and the Washington County (Maine) Vocational Technical Institute (better known as Eastport). Though they are perhaps the best-known programs, the similarities end there.

Eastport has, as a primary requirement of enrollment, the intention to continue in the field as a professional. Preference is given to Maine residents, since the school is funded and operated as part of the state's county-based, voc tech system. In an effort to prepare students for the transition to the yard, students must punch a clock, keep regular hours, and provide their own housing. This last is no small matter in Washington County, Maine.

The Apprenticeshop, on the other hand, is as much a personal growth experience as a boatbuilding program. Apprentices come from many regions and live and eat in a housing community, sharing expenses. Weekly rap sessions are held to ease differences and make decisions. Each participant is there as an "individual," working at his/her own pace with his/her own goals. The program is nonprofit and is run as an extension of the Bath Marine Museum. Relatively few of Bath's graduates to date have gone on to professional boatbuilding, but this trend seems to be changing.

Both schools have undergone substantial change since opening. (In schools of this size, even a change of instructor can cause a major change in, if not wholesale revision of, the program.) At the risk of oversimplifying, Bath has become more time/productivity-conscious while maintaining its self-reliant, small-is-beautiful, human-energy-intensive philosophy. The Eastport school has moved from the coastal beauty of Lubec's Quoddy Head to a more diversified, if less pleasing, steel and concrete industrial park in the town of Eastport. It has added commercial fishing, marine mechanics, and marine finishing to the Marine Trade Center's overall program. Because all the schools have relatively limited resources and strong philosophical positions, the emphasis is on what the individual can make of his/her stay.

The changes at Bath and Eastport are significant, since the shift toward a

An apprentice trims the stem of a rowing/sailing peapod.

more businesslike, comprehensive approach lies at the heart of concerns about labor in general. Opinions of the programs were sharply polarized among alumni many years out of school. Even builders with a minimum of contact often couched their words in the strongest possible terms.

The quotes that follow illustrate the intensity of feeling and diversity of perspective that builders expressed about training and labor in general. Beyond separating commercially oriented builders from recreationally oriented ones, I have let their comments run together. For example, some builders differentiated between those in vocational training programs and

Eastport, Maine: When that rabbet line doesn't sit fairly, a lofting conference may be the fastest way to locate the source of the discrepancy. In this case, it is in the midsections of a 17′ Buzzards Bay sloop.

those getting their training on the job, while others did not. In considering the range of views that follows, that kind of categorizing is of no value. Rest assured, if a builder quoted as saying, "Standards of speed at the schools are low" didn't apply that view to *all* builders in training, another builder did.

In the commercially oriented, less intellectualized areas of the Eastern Shore of Maryland, the Carolina Banks, and the Louisiana Bayous, young people are not interested in boatbuilding. Gerard Ledet of Golden Meadow, Louisiana, said:

> In the past, everyone could do carpentry, splice, etc. The older men have been working for many years and want to take it easy. It's hard to get good men of any age. I'm the only younger one I know.

Others elsewhere have said:

> Labor is a problem. Young people aren't interested in boatbuilding . . . they're out on the water (fishing) where the money is . . . watermen, not boatbuilders. * * * They can make a lot more money on the bay as long as it's clean.* * * The labor pool is very poor. Marine carpenters, loftsmen, machinists, etc., are very rare. This is due, to a great extent, to low pay for the knowledge required. The young people sought higher-paying trades. * * * Commercial fishermen make good helpers and workmen, but most trainees are dreamers. * * * The quantity of labor is low. Lots of young people are getting into it, but *it takes time.* Lots of old-timers have dropped out, and there's a lag between them and the new men. The young men will make just as good builders in the end. * * * There is more to this lag than just a difference in years. Many of the new builders of the last four or five years . . . are returning to skills in lieu of professions. They bring with them the alternativism of the Sixties. * * * The concept of "industry" is nuts—commercialism must be open-minded, not turn people off. Traditional wooden boating is creative, not particularly business-oriented. Training should be slanted that way. There are no jobs for those trained, save in their own shops. * * * Some can and will cut the mustard, in repair yards or on their own. Others tend to move on within a three-year period. The cut-off line seems to be about five years. If they last beyond that, something is right with them. * * * I *am* that labor pool. There are a great number of young men who are willing to learn. * * * Programs should be geared toward learning by *doing,* working on boats with market value—not Indian canoes and guide-boats. * * * There's not enough hands-on experience. They have tool skill, but less practical knowledge. * * * Not enough people know the whole job in all its phases of detail. * * * I have a natural talent for building boats, and my knowledge of wood and structures is my guide. * * * I always have to think of the boat going through the worst weather imaginable. * * * There should be more schools . . . I do not train apprentices because they want to start from scratch. I feel they should have basic woodworking skills before learning boatbuilding. * * * Many people want to work and learn. However, few succeed in becoming fine craftsmen. * * * It takes a lifetime to be a boat carpenter—'til you are 50 years old to know what

you are doing. The younger people don't have the eye or aptitude. You practically have to be born into it. Vocational training is great for keeping interest going, but I doubt it will produce competent boatbuilders. * * * There are very few men who can build a traditional hull as they used to. Their numbers are diminishing as the old-timers depart. There are still not enough young people interested. * * * In the yard, with taxes and insurance and all, one can't afford to pay any starter more than three dollars an hour. How can you keep a man on for that? You can't expect him to live on that. * * * You can't keep the good men, and the bad ones you don't want to keep. * * * Schools keep 'em off the streets . . . but we are turning out a *lot* more builders than there are jobs for. * * * Wooden boats are certainly not getting *less* popular. . . . There aren't any formal, in-yard apprenticeships, and you have to learn somewhere. While building traditional small craft trains people in fits and construction, it might lead them to believe that that's what they are going to be doing. I doubt there are those kinds of jobs available for the products of the boatbuilding schools. The jobs that are, are in *repair, replacing floor timbers, sistering frames, and not in varnish and Whitehalls* [emphasis mine—P.L.]. * * * Newcomers don't understand laws and business . . . they also need more chemistry, as well as economics. * * * I haven't seen a decent program. Vocational students have lousy work habits, don't know %$#&, and want to be primadonnas. I don't think the instructors know all that much either. * * * With rare exceptions, vocational-technical products are no good. Graduates know just enough to be dangerous. * * * I'm 67, so I build boats because I want to. My main objective is to train young men in a skill that is becoming rare. They'll never be out of work. * * * The voc tech products seem to think of themselves as artists. They do not have a cost-effective, get-the-job-done approach. There is a general lack of experience, so vocational training is a good thing. Interested young men with that background will carry on the profession. Without the schools, it will die quickly. * * * Students seem to have good basics. * * * We need the kind of creative training that is found at Bates and Seattle Community College—teachers looking for faster, more accurate means to do the job. The old apprentice/master system is too rigid. For builders to make a living today, they must be able to produce efficiently. * * * The young guys are dedicated as hell. My present trainees are better than those I had 30 years ago. . . . The morale and education of those there are, are excellent. * * * Motivation is an absolute necessity. Everything says you can't do it, so if you listen, you are %##'&!!. * * * Those coming out of the schools will have a tough time without the inner desire and determination. You must be a boatbuilder in heart, body, and soul. Those who will make it must eat, sleep, and drink boats. . . .

Fred Ajootian of White Stone, Virginia, said:

I have been exposed to some of the fine builders, Herreshoff, Minneford, Nevins, etc., and they cut perfect fits quickly and accurately faster than any clown cut a two-by-four. I don't think there are too many like that, but everyone has to produce the best they can toward that standard.

I believe, along with Fred, that men of this potential were no more common in the "good old days" than they are today. For one man to achieve speed and accuracy on the design board, the lofting floor, with a spiling batten, and on into varnish work is no more difficult today than it was then, except for one factor: the number of yards and opportunities to work toward such a goal are far fewer.

> There is excellent potential for a small number of truly professional yards. Right now there are too many amateurs muddying the water. Traditional wooden boatbuilding needs to be seen more as an occupation and less as a romantic endeavor: that is to say, traditional small craft can't take months to build if one is to make a solid living. There's no pension plan. The schools may be saturating the market. It's hard to see what's going to happen. In any case the quantity is fine; to get the quality you have to be very selective. The labor pool is getting better. Seriously interested hard workers, nonromantics, are getting stronger.

The most common remarks are all related to time productivity awareness, dedication, transient workers, and low wages. The root of all the criticism is the desire for a realistic approach to the industry.

Gordon Swift spent 13 years as an apprentice under the much-respected Bud McIntosh. If this seems excessive to some, consider the fact that when he went out on his own, "Swifty," as he is known, was a much more than competent man. Two exquisite 34-foot Warner-designed ketches followed. The younger builders who seem most likely to succeed are for the most part yard-trained, and even those with vocational education backgrounds consider their "five years with Delaney" the vital ones. It is agreed among both builders and instructors that the new graduate, whether formally or self-trained, is ready to begin his true apprenticeship in the yard. It is only the very exceptional student who can even start as a finish man, let alone competently open his own shop. This important point has been recognized all too infrequently.

Former students and builders often may be in conflict simply because their expectations of each other are unrealistic. Some of the institutions are recognizing this as a serious problem for which they are largely responsible, and a few are taking positive corrective measures. In defense of the programs in general, it must be said that professional builders had little to do with getting the programs started, and no organized trade group exists to offer assistance or advice. Schools welcome input, but few builders have taken the time to address their criticism to those in charge. It is hardly remarkable that builders find the focus not always to their liking.

THE LABOR POOL

Number of Builders by Region

(The pool is:)	North-west	Cali-fornia	Gulf Coast	South-east	Chesa-peake	North-east	Great Lakes	National
Good and improving	7	1			1	4	2	15
Good and holding	5	2		3	1	12		23
Good and declining			1					1
Bad and improving	1			4	1	2	1	9
Bad and holding	4	3	8	7	2	6		30
Bad and declining			3	2	7	6		18
Saturated	3					1		4
Total								100

By percentage:

	North-west	Cali-fornia	Gulf Coast	South-east	Chesa-peake	North-east	Great Lakes	National
Improving, good and/or holding	76	50		39	25	60	100	49
Declining, bad and/or holding	24	50	100	61	75	40		51

Nationally, the situation looks somewhat ambiguous. Fifty-one percent saw the situation as declining, or less than satisfactory, with no change in sight. However, if we examine the commercial regions, we get a very different picture. The Gulf, Southeast, and Chesapeake are 75 percent on the negative side, compared with the recreational areas' 66 percent positive outlook. It would seem that the quantity and quality of the work force is declining in direct proportion to the distance from the alternativist, intellectualized centers.

VOCATIONAL TRAINING

Number of Builders by Region

	Northwest	California	Gulf Coast	Southeast	Chesapeake	Northeast	Great Lakes	National
Positive feelings with slight criticism	18	2	1	2	5	33		61
Need for more businesslike approaches	15	2		2	6	13		28
No jobs for graduates, negative feelings	9					2		11
								100

By percentage:

	Northwest	California	Gulf Coast	Southeast	Chesapeake	Northeast	Great Lakes	National
Positive feelings with slight criticism	56	50	100	50	45	68		61
Need for more businesslike approaches	15	50		50	55	27		28
No jobs for graduates, negative feelings	29					5		11

Sixty-one percent thought in generally positive terms, 28 percent said the programs could use overhauling, only 11 percent thought the whole idea was cockeyed and inappropriate, if not downright harmful.

> The market is growing, but the number of prospective builders is growing faster. There are rough times ahead.
>
> *Anonymous*

The tables also show that there are large areas of the country where builders don't even know programs exist. This, as much as all the criticism, points out the need for better communication among the schools, their students, and the builders. Walter Baron's comments on the misleading aspects of training people on traditional small craft are well taken (see page 260). A realistic assessment of the job opportunities available for graduates (repair as well as new construction) should be a routine part of every school year.

Despite the growth of boatbuilding schools, and the increase in the numbers of men and women pursuing boatbuilding careers in general, there are still not enough of either. The southern states lack accessible programs. Boat repairers have slots going begging. With a modicum of experience and stick-to-itiveness, the best positions in the yard can be had in a few years' time. There is room for at least two more schools, particularly in the South, and for as many minor programs for the enthusiast as the public will support. The distinction between them needs to be kept clear, and the realities of "going into boatbuilding" made evident.

A Word to the Wise

As Alan Villiers said, "Don't let the books fool you, my boy, there's no sailor writing them." It is also true that boatbuilders don't usually write books on boatbuilders. I have attempted to break that truism here. To the careful reader, the builders' words about boatbuilding, the market, and so forth, will reveal the substance of their lives. The interviews must be considered the heart of this work. Builders aren't professional speakers or writers, and while many can and have spoken eloquently, some simply have not. To expect them all to be as articulate as the late Pete Culler of Hyannis, Massachusetts, is unrealistic. Furthermore, their normal response to questions about who they are and what they do is:

> Let my work speak for me. Go climb all over that sloop over there; I built her 30 years ago. If you've got eyes to see and a brain to think with, it's all right there.

In our voluble society, the ability to speak or write is often confused with the ability to *do* what one is talking about. The two are hardly connected. When reading the interviews, consider what the builders have to say line by line, and add it up as you go. In one of my briefest interviews, George Saroukas of Tarpon Springs, Florida, said:

> What's that sign say? "Master Builder," that's right. That's all they have to know.

One of the other builders of Greek extraction in Tarpon Springs is Minas Sarris. In his interview (immediately following that of Saroukas), he talks about "dog-eat-dog" competition. Saroukas' brevity and Sarris' comments tell the story in a nutshell. They may or may not be in direct competition, but the tone of their approach to their work, lives, and strangers is clear enough. If a builder wants to develop his own woodlot or join a cooperative, chances are that he's fairly young. If he says he settled in his present location because "I'm from here," that can be interpreted to mean that he has extensive local contacts. If he's just moved, on the other hand, that implies a certain flexibility. The reader should watch for these points.

At the same time, avoid placing too much faith in what you read between the lines, or even taking what is there at face value. (Remember, I paraphrased their answers much of the time. You may not be reading their exact words.) A builder who says, "There isn't any decent lumber left" is not necessarily saying he uses poor lumber. Builders of traditional small craft, custom cruisers, etc., all speak from different perspectives.

Many people have requested that I rate or recommend the "better" builders in this book. I get angry when I hear an aficionado cite a particular flaw in one boat as proof of so-and-so's failings as a builder. I have been in almost all the yards listed here, and talked with almost all of the builders. I have seen their work and often inquired of disinterested parties as to their boats' longevity. I hesitate, even in the privacy of my own mind, to make judgments on the basis of this cursory research. A man's past record, most recent projects, the longevity and diversity of his work—in short, all the variables in all their relative degrees that go into defining what each of us terms "the best for the job"—must be considered by each reader in each situation before passing judgment. This is not possible on the basis of these interviews. What I have presented here are outlines, not detailed portraits.

I intentionally refrained from all but occasional references to a builder's age. I have included a few builders who are young and unproven. I firmly believe that in the interests of a more balanced market, this is the fairest approach. Responsible newcomers must be given the opportunity to break in; older shops will persevere.

In writing the introduction to each region, I made no attempt to cover them all in exactly the same way. I was struck by different things in different places. In the same way, I did not write an introductory paragraph for each interview. There were many cases where there was nothing of note to say. But the absence of such a paragraph is in no way a reflection on the builder in question.

II.
The Northwest and California

The whole of the northern West Coast was my home for the fall of 1977. I drove, walked, and hitchhiked between San Francisco and British Columbia. The variety of the builders' views, their hospitality, and the changing scenery kept the miles from wearing me down. One interview led to another, the second builder would mention a third, and suddenly I'd have to take on another thousand-mile excursion. After I'd been around Puget Sound for more than two months, I began to think I'd located all the builders. Suggestions from new contacts were mostly repetitions of the list I had developed. Then someone would mention four or five people of whom I'd never even heard! More often than not, these would turn out to be amateurs or retirees. Still, it taught me respect for the breadth and idiosyncrasies of the grapevine.

I headed west to Hoquiam and worked my way south toward San Francisco. Most of the coastline consists of 800-foot cliffs with no beach at the bottom. U.S. 101 is carved into the face about 400 feet up. Logging trucks wheel around the hairpin turns on this single-lane "highway," taking up much of both sides of the road. Often it seems as if there's no way to avoid them but to drop into the Pacific.

This coast is almost as forbidding to boats as it is to drivers. There are few "sailable" areas in almost a thousand miles of surf-torn coastline. To pass under the Golden Gate Bridge, or leave for long the shelter of Puget Sound, is not something most sailors take lightly. If you don't fight your way along the coast, where can you go—Hawaii? A lot of cruisers seemed to be stagnating in Grays Harbor, Washington, which didn't make sense to me until I talked with the man behind the counter in the local chandlery.

> Oh yeah, they're here 'cause they've lost whatever it is that brought them *this* far. Old boats come here to die. This town is loaded with old rotters and even new boats whose skippers can't face crossing the bar again.

The Columbia River Estuary is well known for its ability to chew up ships and men. Still, I found a few builders in the area. At Newport, Oregon, on the Siletz River, and at Eureka, California, they build everything from yachts to trawlers.

In an industrial park outside of Newport, Orville Wike and Joe McGlasson are busy in their shops, The Oregon Dory Company and Cape Foulweather Boat Company, respectively. Orville has built his flat- and V-bottomed workboats and cruisers for customers as far away as Saudi Arabia and Australia. A naval architect and builder, Joe gets busier with each passing year. When I visited, he had no fewer than six projects underway, including a 54-foot twin-screw yacht complete with a helicopter landing pad.

California, for all its miles of coastline and talented artisans, also has relatively few builders. The reasons are that same rugged coast, the high overhead caused by incredible land values, and the Longshoreman's and Harbor Worker's Compensation Act of 1972. The Act essentially brought marina employees under the federal umbrella and helped pressure state benefit structures into compliance. For a multitude of "erroneous" and "mysterious" reasons, the insurance market became very constricted and expensive. To complicate matters, the effects of the Act varied from the negligible to the catastrophic from state to state; litigation surrounding the Act was difficult, complex, and contradictory; and boatyards, insurers, and federal bureaucrats could not even agree on whether or not the Act itself was responsible for the tight insurance market. In any case, California boatyards that formerly provided repair and construction services consistently cited the LHWCA as the principal cause for discontinuing these services. Since traditional boatbuilding was a marginal moneymaker and a liability in the eyes of insurers, many yards closed down this part of their operations in order to beef up more profitable services. Some closed completely.

Itinerant repairers and builders of the old pickup, California stereotype exist in abundance, but full-time builders of recognizable longevity and stability are few and far between. Enthusiasts are plentiful. The Traditional Small Craft Association's Santa Cruz group has been very active under the leadership of Steve Zieler and boatbuilders Richard and Laura Kolin. The Kolins have moved to Anacortes, Washington, but it is clear that the Santa Cruz chapter will continue to prosper. Sausalito has a berthing facility for wooden boats *only* (see *WoodenBoat*, No. 25) and a number of permanent and itinerant boatbuilders.

As I worked my way around the Bay area, and Sausalito in particular, I learned that several people I was looking for had moved north. The Kolins were not alone. Just a few weeks after I'd left Hoquiam, I prepared to hitchhike north again.

Sommer's Boat Works in Oakland, California, gutted the interior before taking on this massive replanking and reframing job.

I was not to travel into Southern California for some time yet, but when I did, I entered "plastic boat land." With the help of "the look of real wood" and "the quality of a teak-trimmed interior," plastic had conquered. Pier upon pier of fiberglass boats was unrelieved by so much as a wooden dinghy. The few builders I found were "holed up," and very depressed about the boating public's "level of consciousness, not only relating to wood but to quality in general." The Longshoreman's Act had been a hard blow. Decreasing interest seemed the final straw. I followed the uprooted builders north.

The attitude of the Northwest builders reminds me of the saga of the Port Townsend Centipedes, "World Champions of the Tug of War." Just prior to the first Wooden Boat Festival, PT sent to the tug-of-war championship a team of small, physically unimpressive young men who were pulling together for the first time that summer. In one of PT's happenings of the decade, their team finished ahead of 110 others in a triumph of brains and audacity over brawn. For years, the championship had been won by teams composed of loggers and other burly types in challenges of sheer strength. The Centipedes figured a lot of little guys could do the job better. (The teams are under a weight limit, not a man limit.) But they won as much on their ability to psych out the other teams as anything else. The Centipedes would rest the first man in line in the middle of competition! He'd stand there resting his arms, loosening up, even melodramatically lying down to relax right in the faces of the grunting, straining opponents! A caller would run up and down the Centipedes' line, yelling over the roar of the crowd into each man's ear. The opposition, sure that they were about to receive a big pull, would tighten up and waste energy on a jerk that never came. Two minutes later, the Centipedes might polish them off with a yank that broke upon them without warning. By the time PT reached the finals at Seattle's Kingdome, the team was so revved up that they ordered sneakers flown up from California that were specially designed for Astroturf. PT residents traveled to Seattle en masse to cheer them on. One member told me that while resting after a semifinal match, a lady in her nineties walked up to him and said, "You guys are gonna win, and IT IS SOOOO GREAT!" In celebration of their victory and the $10,000 prize, the team chartered the steam ferry *Virginia V* for the trip home and threw a gigantic party aboard her as they cruised up the Sound. Months later, memories of the championship *and* the party still set eyes ablaze. This is what Northwestern wooden boating is like.

In recent years, there has been a lot of copy devoted to the traditional watercraft revival in the Northwest and how it is taking off. While I found more boatbuilding per se in the Northeast, gatherings of devotees are much more common on Puget Sound than elsewhere. The explosion of information from the Sound is due to this, and to geographics. (More on these later.) Regardless of the reasons, the outburst is valuable, informative, and long overdue. Mystic Seaport, John Gardner, Howard Chapelle's writings, *National Fisherman,* and *WoodenBoat* are all based in the Northeast. Only in recent years has any information on Northwestern indigenous small craft (for instance) been available. Now, active enthusiasts such as Herb Yates of Portland, Oregon, are researching à la Chapelle to put the situation on more equal ground. The Seattle-based Traditional Wooden Boat Society's publication, *Lines and Offsets,* keeps abreast of what is happening around Puget Sound. There is a new Center for Wooden Boats (see the interview with Dick Wagner).

The intense energy and strength of wooden boating in the Northwest are rooted in the individuals involved, and the area's undeveloped potential. With an abundance of islands and bays to cruise, the Sound is close to paradise, particularly for the traditional small craft enthusiast. The thousands of square miles of Puget Sound are relatively compact, and transportation by road and ferry is extraordinarily good. With at least 28 boat shops compressed into the area (just in this listing), enthusiasts and builders are always passing through each other's shops, stopping long enough for refreshment and a chat. A wooden boat "chat" is anything less than an hour and a half; more than that is a "talk"; five or six hours nonstop is a "discussion." No one knows this better than Dick and Colleen Wagner.

Ten years ago, Dick and Colleen started renting and selling traditional small craft from their houseboat on Seattle's Lake Union. Seattle is centrally located on Puget Sound, thus increasing the frequency with which people dropped in. Since they helped found the Traditional Wooden Boat Society in 1976, their home and business, The Old Boathouse, has become a haven for boat "nuts." The flood of callers, inquiries, and visitors is overwhelming. Launch an idea in Anacortes on Friday, and it will have been thoroughly discussed at Dick and Colleen's by Monday, and vice versa. In what must have been an attempt to get just a few of the discussions out of their living room, The Center for Wooden Boats was created. Still, it is doubtful that even the Center will completely prevent some builder from espousing his latest brainstorm in the Wagners' dining-room forum, which is probably the way the Wagners want it.

The Old Boathouse is by no means the only such nucleus. Across Seattle, The Wooden Boat Shop sells traditional small craft and wooden-boat-related tools and supplies, and gives away much good advice. Proprietors Land Washburn and Joe Bucek are attempting what may be a first since the wooden-boat crash—retail sales of wooden boats on a showroom basis. In Anacortes, Bob and Erica Pickett of Flounder Bay Boat Shop and Lumber Sales are roaring along. Long lengths of premium air-dried fir, oak, spruce, and red and yellow cedar lure wood buffs. A block away, Martin Langeland and his wife, Diana, operate Skookum Fastenings, manufacturing copper rivets, clench nails, roves, and galvanized cut nails. Two blocks the other way is David Jackson's Freya Boatworks, which recently started a 45-foot Brewer-designed schooner.

General Information

Number of builders: Thirty-nine, and four sources. The average shop crew consists of 2.8 men. It became apparent after several months of trying to see all the builders in the Puget Sound area that if I were to continue with that goal, I would be a peer to Methuselah before I finished the entire country. The decision to write this book grew out of my struggles with this dilemma, and that early-morning discussion I had with Terry Lesh in Oregon. I refined my goal to a reasonable sampling of each region's builders as "points of access." This is, therefore, perhaps a 75 percent sampling of the builders of Puget Sound, as opposed to the national average of about 10 percent. The builders included from British Columbia are those I found to be working frequently within the American market.

Capacity: The average shop could accommodate a 42-foot boat, with six shops having space for boats 60 feet and over.

Specialties: Of 33 responding, 17 mixed custom sail and power with traditional small craft; eight specialized strictly in traditional small craft; four worked mostly with powerboats; and four built *only* a specialty line, such as Don Hill's river dories.

Nontraditional modes: Fifteen were willing and experienced; 14 were willing to work with them but had not previously done so; six said they would not work with them on the basis of experience; another six rejected the idea without previous contact.

Preferred paints and glues: Sixteen used a combination ("We use what's best"); 12 were strictly traditional; seven preferred the modern.

Sail and/or power: Of 30 responding, 14 had more experience with sailing craft; six with power; 10 said fifty-fifty each way.

Facilities

Design and drafting: Eighteen said they had capabilities in these; 10 limited their capabilities to certain kinds of work, types, sizes, etc.; five had none.

Lumber storage: The average amount of lumber stored was 4,730 board feet, with Orville Wike leading the field with 30,000 b.f. Some shops are so close to suppliers that their stock can be minimal.

Metal working: Twenty said they make their own patterns and then hire one of the new marine-oriented foundries in the area. Grant Sarver of Seattle is making tools of the finest quality, including adzes and riveting hammers.

Recent Projects

The range is awesome. From McGlasson's 54-foot diesel yacht to Carl Brownstein's 9-foot prams, many sizes and types are represented, including Scandinavian boats by Paul Schweiss, No Man's Land boats by Greg Foster, etc. Excluding the ever-present Whitehall, there is so little repetition that virtually every launching represents a first: a 43-foot ketch, a 27-foot St. Pierre dory, four 21-foot gigs, two 17-foot Newfoundland sealing skiffs, 14-foot and 17-foot wherries, 19-foot Swampscotts and three 43-foot power cruisers.

Projects in Store

A 36-foot Culler Presto ketch, a 28-foot Atkin cutter, a 60-foot apple-bowed topsail lumber schooner, a 45-foot gaff schooner, a 27-foot Nelson Zimmer-designed sloop, two 32-foot and one 38-foot McGlasson-designed-and-built sloops, 14-foot Danish beach boats, and more.

Unusual Tools and Methods

Hewing hatchet, Batlodd (a "boat plumb bob"), Norwegian riveting hammer, a revolving jig for building traditional small craft, scribing plates, auto-body sander handles, and caulking rakes.

Lumber

"If the lumber companies would stop selling all the big logs to Japan, we'd be in great shape. Lumber management as in Norway, Europe, etc., is essential, and not happening. The future may be dark without action soon; lumber costs may triple in 10 years."

Roberts and Adams

There is truth in this statement. The timber resources of the Northwest are vast, but the export of high-grade fir has already tripled the price in some areas and has severely limited availability on the lower levels that builders normally use. "Standards will drop off, as in the Northeast, to meet the supply." This was the way Carl Brownstein saw it. Orville Wike went so far as to say, "The only hope I see is in a change of government; reseeding should be mandatory." Nine builders specifically singled out exports to Japan as a problem, others were just as depressed, but on a more general level. "Lumber practices in the U.S. are not conducive to sanity." A third of the 33 builders responding felt prices were inflated over and above the expected annual increases. "Still," Dick Wagner said, "We will always have trees." Paul Glassen and David Jackson followed with, "We need more evidence—like this survey—of our collective buying power so lumber and hardware companies will see the profit in meeting our needs. Lumber availability is on the *increase*. There are more support businesses springing up." The separate tally on price and availability in the Northwest did not disclose quite as marked a disparity as it did in the Northeast, but it was in evidence nonetheless, with six of the 15 positive builders referring to those concerns. I was not able to ascertain why the California builders were 86 percent optimistic, unless it is because Dick Tucker's mill in Oregon began to be well known as a good supplier about that time.

Hardware

Traditional hardware really got the axe in the Northwest. Twenty-five percent were convinced that the situation was improving due to operations like The Wooden Boat Shop and Skookum Fastenings; the other 75 percent complained about overpricing, the inordinate amount of searching necessary to locate a needed item, and declining quality. Some went on to say that casting your own hardware was the only real solution.

Cooperatives

These received considerable support, with a 23-to-4 tally favoring a materials cooperative, although seven of the 23 had some of the usual reservations. Of all the regions, Puget Sound, with its high density of builders and relative freedom from the habits of long establishment, holds the greatest potential for cooperatives.

The Market

The severe weather of the past few years, soaring fuel costs, overcrowding, pollution, and urban decay have all helped to accelerate migration toward more moderate climates. The Northwest has been particularly affected by this because of the lure of all that lush, green, undeveloped land. I found that wherever I went, the locals were anxious about what appeared to be a shift from east to west, particularly the Northwest. In Washington, they complained about the Oregonians arriving in droves; in Oregon, they complained about the Northern Californians; the Northern Californians were very cynical about the Southern Californians, who are "taking over." *Everybody* was set on convincing the "hypertense Easterners" that somewhere *else* was the place to be. "We're too laid back here, you wouldn't like it." Seattle has an organization devoted to talking about how much it rains and how high unemployment is—anything to control growth.

The population boom brings with it a soaring market. Seattle has more boats per capita than any other American city. Forty-six percent of the Northwestern builders foresaw a "no-limit" future. But the same boom brings soaring real estate prices, and boat shops need a lot of space too. The high cost of living, high lumber prices, high wages, and so forth, have driven the price of boats to the national limit. Foot for foot, pound for pound, boats produced in this area are the most expensive in the country. The $5,000, 18-foot row/sail boat is a reality! It would appear that the concerns of Paul Glassen and others about boats for ordinary people are to the point. I foresee that Paul and others will be filling in the gap between the yacht-oriented, top-dollar builders and the less wealthy sectors of the market. If this happens, then the optimism is warranted.

There is a bright future in wood construction. There are as many good reasons to think so as there are people. People come to us mostly by word of mouth and stay because they are impressed.

Dave Acorn

I think there's a chance to develop our own market, particularly in traditional small sailing craft.

Carl Brownstein

I've got a two-year backlog that keeps increasing. We do no advertising. Therefore, the future looks very positive. I hope we are heading toward the return of working sail.

The weird computer/sail concepts being developed are not our cup of tea. Our interest is in the small coastwise merchant and fishing craft that reached the height of the appropriate technology in the 18th and 19th centuries. These seakindly vessels are relatively inexpensive to build and maintain, can be handled by family-type crews, and do not require the use of auxiliary engines. Right now, we are designing an apple-bowed topsail schooner, about a 60-footer, which will supply boatbuilders in this area with red cedar, yellow cedar, fir, and spruce at half the present commercial rates. Subsequent versions will carry shakes and firewood to the population centers, loading return cargoes of bulk foodstuffs and general freight.

Our "advice": keep your shop simple, don't be afraid to make mistakes, work quietly, and concentrate on contentment rather than recognition or wealth.

Gregory Foster

The Labor Pool and Vocational Training

The active and prospering programs at Bates Vocational Technical Institute and Seattle Community College brought to the fore the question of dreamers vs. doers. Twelve builders made specific references to it, either in their statements on vocational technical training or on the labor situation. Despite these concerns, 76 percent of the Northwesterners (50 percent of the Californians) said the situation was at least improving, if not good already. Three builders thought the schools might be flooding the market. Whether this turns out to be the case, and how the labor pool fares in general, depends largely on the willingness of graduates to move to other regions and/or take on work in other facets of the market—putting interiors on glass hulls, doing repair work, and so forth.

The labor pool is pretty amateurish, including ourselves. The lag between the younger and the older builders is largely responsible. We have lots of energy, talent, and ability to learn, but we're really all amateurs, not efficient yet. . . . I see traditional wooden boatbuilding as primarily creative, not particularly business-oriented. Training should be slanted that way, since there are no jobs [in new construction] for those trained—save perhaps on their own.

Sam Connor

Wish I'd had it [vocational training] instead of a college liberal arts degree.

Gregory Foster

Craftsmanship takes dedication, perseverance, and patience. These qualities are not in abundance.

Henry Long

We are developing a core of good people, good technicians.

Carl Brownstein

All these fine young boatbuilders coming along are going to produce a bumper crop of beautiful watercraft that will reeducate the tastes of the boating public.

Paul Glassen

Perhaps we have an oversupply of "boatbuilders."

Bob Coe

Miscellaneous

The Westerners' preoccupation with the present and the near future has helped to give wooden boatbuilding a fresh start there. Builders have not been saddled with practicing a certain technique just because it's traditional or "the way it used to be done." I don't believe that it is entirely by chance that the country's first new boat lumber business, first monthly small craft meets, and first broad-based wooden boat festival all occurred on the West Coast. If the long-established Northeast is the backbone of wooden boatbuilding, the Northwest is the modern, creative nerve center. Unfortunately, high stakes and even higher levels of energy have given the area a competitive note. Whereas in other parts of the country builders tend to be so few and/or long established as to be driven toward each other, builders and others here have tended to be cliquish and distrustful. The harsh fact is that concepts that deserve regionwide support, concepts with benefits to the broadest possible base, are hurt by in-fighting and personality conflicts. While the problem is not yet out of hand, it surely won't help to spur the growth of traditional boatbuilding. This and the declining lumber resources are, I feel, the key problems the region faces.

NORTHWESTERN BUILDERS

Dave Acorn and Cedar Boggins
Acorn and Boggins
Behind Radon Marine
Point Hudson
Port Townsend, WA 98368
(206) 385–4066

This shop is tucked away in a corner, behind a fiberglass boatbuilding shop. It's the sort of place you don't come upon unless you know it's there. The location is convenient for the builders, yet not so convenient that visitors are always dropping in—a good thing considering the amount of work these two have done and have lined up in a relatively short period of time.

General Information

Number of builders: Two.

Capacity: 53 feet.

Specialties: Shoal-draft cruising and workboats, including Presto sharpies and other Commodore Ralph Munroe-style craft.

History

Training: Just doing it.

Selection of location: Good interest and demand here.

Financing: Individually, by grunts and groans.

Recent Projects

A 12-foot by 5-foot sailboat, lapstrake construction; a 20-foot by 6-foot sailing sharpie (workboat style); and a 19-foot by 8-foot cat ketch shoal cruiser.

Projects in Store

A 37-foot R.D. Culler Presto sharpie; a 27-foot shoal schooner designed by us for Puget Sound use; and a 25-foot Lyle C. Hess sloop. Keep building.

Lumber and Hardware

There is less and less timber-style construction, and more laminates, as the quality of wood goes down from overharvest of the timber resources. We are buying whole trees now to get what we want the way we want it. Availability of good-quality hardware (bronze and galvanized) is increasing because of interest and demand, but there sure is need for work in this area. Prices are high, but everyone gets a good deal now and then—including us—and we pass the good deals on when possible.

Cooperatives

Most of the situations we've seen seem to degenerate into debating societies.

The Market

There is a bright future in wood construction. There are as many good reasons to think so as there are people. People come to us mostly by word of mouth and stay because they are impressed.

This 17′ cat-ketch cruiser is almost ready to receive shutter planks. The breadth of her sheerstrake and the newness of the shop machinery are very unusual. (Cedar Boggins)

The Labor Pool

There's lots of unskilled labor looking for work; skilled labor generates its own work.

Vocational Training

If you like school, sign in. If you want to build, hire on! Boatbuilding schools provide good exposure to basic construction techniques, but they pay little attention to business experience and efficient work practices.

Modern and Traditional Design

We prefer to integrate both concepts. For example, a cold-molded spruce cabintop, covered with canvas, works very well on a carvel-planked boat.

Restorations and Replicas

Boggins: I see a lot of "weenie" boats—ones that ought to make the coals for a weenie roast—being restored. I'd rather see a new one built, adapted from old lines. Acorn: Get out the old chain and saw up some good firewood. You can have a good strong sea boat laid down and half-planked by the time you've worried through the reefed seams, rotten planks, and sistered frames of that old beach relic. Save that old bronze hardware and put it on the wire wheel—clean it. They don't cast them like they used to.

Time and Finish

"If you can't make a dead fit, you are not a shipwright. If you choose not to, for time's sake, you don't save anything in the long run." We allow owners to perform finish work as a way to save money on a boat. Strength and integrity should be uppermost in the builder's mind, regardless of regulations; safety is a must.

Open Statement

Our favorite bedding compounds and wood treatments are shingle cement and pine tar. We have a special concoction we snack on with coffee; copper nails add the crunch, pitch gives the stick. We mix it ourselves and rub it in all the joints.

Roland Anderson
Poulsbo Boat Works
P.O. Box 145
Poulsbo, WA 98370
(206) 779-7170

Mr. Anderson is well versed in boat-related chemistry, electronics, mechanics, and financing. While at the University of California at Berkeley, he conducted a study of small cruising vessels that have attempted to circumnavigate. He helped develop a formula, based on their ratios of center of lateral resistance to center of gravity to explain the success or failure of their voyages. He found that boats with ratios outside his formula's limits failed. This kind of study is typical of his approach to building in general. Note the suggestion that the vocational boatbuilding programs need to teach some chemistry.

General Information

Number of builders: One.

Capacity: Has the only railway in the immediate area.

Specialties: Plywood boats to 34 feet (new construction) and repair or modification on all wood boats to 40 feet.

Nontraditional modes: Yes.

Experience: Yes, ferrocement.

Preferred paints and glues: 75 percent modern.

Sail and/or power: Sail.

Facilities

Design and drafting: Yes.

Lumber storage: Yes.

Metal working: No, his brother is a welder.

History

Training: Learned from grandfather in California.

Financing: Self-owned.

Recent Projects

Designed and built a 34-foot by 8-foot by 2½ -foot trailerable ketch based on the lines of a ninth-century Viking ship.

Projects in Store

Just purchased the property and plans to reopen as primarily a repair facility with a marine railway.

Unusual Tools and Methods

Portable polyethylene "roof" for working in inclement weather, a must in the damp Northwest. The shop itself is modular so that it can be lengthened to fit a specific boat. This keeps heating and light bills down to the minimum. Stands for each shop tool are designed to double as shipping crates for the same. What's more, they are stackable. He builds his interiors first—upside down—as structural members. The hull goes on later and then the boat is righted.

Lumber and Hardware

No problem! Japanese exports are a short-range problem only. Money is a national problem; it's difficult to get paid, period. But that's certainly not unique to boatbuilding.

Cooperatives

It would need a responsible and knowledgeable leader. One way around Washington's inventory tax might be to have a storage warehouse run by the coop in Oregon, where builders could simply pay cash.

The Market

The newcomers don't understand laws or business. They're going to have a tough time.

The Labor Pool

Work is available but money is not. Many newcomers get discouraged because the pay is so low. This applies to vocational training, too. They need to teach more economics and chemistry so prospective builders know what they're getting into.

Modern and Traditional Design

What's good is good.

Open Statement

With three railways, I intend to cater to do-it-yourself and amateur boatbuilders. They can haul here to repair or rebuild their own boats. I will offer service and/or advice, if needed. There's a real need for this around here.

Carl Brownstein
Rights of Man Boat Works
Route 1, Box 487
Shelton, WA 98584

In Carl's own words, "I was building a 27-foot dory yacht, going to Bates Vocational-Technical in Tacoma, and working late nights in the shop. I was working weekends, too, struggling with my dilemma, and then Joe Trumbly said, 'You don't even need to be here, why don't you get out?' " This may be a first. There can't be too many people who've been booted out by Joe for being too good.

General Information

Number of builders: One.
Capacity: 40 feet.
Specialties: Lapstrake construction, custom work.
Nontraditional modes: No.
Experience: None.
Preferred paints and glues: Traditional.
Sail and/or power: Equal experience with both.

Facilities

Design and drafting: Yes.
Lumber storage: 2,000 b.f.
Metal working: No.

History

Origin of interest: Through my family; the romance of it fascinates me.

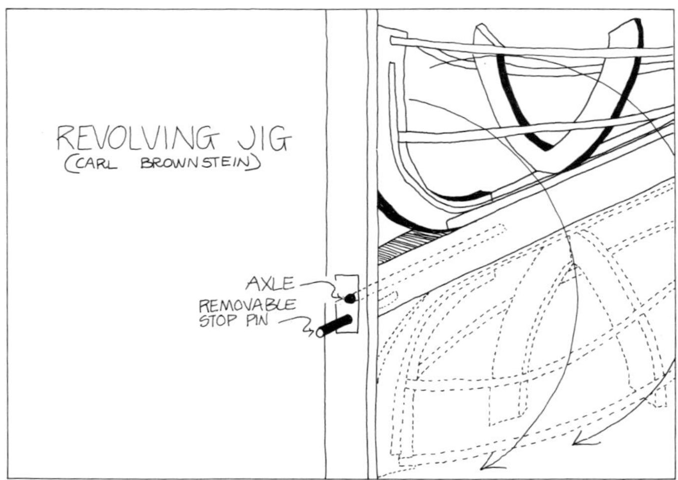

In order for the revolving jig to work, a boat in mold has to be carefully braced internally so as to remain fair when the floor or ceiling bracing is removed. (Rebecca Wheeler illustration)

Training: With Henry Long at Evergreen College [see H. Long interview — P.L.] and at Bates Vocational.

Selection of location: I came out here to go to Evergreen and liked it.

Financing: Boats have paid the rent.

Recent Projects

Work on the Evergreen 38-footer; four 21-foot gigs for Evergreen (Brownstein's design); a 17-foot Chapelle sealing skiff; a 27-foot St. Pierre dory; and two 9-foot Chapelle lapstrake prams.

Unusual Tools

A skew-bladed block-style rabbet plane and a revolving jig. The beam on which I set up the boat I'm working on is held to each leg by two stout pins. By pulling one pin at each end, the boat can be rotated 180 degrees. Very useful when you want to work on a boat both right side up and upside down.

Lumber and Hardware

Japan is a problem. They'll sell it back to us when we are hard up for wood. Standards will drop off, as they have in the Northeast, to meet the supply.

Cooperatives

I would love to go in with other builders on an order of cedar. In a large group (over two people), responsibility is too dispersed. Logistically, someone has to do inventory, order parts, etc.

The Market

Hell, I wish I knew! I think there's a chance to develop our own market, particularly in traditional small sailing craft.

The Labor Pool

It's getting better. We are developing a core of good people, good technicians.

Vocational Training

Most graduates I know are finishing glass hulls. The courses are not demanding enough, even if motivation *is* a necessity. Everything says, "You can't do it." If you listen to anybody but yourself, you are %$#&??!!

Modern and Traditional Design

I prefer traditional, but I'm certainly not closed to modern designs as far as work goes.

Time and Finish

Where wood meets wood, good joints are essential. In general, it's a matter of situation ethics, a balance of what is right, the builder's capabilities, and the owner's money.

Open Statement

I build boats for fun and to keep body and soul together. I enjoy the challenge of doing the impossible and making a living at it.

Miscellaneous

I find working with and teaching students highly rewarding. There is great satisfaction in passing on knowledge of the use of tools, working with one's hands, etc.

Mark Burn and Jim Peacock
Port Townsend Boat Works
Box 577
Port Townsend, WA 98368
(206) 385-1525

This is a somewhat rare yard. It is owned and operated by a relatively young crew with lots of experience in the commercial fisheries and a no-nonsense approach. When I visited the shop, the crew was on an emergency schedule in order to completely re-fasten and build a new transom for a 45-foot fishing vessel that came to the yard in distress. The total job time from water to water was six days.

General Information

Number of builders: Twelve, including metal workers.
Capacity: 45 feet inside, 55 feet outside.
Specialties: Commercial repair and construction.
Nontraditional modes: No.
Experience: None.
Preferred paints and glues: Traditional.
Sail and/or power: Power.

Facilities

Design and drafting: No.
Lumber storage: 4,000–5,000 b.f.
Metal working: Welding in steel and aluminum.

History

Origin of interest: From family and a sailing fishboat.

Training: Freelance.
Selection of location: I'm from here.
Financing: From commercial fishing.

Recent Projects

Complete rebuild of a 45-footer and a new poop deck for a 54-footer.

Projects in Store

Construction of a 40- to 45-foot commercial sail or conventional fishing vessel on speculation. A 42-foot horseshoe-sterned troller. Considering buying peelers (old-growth fir) for retail and wholesale sales.

Lumber and Hardware

The future is good. Supply will increase with demand. There's still a lot of timber left, but Japan is a problem. In any case, we must develop mills that cut boat lumber.

Cooperatives

Positive for buying lumber and hardware, but not in a shop setup. I can see Puget Sound builders getting together on a carload (train car, that is) of oak.

The Market

Steel will eventually beat out wood in the commercial market, but there's all of the thousands of older boats that need repair and some new construction besides. At least another 40 years in wood repair and construction.

The Labor Pool

There are lots of unemployed shipwrights. Boatbuilding takes different disciplines for the different kinds of work. It also takes the ability to grow and improve one's knowledge and skill.

Vocational Training

School is for basics; learn the rest on the job.

Modern and Traditional Design

Traditional.

Open Statement

We are aiming for a very complete woodworking shop. We have 12 good mechanics and great versatility.

David P. Clarke
Box 193
Nordland, WA 98358

General Information

Number of builders: One.
Capacity: 50 feet.
Specialties: Plank-on-frame and plywood-on-frame construction, small lapstrake craft, cold-molding.
Nontraditional modes: Yes.
Experience: Yes, cold-molding.

Preferred paints and glues: Traditional for my own use. For a customer, I match him to a material.

Sail and/or power: Both, probably more experience in power.

Facilities

Lumber storage: 1,500 b.f. on hand. Presently have about 10,000 b.f. for a large pinky.

History

Origin of interest: From a commercial fishing family.

Training: Self-taught.

Selection of location: Lumber is available, proximity to the water.

Financing: By construction of custom parts for glass boats—wooden doors, rails, etc.

Recent Projects

A 14-foot George Calkins wherry; a 22-foot Calkins Bartender; and an 8-foot Knott skiff.

Projects in Store

A 43-foot pinky; two small lapstrake boats; and perhaps another Bartender.

Lumber and Hardware

Lumber is of a lower and lower grade. Good lumber is being shipped off the Olympic Peninsula to Japan in tremendous quantities. Red cedar is practically unavailable here. For hardware, people are starting to make their own patterns again and having them cast. The "traditional" hardware is coming back.

The Labor Pool

The quantity is low, the quality is variable. Very few people want to work a 10-hour day in less than ideal conditions for any amount of pay.

Modern and Traditional Design

I prefer traditional for its reliability, easy repairability, and inexpensive initial cost. I prefer workboats over yachts in all cases. A workboat looks best when she's doing her job; a yacht, on the other hand, looks worst when she's being used, best when tied to a dock with a tarp over her.

Time and Finish

It's never a waste of money to do it right. I bid a boat complete. If it takes longer, I make less. As I become more skilled, I'll make more. I've built some boats for around $1.50 an hour and gained a lot more than money in the skill acquired.

Open Statement

Although there are numerous shops in our area, only one or two are successes. Many others get publicity, but very little of any value is produced. To me, a successful operation is one that keeps its employees active at a good wage and completes a job that satisfies the owner's needs.

I think the recent blowup on wooden boats in probably the kiss of death. Boatbuilders and woodworkers are now being exploited far beyond their capabilities. Wood boats are really, or should be, the poor man's boat; not for everyone but for a few. I'm not interested in putting a shiny new epoxy-saturated boat in every backyard. Most people should not own a wood boat—they are not prepared to deal with it.

I lived aboard my 45-year-old cutter for eight years. I've seen five- to 10-year-old boats destroyed by neglect in the hands of wealthy boating people. On the other hand, I have a friend who earned between $30,000 and $40,000 this season on his fishboat, circa 1920. He'll be sure to take care of that little bucket—he knows what she's worth.

Bob Coe
101 North Bay
Waldron, WA 98297

Bob is perhaps the alternativist's alternativist. Waldron Island can only be reached by a dory-ferry from Orcas Island. There are no paved roads, no running water, and no electricity. When I last visited with Bob in his hand-built house on the beach at North Bay, he had just acquired some power tools and was setting up a tractor-generator.

General Information

Number of builders: One.
Capacity: 20 feet.
Specialties: Whitehalls and Swampscott dories.
Nontraditional modes: No.
Preferred paints and glues: Mostly modern.
Sail and/or power: Sail and oar.

Facilities

Design and drafting: Yes.

Bob Coe's nearly complete 17′ Whitehall eventually will provide transportation to and from Waldron Island. Note the molds hanging over the lofting wall at the back of the shelter. (Bob Coe photo)

Lumber and storage: Yes, limited.
Metal working: No.

History
Origin of interest: I just started building boats as a kid.
Selection of location: It's where I was living.
Financing: Savings.

Recent Projects
A 17-foot Whitehall and two 19½-foot Swampscott dories.

Projects in Store
Another 19½-foot Swampscott. I will continue to concentrate on traditional rowing and sailing craft.

Unusual Tools and Methods
Just the usual wooden lap clamps and other reground odds and ends.

Lumber and Hardware
They're going to get more scarce, but I feel I will still be able to obtain them.

Cooperatives
Very useful if you can find enough people of similar mind.

The Market
Should be growing steadily.

The Labor Pool
Perhaps an oversupply of "boatbuilders."

Vocational Training
Not very effective.

Modern and Traditional Design
I have a great love for traditional designs and construction methods.

Sam Connor
Northwest Boatbuilding and Restoration
Point Hudson Marina
Port Townsend, WA 98368
(206) 385-3628

Sam Connor is best known for his activities beyond boatbuilding—that is to say, the Port Townsend Wooden Boat Festival and Boat Building Symposiums each September. The festival's wide-open atmosphere is a Connor trademark.

General Information
Number of builders: Six.
Specialties: Small rowing and sailing craft.
Nontraditional modes: We have worked in these, but we won't work outside carvel or clinker in the future. We want to work in nontoxic materials only.
Preferred paints and glues: Traditional.
Sail and/or power: Sail, but I wouldn't mind getting into more power craft.

Facilities

Design and drafting: Yes, under 25 feet.

Lumber storage: Limited.

Metal working: No. We have an excellent local foundry in New Found Metals [local firm].

History

Origin of interest: From building a 40-foot cement boat.

Training: Books and on my own.

Selection of location: I like the area and the climate.

Financing: On a shoestring.

Recent Projects

Two wooden-boat festivals and a boatbuilding symposium. Two 24-foot cruising sloops, strip-construction, and more traditional small craft than I care to list.

Projects in Store

More work in the historical and educational aspects of boatbuilding, such as apprenticeships and the symposium.

Lumber and Hardware

Hardware is no problem, nor are softwoods. Fir timbers are easy to get, even dry. In hardwoods we may have to go to Oregon white oak, though it checks a good bit. It is superb for framing.

Cooperatives

For buying lumber? Definitely. The trouble with coops is that nobody's responsible—tools get ruined, for example. You need to delegate responsibility so that nobody can slip up without hearing about it.

The Market

Lord, I don't know. We've thought about jigging up the Handy Andy dinghy for production, but the market is probably not firm enough yet.

Who is Buying and Why

The small craft are bought by city folk, often upper-class. The first 24-footer was the first sold locally.

The Labor Pool

It is pretty amateurish, including ourselves. The lag between the young and the

One of Sam Connor's Whitehalls.

older builders is largely responsible. We have lots of energy, talent, and ability to learn, but we're really all amateurs, not efficient yet. We are new talent.

Vocational Training

I see traditional wooden boatbuilding as primarily creative, not particularly business-oriented. Training should be slanted that way, since there are no jobs for those trained—save perhaps on their own.

Modern and Traditional Design

We need a blend. Time-testing cannot be beat. The need for better handling and speed may necessitate modification of traditional designs and/or new designs along traditional lines.

Open Statement

The concept of wooden boats as an "industry" stinks. Commercialism must be open-minded or it will only turn people off. Otherwise, it becomes just like office work.

Jim Dryburgh
Oak Bay Boat Works Co. Ltd.
1327 Beach Drive
Victoria, B.C., Canada
(503) 598-2912

General Information

Number of builders: Six.
Capacity: 60 feet.
Specialties: Custom building and repair.

One of Jim Dryburgh's crew takes a spokeshave to the toerail of a Monk-designed cruiser and then checks the fit.

Nontraditional modes: No.
Experience: Yes.
Preferred paints and glues: Mostly modern.
Sail and/or power: Power.

Facilities

Design and drafting: Yes.
Lumber storage: Limited.
Metal working: Patterns only.

History

Training: At Vogler Brothers Seacraft, Victoria, B.C. But I've been in this shop 12 years.

Recent Projects

Two 35-foot Monk power cruisers.

Lumber and Hardware

The future of both is good.

The Market

Good.

The Labor Pool

Also good.

Vocational Training

I take on apprentices from the local high school.

Roy Dunbar
Lake Union Boat Repair
3313 Fairview East
Seattle, WA 98102
(206) 329-3324

This is a man who knows what he wants. He's made his own setup and likes it. In the heart of Seattle under a bridge, the yard has an urban, let's-get-down-to-business approach. As in most yards, this atmosphere is an extension of the master's personal view.

General Information

Number of builders: Five.
Capacity: 60 feet.
Specialties: Wood; power craft only. (Sailboat owners are a big hassle.)
Nontraditional modes: No.
Experience: Yes, up to 50 feet in strip.
Preferred paints and glues: Mostly traditional.
Sail and/or power: Power.

Facilities

Design and drafting: Yes.

Lumber storage: 2,000 b.f.

Metal working: Patterns only.

History

Origin of interest: In yards.

Training: In yards. Also, my father was in construction and had lumbering experience.

Selection of location: From here.

Financing: From work in yards, bit by bit.

Recent Projects

Three 43-foot power cruisers in wood, naturally.

Projects in Store

Continue as we have.

Unusual Tools

Adjustable spindle sander, somewhat like a shaper except with a tilting arbor to allow sanding of unusually difficult curves.

Lumber and Hardware

Same as always, you have to pay for quality. Why worry about the middle class, amateurs, etc., not being able to afford it? This isn't their market.

Cooperatives

Not interested.

The Market

The only changes are in repair of foreign-built vessels. Unique problems are occurring, particularly with decking. Traditional small craft are not boats, they are dinghies!

The Labor Pool

It's always been bad.

Vocational Training

I haven't seen a decent program. Vocational students have lousy work habits, don't know $%@! and want to be primadonnas. I don't think the instructors know all that much either.

Modern and Traditional Design

Good is good, whenever it's designed.

Time and Finish

Finish first.

Open Statement

In our shop, I prefer repair and rebuilding. At any point, the owner can pay up and leave if he doesn't like our work. We can say, "Pay up and get out," if we don't like his approach. All work is materials plus labor.

Miscellaneous

The gruffness is deceiving. This is a fair and honest man who'd always give every individual a chance. He also teaches biophysics part-time.

Tom Finch and Gale Shub
28759 Gamble Place N.E.
Kingston, WA 98346

General Information

Number of builders: Two.

Capacity: 15 feet.

Specialties: Solid spruce oars—spoons, flat blades, and shell oars. Light dories, both pulling and sail, are our emphasis and direction.

Nontraditional modes: Glued-strip, yes. We will only work in nontoxics.

Preferred paints and glues: I don't work with items that "smell bad" if I can help it. The quality of a product can overcome that occasionally; I use Aerolite and Thiokol.

Sail and/or power: Equal experience in both.

Facilities

Design and drafting: Not professional quality.

Lumber storage: Limited.

Metal working: No, we use New Found Metals [local firm]. I'm a fair welder but we don't do any here.

History

Training: Repairing and rebuilding fishboats.

Financing: On a shoestring.

Recent Projects

Some repair work, eight of our Port Gamble skiffs [their own design], and the oars.

Projects in Store

A houseboat to put a shop on! Building more traditional rowing and sailing craft.

Unusual Tools and Methods

We check out furniture and sports equipment manufacturers. Scrounging for the most efficient use of materials is important to us.

Lumber and Hardware

Hardware will be more available as individuals get involved. Look at Skookum Fastenings. The grapevine will help bring out needs and bring together the people to fill them. We must divert some of the lumber that is going to Japan.

Cooperatives

Definitely a good idea, particularly in terms of buying materials.

The Market

It will come back over the short and long term. Our market is split about fifty-fifty, locals and yachties.

Vocational Training

I'm basically positive. Some are good and some are bad, as in any other field.

Modern and Traditional Design

Modern designs along traditional lines can be adapted to new, or more available, materials.

Time and Finish

I believe in keeping time in mind, but not at the expense of quality.

Gregory Foster
Whaler Bay Boat Yard
Box 43
Galiano Island, B.C.
Canada V0N 1P0

To my great disappointment, I never made it to Galiano Island. I must say, however, that everything I've ever heard about the Fosters (including the answers in this questionnaire) speaks of self-assurance and ability. They display none of the strident concern for reputation that is so common. They are, in short, rare. Speaking of visitors, the Fosters do *not* encourage casual visitors; there is simply no time for such.

General Information

Number of builders: My wife and myself; a possible third by next year.
Capacity: 60 feet.

A magnificent spot for a boat shop—or, why a lot of young, would-be boatbuilders move to the Pacific Northwest: the house nestled among the trees at upper right looks out over a No Man's Land boat and the Whaler Bay Boat Yard. (Greg Foster photo)

Specialties: Providence boats, tentsail cruisers, ancient Viking small craft, No Man's Land boats, Isles of Shoals boats, Tancook whalers, 18th-century schooners, and pinnaces—museum replicas.
Nontraditional modes: No.
Experience: Our choice is clinker, having tried them all.
Preferred paints and glues: Fifty-fifty each way—modern and traditional.
Sail and/or power: Sail or oar only.

Facilities

Design and drafting: Yes, both.
Lumber storage: 15,000 b.f.
Metal working: Not yet; soon.

History

Origin of interest: How did I get started? By starting.
Training: Chapelle's books and trial-and-error.
Selection of location: It's lovely, on the water, and close to log sources.
Financing: By scraping and saving for several years—odd jobs.

Recent Projects

Sailing replica of the Gokstad faering; Providence boats; a No Man's Land boat; and other traditional small craft.

Projects in Store

A 29-foot Isles of Shoals boat for local farmers (to be used without an engine for basic transportation and hauling of farm goods). Also scheduled for this year are two No Man's Land boats and a clinker Tancook whaler.

Unusual Tools and Methods

We use all hand tools or hand power tools. No bandsaw. We make all our own lumber from choice drift logs. We also make the sails for the boats we build, using treated canvas (Vivatex) and Egyptian cotton. We'd like to see more "how-to" information circulated on sailmaking for boatbuilders. It's no secret art, just a very enjoyable, appropriate avocation.

Lumber and Hardware

No problem on either, but hardware prices are soaring. We'll see more home casting. I can't believe the prices some folks are paying for boat lumber. Their boats must be quite expensive.

Cooperatives

Sounds like a good route. We are trying to encourage the use of sailing/rowing boats by food cooperatives and among small family groups. The old shallops, Block Islanders, Columbia River boats, etc., are just ideal for this purpose, not to mention Orkney yoles, Shetland sixerns, Danish smakkejolles, and what have you.

The Market

I've got a two-year backlog that keeps increasing. We do no advertising. Therefore, the future looks very positive. I hope we are heading toward the return of working sail. The weird computer/sail concepts being developed are not our cup of tea. Our interest is in the small, coastwise merchant and fishing craft that reached the height of the appropriate technology in the 18th and 19th centuries. These seakindly vessels are relatively inexpensive to build and maintain, can be

An Isles of Shoals boat is ribbanded off in the shop at Whaler Bay. (Greg Foster photo)

handled by family-type crews, and do not require the use of auxiliary engines. Right now, we are designing an apple-bowed topsail schooner, about a 60-footer, which will supply boatbuilders in this area with red cedar, yellow cedar, fir and spruce at half the present commercial rates. Subsequent versions will carry shakes and firewood to the population centers, loading return cargoes of bulk foodstuffs and general freight.

The Labor Pool

We don't have any contact with this.

Vocational Training

Wish I'd had it instead of a college liberal arts degree. I certainly do support them. The best I'm aware of is The Apprenticeshop in Bath, Maine.

Modern and Traditional Design

Traditional designs were *developed.* Modern designs are plagiarized, calculated, drawn. Which would you choose? We have an increasing respect for the traditional.

Restorations and Replicas

The preservation of skills is most important. My choice would be to build a new replica rather than restore an original—unless the old one is a famous personality.

Time and Finish

A professional craftsman is always upgrading his work, learning to make dead fits quickly and efficiently. What else is there to say?

Open Statement

We feel that we're apprenticed to the past and that our apprenticeship will never be over. Our "advice": keep your shop simple, don't be afraid to make mistakes, work quietly, and concentrate on contentment rather than on recognition or wealth.

Miscellaneous

We've been in business for 10 years. Our most helpful published sources have been the works of Howard Chapelle, *National Fisherman,* and the National Watercraft Collection at the Smithsonian.

R. Paul Glassen
P.O. Box 535
Port Townsend, WA 98368
(206) 385-2314

I met Paul just three days before the Port Townsend festival as he prepared to plank the sides of a 14-foot flat-bottomed bateau. "A modification of one of Phil Bolger's designs," he explained. "I'm going to enter the rowing race on Saturday at noon with her." Moved by his determination and with some free time on my hands, I gave him a hand for a day. When she hit the water at 12:15 Saturday, the linseed-oil finish was still wet. Friday had been his birthday and he'd worked 14 hours. Very typical of a boatbuilder—missing the race was not half as important as the pleasure of the launching, working birthdays notwithstanding. Just a few days later, Paul was the first builder to complete the questionnaire.

General Information

Number of builders: One.

Capacity: 30 feet.

Specialties: Conventional, plank-on-frame carvel construction of sharpies.

Nontraditional modes: Have done so, prefer not to.

Preferred paints and glues: Traditional, but no purist about it.

Sail and/or power: I like sail and muscle power (oar), but I have experience with engines. [Paul has raced motorcycles and been a top-ranked mechanic.—P.L.]

Facilities

Design and drafting: No.

Lumber storage: Limited.

Metal working: No.

History

I owned and rebuilt a series of undistinguished old rotters. Then with professional career prospects looking gloomy, I turned to maintaining and repairing other people's rotters. To get experience with new construction on a level I could afford, I sporadically built a skiff. All one need do is look at a map or, better yet, a chart to know why I settled here. If I knew anything about finances, I'd be in another trade. Like most builders I live cheaply (on an old boat, in fact) and enjoy reforging the almost-unbroken link in the chain of continuous wooden boatbuilders that goes back several millennia at least.

Recent Projects

Completed Bolger bateau in five working days for Port Townsend Festival; Chapelle St. Lawrence River bateau under construction.

Projects in Store

I'd like to build a bunch of cheap, practical sharpies and the like, so more ordinary fishing and boating folks could take to the water without it being such a big deal (read expensive) and alienating (read complicated motors and unworkable synthetic materials).

Unusual Methods

My only "innovation" is to apply good old workboat construction to skiffs. Open boats can be built of any wood that grows in trees. With ordinary rough usage, a skiff shouldn't last any longer than good galvanized fastenings—two or three decades(!), I'd estimate, in salt water. They are not monuments, just boats.

Lumber and Hardware

We need more evidence—like this survey—of our collective buying power, so lumber and hardware companies will see the profit in meeting our needs.

Cooperatives

I'd be interested in a lumber and hardware buying coop. It would have to be professional—paying its overhead and run by qualified employees. Discounts would be proportional to shares owned.

The Market

Boats will be made out of wood because that's all there's gonna be. There will be more efficient small open boats. The person who can't go on the water without a floating living room doesn't belong there.

Who is Buying and Why

Beats me, that's why I'm not busy full time. [Paul is a sometime employee of Port Townsend Boat Works, a few hundred yards away.—P.L.] Seriously, the money is mostly in repair, as John Gardner says it's historically been. In this area it's largely fishboats.

The Labor Pool

Quantity and quality are getting better all the time. Supply will create demand. All these fine young boatbuilders coming along are going to produce a bumper crop of beautiful watercraft that will reeducate the tastes of the boating public.

Vocational Training

Some good, some bad. Best of all would be a little vocational schooling and lots of on-the-job training with experienced people in thriving repair and construction yards. That's a hard combination to come by today.

Modern and Traditional Design

Modern boat design has degenerated for a number of reasons; a big enough engine will push any box across the pond, and quantity manufacturers haven't got the taste and good sense an individual artisan can, and will, indulge.

Restorations and Replicas

They have to follow the model set forth by that prodigious genius of the field, John Gardner. Skills, value, and taste are what need preservation. Relics serve a very limited function in this.

Open Statement

If the new breed of boatbuilder has to employ Madison Avenue advertising techniques to sell his product or service, the revival will have failed. And yet the "boat keeper" (as opposed to boat owner or user) must have knowledge. Supplying that knowledge is the job of a responsible boat press, museums, and boat festivals (not just shows). Knowledge can only come from information, not promotion. I'd gladly buy a magazine (like those of the first half of this century and earlier) that teaches me something. But, I'll be damned if I'll pay for a magazine or boat show that's just a tedious and interminable advertising hype.

Miscellaneous

On the Coast Guard regulations: Somebody ought to regulate the Coast Guard so they don't hurt themselves or anyone else. The C.G. may guard the coast, but who will guard us from the C.G.?

Darryl Graves and Bill Carter
Salty Bog Boatworks
P.O. Box 1198
Bandon, OR 97411
(503) 347-9284

General Information

Number of builders: Two.

Capacity: 20 feet.

Specialties: Lapstrake guide-boats, rowing skiffs, and custom cruising sail.

Nontraditional modes: We are interested in trying cold-molding on decks and components other than hulls.

Experience: No.

Preferred paints and glues: A little of both traditional and modern, depending on use and application.

Sail and/or power: 40 percent power, 60 percent sail.

Facilities

Design and drafting: Yes.

Lumber storage: 1,000 b.f. of planking stock.

History

Origin of interest: As a child, boats were my first love.

Training: Researched and built scale replica of a steam schooner.

Selection of location: Plenty of local Port Orford cedar, white oak, ash, Douglas fir, spruce, yew wood, red cedar, and every once in a while, something exotic washes up on the beach.

Recent Projects

A 36-foot replica steam riverboat with a Chicago Iron Works steam engine (rebuilt). It's ready for planking and decking, oil tank is in, boiler is three-quarters done, shaft and propeller are in—but we're short of funds to finish. Historically, it's an important boat for the area. An 11-foot lapstrake salmon wherry (Stimson Rhodes model) in Honduras mahogany, Philippine java, Port Orford cedar, oak, and copper.

Projects in Store

A 14-foot version of the same wherry; a 14-foot Lincolnville wherry; an 18-foot double-ender (our design); and a lapstrake skiff from a 1916 magazine, used for exploring the upper reaches of the Columbia River. Completion of the 36-foot riverboat.

Lumber and Hardware

No problem.

Cooperatives

There's nobody else in our area building traditional wooden craft.

The Market

On Oregon's southern coast, there are so many lakes, rivers, and estuaries, yet my partner and I have seen one sailboat each in the two years we've been here!

Who is Buying and Why

Our market is geared toward the bicycler/backpacker set. Our 18-foot model is nicknamed "The Backpacker's Yacht."

The Labor Pool

Here, it's just the two of us turning a labor of love into meaningful, "gainful" employment.

Vocational Training

The nickname for Salty Bog Boatworks is the "self-apprenticeshop."

Open Statement

We are developing skills, combining the best possible "state-of-the-art" craftsmanship, and utilizing the abundant natural resources to produce a product almost unknown to the local people. Hopefully, interest generated by our projects will promote not only appreciation of our craft, but also a positive recreational experience in an area where both are very much neglected.

Don Hill
Don Hill Custom Built Riverboats
P.O. Box CC
Springfield, OR 97477
Shop: 4579 Jasper Road
Springfield, OR
(503) 746-7281

Don's business is expanding rapidly. A licensed whitewater guide and former politician, his business has grown from his backyard to up to 70 boats a year and possible dealerships in Idaho, Montana, Wyoming, Washington, Oregon, Northern California, Mexico, Nevada, and Canada. Some are in operation already; others are in planning. The shop is beautifully organized and almost spotless. It is difficult to believe he actually builds boats here, but that he does.

General Information

Number of builders: Three.
Capacity: 28 feet.

Don Hill's dories have specially designed and built trailers.

Detail of a Don Hill river dory: note the rope stern seat, sliding forward seat, and netting for fishing gear. Don pays attention to every detail. When he realized that the regular hex nuts on the inwales snagged a lot of lines, he switched to round-headed nuts, even though it was expensive to have them galvanized.

Specialties: Production riverboats (dories) for oar or power propulsion, and river sleds (highly powered, flat-bottomed river craft).
Nontraditional modes: No.
Experience: No.
Preferred paints and glues: Mostly modern.
Sail and/or power: Oar power and outboards.

Facilities

Design and drafting: Yes.
Lumber storage: 4,000 b.f.
Metal working: Patterns. We have a separate shop building all-aluminum dories as well.

History

Origin of interest: I built my first boat as a kid.

Recent Projects

Up to 70 boats a year. We recently moved to a new location—a major operation in itself.

Projects in Store

Dealerships (see Introduction).

Lumber and Hardware

There is some problem with the high-grade ply that I need. It can be a hassle to get it. We buy hardware only in bulk, as we supply parts and materials to others as well. [All the Hill boats are standardized and Don maintains a complete supply of spares. He will repair, refinish, or simply supply materials for the owner to do so.—P.L.]

Cooperatives

We have already tried it, and still use it for certain parts of the boats now. We have bought screws in lots as large as 15,000.

The Market

Unlimited in this field. Good-quality merchandise at good prices will always be the key.

Time and Finish

The safety factor is primary. These are not yachts. These boats are fished or whitewater run. Finish is good, but secondary.

Miscellaneous

We do more than build boats. Our brochure of accessories runs from trailers (specially designed) to fishing rods to hardware to marine finishes. We also run the Northwest Guide Booking Service.

David Jackson
Freya Boat Works
909 3rd Avenue
Anacortes, WA 98221
(206) 293-6143

The picture of David's shop—Smokey's Grocery sign and all—belies the down-to-earth productivity that is his trademark.

General Information

Number of builders: One to three.
Capacity: 12 to 50 feet.
Specialties: Round-bottom oar and sail.

Nontraditional modes: Maybe, it would depend.

Experience: Yes.

Preferred paints and glues: Fifty-fifty. I use what's around and seems best.

Sail and/or power: Sail and oar.

Facilities

Design and drafting: No. I am working on developing them, though.

Lumber storage: No, Flounder Bay Lumber is down the street.

Metal working: No, there's an excellent machinist in town.

History

Origin of interest: My family is full of traditional wooden-boat nuts.

Training: I've spent time with Aubrey Marshall at Strawbery Banke, Portsmouth, New Hampshire; Goudy and Stevens in Boothbay, Maine; the Apprenticeshop, in Bath, Maine; Stan James and others. I try to pick up what I can wherever I can.

Selection of location: The Picketts drew me here from the Spokane Festival where I'd been building a Friendship sloop for five months with Stan James and others.

Recent Projects

A 17-foot Swampscott dory; a 16-foot Boston Whitehall; new bow sections, guards, covering boards, etc., on the 85-foot tug *Fearless.* Incidentally, she was built in 1900. A traditional Norwegian oar and sailboat, the *Vandrafalken,* for Ginger Cox and Tish Davis to row from Seattle to Alaska and back. Lastly, a 17-foot sealing skiff.

Projects in Store

A Brewer-designed 45-foot schooner; possibly a 54-foot trawler.

Lumber and Hardware

They're on the increase. There are more support businesses springing up: Flounder Bay Lumber Sales, Skookum Fastenings, Grant Sarver's toolmaking business.

Cooperatives

There is definitely interest in Anacortes. We have, for instance, a three-man caulking gang.

The Market

The market is on the increase also. It's going to be easier to sell wooden boats, partially because glass is becoming too expensive when built *right.* A well-built glass hull is costly. Generally, the cheap glass hulls are just that, cheap—particularly in the larger boats.

The Labor Pool

We have an excellent labor pool in Anacortes.

Vocational Training

Boatyards are best.

Modern and Traditional Design

I tend toward traditional design. I have little interest in fin keels and high-aspect-ratio rigs.

Restorations and Replicas

Replication is cheaper and the boats can be *used* afterward.

Bent Jesperson
Bent Jesperson, Boatbuilder
Kingfisher Marine, Harbour Road
Sidney, B.C., Canada
(604) 656-5096 (home)

Of all the yards I entered, this has to be one of the most cheerful. As he put it, "We try to make a living and enjoy our work." Located in the corner of a busy marina, the riot of activity around doesn't seem to have slowed down Bent or his small crew a bit. They have turned out four good-size boats and started a fifth in the three years they have been at Kingfisher Marine. Here is a shop that has found a good balance. Note, for instance, that the boats' owners locate hardware, thus ensuring their own satisfaction and relieving Bent of this time-consuming chore. He recommends sources and prices, they do the legwork.

General Information

Number of builders: Three—myself, one journeyman, one apprentice.

Capacity: 50 feet.

Specialties: Custom construction.

Nontraditional modes: Yes, glued-strip and cold-molding.

Experience: Yes, both of the above.

Preferred paints and glues: Mostly traditional.

Sail and/or power: Sail.

Facilities

Design and drafting: We do interior design only, but we also do a fair amount of work for clients of Bill Garden.

Lumber storage: 3,500 to 4,000 b.f.

Metal working: Patterns only.

History

Training: I apprenticed in boatyards in Denmark.

Selection of location: I was living here.

Financing: I started with one order and worked up from there.

Recent Projects

In the last three years we've built three of Bill Garden's sailboats and a one-ton, Peterson-designed racing sloop.

Projects in Store

We have three boats on order now.

Lumber and Hardware

Wood is available if you can keep a standing order with the mill. Supply will meet demand. The owners have to look after the hardware, which often means going to Seattle to find it and/or get it on time.

Cooperatives

They're only sensible where the concentration of yards is high.

The Market

I've got all the work I can handle.

The Labor Pool

It's fairly strong, but journeymen are hard to find. I do take on apprentices regularly, and that helps.

Vocational Training

I feel it's a good program. We have governmental supervision and some subsidy, and that helps.

Modern and Traditional Design

I have no preference, "as long as it's wood."

Time and Finish

I'm inclined toward nice finish, but after the basic structure is up, finish work is by the hour.

Open Statement

We try to make a living and enjoy our work, which includes working with the customer to mutual satisfaction.

Richard and Laura Kolin
Kolin Boat Works
1314 15th Street
Anacortes, WA 98221

As editors of the Traditional Small Craft Association's newsletter, *The Ash Breeze,* the Kolins have worked well beyond the call of duty. As members of the Association's National Council they have represented the West Coast at a number of meetings.

I spoke with Richard in their previous shop in Santa Cruz, California. The Kolins planned to use the garage of their new home in Anacortes as a shop.

Richard and Laura chose specifically not to answer most of the opinion-oriented questions on the form.

General Information

Number of builders: Two.

Specialties: Traditional small craft, and small open boats in general.

Nontraditional modes: No.

Experience: Yes.

Preferred paints and glues: We use what works and have found that the older stuff generally works best.

Sail and/or power: Sail, oar, and outboards.

Facilities

Design and drafting: Yes.

Lumber storage: We buy on opportunity, so the amount varies tremendously.

Metal working: Patterns only.

History

Origin of interest: Grew up on the water.

Training: In yards.

Selection of location: We like the area.

Financing: From work on boats. Getting a shop was an evolutionary process. Working on boats created a need for a shop, since we couldn't do certain kinds of work without one. The one supported the other.

Recent Projects

Lots of traditional small craft, the last two being Pete Culler's *Long John* and *Dancing Feather.*

Projects in Store

Further development of the Traditional Small Craft Association.

Lumber and Hardware

Lumber will always be available, even if expensive. The same is true of hardware.

Modern and Traditional Design

We use what's best for the needs of our clients.

Despite many extracurricular activities, the Kolins remain boatbuilders first, as is evidenced by this Culler-designed Long John.

Peter Landon
Harbour Road
Sidney, B.C., Canada
Or: 2322 Malaview
Sidney, B.C.
(604) 656-4220 (home)

I think these "before-and-after" photographs taken by Peter say it all.

General Information

Number of builders: One.
Capacity: 40 feet.
Specialties: Recovering older boats.
Nontraditional modes: No.
Experience: No.
Preferred paints and glues: Mostly traditional.
Sail and/or power: Power.

Facilities

Design and drafting: Yes.
Lumber storage: 3,000 b.f.
Metal working: Patterns only.

Recent Projects

New transom and deck on a 46-footer, complete rebuild of a 34-foot bowpicker (halibut boat).

Projects in Store

I have a 22½-foot tug to build for myself. Some day I'd like to build a 60+-foot traditional tug.

Lumber and Hardware

I am worried about lumber. While the economy is good, it's OK. If it goes down, the leisure industry will go with it. The small man can't get the capital to combat it, particularly in things like lumber. Hardware's all right; it'll keep going.

The Market

Barring the problems above, *small* concerns can do well.

Peter Landon

Peter Landon

The Labor Pool
Very few and far between.

Vocational Training
One-on-one in a yard is best.

Modern and Traditional Design
Traditional.

Restorations and Replicas
I believe in recycling boats.

Time and Finish
It depends on the builder/owner relationship—situation ethics.

Open Statement
If a man is good, he doesn't have to advertise. Business and people will find him.

Cecil Lange
Cecil M. Lange & Son Inc.
Route 3, Box 202
Port Townsend, WA 98368

Tucked away on a back road outside of Port Townsend, this former New Zealander and his crew have quietly built a fine reputation. In one of the first interviews I conducted, I was impressed with Cecil's quiet, unassuming manner. Like many builders, he prefers to let his work speak for itself.

General Information
Number of builders: Four to six.
Capacity: 50 to 60 feet.
Specialties: A 41-foot strip-planked sloop. Every strip is custom beveled.
Nontraditional modes: Yes.
Experience: Yes.
Preferred paints and glues: Whatever's best. I've found Aerolite makes the best laminations, for example.

Facilities
Design and drafting: Yes, on power only.
Lumber storage: Limited.
Metal working: Patterns.

History
Origin of interest: Father was a builder.
Training: From Pa in New Zealand.
Selection of location: Cheaper! Land is cheaper and we're away from unions and/or insurance types.
Financing: Cash in hand, never owed a cent.

Recent Projects
A 45-foot cutter for a Hawaiian.

Projects in Store

A 41-foot sloop for cruising is next and maybe a 60+-foot powerboat. One wood boat a year while maintaining our work in glass.

Lumber and Hardware

Lumber is available at a price. Amateurs need to look out for cheaper businesses like the Costa Mesa coop, Boatbuilders and Sailors.

Cooperatives

Positive for amateurs, not for builders. It's too hard to delegate responsibility.

The Market

We may get into making fiberglass hulls for kit finish. Foreign labor is a problem in competition for customers. There'll always be a demand for wood boats from those who can pay.

Who is Buying and Why

People as crazy as I am. People who look for custom builders are dreamers, professionals, and city people—millionaires even.

The Labor Pool

Not enough people know the whole job. Very few understand all the pressures and strains on a vessel underway. Few builders today have the full range of knowledge and experience necessary to be a true "boatbuilder."

Vocational Training

Not enough hands-on experience. They have tool skill but less practical knowledge.

Modern and Traditional Design

I'm not a modern racing man. Some older ideas are inefficient, though. Traditional designs must be balanced with efficiency.

Miscellaneous

On the Coast Guard regulations: Why buck it? Do it right and then you are clear.

Henry Long
H.A. Long Boat Works
7719 Bobcat Drive S.E.
Olympia, WA 98503
(206) 491-2212

To quote Mr. Long, "Craftsmanship takes dedication, perseverance, and patience." These are attitudes Henry Long needed in abundance in order to come back from the fire that devastated the shop that was his father's before it was his. The loss was incalculable. Not only were many tools, plans, and so forth lost, but the Evergreen 38, ready to plank, burned as well. This was a joint project of Mr. Long's and the students of Evergreen State College's Marine Studies and Crafts program.

General Information

Number of builders: Three.
Specialties: Our 12-foot and 15-foot clinker wood boats, period.
Nontraditional modes: No.
Experience: No.

Preferred paints and glues: Traditional unless *proven* inferior.
Sail and/or power: Formerly sail, now power. About fifty-fifty.

Facilities

Design and drafting: Yes.
Lumber storage: Very limited.
Metal working: Patterns only.

History

Origin of interest: My father was a builder and I did it as a hobby.
Training: Bremerton (Washington) Navy Yard.
Selection of location: I liked Olympia.

Recent Projects

Getting back on our feet after the fire.

Projects in Store

See Specialties, above.

Lumber and Hardware

Quality red cedar is scarce and expensive. Manufacturers are discontinuing wooden boat hardware due to low demand.

The Market

It should improve due to the resurgence of appreciation for craftsmanship in wood.

Who is Buying and Why

Rowing buffs.

The Labor Pool

Difficult. Craftsmanship takes dedication, perseverance, and patience. These qualities are not in abundance.

Vocational Training

See The Labor Pool, above. Bates (Joe Trumbly) is good.

Modern and Traditional Design

There's room for both.

Restorations and Replicas

Either is acceptable if done with pride and excellence.

Open Statement

Love craftsmanship, no matter what.

James C. Lyons
P.O. Box 684
Port Townsend, WA 98368
(206) 385-4903

In a town that is commonly considered boat-crazy, James is soft spoken and to the point. His is an uncommon voice—calm and assured.

General Information

Number of builders: One.
Capacity: 40 feet.
Specialties: Custom woodworking.

Nontraditional modes: Yes.
Experience: Yes.
Preferred paints and glues: Traditional by far.
Sail and/or power: Sail.

Facilities

Design and drafting: No.
Lumber storage: No.

History

Training: Seattle Community College under Earle Wakefield.
Selection of location: Lots of boating activity here.
Financing: Cash.

Recent Projects

A 25-foot Pemaquid Friendship, red cedar on oak. [It was a hit at the 1977 Port Townsend Festival.—P.L.] I've also been building Ingrid interiors.

Projects in Store

Setting up a new shop, and possibly some of Calkins' Bartenders.

Unusual Tools

A small caulking mallet. The ones available are generally much too big and heavy for the work on hand. This one has a head only 1½ inches in diameter and 11 inches long.

Lumber and Hardware

Good-quality boat lumber will be available for many years to come in the Northwest. Both hardware and lumber will become much more expensive.

Cooperatives

The right combination of personalities makes or break a coop. Most coops end in bad feelings.

The Market

The boat market will continue to grow, mostly in plastics and epoxy-oriented construction.

The Labor Pool

Presently, there's less skilled labor and more emphasis on sheer quantity.

Vocational Training

It is a good way to get a start in boatbuilding for those without previous experience.

Modern and Traditional Design

Modern design is essential for progress, yet, at the same time, there are many traditional designs (still unexplored) suited to most needs.

Restorations and Replicas

Both are important to the tradition of boats and boatbuilding.

Open Statement

Building boats is one way to express oneself. Boats are both functional and aesthetic.

David McFadden
Waldron Island, WA 98297

Like Bob Coe, David is basically an alternativist. His farm is largely self-sufficient. His interest in boats is as much a personal expression of deep conviction as it is a vocation. Note his succinct, but meaningful, Open Statement.

General Information

Number of builders: One.

Capacity: 30 feet.

Specialties: Traditional craft—sail or power.

Nontraditional modes: No.

Experience: No.

Preferred paints and glues: About fifty-fifty, but I tend toward the traditional.

Sail and/or power: Fifty-fifty.

Facilities

Design and drafting: No.

Lumber storage: Unlimited. This island is covered with good timber. Availability is not a problem.

Metal working: No.

History

Origin of interest: Living on the waterfront in Sausalito, California.

Training: Repairing boats on my own.

Selection of location: My wife and I were camping in the mountains and realized we wanted to sleep under a cedar tree every night. We do that here in this house.

Financing: We built and then sold a houseboat.

Recent Projects

A 14-foot Whitehall. I selected, felled, hewed, etc., spars for the 75-foot sardine carrier/schooner *Helen McColl.*

Projects in Store

To sustain myself on new construction and have not only my own boat, but the time to enjoy it as well.

Lumber and Hardware

The wood is there (beyond this island) but hard to get. But although cold-molding may relieve some pressure in making the use of second-growth lumber possible, there is *not* enough to sustain a full-fledged traditional wooden boat revival on the level of things like this survey, *The Mariner's Catalog, WoodenBoat,* etc.

Cooperatives

They are an intellectual exercise in what the small community does (ideally). I see a "community" forming: a rural, self-sufficient, tribal American subculture! This will need local mills, foundries, and blacksmiths.

David McFadden prepares for an afternoon of fishing with his Whitehall.

The Market

Despite the semicommercial leanings, amateurism is where it's going.

The Labor Pool

There is tremendous energy and interest; a lot of learning going on.

Vocational Training

It's right on!

Modern and Traditional Design

Traditional.

Restorations and Replicas

This question will be solved by reality itself.

Time and Finish

The relationship between builder and client is there so that they can communicate on this.

Open Statement

The traditional wooden boat is a series of personal victories in skill, knowledge, and quality, in an increasingly impersonal world.

The ferry that runs to Waldron, northernmost of the American San Juan Islands, from West Beach, Orcas Island, is a dory. Waldron has no power, no running water, no telephones, and just a few dirt roads. The handful of cars there have come by hired barge at great expense. (Should their owner leave, they stay. Like everything on Waldron, the car would simply be recycled into someone else's life.) Waiting for the ferry, I mused and watched the sun steam the dew off my pack. Self-sufficiency and wooden boatbuilding—perfect.

As I passed through the open gate to McFadden's farm, there was laughter. Seated on a log, keying out wild mushrooms with a bunch of young children gathered around, was a man of middle height with a long beard and a clear eye. In a corner of the field stood an open shed built of logs, and in it were three boats in various stages of construction. On the basis of 30 seconds' contact, David said, "Of course you'll stay a few days. Somebody go tell Momma that Paul will join us, please?" From someone else came the request, "Can I wear your black cowboy hat?" (On the drive to the West Coast, I'd stopped in Wall, South Dakota, long enough to fulfill a childhood dream. I wanted a black cowboy hat like one an older brother had bought there 15 covetous years before.)

By kerosene lamp at night, and in the brilliant, warm autumn sun, David and I talked boats and alternatives. Standing amid the boats and shavings, I told him of a solar-heated boat shop I knew of in Maine. Back in the woods David showed me two huge, solid spars that he had selected, felled, barked, cured, and hewed out for a friend's schooner. A team of men and horses would move them to the water later on. The caring and generosity of his family was like the Indian summer. The days were of those life-remembered, perfect few.

Weeks later, in Vancouver, British Columbia, I suddenly realized I didn't have my Stetson. I called the bar in Westsound where I was sure I'd left it. The barmaid thought she'd seen it, but no, it's gone. I moved on south to Olympia, Newport, Eureka, and San Francisco Bay. Then came the trek north again.

I missed the hat so much that while on Orcas and Waldron Islands (for the second time in two months) I watched for someone wearing my cowboy hat. No luck, I gave up. Later, as I was leaving McFadden's, Dave stopped me. "You said you might be going through San Juan Island. Could you stop off at Tate's boat shop with this hat?" In a flash I remembered his kids playing with my Stetson and my heart leaped to my throat, but . . . it was only a red cap. "It's his apprentice's favorite."

As I stepped through the door at Tate's, before I could say a word, his apprentice looked up and said, "You've come back for your hat!" From under the workbench he whipped out my hat, sawdust and all. I had given him *his* before I realized just what had happened. I had inadvertently traveled several thousand miles, from San Francisco in fact, in order to unite a friend of a friend of a friend, and myself, with our respective hats. The circles of the world, and the maritime grapevine, grow ever smaller and more interconnected each day.

J.H. McGlasson
Cape Foulweather Boat Co.
P.O. Box 748
Newport, OR 97365
(503) 867-6705

Joe and the operation at Cape Foulweather can be summed up in one word—competent. McGlasson's had five different boats, in various stages, going at one time—from a Stone Horse to a 54-foot diesel yacht. Four of the five were Joe's designs. Evelyn McGlasson, an integral part of the business, wrote, "In 35 years we've had shipyards, fiberglass plants, and now again back to wood—and happy to *be* back."

General Information

Number of builders: Ten.

Capacity: 65 feet.

Specialties: Custom boatbuilding—in particular, the Bahama 31- and 38-foot sloop line.

Nontraditional modes: Nailed and glued-strip.

Experience: Yes, lots.

Preferred paints and glues: 50 percent modern.

Sail and/or power: Equal experience with both.

Facilities

Design and drafting: Yes, I'm a marine architect and a marine engineer.

Lumber storage: 4,000 b.f.

Metal working: Patterns, aluminum welding.

History

Origin of interest: Woodworking is in my family; everything from bow and arrows to backyard building.

Training: In yards.

Selection of location: We like the people and the climate.

Financing: Through banks, our own cash, and our excellent credit reputations.

Recent Projects

Evelyn: "Oh, have you got an hour?" A 25-foot Stone Horse, two quarter-tonners (25-foot and 31-foot), a 54-foot pleasure yacht, two 32-foot strip-planked sloops, and a 38-foot sailboat.

Projects in Store

More of the same! As a matter of fact, we have an order for a gondola, too.

Lumber and Hardware

I think the future is good.

Cooperatives

I doubt it, in Oregon. With the young builders they may have a great future—they're more aware.

The Market

Better every day! We have more and more inquiries as time goes by.

The Labor Pool

The situation is very bad in Newport; we have to train our own. Those that are interested have excellent morale and education, just as good as 10 years ago, if not better.

Vocational Training

We have no contact with the schools.

Modern and Traditional Design

No preference, or perhaps my preference is for traditional lines modified to suit present needs.

Time and Finish

We won't build a boat we wouldn't go to sea in. There is a limit as to how far we will go in any direction, fancy or plain. It's common sense.

Open Statement

We build custom boats, designed or modified to suit an individual customer's needs and desires.

Robert E. Nixon
Nor-west Boat Works
P.O. Box 641
Gig Harbor, WA 98335
(206) 858-8043

General Information

Number of builders: One.
Capacity: 35 feet.
Specialties: Custom cruising sail.
Nontraditional modes: Yes.
Experience: Yes, strip-planking.
Preferred paints and glues: Mostly traditional.
Sail and/or power: 90 percent sail.

Facilities

Design and drafting: Drafting only.
Lumber storage: 2,000 b.f.
Metal working: Patterns and welding.

History

Origin of interest: In boatyards as a child.
Training: In yards and at school.
Selection of location: It has a 12-month boating season.
Financing: On my own with a lot of hard work.

Recent Projects

Rebuilt Bill Crosby's *Osprey;* built Bill Atkin's *Eric Jr.;* built Bill Atkin's Nordic Folkboat; and rebuilt a 25-foot Blanchard-built sloop.

Projects in Store

Rebuild Hanna Tahiti ketch and build a strip-planked, Nelson Zimmer-designed 27-foot sloop.

Unusual Tools

I make and alter tools as I need them.

Lumber and Hardware

I do not have any trouble obtaining all the lumber I need.

The Market

Back to wood boats. The younger generation are buying wood boats and older people are buying combined glass and wood.

The Labor Pool

Well-trained boatbuilders are in this area because there's a very good vocational technical school here. The schools are doing a good job.

Modern and Traditional Design

I think the best designers were Alden, Atkin, and Hanna.

Restorations and Replicas

If you do not have the preservation of skills, you won't have restorations or replicas.

Time and Finish

There is only one quality to use when building a boat. If this requires extra work, you have to do it whether you get paid for it or not.

Open Statement

My shop builds and rebuilds wood and glass/wood boats of top quality.

SOURCE **Bob and Erica Pickett**
Flounder Bay Boat Shop and Lumber Sales
3rd and O Streets
Anacortes, WA 98221
(206) 293-2369

The Picketts, like their almost-neighbors Martin and Diana Langeland of Skookum Fastenings, have set up a fine "support industry" business. Flounder Bay Lumber Sales grew out of Bob and Erica's wooden-boat repair shop when a local mill asked if they would handle the mill's high-grade stock. One thing led to another. "Our principal business (now) is selling boat lumber and doing a small amount of custom milling and repair. Our background in boatbuilding, refinish work, and light repair has stood us in good stead to advise customers on doing their own work. We can be very involved with a customer's project at times, particularly with amateurs and boatbuilding students. Don't be misled, though; about a third of our business is out of state, so we are not strictly local. A good bit even goes to Alaska."

General Information

Number of builders: Two.

Specialties: See above. Also building small craft when we can find the time.

Facilities

Design and drafting: No.

Lumber storage: About 40,000 b.f. and expanding. We are looking at forklifts and more storage space.

History

Origin of interest: See above and Volume 17 of *Lines and Offsets,* the journal of the Traditional Wooden Boat Society, for a good portrait of the Picketts and Flounder Bay.

Lumber and Hardware

There's no shortage of resources; it's distribution that is poor. Remember, the big mills aren't interested in the relatively small quantities that traditional wooden boatbuilding requires. Also, much of what is left is not easy to get at, being on bad terrain or in the national forests. Looking at the long range, we have a tough situation with a lot of export, and cross purposes between environmentalists and reasonable lumber utilization. The environmentalists' arguments are weakened by the fact that some of them insist on all-wood houses and wooden boats. Wilderness designations preclude the possibilities of multiple use and proper forest management. I would say, even so, that on a small scale like ours, there is certainly room and materials for others in this business (boat lumber), particularly in other parts of the country.

Cooperatives

I think the highly competitive nature of the lumber business requires that a setup have a professional in charge; someone with a relatively free hand to select, buy (wheel and deal), and generally establish priorities.

The Market

It's good. It will increase dramatically sometime in the next five to 20 years as a result of the oil situation.

The Labor Pool

No problems.

Vocational Training

I like the quality of the student population; their motivation is excellent.

Open Statement

There is a future in selective logging of privately owned land, particularly for those with a sense of ecology, those who like logging with horses.

Miscellaneous

Here is an excerpt from Flounder Bay's excellent five-page pamphlet titled *West Coast Lumber for Boat Building*. In keeping with an irreproachable standard of service, they sell this, and a second five-pager on air drying, for 25 cents and 15 cents, respectively.

Western Red Cedar, Thuja Plicata. Those in the east will recognize the first name as being the same as that for their Northern White Cedar, Thuja occidentalis. Red Cedar is commonly used for strip-planking, cold-mold laminating, small boat planking, and thwarts. [I have seen a fair bit of it in the interiors of recently built, larger boats, too.—P.L.] It is highly rot-resistant because of the toxic resins and oils in the wood. These oils give the wood a distinctive fragrance. Red cedar crooks can be very dense, and rock hard, and may be used for natural knees in small boats.

Knots and Pitch. Knots in the old-growth cedar are generally loose or rotten. This is because the trees grow so close together that the lower limbs die for lack of sunlight, then hang on while the rest of the tree grows around them. Dead limbs make for loose, unsound knots. Pitch pockets are practically absent in red cedar.

Common defect. In cedar, these are fall shake and pocket rot. This is rot in small patches of the plank, and is present in the tree before it is cut. It is nearly impossible to detect this rot in a wet, newly sawn board. As the board dries, the rot remains a very dark brown color, darker than the rest of the plank. This defect seems to occur most frequently in the butt cut of the log, that is, the first section of the tree from the ground. Bad slope of grain is also a problem in the butt cut because of the flare of the tree.

The red cedar used for boat stock comes, like the fir, from old-growth trees. Long clear planks are available, though not common. The cedar is soft, easy to work, and straight-grained. It holds paint fairly well, and definitely needs a finish film, like paint or varnish, or it will soak up and retain water, especially in flat-grain planks.

Many of the flatiron skiffs, lapstrake rowing boats, and rental boats of this area were planked in red cedar. It does not resist abrasion as well as fir, but if properly maintained will give years and years of good service. It is a popular planking material for small boats because it is so light. It has been used in planking as thin as $\frac{3}{16}''$ in canoes and shells, but does tend to split, especially along a fastening line. It will not hold fastenings very well and should not be used for framing.

Stanley R. Pocock
George Pocock Racing Shells, Inc.
Home address: 602 12th Avenue North
Edmonds, WA 98020
(206) 633-1038 (business)

The strict demands of athletic competition make racing shells a specialty unto themselves. Mr. Pocock and family have been leading names in this field for 60 years.

I must add that since the shells are neither technically plank-on-frame, nor without skin (they use a glass cloth for reinforcement), I decided to include them only after much inner debate. Mr. Pocock and his fine shells are a reminder of just how diverse the wooden boatbuilding field can be. Reading the interview below, the reader becomes aware of how little some of the questions apply to this situation, and how others remain valid—such as with materials. This point can be extended to include wood-canvas canoe builders, birch-bark canoe builders, and other specialty shops. Note the entirely different perspective.

General Information

Specialties: Racing shells and oars, also training equipment.

Nontraditional modes: No.

Experience: Yes.

Facilities

Design and drafting: Yes.

Lumber storage: Unlimited.

Metal working: No.

History

Origin of interest: Family business.

Training: Here in the shop.

Selection of location: Availability of lumber.

Recent Projects

[This, as with much other information, is not available due to the stiffness of competition among builders.—P.L.]

Lumber and Hardware

In the future it is going to be difficult to get high-grade lumber, and it certainly won't get better further along.

The Market

Our market is primarily to universities, colleges, high schools, prep schools, rowing clubs, and a few individuals.

The Labor Pool

There seems to be an increase in the number of young people who want to work with their hands. Most want too much money.

Open Statement

I think the universities could perform a great service by combining technical training with actual shop experience. This would help bridge the gap between the theoretical and the practical.

Jim Prier
Raincoast Boatshop
Hornby Island, B.C., Canada
(604) 335-2527

Prier came to Port Townsend for the festival (1977) with what turned out to be the hit of the show, or one of them. This was a 40-foot strip-built Tancook whaler complete with tanbark sails.

General Information

Number of builders: Two to four.
Capacity: 50 feet.
Specialties: Traditional schooners, especially Tancook whalers, and custom sail.
Nontraditional modes: Yes.
Experience: Yes, strip.
Preferred paints and glues: Mostly modern.
Sail and/or power: Sail.

Facilities

Design and drafting: Yes.
Lumber storage: 8,000 to 10,000 b.f. covered.
Metal working: Patterns and stainless welding.

History

Origin of interest: Temporary insanity.

Jim Prier's 40-foot Tancook whaler.

Training: As a pattern maker.
Selection of location: There is good wood readily available.
Financing: By the skin of the teeth.

Recent Projects

A 45-foot Nova Scotia schoonerboat; a traditional, Prier-designed five-ton-cutter; a 40-foot Tancook whaler; and five cold-molded dinghies. Rebuild of 20-ton trawler.

Projects in Store

Earn a living constructing sailing vessels of high standard.

Unusual Methods

Interiors are finished off before the decks are laid on. [This is fairly common in the Northwest. Some builders even complete the interior before they build the hull around it. —P.L.]

Lumber and Hardware

It's available if you know where to look. I use local loggers a good bit and import most hardware from Europe or manufacture it myself.

Cooperatives

A mistake.

The Market

Excellent potential for a small number of truly professional yards. Too many amateurs are muddying the water. The big future may well be in cold-molding, mainly racing.

The Labor Pool

Poor and unreliable for the most part. Traditional wooden boatbuilding needs to be seen more as an occupation and less as a romantic endeavor. Traditional small craft can't take months to build if one is to make a solid living. There's no pension plan.

Modern and Traditional Design

I prefer traditional designs, but I'll build whatever comes along. I'd like to put together a really strung-out racer.

Restorations and Replicas

Both. Government or foundation money may be required.

Open Statement

I aim to provide high-quality custom wooden boats in continuation of a long-standing tradition.

Miscellaneous

The fall of the Canadian dollar makes our quotations more attractive for U.S. markets.

Myron Richards
Pleasant Bay Boats
6555 102nd Avenue
Kirkland, WA 98033
(206) 822-3907

My instincts notwithstanding, there are always times when boat shops turn up in the least expected places. Myron's shop is out behind his home on a street so split-level-suburban-ordinary that I checked twice to be sure I had the right address.

General Information

Number of builders: One.

Capacity: 24 feet.

Specialties: Traditional oar and sail, also steam launches.

Nontraditional modes: Prefer not to.

Experience: Very limited.

Preferred paints and glues: Mostly traditional, but I have recently begun experimenting with more modern materials.

Sail and/or power: Have done both, but plan to stick with row and sail in the future. Perhaps some steam.

Facilities

Design and drafting: Yes.

Lumber storage: 1,000 b.f.

Metal working: I have made patterns and castings, but have no facilities at present.

Recent Projects

A 10-foot lapstrake sail/rowboat of my own design; a 14-foot steam launch; and an 8-foot lapstrake sail/row dinghy.

Projects in Store

A 12-foot lapstrake sailboat and a 20-foot sharpie. Both are on speculation; both have been spoken for.

Unusual Tools and Methods

A bench jig with which to resaw boat lumber, particularly planking stock, on my bandsaw.

Lumber and Hardware

There is no shortage except for copper-cut boat nails. These are evidently not available in the U.S.; perhaps they are in England.

Cooperatives

I have bought lumber this way; it's a good idea.

The Market

Limited but there. Some of us won't make it!

The Labor Pool

Quantity is okay. The quality is unknown.

Vocational Training

The schools I know about are doing a good job.

Modern and Traditional Design

Traditional! I grew up enjoying the beauty of line and form that are traditional. I see a boat as functional sculpture. I built a pregnant-elephant-type once and it wasn't much fun.

Time and Finish

My building has been my own choice of design, to suit me. If it will sell at my price, okay. If not, I may be out of business. Obviously, the parts must fit, especially if one speculates.

Open Statement

My plans are to build my own designs and sell to those who want a boat that will be distinctly theirs. I don't want to bid on work that others could do! I just want to do what I enjoy: develop an idea, then put it together.

David Roberts and Martin Adams
Roberts and Adams
3816 Railway Avenue
Everett, WA 98201
(206) 252-8330

Notice their concern for forest management and the overall quality of their medium. Everett has several large operations cutting lumber, much of it for Japan.

In partner Nancy Sosnove's own words, "*Teach* is an incredibly beautiful, expensive, overbuilt little gem . . . and a way to show other people our work." Whether it's the basic materials or their own skills, they care.

General Information

Number of builders: Three.
Capacity: 50 feet.
Specialties: Custom sail and auxiliaries.
Nontraditional modes: Yes.
Experience: No.
Preferred paints and glues: Mostly modern.
Sail and/or power: Sail.

Facilities

Design and drafting: Yes, some.
Lumber storage: 2,000 b.f.
Metal working: No.

History

Roberts went to Seattle Community College's boatbuilding school and then started a repair business, originally in Mukilteo. Adams went to Seattle Community for a while, then quit to work and gather capital for the business.

Sosnove started as a part-time apprentice and worked her way up to full-time employee. She's from Massachusetts, Roberts is from Alaska, Adams is a native. All are there because they prefer the Northwest in general.

Recent Projects

The 16-foot Atkin daysailer *Teach.* (See introductory paragraph.)

Projects in Store

When our current job is finished, we are planning to start one and maybe two 30- to 35-foot wooden cruising sailboats.

Unusual Tools

Scribing plates. Pieces of sheet metal 2½″ x 1″ with tabs 3/16″ deep bent as follows or as needed. ⌐¬ Auto-body hand sanders for fairing off. These basically have a plane's configuration for easy handling. They are usually made of wood and very cheap. [A few yards I visited had compressed air-powered models. —P.L.]

Lumber and Hardware

If the lumber companies would stop sending all the big logs to Japan, we'd be in great shape. Lumber management, as in Norway, Europe, etc., is essential and not happening. The future may be dark without action soon; lumber costs may triple in 10 years.

Cooperatives

Coops are a great idea but we have none in operation around here. We have coops for food, health care, and recreational equipment, so we have some knowledge of the problems involved.

The Market

If lumber is properly managed, we'll have a great "market." Otherwise, no wood—no wood boats.

Who is Buying and Why

Most of our inquiries come from young people who want to get away and "retire" early.

The Labor Pool

There is a lot of labor available, but we can't judge the quality since we haven't any other employees.

Vocational Training

David says it "keeps 'em off the streets." They are turning out a lot more "builders" than there are jobs for.

Modern and Traditional Design

A good idea is a good idea, and a bad idea is a bad idea. Some traditional designs are fantastic. So are some modern innovations. We favor tradition where it means quality or performance or beauty.

Miscellaneous

On the Coast Guard regulations: We love seeing the other guy regulated! Control plastic powerboats and leave wooden sailboats alone.

All this is a bit cursory, but we have deck beams to put in, you know. Hope this is some help.

Paul Schweiss
Clinker Boatworks
8906½ 35th West
Tacoma, WA 98466
(206) 564-1424

Mr. Schweiss is getting quite a reputation as a fine, serious young builder. He is coming into full stride, potential unlimited, with his increasing speed in the shop. This is the more remarkable since he already has a reputation for fast work of first-rate finish.

General Information

Number of builders: One, soon to be three.

Capacity: 40 feet. At least once, I'd like to try a 60- to 70-footer!

Specialties: Ancient Norwegian skiffs, traditional Scandinavian rowing, sailing, and power vessels. Also custom work in regular lapstrake and carvel construction, all designs.

Nontraditional modes: No.

Experience: Double-planked carvel only.

Preferred paints and glues: Mostly traditional.

Sail and/or power: Equal experience with both.

Facilities

Design and drafting: Yes, to the extent of modifying existing designs.

Lumber storage: Yes.

Metal working: No.

History

Training: Seattle yacht yards and yards in Norway.

Paul Schweiss has found good challenges to his skill in such projects as this beamy little "bathtub," which shows clean lines and close work. Paul's sawn frames and natural crooks come from a variety of sources: he has been known to drive around Tacoma after a storm, chainsaw in hand, offering to remove and/or saw up fallen limbs.

Selection of location: I found good shop space, a place to live, and a source of tools upon returning from Norway.

Financing: Family loan.

Recent Projects

A 32-foot Cornish pilot gig for a rowing club; several 14-foot Danish beach boats; a 20-foot Norwegian double-ended fjord boat; an 18-foot Danish pram; another Viking boat; and an 18-foot Cornish gig of Culler's design.

Projects in Store

Build some larger cruising vessels; promote camping-cruiser types; encourage rowing, sailing, and sensible powerboats.

Unusual Tools and Methods

A hewing hatchet [with which he cuts beautiful planking scarfs—P.L.], Norwegian riveting process, and bucking iron. Moldless Norwegian (Viking) construction process. (See Chip Stulen interview for description.)

Lumber and Hardware

Lumber is very good. Hardware for these simple boats is mainly custom-made locally. Ideally, local craftsmen could become part of an ongoing, mutually supportive exchange of skills and services.

Cooperatives

Positive for shops for the amateur. To run a lumber cooperative would be difficult due to quantity of work (sticking, etc.) involved. You'd need a full-time man to run it and keep charge.

The Market

The future of small boats may be cloudy. I don't always see short-term demand for traditional small craft. Big stuff is strong in both long and short term.

The Labor Pool

Good all around.

Vocational Training

Speed at the schools is slow. Schools are good for teaching lofting and certain technical work, but, ideally, the bulk of learning takes place in a yard.

Modern and Traditional Designs

Traditional designs need some changes, such as when you convert a working hull to a cruising one. Traditional materials are cheapest and best, barring racing or other special needs.

Restorations and Replicas

Replicas, barring the real historical significance of a particular vessel, because they are cheaper.

Open Statement

We are attempting to bring back custom boatbuilding by shaping a boat to a person's individual needs.

Tom Tucker
The Marvel Boat Farm
P.O. Box 116
Port Ludlow, WA 98365
(206) 437-2894

Tucker is one of a number of young builders who've moved north from California in recent years. I can think of no better introduction than to quote from his own article on his most successful design, the 20-foot trailerable, hard-chine, gaff sloop *Lyra*. "At the time, my boat shop was located between the dog food and the alfalfa in the local cooperative hardware, feed, and grain store in Santa Cruz. I was contemplating whether perhaps I should do something economically realistic like house carpentry when Gary Frederick walked in. Proving that appearances aren't everything, he asked me if I would be interested in building a small boat from a 1930s design. I promptly refused on the ground that said design was too ugly to build. Out of this came my first commission." (*WoodenBoat,* No. 10)

General Information

Number of builders: One.

Capacity: 45 feet.

Specialties: Custom cruising sail. Plans and boats from *Lyra*'s design. See also Projects in Store.

Nontraditional modes: Yes.

Experience: Yes.

Preferred paints and glues: Whatever is suitable, proven, and economical, which means about 50 percent modern.

Sail and/or power: Sail.

Facilities

Design and drafting: Yes.

Metal working: Patterns only. I use a lot of stainless because I can often find what I need there, if not in bronze.

History

Origin of interest: I had an early interest in designing and spent a lot of time in boats and around boat nuts.

Training: Just doing it! I've been at it about 10 years. I built a lot of El Toro dories, too.

Selection of location: I recently found a good space here on Mats-Mats Bay. There's more interest here than in California.

Financing: Loans.

Recent Projects

Purchased aforementioned shop. It's 50 feet by 60 feet and on the water.

Projects in Store

Rebuild a 27-foot five-ton Crosby yawl. I have the interior to design and build into an Ingrid. I am designing a keel centerboarder along *Lyra*'s lines; a 27-foot, three-ton gaff sloop.

Lumber and Hardware

Good trees are getting scarce, the price is constantly rising at frightening rates. Good wood will be available, if expensive. Traditional hardware is hard to get, but since new people seem to be getting into producing it (on a small scale, at least) things may improve slightly.

Cooperatives

Coops are fine as long as the goals are mutual, centralized. A cooperative sawmill would be great but difficult to execute. In any case, local builders should be working cooperatively, not competitively.

The Market

I don't know.

The Labor Pool

It's getting better. Seriously interested hard workers—nonromantics—are getting more numerous.

Vocational Training

I haven't had any contact with the schools here, Bates and Seattle Community, but I'm positive about the concept of vocational training.

Modern and Traditional Design

We need combinations—the best of both worlds.

Time and Finish

Depends entirely upon the situation, money, etc. Personally I lean toward high finish.

Open Statement

What I try to do here is just build good boats.

Gilbert Vik
Vik Boat
Route 1, Box 129
Cathlamet, WA 98612
(206) 849-2942

Few young men are as methodical as Gilbert in their pursuit of a shop. He has built the space himself, bought lumber as much as two years ahead to allow for seasoning, devoted a good part of several years to developing his design skills, and so forth. Both feet on the ground, and very dedicated, he knows where he is going.

General Information

Number of builders: One.
Capacity: 40 feet.
Specialties: Custom design and construction of sailing craft under 45 feet.
Nontraditional modes: Yes, cold-molding.
Experience: No.

Preferred paints and glues: Traditional, most of the time.

Sail and/or power: My experience is about split between them, but the emphasis has always been on sail.

Facilities

Design and drafting: Yes.

Lumber storage: 15,000 b.f.

Metal working: Patterns only.

History

Origin of interest: Mine comes from a life in and around boats.

Training: I learned from my father, who did quite a bit of building when he wasn't fishing or farming. I've had enough experience with building to consider myself thoroughly competent, by any real standard.

Selection of location: This is my home town.

Recent Projects

Building and setting up this shop.

Projects in Store

A 42-foot traditional schooner, gaff rig and all. Originally it was going to be 47 feet. You will note that my capacity is really 40 feet. Typical of what the business is like, don't you think? It's a case of contradictions.

Lumber and Hardware

Okay, but occasionally it takes a lot of time to get building supplies, in fact, most of the time. But there is still some good wood around.

Cooperatives

It'd be great for lumber.

The Market

A certain percentage of the glass market will switch over. That percentage isn't large, but it is firm.

Modern and Traditional Design

I have little interest in racing boats, as I feel that life is too short to spend a lot of time working on something that is going to be obsolete in two years. As far as more general designing goes, I'm fifty-fifty on modern versus traditional.

A functional vessel is definitely where the emphasis is, but the quality of the design is not enough. The materials involved have to be every bit as good. If I can't get decent materials, I won't build boats. And my standards are tough.

Open Statement

It is important to realize the lead time required to set up a shop. It is the designer/builder's obligation to be ready to really go when the time comes. At the same time, the client must *know* what he wants, or be ready to accept what the designer thinks he should have.

SOURCE

Dick Wagner
The Old Boathouse
2770 Westlake N.
Seattle, WA 98109
(206) 283-9166

Dick's position is unique. As proprietor of The Old Boathouse, he has been renting (by the hour, day, week) wooden Whitehalls, wherries, Beetle Cats, Rana sloops, and the like for 10 years on Lake Union. As President and a founder of the Traditional Wooden Boat Society, he is the West Coast's foremost authority on traditional small craft, and Puget Sound boating in general. Dick has been known to complain about boatbuilders who demonstrate their technique for making plank scarfs (with a fairing hatchet) on his living-room rug. Secretly, he rather enjoys it. As this incident shows, here is a boat man, gentleman, and enthusiast. Warning: his excitement is contagious. People who visit the Boathouse are likely to come away with boat fever.

Dick and Colleen Wagner's "front yard." The Old Boathouse itself is on the left, obscured by the canoe and the sail of a Concordia Beetle Cat.

General Information

Number of builders: Two.
Capacity: 16 feet.
Specialties: Lapstrake traditional small craft, rudders, tillers, spars, and oars.
Nontraditional modes: No.
Experience: Yes.
Preferred paints and glues: Traditional.
Sail and/or power: Sail, oar, and paddle constitute 99 percent.

Facilities

Design and drafting: Yes.
Lumber storage: No.
Metal working: No, but have access to a good blacksmith.

History

Origin of interest: Permanent and incurable.
Training: Observation and practice. I first got into boat work in order to save money on the repairs of all the boats I owned, particularly the rental fleet.
Selection of location: There's lots of water, great cruising.
Financing: Savings, renting boats. (See also *WoodenBoat,* No. 24.)

Recent Projects

New afterdeck on a 40-foot schooner; replaced stove plank on a 40-foot steam boat; repaired split planks, lapstrake dinghies.

I helped start The Center for Wooden Boats in the Northwest. The purpose of

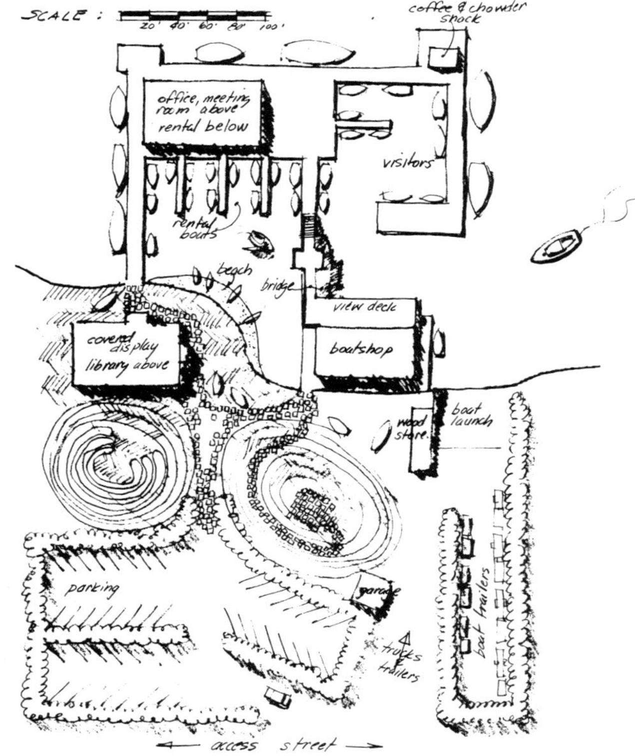

Dick Wagner was asked to dream up a cost-no-object master plan for The Center for Wooden Boats, which has no site, let alone a cost-no-object budget. The Northwest's big dreams have a habit of becoming realities. (Shavings)

the Center is to obtain, preserve, and disseminate knowledge of traditional small watercraft; to offer educational displays and services related to traditional wood boats; to build, restore, and preserve traditional small craft, particularly those unique to the Northwest region of the United States; to share information, boat plans, small craft history, and woodcraft skills with others. Our newsletter's first issue came out in November 1978. We welcome assistance and input of all kinds, so if all this interests you, write us at the address above.

Projects in Store

Building some yacht dinghies on speculation, also some utilitarian skiffs on speculation—a Swampscott model, maybe. I'd like to develop a high-quality kit rowing boat. Further development of The Center for Wooden Boats.

Lumber and Hardware

We will always have trees. We don't use much hardware on small boats, but the supply seems better now than 10 years ago.

Cooperatives

It's a good idea in reducing the cost of power tools and space. Very likely to increase in number.

The Market

There is a groundswell of demand for quality and integrity in all products. Traditional wooden boats will be in increasing demand. The buyers of wooden boats have a love of quality in design and craftsmanship.

The Labor Pool

There are plenty of good builders in Puget Sound now.

Vocational Training

We need the kind of creative training that is found at Bates and Seattle Community College. The teachers are always looking for faster and more accurate ways to do the job. The old apprentice-master system is too rigid. For boatbuilders to make a living today, they must be able to produce efficiently.

Modern and Traditional Design

There is nothing new about fin keels and spade rudders—or cold-molding, for that matter. I think the traditional designs will always fare well.

Restorations and Replicas

I would prefer restoration if the boat can be economically restored and then used; otherwise, forget it. Skills preservation is more important than boat preservation.

Time and Finish

If by "time and finish" you mean that form should follow function, the answer is "yes." If in doubt about design, follow the traditional form. It will produce a more-than-functional boat. The old forms were developed pragmatically to give the best performance for the parameters of budget, materials, and function.

Open Statement

A new era is beginning; demand for high standards in appearance, workmanship, and performance. I feel we established our position 10 years ago, and the rest of the folks are starting to catch up to us.

SOURCE

Land Washburn and Joe Bucek
The Wooden Boat Shop
1007 Northeast Boat Street
Seattle, WA 98105
(206) 634-3600

Lake Union and Boat Street acquired a new business in February 1978 when Land and Joe opened their doors for the first time. The Wooden Boat Shop carries tools, books (including European publications), hard-to-find hardware, and "honest boats." That's right, boats. Land and Joe began their endeavor with a plan to sell wooden boats from a showroom, something of a first. In the time since they opened, their purposes have evolved and grown.

The Shop is the area's authorized dealer and service center for Seagull motors, and recently they announced the addition of the Greenlee line of tools. Touring the well-lit showroom always inspires conversation, and that's where Land and Joe have come into their own. The Shop's long-range purpose, in addition to selling boat-related materials, is to be an old-fashioned chandlery—providing as much advice and assistance to boat people as they want and need. "We have a good number of people through here every few days with boat problems, like leaky skiffs," Land remarked. "It is a good part of our business to talk over problems before providing the supplies needed to deal with them. But for now, we frankly admit to doing more advising than selling. It will take some time before our reputation expands sufficiently to pay off."

Between the Shop and the expanding Center for Wooden Boats in the Northwest (see Dick Wagner interview), Seattle should be in a fine position in years to come. The two would seem to be a complementary combination of an active center for traditional watercraft and a retail outlet supporting that center. In a hypothetical scenario, the Center will introduce the public to the boats and gradually educate and entice them toward full involvement. The Shop then provides the boat and/or supplies to boatbuilders, and, finally, the Center will offer a focal point and historical context for their wooden-boat activity.

By mid-1979, Land Washburn and Joe Bucek were going full tilt at The Wooden Boat Shop. Their stash of oars is visible through the window at far right. (Land Washburn photo)

Stephen Webster and Janet Gray
Siletz Boat Works
Box 192, Kernville Route
Lincoln City, OR 97367
(503) 996-3208

Webster is a private person. He feels his boats speak for him. In a rare moment, late one night, he made this comment: "I want to be free of financial and emotional limits. The seas are still relatively free of population and restrictions. I want the opportunity to enjoy every aspect of the sea, while working in my own medium."

General Information

Number of builders: Two.

Capacity: 65 feet.

Specialties: Traditional small craft.

Nontraditional modes: No.

Experience: No.

Facilities

Lumber storage: 2,700 b.f. and covered space for 10,000 or 12,000 more. We also have a mobile dimension saw available at the shop.

Metal working: Limited.

Recent Projects

[The shop Stephen has renovated contains what is undoubtedly the biggest bandsaw I have ever seen. I never measured it, but I do know that Stephen had to replace a goodly number of the pilings under the building before he could even begin to contemplate moving it in. — P.L.] Since we've restored the shop, we've turned out 18½-foot and 16-foot Culler skiffs.

Projects in Store

Nothing definite.

Lumber and Hardware

Good, if we can slow the log exports. Otherwise, the rape and pillage of Brazil ought to produce competitively priced hardwoods on this coast. The same goes for Central America.

Cooperatives

This has to be a great idea, but in practice I haven't met anyone with the organizational abilities.

The Market

The future looks good, next to the rising costs of steel, polyester resin, etc. There appears to be a good market for trailerable, shoal, inexpensive rowing and sailing craft for fishing or pleasure.

The Labor Pool

I think a good foreman can bring it together, with less than the best help, as long as he directly oversees all the work.

Vocational Training

This is a difficult question to assess if only because a lot of this kind of training is geared to the employment available in the field. Woodworking skills often get down-played.

Modern and Traditional Design

You can argue with me, but I can't argue with my own eye. It seems to choose the traditional types and their derivatives.

Restorations and Replicas

Skills preservation first.

Time and Finish

I definitely set a standard and try to keep to the basics in finish.

Open Statement

The future looks good from here. I only wish that the builders and their public would identify themselves as high-priority users of prime-grade domestic lumber. Only this way will it remain available at a competitive price and not be sold off to balance an already sick trade deficit.

Orville Wike
The Oregon Dory
P.O. Box 573
Newport, OR 97365
(503) 876-6161

Wike is a true shipwright of the old school, examinations and all. The range of his experience is profound. He has sold boats to Saudi Arabia, Egypt, and Australia. Buyers don't travel that far for nothing. His boats are not yachts, but that is not to say they can't be, and haven't been, used as pleasure boats.

Construction detail of a 24′ cruiser in Orville Wike's shop. Orville is well known for the diagonal run of his plywood bottoms and the careful fits on his boxed beams. He uses a very fine grade of plywood—voids are virtually nonexistent.

An Oregon Bar Runner receives the finishing touches in Orville Wike's big shop. Treenails are used in the forward sections of the deadwood—part of what Orville calls "the boat's Viking heritage."

General Information

Number of builders: Four.

Capacity: 25 feet.

Specialties: Flat- or V-bottomed, square-sterned, working craft.

Nontraditional modes: Yes.

Experience: Yes.

Preferred paints and glues: 50 percent traditional.

Sail and/or power: Power.

Facilities

Design and drafting: Yes.

Lumber storage: 30,000 b.f.

Metal working: Patterns only.

History

Origin of interest: In 1927, at age 17, I got started building a boat for a friend. He had been badly hurt when his boat got caught between the surf and a pier. We pooled together to build him a new boat, and then one thing led to another.

Training: On my own and then in yards.

Selection of location: Lumber is available, good sources for plywood.

Recent Projects

Fifteen to 20 boats a year; the Oregon Dory (22 feet); the Oregon Bar Runner (24 feet); the Newport Offshore Express Cruiser (25 feet 4 inches); and others. I use box-beam (aircraft) construction, and all the boats are available at various stages of completion. Prices are reasonable.

Projects in Store

More of the same.

Lumber and Hardware

I used to have my own mill; friends now make up my plywood, since it's the only way to get the necessary quality. With the stupidity and selfishness in government bodies, and all the shipping to Japan, the only way to be set with lumber is to keep two years ahead. The only hope I see is in a change in government. Reseeding of quality woods, not just pulp, should be mandatory.

Cooperatives

Yes, if you can find a source for the lumber, they could work.

The Market

As long as people live, they'll need boats. Glass will be too expensive. Aluminum has a future, but it is too cold, brittle, etc., to go too far.

The Labor Pool

Very scarce; we have to train our own men. Ten percent of all the applicants are any good. They are doers and leaders, not watchers and sheep. When an "apprentice" is helping me at the planer, and he doesn't move around to the other side without being asked, I know he's not thinking for himself. *That's* what I mean.

Vocational Training

With rare exception, no good. The graduates generally know just enough to be dangerous. Only rarely can a builder find an experienced man. As I said, you must train them yourself.

Modern and Traditional Design

Traditional.

Time and Finish

Both workboat and yacht finish are fine, and they each have their place. The trick is to be honest in the representation of what you are doing.

Open Statement

I am 69; I do it because I want to. My main objective has been to train young men in a skill that is becoming rare. They'd never be out of work. I was looking forward to many more years of my favorite work. But now I am no longer able to get apprentices. The government has abandoned all these training projects so that we may give the congressmen a raise, or Lower Slobovia another million for lost causes.

The scare of limited entry is dying down now, and we are getting some more possible buyers looking around. The boats that most fishermen are interested in are the most versatile types; salmon trolling is not, and cannot be, the only resource for them.

L.H. Bates Vocational-Technical Institute
of Tacoma
1101 South Yakima Avenue
Tacoma, WA 98405
(206) 597-7220

Until the spring of 1979, when Joe Trumbly retired, boatbuilding at Bates was always referred to as "Trumbly." That is no misnomer. Monday through Friday at 8:15 A.M., for 23 years, Joe was ready and waiting to dig into some fresh teaching project. This man could run a greyhound ragged. The Institute's superb reputation has only been improved by his remarkable handling of the boatbuilding course. Joe reassured me by phone that the curriculum and approach of the program would not change substantially with his departure.

The Institute's plant on South Yakima covers several blocks and trains about 2,000 students daily in 51 different trades! For large projects, such as the 40-foot ketch recently completed, the whole school has been known to contribute something: welding work, upholstery, stainless steel hanging knees, the works.

The boatbuilding course runs 22 months, or 2,574 hours of instruction. The course outline includes everything from occupational and safety information, to the study of propellers and rudders, to joinerwork and fiberglass construction. This is a program where you get quite a grounding in the basics, but to get a diploma you need a recommendation from your employer not less than six months after you have started on the job.

Anyone over 16 years of age may apply, from anywhere. There is no tuition charge for students under 21, others pay $50 a quarter plus a $15 registration fee. Total tool, book, and supply requirements run about $70, all of which are available through the Institute's store. Yes, they *are* thorough.

Large boats (power and sail) are built either as class projects or as individual efforts by the students. Students have the opportunity to bid on the class projects or build their own boats.

When I visited Bates, I was struck by the caliber of the program's 20 students and the intensity with which they applied themselves to their work. It stands to reason. The program has a waiting list of about 125. In May 1979, the top name on the list had applied on August 31, 1976! The students come from all parts of the United States, including Hawaii and Alaska.

A hallmark of Bates and Trumbly has been an awesome amount of creativity. (Joe is presently at home on Raft Island, writing a book on lofting based on his many innovations.) The inside-and-out framing method they teach is not a Bates original, but it is typical of what has kept boatbuilding at Bates flourishing for 30 years. A Yankee builder once said to me, "The only way to frame up alone is with two other guys." While this method requires good lofting skills, it does make it possible for one man to frame up a good-sized hull alone.

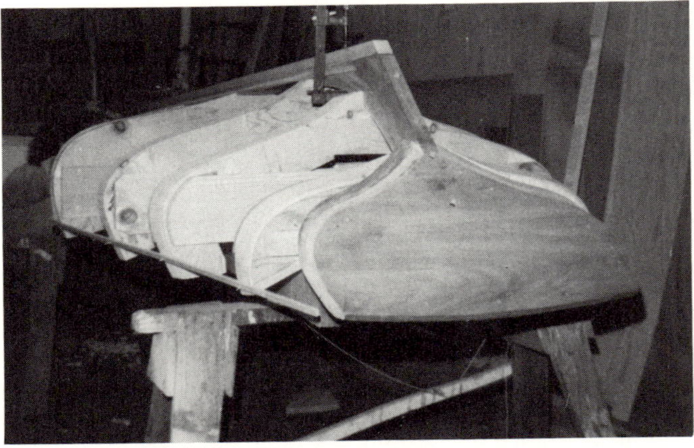

Some nice work by an apprentice boatbuilder at Bates shows efficiency of effort. The oversize molds will be reshaped into sawn frames.

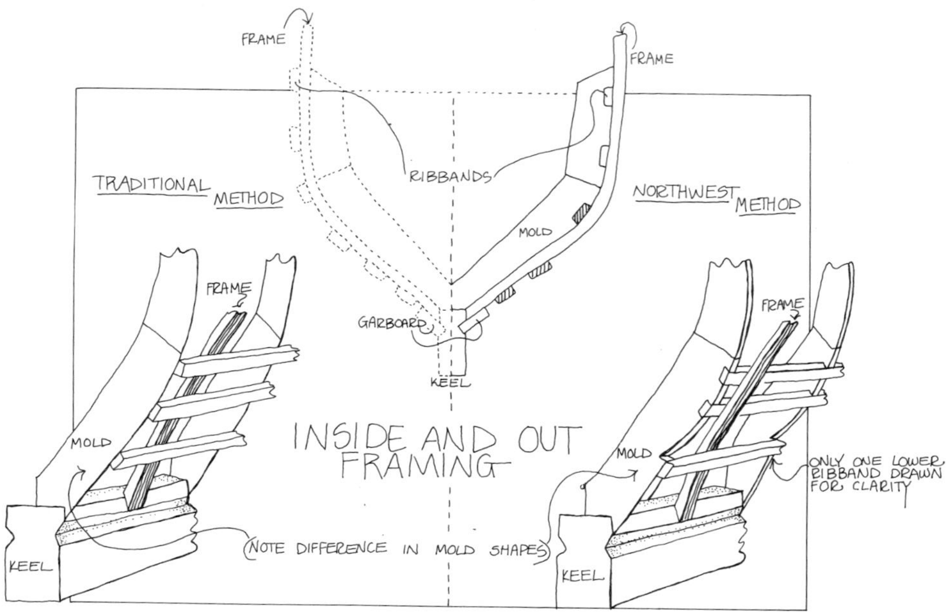

The framing technique taught at Bates. In the Northwest, the loftsman deducts the plank thickness and *the thickness of the framing from the mold's upper section while deducting only plank thickness in the lower sections. Permanent members, such as sheer clamps and stringers, can be notched into the molds, cutting down the number of ribbands necessary, adding stiffness and locations to permanently fasten the frames at the outset. Hot frames can be slipped to the keel through the slot between the ribbands and then bent to the upper sections* all from outside of the hull. *(Rebecca Wheeler illustration)*

Miscellaneous

Joe welcomes serious correspondence at his home at 197 Raft Island, Gig Harbor, WA 98334. Area boat buffs and enthusiasts at large will continue, no doubt, to enjoy the benefits of his expertise through his presence at boat shows and gatherings, and in his forthcoming writings.

Seattle Central Community College
Roy Kobayashi, Instructor
2310 South Lane Street
Seattle, WA 98144
(206) 587-5460

Former instructor Earle Wakefield was fond of saying that the difference between boatbuilding and other trades is that builders *make* the part before they assemble it. Roy Kobayashi added, "Our main objective is to make the student employable, so they have to be pretty sharp, and they *are* sharp."

The deadwood for another Whitehall gets careful measurement at Seattle Central.

General Information

Number of builders: 35 to 40 students with open enrollment.

Capacity: 20 feet.

Specialties: We start with tools and equipment and move on right through joinerwork. We have an additional, optional section that covers wiring, tanks, controls, exhaust, struts and bearings, plumbing, and so forth.

Nontraditional modes: Yes, we cover fiberglass, too.

Experience: Yes.

Preferred paints and glues: We advocate that they use what is best in *their* best judgment.

History

In 1965, the old Gompers-Edison Technical Institute became part of the Seattle Community College system. Tuition is now about $100 per quarter for residents of the area, about $400 a quarter for others. A three-year waiting list was closed not too long ago, the students on it given priority, and a new policy of first-come, first-served initiated.

Recent Projects

You name it. We've had everything from 17-foot Hampton boats to mini-trawlers.

Projects in Store

More of the same. We are not purists, mind you. Our students build a good proportion of fiberglass hulls that they finish off in wood. The course is structured for maximum flexibility.

Lumber and Hardware

The wood situation is almost impossible, and wood is only getting harder to get. A lot of our students go up to Picketts' Flounder Bay Boat Shop and Lumber Sales. We put a fair amount of emphasis on making patterns, which tells you how we feel about the hardware situation.

Cooperatives

The possibilities are very limited. Boatbuilders are usually the wrong type of person for coops—too individualistic.

The Market

It's moving toward well-to-do types who want a special boat, at least as far as wood is concerned.

The Labor Pool

The labor pool is good. It is a matter of connecting the supply with the demand, the builder to the school. Our graduates are picked up very quickly, as a rule, by the repair and finishing-off facilities. No shortage of work *there.*

Vocational Training

The majority of our students are aware that it takes 10 to 15 years to become a real "boatbuilder." Many are college graduates with time in other fields, older people who know what they want. They'll match the old-timers for quality with fewer years on the job. Here, we emphasize the basics because we can't take the time to go through each individual builder's way of doing a given job.

Time and Finish

The student will pick up speed; the old-timers were slow once, too. I've never heard of a decent boatbuilder who was out of work and hungry, at least not for very long.

Open Statement

I can't say enough for these students. They are more rounded than those of, say, 30 years ago, and worldly. Most of them will be lead men in 10 to 15 years, though not all in wood-only work. Only the best of the best of these will be able to do that. What we push for here is reliability—it is in short supply these days.

CALIFORNIA BUILDERS

Greg Baker
514 Waldo Point
Sausalito, CA 94965
(415) 332-6824

Baker's shop is not far from Ray Speck's at Waldo Point. If memory serves me right, the fastest way to get from one to the other is to walk through the Gate Three Boatbuilding Cooperative.

General Information

Number of builders: One.
Capacity: 45 feet and/or 12 feet of beam.
Specialties: Spars up to 60 feet long and 9 inches square.

A replica of the Spray *has her deck caulked at the Gate Three Boatbuilding Cooperative.*

Nontraditional modes: Yes. Any construction as long as it's wood.

Experience: Yes.

Preferred paints and glues: Fifty-fifty.

Sail and/or power: Sail 25 percent, power 10 percent, oar 65 percent.

Facilities

Design and drafting: Yes, also photo reproduction.

Lumber storage: Space for 6,000 b.f.

Metal working: We have a small smith's shop and metal lathe.

History

Origin of interest: I was 12 when I built my first skiff (I'm now 37).

Training: From old-timers and working in boatyards.

Selection of location: This is just my home area.

Financing: House carpentry and working at repair in other boatyards.

Recent Projects

A 30-foot cathedral-hull powerboat of my own design; the interior on a 20-foot sloop; construction as far as the third strake of a 28-foot sloop for a fellow boatbuilder; and restoration of a 12-foot Whitehall skiff.

Projects in Store

A 46-foot Herreshoff schooner (already set up) for myself. I am discussing the possibilities for semiproduction of Whitehalls for a customer who wants to handle them.

Unusual Tools

My bandsaw is a Butcher Boy meat saw (from a butcher shop) and it is quite strong.

Lumber and Hardware

Lumber has been in a slump as far as accessibility goes, but the situation is get-

A modified Kingston lobsterboat gets her masts stepped by builder Kit Africa.

ting better. Good hardware just *has* to be specially cast for all but a very few items.

Cooperatives

There is one in this area that seems to work well, but I personally prefer to stick to a small shop. I'm not much interested in that kind of extra effort; I've got my hands full.

The Market

More and more people want wood boats. Work in this area (all around the Bay) is quite plentiful.

The Labor Pool

It looks like there are enough boatbuilders for the people who want boats. I should add that if a person doesn't build a boat of good quality, he isn't a boatbuilder.

Vocational Training

Some of the schools are working, and vocational schools in general are a good idea. I'd like to have had some regular schooling instead of learning bits here and there. Of course, I'm still learning and I don't think I'll stop.

Modern and Traditional Design

As a rule, traditional designs make a better sailing and handling boat than those of the last 10 or 15 years; call them modern or IOR, it's no different. Under that same rule, they also look better.

Restorations and Replicas

Sometimes a restoration turns out to be a new boat with a lot of extra work. Obviously, there's a limit.

Time and Finish

You have to balance your time so that you get a good finished product, and yet it can't cost a fortune.

Open Statement

I like to work with wood and create something useful and nice to look at. Boatbuilding fills that bill. I have fun, and get paid for my time. As my own boss I can set my own timetable so that I can go sailing or take trips.

James Blaiklock
70 Carmel Valley Road
Del Mar, CA 92014
(714) 755-8361

James' philosophy is evident throughout the interview. As he openly admits in his Open Statement, he moves beyond practicality to fanaticism. His living situation underscores this. He lives over his shop, which is located at the back of a farm. This intense home/work arrangement allows Blaiklock not only the time he needs to pursue his perfectionism, but the flexibility of low overhead as well.

General Information

Number of builders: One.
Capacity: 30 feet.
Specialties: Workboats and repair (remember that this area is known to many as "plastic boatland").
Nontraditional modes: Only if the specific boat interests me.
Experience: No.
Preferred paints and glues: Mostly traditional.
Sail and/or power: 50 percent each way.

Facilities

Design and drafting: Yes.

James Blaiklock's meticulous Eaglet, *a Thomas Gillmer* Blue Moon.

Lumber storage: 1,000 b.f.

Metal working: Patterns and keel-casting.

History

Origin of interest: I was constantly building things: tree houses, skiffs, anything! My father was an amateur builder and my family has a long history with the sea in general.

Training: Any way and every way possible, but mostly in repair.

Selection of location: It was available.

Financing: Through tightening my belt and long hours of work. Things always worked out somehow.

Recent Projects

A 22-foot 10-inch *Blue Moon* by Thomas Gillmer (see *WoodenBoat,* No. 2). This one is to be renamed *Eaglet.* Planking is 1⅛-inch Philippine mahogany on white oak laminated frames 2 inches by 2½ inches. Keel and deadwood are apitong, with 2,200 pounds of lead outside ballast, through-bolted with ¾-inch bronze. All fastenings and fittings are bronze, all decks and joinerwork will be teak. Philip Bolger's Folding Schooner; a *Seguin* (stretched to 17 feet); an Atkin Rinky Dink; and a Swampscott dory have been my projects in new construction before *Eaglet.* Oh yes, I also built a plywood Boston Whaler-type entirely by eye. The owner insisted that I do it that way.

Projects in Store

Finish *Eaglet*, and then more of the same.

Unusual Tools and Methods

Well, I make most of my tools, not just planes. It pays to do as much as you can yourself. I've designed and built a system for greater ease in folding and unfolding the 31-foot Folding Schooner. It's a simple A-frame, two-part tackle and sling that provides much better purchase and a margin of security, with minimal additional time and trouble in construction overall.

I believe the composer writes the score, the conductor interprets it, developing phrasing and tonality to its fullest, giving the piece life! I believe that the designer develops the boat, but the builder interprets and works with it to give it life. That's why I've changed things on Gillmer's design. I've added knightheads and a housing bowsprit. These lifting eyes are also my idea. The lifting eyes consist of two heavy bronze "arms" bolted through the keel at equal distance from the boat's center of gravity. A sling, complete with shackles, will be kept aboard. The shackles can be attached to the arms, and the sling, exiting through the cuddy directly over the center of gravity, need only be hooked into a crane for easy hauling.

Lumber and Hardware

The quality of wood has decreased, particularly softwoods. Lumber practices in the U.S. are not conducive to sanity. We are doing permanent damage to the environment. Hardware is not a big problem.

Cooperatives

Builders are generally too diversified for a formal coop to work. However, the "grapevine coop" provides a good many jobs.

The Market

There will always be a market for the few. As long as they *want* to, builders will

Laminated oak frames and mahogany planking. The top of a bronze lifting eye can just be discerned at dead center.

make it. I'll admit, though, that Southern California seems to have a market factor of nil. It's tough here.

The Labor Pool

It's pretty low, almost nil, too. There are very few knowledgeable souls.

Vocational Training

Those coming out of the schools will have a tough time without inner desire and determination. You must be a builder in heart, body, and soul. Those who will make it must eat, sleep, and drink boats.

Modern and Traditional Design

I prefer the traditional, but not exclusively.

Restorations and Replicas

Individual situations require individual solutions. Both of the above have their applications. But I would say I'd lean toward getting the most variety and quality of craft possible for the money, as opposed to one large boat that will probably also be one big headache to keep up.

Time and Finish

A boat is made of thousands of interlocking parts. Anything but the finest fit weakens the whole. It sometimes goes beyond practicality to fanaticism. Like not shining the back of your belt buckle—perhaps nobody else will know, but it's not the same as if the job is done right. It isn't necessarily logical, but it *is* right boatwise and spiritually.

Open Statement

I can remember being four or five years old, seated in the bottom of a leaky skiff, bailing just as fast as I could. My arms got tired because I had to reach up as high as I could just to dump the water over the side! If a person is a boatbuilder, he will build boats in the face of all that is against him. Lack of knowledge, tools, money, materials, and markets will always plague him. If you *are* a boatbuilder, then *be* one. Build a boat, it's worth it.

Edward Frey
Frey's Boat Works
1707 Main Street
Fortuna, CA 95540
(707) 725-5212

I arrived at Frey's late one evening, and I had to leave before daylight. We chatted away in the darkened shop, surrounded by dories, prams, and tools. A car passing by on the street sent headlights flickering through the shop, and I caught a glimpse of a hard steel edge. Investigation revealed a meticulously maintained gyrocopter that Ed had built. His fight to get legal permission to fly the open single-seater was the usual Man vs. Bureaucracy struggle. Yet it proves the depth of his tenacity in the face of difficult odds—and the diversity of his interests as well.

General Information

Number of builders: One.
Capacity: 30 feet.
Specialties: Commercial fishing boats, dories, and skiffs.
Nontraditional modes: Yes.
Experience: Some.
Preferred paints and glues: Mostly modern.
Sail and/or power: Power 60 percent, sail the rest.

Facilities

Design and drafting: Yes.
Lumber storage: Limited to the equivalent of one or two boats.

History

I worked for many years as a carpenter around the docks of Portsmouth, N.H., after developing (even earlier) an interest in boatbuilding with wood (the only material that'll float). I am self-taught as a designer/builder. I like the West Coast and moved out here six years ago. After working here and there, I decided I'd stop thinking about it and really build boats. The effort is owned and financed entirely by myself.

Recent Projects

An 18-foot St. Pierre; a 22-foot deadrise fishing boat (plywood); three 19-foot Carolina dories; assorted prams, skiffs, and a miniature 16-foot Tancook whaler, the *Yarrow,* by Phil Bolger.

Projects in Store

Just building boats. I will eventually build only custom, conventional plank craft.

Lumber and Hardware

I select and cut my own timber, for the most part. Some materials are returning to the marketplace; prices are soaring, however.

Cooperatives

Not a bad idea. As for myself, I work independently and would rather not get involved in a large venture.

The Market

It looks as though wood is coming back, especially wooden sailing yachts.

The Labor Pool

Many people want to work and learn, few of these succeed in becoming fine craftsmen.

Vocational Training

There should be more schools for boatbuilding. I do not train apprentices because they want to learn from scratch. They should have basic woodworking skills before learning boatbuilding.

Modern and Traditional Design

I am mainly interested in the traditional, but there is certainly room for both.

Open Statement

All I want is a Little Olde Boat Shoppe that pays its way. It looks as though we will make it, too.

Bill Grunwald
Aeolus Boat Works
Old Coast Road
Davenport, CA 95017
(408) 423-5681

Bill had just built a 19-foot fantail launch "under this ancient 'make-and-break' I've rebuilt. If you'll crank that flywheel with your foot for a while, I'll do some last-minute tinkering." One tired foot later, we were under way. The engine was minus its muffler and the sporadic explosions brought half the marina out to watch. This questioning was begun under inquisitive stares and completed in Bill's cavernous shop, several days later.

General Information

Number of builders: Myself and an apprentice/helper.

Capacity: 20 feet.

Specialties: Peapods, yacht tenders, dories, Whitehalls, and other traditional small craft.

Nontraditional modes: No.

Experience: No.

Preferred paints and glues: Mostly traditional.

Sail and/or power: Mostly oar.

Facilities

Design and drafting: Minimal.

Lumber storage: 2,000 to 3,000 b.f.

Metal working: No.

History

Origin of interest: I've been a boat buff since childhood.

Training: I was an amateur, and then went professional. I sometimes call it boatbuilding-by-default; it's what I can do well.

Selection of location: There was just this big old shed available.

Financing: From hard work.

Recent Projects

A 19-foot fantail skipjack launch. We get out about 30 boats a year. Most are ¼-inch or ⅜-inch plywood-on-oak; the fancy ones like Whitehalls can be Philippine-mahogany-on-oak. Bill's helper chimed in: "There are some dories down in the harbor that Bill sold close to 20 years ago. A couple seem to have had almost no maintenance, or at least only sporadic attention; they get banged around and drawn over rocks, and they are very sound little boats." Bill: "My boats may often be plain, but they're honest."

Projects in Store

We'll carry on with most anything. I'm amenable. I have a man talking about another one of these [the launch] but for a steam engine.

Lumber and Hardware

As far as I know, ply will always be available, but the quality of it sure is dropping.

Cooperatives

That's a good idea!

The Market

I don't really know, the present one is steady and strong.

Who is Buying and Why

Of course, with oar power one doesn't reach the "great unwashed" much. These folks are mostly higher educated.

The Labor Pool

It's less and less a factor for me. Having had as many as five people working for me, I've cut back. It just wasn't much fun. I get less trouble and more pleasure out of working alone. Most of the young guys who come in here don't have the potential.

Time and Finish

I'm in the middle. A good balance between cost and utility is essential.

Open Statement

We should keep a close watch on the Coast Guard. Last I heard, they'd managed to devise a test the Bank dory couldn't past. What next?

Ken Mobert, Mary Mobert, and Kazan Mohrs
Doghole
P.O. Box 273, 36210 Old Stage Road
Gualala, CA 95445
(707) 884-3368

Ken has been in and out of boats since he was a few years old. He knows boatyards well enough to have drawn the cartoons sprinkled through this book. Wit lightens the difficulties of running both a small farm *and* a boat shop. He has been known to work in the shop for stretches as long as 24 hours, and still have his sense of humor when he finds himself back at the bench the next day, with too little sleep.

Hey, Roger, on your way down get me a scraper.

Ken Mobert

General Information

Number of builders: Two.

Capacity: 26 feet.

Specialties: Lapstrake craft are our specialty, both traditional sail/row craft and powerboats under five h.p.

Nontraditional modes: Yes.

Experience: No.

Preferred paints and glues: 60 percent oldies-but-goodies. We only switch to more recent stuff if it has been thoroughly proven more effective.

Sail and/or power: 30 percent power, 70 percent sail/oar. Kazan is a fine mechanic.

Facilities

Design and drafting: Yes.

Lumber storage: 12,000 b.f.

Metal working: Patterns.

History

Origin of interest: From childhood. I had my first bomber at age nine.

Training: In boatyards. Much of my life has been spent as a yard guerrilla. Mary and I have lived on boats for seven years.

Selection of location: Overhead is low, and those who want a boat can find us. Chatterers are unwelcome.

Financing: Work in boatyards and a small inheritance.

Recent Projects

We have been busy! There's been a replica of a 16-foot Norse pram for the San Francisco Maritime Museum, and half a Whitehall for them also. Yes, that's "half," slit the long way, to show construction details and all. Try building half a boat sometime; it's got some neat challenges. Since then it's been tenders, foys, sharpies, and on and on. This is after we built the shop and a new home for ourselves, of course.

Projects in Store

I've got 16 pairs of Port Orford oars to make and no time to do it. In general, I intend to promote a lifestyle I enjoy.

Unusual Methods

We've built some Whitehalls here and found that on one model all the planks were variations on the second strake. By turning it one way or another, all but the garboards could be fitted pretty closely. My guess is that it was a production or factory boat.

Lumber and Hardware

A yard like ours doesn't need that much, so it's not too bad. Hardware is just plain difficult. Difficult to find, get delivered, and even hard to get cast sometimes.

Cooperatives

Buying lumber has possibilities, although getting together will have its difficulties. No one is really cooperating terribly much these days. When we sent out a call for action on the Coast Guard mess, the response was, "Oh, great!" but it went nowhere after that. Things seem to have cooled a little, but I still feel at times that our motto ought to be, "Hang together, or hang separately."

The Market

Small boats have a strong market. I feel the larger boat market in wood would be very weak without cold-molding.

The Labor Pool

Not too bad! It's shaky but growing fast. There are the usual kids who don't really care to learn or care to do it right, but otherwise it's pretty good.

Modern and Traditional Design

Traditional.

Restorations and Replicas

Both are altogether inadequate in the area of small working craft. What's been done is a drop in the bucket. I'd like to pursue this further personally someday, too.

Time and Finish

You have to do the very best you can everywhere in the boat. Otherwise, you won't enjoy the job. I do the best work possible at a professional rate. If it weren't at boats, it'd be something else.

Phillip Philbrick
Philbrick Boat Works
603 Embarcadero
Oakland, CA 94606
(415) 893-9443

It has taken Mr. Philbrick 44 years of boatbuilding to get to this new shop and a regular production system. As a high-schooler he started working on boats; since then, his principal interest has been runabouts. Keeping in mind that speedy production and fine work are sometimes at odds, he has limited his schedule to 12 boats a year. The big shed where he has set up is well laid out.

General Information

Number of builders: Three.

Capacity: 30 feet.

Specialties: Semi-production of our 20-foot six-inch Honduras-mahogany motor runabouts.

Nontraditional modes: No.

Experience: Yes.

Preferred paints and glues: Fifty-fifty modern and traditional.

Sail and/or power: Strictly power.

Facilities

Design and drafting: Yes.

Lumber: 2,000 b.f.

Metal working: Patterns only.

History

Origin of interest: See above.

Training: Building boats on my own.

Selection of location: I live here.

Phillip Philbrick's legs are just visible beneath the foredeck and dashboard of his first painstakingly finished, production-built runabout. Someone once said boatbuilders are frustrated contortionists—this photograph offers ample proof of the statement.

Recent Projects

Our first production-built runabout after several months of setting up.

Projects in Store

Really get the ball rolling.

Lumber and Hardware

Remember, we use imported woods 90 percent of the time, so we don't foresee any real problems with quality or availability.

The Market

I'm gambling; it looks good.

The Labor Pool

Not very good. I'll train my own.

Open Statement

I don't have a philosophy of boatbuilding.

Ray Speck
722 Waldo Point
Sausalito, CA 94965
(415) 332-6529

Ray is located smack in the middle of Waldo Point and its polyglot lifestyles. In this one small area, there are exotic Bohemian houseboats with bubble windows and hanging plants; the Bank of America with its manicured parking lot (the Establishment and all); and a third section with dozens of classic and not-so-classic cars, trucks, and boats in various stages of reconstruction and neglect. Amid the chic hipness of this ultimately Californian collage, Ray is a bedrock pragmatist with only a touch of romanticism about his vocation.

General Information

Number of builders: One.

Capacity: 32 feet inside; outside it's unlimited.

Specialties: Lapstrake traditional small craft. The Sid skiff.

Nontraditional modes: No.

Preferred paints and glues: 50 percent traditional.

Sail and/or power: Sail and oar.

Facilities

Design and drafting: Limited.

Lumber storage: 1,000 b.f.

Metal working: No.

History

Origin of interest: From childhood.

Training: I apprenticed to Jack Lowther at Spittle Bridge, Whitby, Yorkshire, England.

Selection of location: I built my first shop out of scrounged materials and I had the opportunity to squat with it.

A rowing/sailing Sid skiff planked with Port Orford cedar nears completion in Ray Speck's shop.

Financing: Scrimp, save, starve, and eliminate house rent by living aboard our boat. Early on I returned 85 to 90 percent of the shop's earnings back into materials and fastenings.

Recent Projects.

About a dozen Sid skiffs of various sizes, for sail and/or oar. Also three Herreshoff 10-foot prams, complete with ten 3-inch planks to a side. And the Boston Partelow Whitehall, 14 feet—I almost forgot that.

Projects in Store

The recent Sid skiffs have been larger, and in that vein, I am now looking forward to some larger boats. Building boats has a snowball effect. I get more inquiries than three years ago, plus I now seem always to have a boat on order.

Unusual Tools and Methods

Ray's construction methods are those he learned in Yorkshire. He works to an overhead beam like the Scandinavians (see Chip Stulen interview), but unlike the Scandinavians, he uses removable molds.

Lumber and Hardware

I've grown dissatisfied with the mill that I used to get Port Orford cedar from—too many defects. Rather than pay $2,000 per thousand board feet for better cedar, I'm thinking of going over to Honduras mahogany. I'm looking for a new future in crook material. If we can interest the "redwood burl" people in milling locust, oak, or cedar crooks, the boat lumber market will be greatly enhanced. Maybe 1980-81 will bring us a supplier of this much-needed material.

Cooperatives

I think that for those building boats for themselves, sharing time is less of a problem. Amateurs could get a lot out of working together. As for a purchasing coop, obviously we'd all benefit from that.

The Market

There is definitely a growing market for traditional wooden boats. It is an impossible way to make a living, though. In England I was told, "You can't make a

The Sid skiff Faamu Sami *("Makes the Water Burn"), with the pleased owner at right. (Ray Speck photo)*

living building boats under 22 feet." They were right. If it wasn't for the fact that we live on a houseboat and pay minimal rent, I could never have gotten started.

It's worth it, though, because of two things. First, the public appreciates all this wood tailoring. I've done a number of shows and the public response has been amazing. Boats that I've had in shows have become hand rubbed; people from machos to grandmothers are humbled by the sight of a "real" boat. Not that plastic or aluminum or epoxy boats are less real, but wooden boats have a strong, visible heritage. The second satisfaction is when you're pushing your freshly sharpened plane down a piece of planking stock. Curls the width of the plane blade, a couple of yards long, pile up on the floor. It's actually work, but it's the payoff.

The Labor Pool

By the nature of the beast, boatbuilding doesn't hold dilettantes. The work is too demanding. It takes a couple of years of long, steady work to achieve even a modicum of skill and efficiency. Yet the people this business attracts are not into a nine-to-five routine. And seeing that my routine is eight-to-six, I find myself alone for the most part. It takes a special fiend to roll this boulder uphill; my hope is that I will soon find another fiend, since it takes two to make a truly efficient shop.

Modern and Traditional Design

There's room for both. It's *quality* that counts!

Open Statement

I think what I said before says it all.

III.
The Gulf Coast, the Southeast, and the Chesapeake Bay

INTRODUCTION TO THE GULF

My uncertainty about how a vagabond would be received in the Deep South was intensified by an almost total lack of information on boatbuilding there. I could count my entire list of contacts for a thousand miles of coastline on one digit of one hand. In a long, lonely drive across the West Texas desert, on a road where the dotted lines disappeared over the horizons in both directions without so much as a bend, I found myself shaking with fear. I didn't even have a place to start looking, a yard at which to make contact. Not even a brilliant sunset of orange, purple, and gold, in which the dark clouds blended with a distant mesa, softened my anxiety. I would just have to start at Brownsville and work eastward.

All across the Texas coast I was warned, "Watch yourself with those backward, no-good Cajuns." One Texan, formerly of New England, remarked, "If you think Downeasters are insular and troublesome, wait till you hit the Louisiana bayous. In Lafitte, anyone born north of Interstate 10 (Baton Rouge) is a 'Damn Yankee.' " If true, I was many-times damned.

Cruising the road that winds beside Bayou Lafourche (pronounced *la-foosh*), I rolled around a bend and saw a police car, poised. The speed limit dropped from 50 to 30 in little more than a car's length. My foot was hard on the brake, but it was already too late. I never object to being caught for speeding, but this was ridiculous. Even before I'd stopped moving, I decided to object. My comments died in my throat when the policeman stood close beside the car. He was so tall that I couldn't see his head. And, as I rolled down the window, a tag next to his badge caught my eye: "To Err is Human, To Forgive

Three Lafitte skiffs show just how versatile the hull can be. On much of Louisiana's Bayou Lafourche, the boats seem to outnumber the cars on the road that runs beside it.

is Not My Policy." That sealed it. In silence, he escorted me to the town hall and wrote up the $40 ticket with the carbon proof sheet between the copies. I figured I was paying for a night on the town, but I never said a word in protest—not wishing to examine the cracks in the ceiling of the town jail.

I drove on at 25 miles an hour with my stomach in knots. It was a threatening introduction to the bayous—and it was not representative. With that one exception, the Cajuns were reasonable, friendly, cooperative, and unbelievably busy building shrimpboats. Launchings along Bayou LaFourche and Bayou Aux Chien (*oh-sheen*) were common enough that it took a 50-footer to turn heads. I learned that small family operations had built about 300 vessels in less than two years, using steel or cypress, Douglas fir, and Brazilian Spanish cedar.

Wooden boatbuilding from West Texas to western Florida has seen very little of the renewed interest in wooden pleasure boats observed elsewhere. On a coast with very warm sea water, a damp climate, teredo-infested inlets, and a booming shrimping industry, a wooden boat that can't pay for itself—and its maintenance—is difficult to justify. Pleasure boats are almost exclusively steel, ferrocement, or fiberglass. Cold-molding, remarkably enough, is virtually unknown.

Beyond its strictly commercial orientation, the most striking differences between Gulf Coast boatbuilding and that in the rest of the country are in construction methods. Building by eye is the rule, not the exception. Like their counterparts on Harkers Island, North Carolina, or Beals Island, Maine, builders keep what plans there are in their heads, or occasionally on models. They set up according to a well-developed feel for what is right. This is nothing more or less than an uninterrupted evolutionary process responding to local conditions, both at sea and in the economy

The best example is in the planking of the Lafitte skiff. These are the Louisiana bayous' beamy, hard-chine vessels of 15 to 60 feet, known particularly for

The open deck of a new 57′ shrimper serves as a work platform for repairs to an older boat in the Lyons brothers shop on Bayou Au Chien.

the extreme flare in their bows, strong sheer, and extended afterdeck. Because of the bayous' inherent marine-borer and rot problems, these boats are hauled as often as three times a year for maintenance. Nevertheless, the borers move rapidly, and once they get started, replanking is the only real solution. Except for the garboard, chine, and sheer strakes, planks are not spiled, nor given shape or taper. (Some builders do taper a few other planks, but this is not common.) Some of the skiffs have no shelf or sheer clamp. Deck beams are tied directly into the massive frame heads, and the planking serves to tie the boat together. This affords an open, less rot-prone area. Since replanking is so common, planks fatigued from the strain of holding the sheer can be replaced regularly. And since there is no shape or taper, replanking is that much faster for the less-skilled fishermen who maintain their own boats. All this is made possible by the shape of the Lafitte skiff itself. There is not a lot of shape to be sprung into the planking, yet you will not find a prettier sheer anywhere. The sheer, in fact, is just one more example of bayou pragmatism. The extended deck provides greater working area, while contributing greatly to the appearance of the skiff.

For the most part, Gulf Coast fishermen build their own boats, perhaps even more frequently than in the Carolinas or in Maine. Of all the people on Bayou Lafourche and Bayou Aux Chien producing those 300 new wood and steel shrimpers, there are only two dozen or so professional builders. This fact, combined with the shortage of any kind of wooden-boat builders in some other areas, are the main reasons why I list only 14 builders for those many miles of coastline.

Gerard Ledet is a third-generation boatbuilder from Golden Meadow on Bayou Lafourche. He is, in fact, the only young professional I was able to locate. His attitudes and products are representative of the Lafitte skiffs and their builders; as much a story of the Cajun attitude about life, people, and the bayou as it is one of cypress, Spanish cedar, and iron.

One member of Louisiana's Cheramie clan was pushing to complete this planking job of Spanish cedar over fir. It is standard practice there simply to notch the stem over the preservative-treated keel.

Ledet spoke of his start in boatbuilding as a simple evolution. In fact, like most Cajuns, Gerard has an immense wealth of experience from which to draw. As he put it, "I am in a boat, at least briefly, almost every day of my life. If you took the water, the sea, from us here, most of us would just die away. It is our life."

In addition to boatbuilding, Ledet has skills as a welder and diesel mechanic. At 20, he took just seven months to complete his first building project, a 52-foot by 18-foot shrimper in Brazilian Spanish cedar, cypress, and galvanized fastenings. Powered by a 165 h.p., 671 G.M., and built in his yard just off the bayou, it was designed to test his own capabilities. The boat fit through the alley leading to the bayou by a matter of inches. He followed that feat with a 40-foot by 16-foot skiff of the same materials. Working seven long days a week, he completed the hull in 3½ months. The rush was due to the owner's desire to make the 1978 shrimping season.

There is more to the bayou than shrimpers. Almost every backyard contains a home-built pirogue for hunting, fishing, and cruising the backwaters of the bayous and the flood plains of the Mississippi.

The Gulf, despite the difficulties of wooden boat ownership, provides as much diversity as any other area, if on a much smaller scale. Retired builder Pete Flores is working on giving life to a number of old rotters, at the same time

Gerard Ledet's latest project looks remarkably like a piece of modern wood sculpture. Contrary to standard practices elsewhere, some Gulf Coast builders start planking in the middle and work outward. The first strake to port underscores just how much shape there is, even in the lower strakes.

giving knowledge and inspiration to the Sea Scouts he has helping him in Donna, Texas, near the Mexican border. Farther east, W.T. Holland of Biloxi, Mississippi, designed, lofted, and "cut out" (keel, deadwood, ballast, and frames) a 52-foot gaff-rigged schooner for a local enthusiast, who has since completed the planking, bulkheads, and decks. He has orders for five more boats, all workboats, to keep him busy.

Joseph C. Landry of Bayou La Batre builds custom round-bottomed, 85-foot shrimpers. The Landry family is heavily involved in these mahogany-on-cypress moneymakers.

> We build . . . a shrimper at a good price, using the best possible materials and workmanship. We try and make a boat a poor man can live with for his entire working life.
>
> *J. Landry*

A philosophy like that is hard to beat.

Over the border, in Florida, George Stevenson is working on what he calls the Philip Bolger/Henry Chatfield Compromise:

> Mr. Chatfield is an older sailor/gentleman who's got quite a set of ideas about this boat, which is to be his ultimate cruising boat. She's 40 feet long, draws 18 inches with her leeboards up . . . and has a 4,000-mile cruising range.
>
> *George Stevenson*

After Stevenson's shop in Panama City, there is little of note until Tarpon Springs. There, three Greek builders are cranking out commercial vessels. Clearwater's Clark Mills and Sarasota's George Luzier have been turning out fine pleasure boats, power and sail, from Optimus prams to a 51-foot marconi ketch.

A heavily built, knuckle-bottomed workboat takes shape in William Holland's shop in Biloxi, Mississippi. The term "knuckle bottom" comes from the special plank at the chine, the joint between the two distinct planes. The frames have been beveled to receive the knuckle.

As long as the present shrimping bonanza continues, men like Landry and Ledet will have an overabundance of work. Recreational wooden boats, excepting the useful pirogues, are so rare as to be nonexistent here, and they will remain so unless cold-molding can make a dent in the problems inherent in the climate.

General Information

Number of builders: Sixteen, and three sources; average shop crew, 3.86 men.

Capacity: The average shop has a 50-foot capacity.

Specialties: Six builders of Lafitte skiffs; three "Greek" work- and partyboat builders in Tarpon Springs; four custom sail and power; one custom power only; one round-bottomed shrimper builder; one in large traditional sailing craft and traditional small craft. Four out of the 16 can build round-bottomed boats.

Nontraditional modes (not applicable to many): Six had worked in them and were willing to do so again; one had and wasn't. Three other builders had not worked in nontraditional modes and had no interest in doing so.

Preferred paints and glues: Three use a combination of traditional and modern materials; four use mostly traditional, four modern.

Sail and/or power: Eleven were strictly power-oriented; three worked in power and sail. Two said most of their experience is with sail power.

Facilities

Design and drafting: The Lafitte skiff builders and some others have continued

Pirogues are so common that they can be found stashed among the odds and ends of boat shops. Regular galvanized finish nails are used throughout, even as clench nails.

the tradition of building by eye. Seven of the builders had reason to develop formal designing skills.

Lumber storage: The average was 6,500 board feet, excluding J. Landry's 75,000 board feet.

Metal working: Of the seven who answered, four had welding facilities and skills; three had reason to do pattern work.

Recent Projects

The six builders of Bayous Lafourche and Aux Chien are responsible for a dozen Lafitte shrimpers over 40 feet in the last year and a half. This is in addition to Valcour Rodrigue's 36 mud boats. The Tarpon Springs clan have turned out 57-and 60-foot partyboats, and several commercial fishing boats. Bill Perry has turned out a 21-foot tug and some glass-over-plywood shrimpers. George Luzier has built a 51-foot marconi ketch and a 20-foot marconi centerboard sloop.

Projects in Store

W.T. Holland has about five projects underway. A couple of these are being built principally by their owners—"cut outs," as he calls them—the rest are his own doing. These include a 42-foot workboat, a 34-foot schooner, and a 45-foot shrimper. There are another dozen shrimpers planned on the Lafitte model, and Joe Landry has 12 round-bottomed 85-footers in the works. Steve Janovsky is working on his goal of two dozen dories a year, in addition to one large boat of undetermined model. Clark Mills plans a 25-foot displacement cruising sailboat.

Unusual Tools and Methods

Valcour Rodrigue's weedless propeller, and the bayou's unusual building methods described earlier. The Flintstone sander by George and Homer Luzier.

Lumber

Cheap Japanese steel has meant a lot to boatbuilding in the South. With the

Panama Canal "across the bay," delivery costs are not as high here as elsewhere. I saw various craft as small as 30 feet built of steel, even though welding distorted the thin plates significantly. Yet even steel is suspect in this climate, since it sweats, rusts, and is very noisy if one has to live with it for days on end at sea. Construction of Lafitte skiffs is about split between wood and steel. In parts of Louisiana, they say that teredos will crawl up onto the ways in their haste to "get started" on a boat still under construction. Without exaggeration, wood's comfort and ease of repair are all that has kept it a viable alternative, because supplies of good cypress and juniper have decreased. Many Cajuns now plank up with imported Spanish cedar, $1,300 a thousand notwithstanding. They are still using cypress for framing, however. In Alabama, it is generally Philippine mahogany over cypress. Due to a complete lack of local timber, Texans are using plywood over sawn Philippine mahogany frames, often glassed to keep teredos out. Eighty-three percent of the builders felt the lumber situation was on its way to a permanent low.

They're chopping them down before they have a chance to grow.

Roy Guidry

There's nobody to cut it, and beyond that, the private landowners and paper companies won't let it go.

William Holland

There are no big trees left, lamination is the future. Sometime in the next hundred years we may have trouble getting two-by-fours.

Minas Sarris

There is talk of import quotas on steel; and since the southern lumber situation "looks bleak," Walter Lyons' comment that there is "no telling how it will develop" seems particularly apt.

Hardware

Except for three builders who mentioned a rise in prices, and a comment by Valcour Rodrigue on discontinued lines, these commercial builders had no troubles with hardware.

Cooperatives

Thirty-three percent of the builders were positive about the idea of a lumber-buying cooperative, but even these felt builders were too dispersed and/or independent to make a go of it. I suspect that some of the interest in coops was sparked by recent price increases at Robichaux's lumberyard. Robichaux's is an excellent yard carrying a wide variety of boatbuilding woods. (The switch to Spanish cedar is largely Francis Robichaux's doing, since he advised builders on the declining cypress situation.) Since he is the only major supplier in the area, he bears the brunt of builders' complaints. (See *WoodenBoat*, No. 26, for more on this interesting lumberman.)

The Market

The shrimping cycle runs from good to bad, and back again, every three to five years. When shrimping is good, builders can't produce enough boats. It will only

In 1969 this boat was taken out of service and set up as a monument to the early fishing industry of South Lafourche. She was then 118 years old and had been in active use by the Theriot family for over 70 years. She was the first boat in the region to be motorized, around 1899. Bayou Lafourche has a long history in the cycle of shrimping and fishing.

be a matter of time before the present boom ends and those 300 new boats become a glut. It is possible that the older builders are anticipating this and finishing up their careers now, while the going is good. In an off year, a smaller skiff might haul off a dozen bushels in a week. Right now, the haul is as high as 30 bushels a day. In good times like these, there are many fringe people working the grounds looking for a quick dollar.

When this cycle drops off, many of the doctors and lawyers will leave off fishing, and boatbuilding will drop off too. There'll be a slow time when just the bayou people will be working. We don't give up on it easily.

Gerard Ledet

People want boats that are bigger, fancier, etc., with no end in sight. They . . . want the best that money can buy.

George Luzier

Sixty-nine percent of the builders surveyed foresaw—after accounting for the usual fluctuations—a small but stable market.

The Labor Pool

Not one builder was positive in his outlook for the future.

In the past, everybody could do boat carpentry, splice a line, etc. Now that the older men have been working very hard for many years, they rightly want to take things easy a little bit. It is getting much harder to find good men.

Gerard Ledet

Contributing to the shortage are two things: the fact that Ledet's peers can make better money shrimping, and the increase in steel construction. After "breaking in" on shrimpboats, a good man can get work in a union yard. In this financially depressed region, that's a tremendous step upward. Most of the operations are still family run and manned. If you ask along Bayou Lafourche for the builder named Cheramie, you have a choice among three or four shops! That the above aspects have eaten into this normally secure labor pool is indicative of how serious the situation is.

Vocational Training

Steve Janovsky mentioned the Port Aransas high school's small skiff-building program, but all the builders were unaware of the programs elsewhere in the country. There would appear to be a serious need for a school in light of the labor situation.

GULF COAST BUILDERS

SOURCE

Weldon Drennan
Drennan Boat Supply
Box 3434, Highway 87
at Rainbow Bridge Marina
Port Arthur, Texas 77640
(713) 962-8747 or 962-5491

Both Mr. Drennan and Pete Flores (following) work with the Sea Scouts a good deal. As mentioned earlier, they assist and advise the Scouts on various restoration projects. It is their openness, as well as their knowledge, that makes them good sources.

General Information

Number of builders: One.

Capacity: Five feet of draft is our maximum by water. We've had much larger boats trucked in.

Specialties: Restoration and repair only.

Recent Projects

Complete restoration of Mystic-built *Stout Fella*; the same with a 42-foot Atkin design. Over the years, we've worked on about 20 others.

Projects in Store

Apart from more boat work, we are expanding. We have a 60-foot shed going up soon.

Pete Flores
Flores Boat Works
218 South Boulevard
Donna, TX 78359
(713) 464-4365

Mr. Flores lightly sketched the story of the present project as about a dozen Sea Scouts gathered round. After locating both an open workboat and a sailboat lying on a marshland, the Scouts watched (and helped) as the boats were salvaged by a professional crew. Transported to Pete's yard, the boats were carefully picked apart, rebuilt, and modified by the Scouts. In later trials, the Scouts will learn seamanship, as well as just how good a job they have done.

SOURCE

John B. Dzerk
Aransas Bay Boats
Box 693
Fulton, TX 78358
(512) 729-0131

At last report, John and crew were busy with repairs in wood, steel, and glass. That is not to say they wouldn't be happy to do some new construction in wood again. As John put it, "I'm not a wood-boat romantic, but we are equipped and willing to do good work at fair rates."

General Information

Number of builders: Two.
Capacity: 50 feet.
Specialties: None, we take what comes: wood, wood-strip, glass, or steel.
Nontraditional modes: Yes.
Experience: Yes.
Preferred paints and glues: Mostly modern.
Sail and/or power: Fifty-fifty, but prefer sail.

Facilities

Design and drafting: No.
Lumber storage: Limited.
Metal working: Welding.

History

Origin of interest: From cruising.
Selection of location: Shop space available, low cost of living, and low overhead in general.

Recent Projects

A 42-foot Cross trimaran; a 40-foot Chris-Craft restoration; a 31-foot Culler lapstrake power craft; and a 20-foot sharpie sailboat.

Projects in Store

More repair, and I have a 50-foot Calkins cutter to rebuild for myself.

Lumber and Hardware

Looks bleak.

Cooperatives

Possible, but tough to organize in this area because of little interest.

The Market

Where are we going from here? *Steel.* The only buyers in wood are a few eccentrics.

The Labor Pool

Cheap, unskilled labor is all that's available.

Vocational Training

As long as people enjoy working with wood, it's a good idea.

Modern and Traditional Design

I don't have a preference except for good designs, new or old.

Time and Finish

We can work to fit the job requirements, time, and money available.

Roy Guidry
P.O. Box 231
Lafitte, LA 70067
(504) 689-3658

Mr. Guidry (*geedree*) has a new, airy shed and lots of work scheduled. I counted four boats under construction both inside the shed and out—almost invariably a sign of good work.

General Information

Number of builders: One.

Capacity: 55 feet.

Specialties: Lafitte skiffs.

Facilities

Lumber storage: 3,000 b.f.

History

Origin of interest: It's in the family.

Training: The same place.

Selection of location: It's home.

Recent Projects

About six skiffs a year, averaging between 25 feet and 30 feet.

Projects in Store

More of the same. I've got a 25-foot cypress-and-Spanish-cedar one to do next.

Lumber and Hardware

They're chopping them down before they have a chance to grow.

Cooperatives

No. I've dealt with them (Guydan Lumber Co.) for 20 years. They treat me well.

Down the road from Roy Guidry is one of the oldest shops in his area—still building pirogues and plywood skiffs.

The Market

It is becoming extinct. When shrimping is bad, the market is bad. There are so many people on the grounds.

William T. Holland
W.T. Holland, Boatbuilder
5912 St. Martin Road
Biloxi, MS 39532
(601) 432-0864

Don't be surprised—even in Biloxi, Mississippi, there are people building schooners. As a friend of mine once quipped about wooden-boat devotees, "They're everywhere! Maybe we ought to kill them off before they multiply!" To this I respond, "It's already too late, they're in Biloxi."

General Information

Number of builders: One.

Capacity: 45 feet.

Specialties: Custom shrimpers, partyboats, traditional powered watercraft, "cut outs" (see below), and some sailboats.

Sail and/or power: Power, 90 percent.

Facilities

Design and drafting: Yes (includes lofting).

Lumber storage: 15,000 b.f.

Metal working: I'm a welder, too.

History

Origin of interest: From childhood.

Training: Various relatives taught me, and I have a natural gift.

Financing: From working on boats, repair.

Recent Projects

A 32-foot shrimper; a 52-foot gaff schooner as a "cut out"; a 40-foot pleasure boat; and various other small jobs.

Bill Holland's yard: note the unusual arrangement of the ballast and the slack-bilged transom.

Projects in Store

A 42-foot by 14-foot displacement hull, and one 38 feet by 13½ feet of the same model. As "cut outs": a 34-foot by 12-foot schooner, a 34-foot powerboat, and a 45-foot powerboat as well.

Unusual Tools and Methods

What I call a "cut out" is usually the lofting, patterns, molds, and sometimes framing for a given hull. Usually, I do this much and then instruct the owner in how to finish the boat, right down to the rigging. I recently had as many as eight owner/builders going at once, in addition to my own project.

Lumber and Hardware

Bad. There's nobody to cut it, and beyond that, the private owners and paper companies won't let it go.

Cooperatives

Builders would just be fighting all the time.

Verification of W.T. Holland's philosophy: the extended work area, an adaptation from the Lafitte skiff, is about to be decked in; the cabin and deck gear will be installed after launching.

The Market

The future is good, provided you are talking *custom*. "If you give them what they want, they have to like it."

The Labor Pool

The reason I work alone is that nobody else is good enough.

Modern and Traditional Design

Traditional.

Time and Finish

My knowledge of wood structures is my guide. Dead fits are the only way, all members notched and faired.

Open Statement

I have a natural talent for building boats. The greater the challenge, the more I can put into a project, and the more I can enjoy it. That is, I can enjoy it if I'm not back-to-the-wall for time. I do welding for the same reason—I *enjoy* it.

Steve Janovsky
Steve's Boat Works
Box 559 Avenue C
Port Aransas, TX 78373
(512) 749-6000 or 749-6448

General Information

Number of builders: Three to five, depending on orders.
Capacity: 45 feet.
Specialties: Wooden boats, particularly glass-on-ply.
Nontraditional modes: Yes.
Experience: Yes.
Preferred paints and glues: Mostly modern.
Sail and/or power: All power.

Facilities

Design and drafting: Limited.
Lumber storage: 2,000 to 3,000 b.f.
Metal working: No.

History

Origin of interest: I built my first boat at age 15.
Training: I never stopped after that first one.
Selection of location: I knew the builder who had this space before I did. I had the opportunity to buy him out.
Financing: Boat work.

Recent Projects

A 33-foot sportfisherman, and many 19- and 24-foot dories. Both the dories and the cruiser were glass over fir plywood.

Projects in Store

I'm planning a 50-footer for myself. We'll keep a couple of dories ahead at all times. Our eventual goal is to build about two dozen a year. [These "dories" have

A 33′ sportfisherman is carefully tied together by fir stringers and a heavy sheer clamp.

a broad transom and outboard well. —P.L.] The dory is pretty new to people down here, but they like them for both commercial and sportfishing.

Lumber and Hardware

It's going from bad to worse. Ply is getting poorer and poorer in quality, and now the companies don't want to sell it in lots smaller than a hundred sheets at a whack. It's volume or nothing. Fastenings, both bronze and Monel, are going out of sight.

Cooperatives

Builders are too far apart.

The Market

I think it's going to swing, and people will be going back to wood because of its better qualities. It has better ride, handling, and feel. It's generally better constructed and the price is increasingly competitive.

The Labor Pool

The labor pool is lousy. There aren't any craftsmen, any boatbuilders left. The best one can hope for is a cabinetmaker you can train.

Vocational Training

There may be hope for the labor situation in this program that the high school has, teaching skiff-building to the kids. In any event, that's many years away.

Modern and Traditional Design

I have no preference.

Time and Finish

It's got to be fitted properly. When people want a lot of boat for a little money, they have to realize that you really get your money's worth in tight joints and quality work, not size. We won't build a shoddy boat.

George and Bill Kalodoukas
Neptune Boat Works
P.O. Box 1251
Tarpon Springs, FL 33589
(813) 934-1072 or 937-0672

The Kalodoukases are gradually establishing themselves as contributors to, not competition for, a strong local tradition of boatbuilding. With their plans for expansion (see Projects in Store), they surprised a lot of locals who didn't expect this from men in their twenties. The shock has taken some time to overcome.

General Information

Number of builders: Technically, the two of us and a helper.

Capacity: 36 to 65 feet.

Specialties: Deep-V trawlers for fishing or shrimping, including knuckle-bottom construction.

Nontraditional modes: Yes.

Experience: No.

Preferred paints and glues: Mostly traditional.

Sail and/or power: All power.

Facilities

Design and drafting: Just by eye.

Lumber storage: 4,000 to 5,000 b.f.

Metal working: Not yet.

History

Origin of interest: I had a guy building a boat for me, and eventually I had to finish it myself. My training just continued from there.

Selection of location: This was the available property at the time.

Financing: We turn our capital back into the yard. Before, we turned money from other boats into working capital to get this place.

A typical Tarpon Springs partyboat of cypress, fir, and Greek extraction is a good measure of George and Bill Kalodoukas' work. The pads at the base of the stem held in the hood ends of the lower strakes until they could be fastened.

Recent Projects

A 57-foot by 18-foot partyboat. She's 1⅝-inch cypress on three-by-four frames, all stainless- or Monel-fastened.

Projects in Store

Either a 53-foot or a 63-foot shrimper on speculation. One thousand feet of docking space; repair facilities; a diesel shop; and a small boat ramp are all in the works.

Lumber and Hardware

There's been a steep increase in price. Quality is hard to get.

Cooperatives

No.

The Market

There's a slim chance that wood will be priced out of the market in the next few years. Still, it's got character, ride, and durability to beat the others.

The Labor Pool

It's bad and getting worse. Younger people can't work with their hands. Everybody wants a buck but nobody wants to work for it.

Time and Finish

I build a boat as if it were my own. We've been here only six years, so our reputation is not very big, but it *is* very fine. Our boats sell themselves because of the workmanship.

Melvin Kiff
6311 W. Main
Galiano, LA 70354
(504) 632-6267

Melvin Kiff's shop sits right on the main road along Bayou Lafouche—so close, in fact, that the stern of the second shrimper almost overhangs the road. It is quintessential bayou building.

General Information

Number of builders: Two, and sometimes an owner.
Capacity: 40 feet.
Specialties: Shrimpers, about two or three a year.
Nontraditional modes: No.
Experience: Just ply-over-frame.
Preferred paints and glues: Mostly traditional.

Facilities

Design and drafting: By eye.
Lumber storage: 4,000 b.f.
Metal working: No.

History

Training: I worked for Roland Duet for three years before going out on my own.
Selection of location: I'm from here.

Detail of the stem of Melvin Kiff's 55-foot shrimper from the inside shows that heavy, rough work still demands good fits. Sheer mass is no substitute for integrity.

Massive cypress timbers make up the backbone of this 54′ Lafitte skiff. Melvin Kiff and a helper are barely visible at lower left, hefting the first plank above the chine into place.

Recent Projects

These two shrimpers, 54 feet and 55 feet. They are Spanish cedar on cypress. I've built a total of about 60 boats in the last 10 years, most smaller than this.

Projects in Store

A couple more big ones, but the sizes aren't nailed down yet.

Lumber and Hardware

No problem.

Cooperatives

Not much chance for survival.

The Market

Good, couldn't be better.

Joseph C. Landry
60 Davenport Street
Bayou La Batre, AL 36509
(205) 824-4121

The citizens of Bayou La Batre were in an uproar when I visited there. Reverend Moon's organization had continued its growth into the fish business by buying up hunks of the town for a combination processing plant and boatyard. Amid the talk of Moonies and competition from unpaid volunteer labor there was an ugly undertone. A complete stranger approached me on the street and sincerely suggested that as a stranger in town I was best off staying someplace else that night. Mr. Landry exhibited little concern over the goings-on; his manner was of one whose business and family have been in town long enough to know they will endure. I consider him a true gentleman.

General Information

Number of builders: 30.
Capacity: 85 feet.
Specialties: Custom shrimpers, round bottomed.
Nontraditional modes: No.
Experience: No.
Preferred paints and glues: Mostly traditional. We don't believe in using glue to hold things together, either.
Sail and/or power: Just power, of course.

Facilities

Design and drafting: Yes.
Lumber storage: 75,000 b.f.
Metal working: Yes. All kinds of welding and machining.

History

Origin of interest: We are shrimpers-turned-boatbuilders.

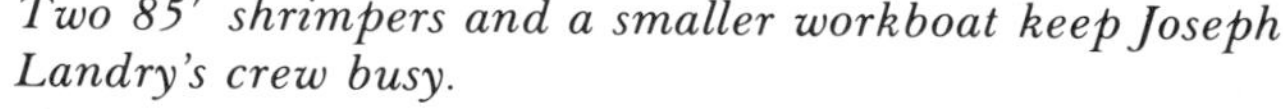

Two 85′ shrimpers and a smaller workboat keep Joseph Landry's crew busy.

Top: *Landry's second 85-footer,* Apache Belle, *displays a nice paint job as a finishing touch.* Left: *Carefully fitted sawn frames, deck beams, and mahogany planking are just a few of the reasons why fishermen will wait years for a Landry-built shrimper.*

Training: Working on the first few boats for ourselves.

Financing: Things were cheap in those days.

Recent Projects

Two 85-foot by 21-foot by 10-foot mahogany-on-cypress shrimpers. For the time being, we are building nothing under 75 feet.

Projects in Store

We're going to build about a dozen 85-footers on speculation. I have little doubt that each one will be sold before it's too far along.

Lumber and Hardware

Lumber is always a problem. We have to make a serious effort to obtain it, time after time. Cypress will eventually be a serious problem; actually, it already is one.

Cooperatives

One day it may come to buying carloads, and that's too much money for one concern.

The Market

We've never had any trouble selling boats. The future looks good, too.

The Labor Pool

Our worst problem is getting good labor. Since it's a craft all its own (not like steel), we have to train our own.

Open Statement

We feel we build the best shrimper on the Gulf at a good price using the best materials and work. We try to make a boat a poor man can live with for his entire working life. We've sold boats on the East and West Coasts by nothing more than word of mouth. Just check our reputation.

Gerard Ledet
302 S. Bayou Drive
Golden Meadow, LA 70357
(504) 475-5476

If you've read the Introduction to the Gulf Coast section, Gerard needs no further introduction.

General Information

Number of builders: One.

Capacity: 50 feet

Specialties: Lafitte shrimpers.

Sail and/or power: Power.

Facilities

Design and drafting: By eye.

Lumber storage: 3,000 b.f.

Metal working: I've done some welding.

With the old and the new, the life cycle of the bayou continues. What may have originally been a Lafitte-style tugboat lies abandoned as the crew of a new 48-footer prepares to head out to sea.

History

Origin of interest: Years ago a cousin and I took a couple of nine-foot dinghies out into the Gulf! Later, we slipped back in through the cut, on the tide, with the main fleet . . . just as if we were big boats. We thought nothing of it. We are water people.

Training: I built a model one day, defining the lines I liked. People said I could build a large one if I could build a model—just like my father, and his before that.

Selection of location: I'm just another bayou person; I'm from here.

Recent Projects

A 52-foot by 18-foot shrimper, Spanish cedar on cypress, 165 h.p., 671 G.M. I wanted to see just how big a boat I could build. It fit through that alley by inches. A 40-foot by 16-foot boat in 3½ months. I wanted the owner to make the shrimping season.

Projects in Store

A 42-foot by 17-foot by 5-foot flat-bottomed boat, ¾-inch cedar on 2-inch by 6-inch cypress. I have three boats to remodel the cabins on.

Unusual Tools and Methods

Just this hatchet that we all use around here for fairing.

Lumber and Hardware

Quality is really going down. It may be a serious problem with time. Hardware is no problem if you don't mind the price going up all the time.

Cooperatives

I like the idea.

The Market

Now, it's good. Shrimping goes in cycles, you know; we have to watch Nature closely to see how it will go. A lot of people are counting on a big season, but I think it's just going to be normal, nothing special. I think a lot of new boat owners may get burned soon; they've bitten off more than they can chew. After a while, we are going to run out of places to put all these boats. Seriously, though, I think we'll manage.

The Labor Pool

In the past, everyone could do boat carpentry, splice a line, etc. Now that the older men have been working very hard for many years, they rightly want to take things easy a little bit. It is getting much harder to find good men. I'm the only young builder I know of on all Lafourche!

Open Statement

I can't believe I'll ever see Mother Nature completely destroyed. When this cycle drops off, many of the doctors and lawyers will leave off fishing, and the boat-building will drop off too. There'll be a slow time when just the bayou people will be working the grounds and Nature can catch up. We on the bayou are like a big family or close, close friends. We help each other out all the time. The water is our way of life, and we don't give up on it easily.

I build a good boat. I like to study and learn how my grandfather did it. They used two pieces of wood where we use one. [Note: He is speaking of double strength.—P.L.] I return to his practices when I see something that has made a difference over the years.

If I put $20,000 into a boat, I want a fair $35,000 or $40,000 for it. You know, we start from scratch and we work hard, and we probably won't make a fortune. But, in the end, we can say we have done it all ourselves. We owe nothing to anybody. We are free men.

George Luzier

George Luzier Boatbuilder, Inc.
2135 Princeton Street
Sarasota, FL 33577
(813) 953-4989

The picture opposite of a 51-foot ketch that George designed and built is a fine example of his often innovative, always sensible approach. Strip-planking to a female mold produces a cleaner boat faster—in both the lofting and the construction phases. Using a female mold is not all that unusual, but some of George's creations are, such as the Flintstone sander shown on page 174.

General Information

Number of builders: Five.

Capacity: 50 feet.

Specialties: Batten-seam construction. We build power and sailing craft, often my designs. Sportfishermen have been built here with some frequency.

Nontraditional modes: Yes, glued-strip.

Experience: Yes.

Preferred paints and glues: We have a modern slant.

Sail and/or power: Fifty-fifty. I like them both, run them both, and have owned them both.

Facilities

Design and drafting: Yes.

Lumber storage: 10,000 b.f. of juniper and cypress.

Metal working: We do our own keels, patterns, and welding.

History

Origin of interest: My great-grandfather was from Prince Edward Island and built schooners. After my uncle built a boat, I started on my own under a tree at age 14.

Selection of location: I'm from this area.

Financing: I started building prams in production after I left the merchant marine.

Recent Projects

A 51-foot marconi ketch (own design) in 1976. After that there was a 20-foot marconi centerboard sloop and a 46-foot sportfisherman, both my own designs.

Projects in Store

Refinish a 30-foot sloop, and then build a 33-footer for myself. She'll be strip-planked, juniper-on-mahogany laminated frames.

Unusual Tools and Methods

Methods first; we use a female mold for strip hulls. I've also noticed that painting the bilges stops woolly rot very effectively. My favorite idea is the Mark I/4 Flintstone hull sander, designed and built by my brother Homer. It can be used in either a horizontal or a vertical position by one man who wears the switch on his belt. The operator directs the sanding pad (of which there are several with different amounts of flex) and its reciprocating action with the remote control,

George Luzier's Mark I/4 flintstone sander.

the notched piece with the padded ball. This last saves him from getting the full effect of the sanding action.

Lumber and Hardware

Getting better! Teak and mahogany prices are up, but the quality is stable. Juniper and cypress have to be ordered in advance, of course, but they're there. Brass and bronze seem to be coming back a little bit, and the quality is getting better also.

Cooperatives

Not around here; there aren't enough people to do it.

The Market

People want boats that are bigger, fancier, etc., with no end in sight. The people who are buying have had boats before and want the best they can buy.

The Labor Pool

You don't know until new help has been in the shop for a couple of months. Generally, it's a matter of luck if you get someone good, that is to say, two out of a hundred are worth keeping on. Mostly the glamour wears off, so they don't stay.

Vocational Training

I really have no contact with the schools.

Modern and Traditional Design

I like them both if they are done within the bounds of taste. Either can be lousy!

Restorations and Replicas

If a museum or an individual is going to *use* a boat, they should take the hardware and build a replica. If they want to let it *sit*, that's something else again.

Time and Finish

My fits are always first-class, from keel to finish work. However, it's up to the owner how far we go with the finish itself.

Walter and Wilbur Lyons
Lyons Brothers Boatbuilding and Repair, Inc.
Star Route 697
Chauvin, LA 70344

The Lyonses' 57-footer was one of the few Lafitte skiffs that I saw that had both a shelf clamp and a keelson. The Lyonses seemed dedicated to keeping the family tradition intact, right down to the clamp most builders have dropped.

General Information

Number of builders: Five—Walter, Wilbur, Albert, Barry, and Sidney.

Specialties: Shrimpers and V-bottoms in general.

Nontraditional modes: No.

History

Origin of interest: Obviously, it's in me.

Training: Through the family, particularly my father.

Recent Projects

57-foot by 16-foot and 50-foot by 15-foot shrimpers, Spanish cedar on cypress.

Projects in Store

A 50-foot by 16-foot shrimper; this one has a nine-foot stem.

Lumber and Hardware

Any trouble we will have will be in plank stock. There's no telling how the whole thing will develop. Hardware is not a problem to obtain; the prices are just way up.

The sternpost of a shrimper lends weight to Walter Lyons' words about the value of a wooden boat.

Cooperatives

I'd be doubtful. We're too independent.

The Market

Good! In 10 to 15 years, when these cheap steel hulls start going to pieces, people will come back to realize that you can't beat a wood boat.

The Labor Pool

Strictly family. [Never was a truer word spoken. — P.L.]

Open Statement

We do a lot of repair work, and we've found the ice holds always go first.

SOURCE **Clark Mills**
Clearwater Bay Marine Ways, Inc.
900 N. Osceola
Clearwater, FL 33515
(813) 443-3207

It is a measure of the respect Clark commands that his yard is really known by his name, not by Clearwater Bay Marine Ways. When I was asking another builder for directions to Clark's shop and yard, he said, "Clearwater what?"

General Information

Number of builders: We have 20 employees, including the machine shop, chandlery, etc.

Capacity: 40 feet. It'd have to be a 40-foot sharpie or a 20-foot launch so I could reach the sheer from the floor. With my gout, I don't care to climb around all day.

Specialties: I'm responsible for the original Optimus pram, Windmill class, Suncat, Compac, and some others. Now we do custom design and construction.

Nontraditional modes: Yes, glued-strip.

Experience: Yes.

Preferred paints and glues: Some of both.

Sail and/or power: Sail.

History

Origin of interest: Playing in the backyard.

Training: In, around, and through boatyards, constantly.

Selection of location: I'm from here.

Financing: On a shoestring.

Recent Projects

A 38-foot fishing launch and a 23-foot plug for a sloop. The tug shown was designed and built by Mills some 10 or more years ago. When the original owner sold her to a close friend of Clark's, after nine years of happy ownership, the friend renamed her in tribute. (There is a hilarious story in connection with this. If you ever meet Clark, ask him about it. He is a man of rare wit and humor.)

This tug was designed and built by Clark Mills in the 1960s. The current owner named the tug in honor of the builder. This photo shows that proportion can be everything.

Projects in Store

A set of plans for a 65-foot power catamaran, and a 25-foot cruising sailboat for my business partner.

Lumber and Hardware

It is available if you want to be patient and pay the price. I don't know about the future.

Cooperatives

Most builders are as individualistic as a %$#&! mule. They don't want anyone to tell them what to do.

The Market

I can't tell where it's going to go; there's too much up in the air.

The Labor Pool

The bureaucrats have really messed it up with the minimum wage. I can't afford to teach a man at that rate.

Modern and Traditional Design

I prefer traditional, but I'm not puritanical about it.

Time and Finish

I always fit it as well as I can, regardless. The customer is paying me for that. If they wanted a wood pile, they'd go to someone else.

Open Statement

The boatbuilding business doesn't make a lot of money; the margin of profit is slim. If you want to go into the boat business, you'd better be able to laugh at yourself. I've had more fun with my trouble, and trouble with my fun, than anybody you know.

On a tougher note, I tried to run a seminar on wooden-boat construction in 1976 or so. We lost 33 out of 36 students in the first six months. What we taught them was that they weren't cut out to be builders.

Billy M. Perry
4437 20th Street
Bacliff, TX 77518
(713) 339-2156

Mr. Perry is one of the few builders on the Gulf who regularly lofts. I spoke with him and his wife, Jill, late one night in their trailer. I was impressed with both their knowledge and their sense of perspective. This awareness extended far beyond the situation around Bacliff—no small thing when you consider the paltry amount of information available on Gulf Coast doings.

General Information

Number of builders: Two. My wife, Jill, has lofting and master-finisher capabilities. She has served a 16-year "apprenticeship" with 11 sailboats to her credit.

Capacity: 35 feet.

Specialties: Glass-over-plywood and strip-planking. Also sailmaking and self-steering mechanisms.

Nontraditional modes: Yes, including one-off glass and sandwich.

Experience: Yes.

Preferred paints and glues: Mostly modern.

Sail and/or power: Sail, about 75 percent.

Facilities

Design and drafting: Limited.

Lumber storage: Up to 10,000 b.f. of yellow pine.

Metal working: Yes, welding.

History

Origin of interest: As a hobby in 1952.

Training: Kettenburg's Marine, San Diego.

Selection of location: Very popular boating area.

Financing: With lots of desire.

Recent Projects

A 22-foot custom, strip-planked, epoxy-saturated sailboat for the Seabrook Shipyard. Last summer I built a 31-foot bay shrimper of my own design, and at present, I'm finishing a 21-foot tug.

Projects in Store

Between other projects, I'll start another shrimper this spring. (See Open Statement.)

Unusual Tools and Methods

I am not inventive by nature, but I pick up whatever I can by reading and watching other people and boats, especially in repair work.

The Market

Wooden construction is expensive and wooden boats are costly to maintain. Couple this with a crippling lack of experienced repairmen and the future of all wood boats looks dark. On the other hand, the need for individualism in the boat-buyer's world is, happily, asserting itself. No longer are people satisfied with one of 10,000. This will lead to more opportunity for small, one-of-a-kind builders.

The Labor Pool

Very poor. Marine carpenters, loftsmen, machinists, etc., are very rare. This is due, to a great extent, to low pay for the knowledge and skills required. The young people have sought higher-paying trades.

Vocational Training

No contact with the schools.

Time and Finish

One must realize that no boat is perfect, and the so-called perfectionist is doomed to a long life of drawn-out failures. There is a fine line between prudence and sloppiness, so one must do the best fit he can do in a reasonable length of time, and move on to the next step.

Open Statement

I would like to involve myself with six or eight do-it-yourselfers and share my experience with them. Glass-and-ply construction is a good medium for this area and well within the reach of the average man.

Miscellaneous

There are still some excellent pines, *real* yellow pines, if you know your area. By watching for these, and old wooden buildings being demolished, some very finely grained pine and cypress can be had.

New construction is what all builders favor, but like everyone else, we must eat and pay taxes. Repair work then enters into our lives, but it's not all bad, since repair has its interesting points also.

Tessie Plaisance
Box 493
Lafitte, LA 70067
(504) 689-2737

Like many builders in the bayou country, Mr. Plaisance builds in a space beside his home; often a fenced-in yard with a tool shed is all that constitutes a shop. Tessie has an open shed to build under, squeaked in between his house and his neighbor's back porch.

General Information

Number of builders: One.
Capacity: 30 feet by 12 feet. If it gets any wider, I can't get it out of here.
Specialties: Lafitte skiffs.

Recent Projects

A 27½-foot by 11-foot all-cypress Lafitte shrimper.

A few more like the last one, if I can find some decent cypress.

Skiffs of about this size (with various arrangements) are the bread and butter of many builders like Tessie Plaisance. A few of these were spruced up for the New Orleans market.

Lumber and Hardware

Quality lumber is both hard to get and expensive. Cypress holds swelling better than Spanish cedar for short haulouts, and it's cheaper. It hurts to have so much trouble getting it.

Cooperatives

Hard to get builders together.

The Market

Glass is our biggest competitor, but I don't believe it will ever completely replace wood.

The Labor Pool

As it's always been, it's hard to get *knowledgeable* men.

Open Statement

All I can do is use the best materials I can get. I go to extra trouble to design the boats to the owner's needs and/or desires. I won't build a cheap boat—a reputation for quality is too important to me.

Valcour Rodrigue
Rodrigue's Boat Shop
119 N. Main
Lockport, LA 70374
(504) 532-2787

This small shop on upper Bayou Lafourche turns out well-built, shapely little Lafitte skiffs. Valcour (*valcor rodreegay*) gradually warmed as we talked. It's a rare builder whose fire isn't fueled by discourse on the subject he knows best.

General Information

Number of builders: One.

Capacity: 17 feet.

Specialties: 17-foot shrimpers and motorized mud boats. Also pirogues. I am the distributor for air-cooled Kohler engines, 4–23 h.p.

History

Origin of interest: In the blood.

Training: I learned from my father, who had this business before me. It's been "Rodrigue's Boat Shop" since 1962.

Selection of location: I'm from here.

Recent Projects

In the last year or so? Thirty-six skiffs and about a dozen pirogues.

Projects in Store

More!

Unusual Tools and Methods

I use a weedless construction in which the skeg does not continue aft under the propeller to meet the bottom of the rudder stock. The rudder is free-standing. Even the 17-footer can move in a few inches of water over a soft bottom.

Lumber and Hardware

I've seen 12-foot sheets of plywood with two scarfs in the length. It's impossible to build pirogues and the smaller skiffs with it, and I won't put it in the 17-footer! I try to buy the best, which means shopping around, picking it yourself. Smaller companies are discontinuing lines of hardware so fast that it's hard for professionals to keep up.

Cooperatives

For purchasing, definitely!

The Market

Good. The man who comes here wants something different. This is growing.

The Labor Pool

Terrible! To train one takes a year or more, and then they quit.

Open Statement

Most of my boats are sold to trappers and duck hunters. I have boats everywhere from here to Texas, and even a few in California.

George Saroukas
George Saroukas, Master Builder
1056 Hibiscus
Tarpon Springs, FL 33589
(813) 937-1103

After waiting wordlessly for half an hour while Mr. Saroukas finished planing some cypress, I had the opportunity to explain my business. I was halfway through the first sentence when he pointed at a sign on the gate and said, "What's that say?" I read out loud, "George Saroukas, Master Builder. Work, party, or sail boats, 10 to 100 feet." He looked me square in the eye and said, "That's all they have to know."

Minas P. Sarris
Sarris Marine Enterprises
Route 1, 322 Anclote Road
Tarpon Springs, FL 33589
(813) 937-7785

Like the other Tarpon Springs builders, Sarris is all business. There is no time whatsoever for idle conversation, and little enough for "surveys." The fierce competition for the booming shrimp market is largely responsible. While we talked, Mr. Sarris was busy running around his outdoor "shop" keeping things going. All the traffic on the water 50 feet away was very much in keeping with the rush of his business and the shrimping boom in general.

General Information

Capacity: 40 to 70 feet.

Specialties: Workboats of knuckle, flat, or round bottom to any stage of construction.

Nontraditional modes: Yes.

Experience: Yes.

Preferred paints and glues: Mostly traditional.

Sail and/or power: Power.

Facilities

Design and drafting: Yes.

Lumber storage: 5,000 b.f.

Metal working: No.

History

Origin of interest: It's a Greek tradition.

Training: From my father, and his father before that, for more than 50 years right here in Tarpon Springs. I learned from them.

Selection of location: I was born and raised here.

Recent Projects

A 40-foot boat for snapper fishing and a 55-footer for shrimping.

Projects in Store

A 60-foot shrimper, cypress or fir planking, pine and oak framing.

Lumber and Hardware

There are no big trees left; lamination is the future. Sometime in the next hundred years we may have trouble getting two-by-fours.

Cooperatives

There is more competition today than ever. Nobody works together anymore, mostly it's dog-eat-dog.

The Market

We build all we can. If we had a hundred boats here in the yard, we could sell them all, and quickly. There's a huge demand.

The Labor Pool

It's a very difficult situation. We'd train our own if they'd stay long enough.

Modern and Traditional Design

Traditional.

Time and Finish

We work to good workboat finish and let the owner put in equipment. That saves us time and him money.

Open Statement

"Reputation is our recommendation." All I can add to that is that we are making a living doing good work, and we work *hard*. The threat of hard work never stopped us from doing anything!

George Stevenson
Saint Marydeth Boat Works
3A Mercer Avenue
Panama City, FL 32041
(904) 769-3115

General Information

Number of builders: One.
Capacity: 40 feet.
Specialties: Designs in wood, steel, or aluminum.
Nontraditional modes: Yes.
Experience: Yes.
Preferred paints and glues: Modern, for the most part.
Sail and/or power: 80 percent sail, 20 percent power.

Facilities

Design and drafting: Yes.
Lumber storage: The building is 40 feet by 70 feet; there's no limit to what we could handle.
Metal working: No.

History

Origin of interest: I managed a repair yard.
Training: Bat Marine and Propeller.
Selection of location: It's home.
Financing: By myself.

Recent Projects

A modified Sharpstown barge; a 24-foot pulling boat; and a Herreshoff double-paddle canoe are the last few.

Projects in Store

We are completing a cruising sailboat we call the Philip Bolger-Henry Chatfield Compromise. She is 40 feet long, drawing 18 inches with her leeboards up, yet she has standing headroom. Among her many unusual features are grain bins and a 4,000-mile cruising range. She is strip-planked and epoxy.

Lumber and Hardware

We are not reforesting boatbuilding woods, which is the key to the future of wooden-boat construction. The paper companies cut all the timber and reforest (when they do reforest) only fast-growing pines. We must start new trees, especially juniper.

The Market

It's all in what I just said.

The Labor Pool

Should be encouraged.

Vocational Training

Needed and should be encouraged.

Modern and Traditional Design

Neither one is much good without the other. Both must be used—how else can we grow? The problem is to separate the junk from what's valuable in both worlds.

INTRODUCTION TO THE SOUTHEAST

In the Southeast there are two distinct regions. The first is tourist-plagued Florida. All the common clichés about rushing buses of blue-haired ladies and men in clashing Bermuda shorts apply. Every piece of land that can be built upon is either overdeveloped or rapidly becoming so. What cannot be built upon is either landfilled until it can be or surrounded by condominiums ". . . with a beautiful view of Wapaloosa Swamp." As one native of the Florida Panhandle put it, "Anything west of a line from Tarpon Springs to Jacksonville is Florida, everything east of there is a suburb of New York."

The boatbuilding situation has a split as dramatic as, and not entirely unrelated to, this dichotomy. With the one exception of St. Augustine's trawler-building yards, the eastern sector of Florida contains recreationally oriented yacht yards. Boatbuilding in the western sector and the entire Southeast north of Jacksonville is primarily commercially oriented. Sociologically and boatwise, eastern Florida is a pocket of contradictions to the southern norm. What I found in St. Augustine was not uncharacteristic. I arrived on the Sunday afternoon after Easter week. There was an excellent craft fair in progress, and the town was jammed with tourists sporting the 10-day tan for which this Gold Coast is famous. When I wasn't at the fair, I was doing touristy things like climbing around Castillo de San Marcos National Monument. On Monday, I visited two of the largest wooden boatbuilding firms in the country.

The St. Augustine yards of Desco Marine and St. Augustine Trawlers mass-produce wooden shrimpers between 60 and 80 feet. A complete shrimper leaves each carefully laid out yard about once every four working days! In contrast to the city's vacation atmosphere, these yards are all business. Security is

Top: *At Ancient City Boatyard, a workman prepares to finish off a fir keel and stem with a power hand plane. Two more shrimpers are in the skeletal stages in the shed at far right, and still another pair are getting their houses and deck gear.* Left: *The lead man in the team at Desco Marine bevels the foot of the still-steaming frame with three or four strokes of a hatchet and then spikes it into the keel for his acrobatic partners.*

tight. Cameras are forbidden or restricted, as is contact with low-level personnel. Competition between the two giants is fierce, to say the least. Both firms also build in steel, and St. Augustine Trawlers builds in fiberglass as well. With the present shrimping boom, they have their hands full, even with crews of 350 for wood construction alone. There are two other trawler-building operations in St. Augustine, working on a much smaller scale. Even so, one of them, Ancient City Boatyard, keeps seven boats under construction at all times. Their production rate is still way above wooden boatbuilding's averages.

Lumber arrives by the train-car load. At each yard, there are separate crews for each stage of construction. One of the larger yards discourages their employees from learning the ropes at more than one or two stations. At Desco, I watched a crew putting in steam-bent oak framing as if it were second nature. As the photos attest, these are very full hulls, generally fir over oak, though some use pressure-treated pine for certain parts of the deadwood. Most strakes have no shape or taper, and the differences are made up between the dozen or so spiled planks at the garboard, turn of the bilge, and sheer. Though boat size ranges from 62 to 75 feet, most of the yards have just one or two sets of molds. They space them differently to get as many as six different hulls for 135 cabin/house/deck layouts. It takes approximately eight weeks for Desco or St. Augustine Trawlers to complete a vessel. Anywhere from 10 to 15 boats are underway at the half-dozen stations: (1) setup; (2) framing out; (3) planking; (4) pilothouse, interior, propeller, shaft, and fairing of the hull. From there the boats are launched and the galley and rigging are completed at the two stations along the docks. To talk of wooden boats in St. Augustine is to talk of these shrimpers and nothing else.

The rest of Florida's eastern sector is much more diverse. The Florida Keys used to have half a dozen builders, though I found they had all closed up or switched to fiberglass. And in Miami and Stuart, there are the two sportfisherman builders, Andy Mortensen and G. C. Whiticar.

North from St. Augustine, professional building in wood is very sporadic until Harkers Island, North Carolina. In among the string of islands and backwaters of Georgia there are supposed to be a number of fishermen/builders. A shortage of time and a recent raid on a number of stills discouraged me from trying to locate them. With the short fuses caused by the raid, I was wary of snooping around the inland waterway, looking into the locals' nooks and crannies. As a local land surveyor put it, "I'm on vacation for a few weeks. I know where I'm going and a lot of people know me, but foolish I'm not. They'll use both barrels first and ask questions later—and I'm not talking about aging vats."

At last report, Georgia's Albert Sidl and Gerhard Schwisow (S and S Boatbuilders) were working on financing for a proposed replica of the S.S. *Savannah*, the first steam/sail ship to cross the Atlantic. Ninety-eight feet on deck,

151 feet overall, the three-master would be built by S and S and a volunteer/trainee program. In the meantime, they have been busy building new spars for the *Barba Negra* and turning out dories and dinghies when fund raising allowed them spare time. Savannah has a number of other very determined boat buffs who have even contemplated a Southern states wooden boat gathering.

Just across the state line at Hilton Head Island, South Carolina, there is plenty of yachting and sportsfishing, and the usual contingent of itinerant builders and sailors that can be found all along the Inland Waterway.

The Beaufort (South Carolina) Marina is the center of local activity. Foreman Jack Ford has turned out an array of boats from dinghies to power yachts, including a Jerry Gallup-designed trimaran. From there I had to search my way along the coast as far as Shallotte, North Carolina, before finding anything of note. There and at Holden Beach, I visited a number of family-run shrimper-building firms. They were so busy that they didn't have time to hear me out, which was unusual. It speaks well for business, if not for my survey.

At Wilmington, North Carolina, one man's dream of a mini-Mystic Seaport is coming to fruition. Chandler's Wharf has amassed an impressive sampling of vessels, including the tug *John Taxis*, built in 1869, a 1908 Chesapeake Bay skipjack, and a 147-foot Nova Scotia-built two-masted schooner.

The Hampton Mariners Museum in Beaufort, North Carolina, is small, but it is a gem. Resident genius Charles McNeill has set a fine example of how to do more with less in conceiving and developing an active, participatory program. The Museum has built and restored small craft; developed a program combining natural history, oceanography, and the maritime traditions; sponsored a small craft meet; and cheerfully handled an endless flow of school children from the area. Hats off!

Just east of there, behind the shelter of the Shackleford Banks, sits Harkers Island, the first major concentration of professional boatbuilders after St. Augustine. A low, flat island with a winding road around its perimeter, Harkers boasted a skiff in every yard and a boat shop around every bend in the road. Since spring was coming on, each shop either had two or three boats near completion or was empty. The area reminded me strongly of Louisiana—the flatness, the concentration of builders, and most of all, the striking similarities between the Lafitte skiff and the Harkers type. The boats' extreme flare, strong sheer, and broad beam are all of the same origin, if my eye is any judge. There is some evidence that Carolina fishermen have migrated to the Gulf during difficult fishing years, particularly in the menhaden fisheries. Also, the insular qualities of each area, their attitudes about the sea, etc., are too much alike to pass over. Among the bayous, Harkers, and Beals Island, Maine, I might go so far as to say that the only differences are the types of boats and the accents of the speech. At Harkers, as elsewhere, there are families with several

The powerful hull of a Harkers skiff. The foot of the bit is clear of the sole and is through-bolted to the first pair of frames—a rotless alternative to a chronic problem area.

boat shops to their names. Like the Cheramies of Bayou Lafourche, the Rose family of Harkers is everywhere. Not all are directly related, of course, but all are wed to the sea.

Juniper (white cedar) over yellow pine is the common building combination of Harkers Island. The closing of the 750-square-mile Dismal Swamp to logging had serious consequences to local builders. Several mills cutting boat lumber were using the swamp as their main source of timber. The resulting decline in availability and increase in cost has hurt. Much of what is now available is coming from other areas or is being cut illegally in the more remote parts of the swamp. It may be that Carolina builders will have to go the route of their southern cousins, in spite of the costs of fir, mahogany, and Spanish cedar. Several builders mentioned going over to cypress, but this seems impractical, since cypress stocks are also low. One advantage of the Harkers type of boat is that it is strip-planked, so the need for wider, longer, clearer boards is less pressing. Some builders have tried to fight off the lumber-induced higher boat prices by gearing up to air tools, others by going the low-overhead route.

All across the country, decreased availability of favored species has raised to fever pitch the old arguments concerning the durability of other woods. There is the favorite argument concerning red vs. white oak. Valid, scientifically based data is sometimes available through a variety of sources, but few builders have found the time to pursue it. Builders on Harkers (and all over the Southeast) frequently say that they are using longleaf yellow pine, though they call it simply yellow, hard, or heart pine. Aside from the confusion caused by varying definitions, there is some evidence that much of this is not longleaf yellow, but one (or more) of the other pine genera. The builder one is talking to is always the one builder in town who is *really* using true longleaf yellow pine. . . .

General Information

Number of builders: Seventeen and three sources. Average shop crew is 5.3, not including the St. Augustine yards.

Capacity: The average shop capacity is 59 feet.

Specialties: Twelve in commercial power; two sportfisherman builders; four in custom sail and power.

Nontraditional modes: Thirteen would use these modes and had done so in the past; three had not and would not; one had not and would be interested in doing so. 5200 or equivalent filler/glues are used liberally by a number of yards; others disdain it as an excuse for bad fits.

Preferred paints and glues: Seven use a combination of the traditional and modern; seven prefer the modern; five prefer traditional.

Sail and/or power: Fourteen power; three sail; one had equal experience with both.

Facilities

Design and drafting: Eleven builders had skills in both; five had neither; one was limited in those skills but did use them.

I noticed that, as a rule, the wider the flare in the bow, the better the bet that the boat was going to be for recreational use. What most people find is the boat's most beautiful and distinctive feature, the professional watermen find is a trap for water. With a really stiff wind off the forward quarter, slop works its way up the flare and into the pocket, only to be blown into the face of the crew at the next big gust.

Lumber storage: Excluding St. Augustine, the average amount of lumber stored was 7,620 board feet.

Metal working: Eleven had welding facilities; two did pattern work only; four said they had no on-site facilities but regularly hire the work out.

Recent Projects

An estimated 91 round-bottomed shrimpers between 60 and 75 feet. Thirty Harkers types between 18 and 57 feet in length were built for anything from the charter-boat business to run boats. (A run boat transfers catches from fishermen to wholesalers.) In recreational craft, there were three sportfishing cruisers built; two 32-foot power cruisers; a 20-foot cutter; a Jerry Gallup-designed trimaran; a 24-foot pulling boat; a Herreshoff double-paddle canoe.

Projects in Store

More, more, more, more, more, and more shrimpers. At least seven Harkers types from 20 to 55 feet, a 53-foot trawler yacht; a 30-foot, deep-V, offshore power yacht; a possible 42-foot all-teak Herreshoff yawl; a 26-foot Presto-style cat ketch.

Lumber

Six said the situation is improving or good, eight said the opposite. Eight, by separate tally, mentioned a price/availability problem.

As part of St. Augustine's pushed production schedule, precut panels are jigsawed into place to form a pilothouse in short order.

Lumber is no problem! Preservatives make boats longer-lasting than at any stage in traditional boating history. It's just that most builders don't take the time to do it.

Ancient City Boatyard

There'll be a problem getting quality juniper, cypress, and pine because there's no program to replant. We've got to get something started in this line.

Bryan Blake

The price has doubled in a year, and where I used to buy 2,000 board feet to go in a boat, I now have to buy 3,000 feet to get the same amount of usable material. I think the small mills have been bought out by big business.

Edward Davis

The good timber has all been cut in the U.S. The only worthy materials are coming from foreign sources.

Jack Ford

Let's not forget about the quality of lumber as a renewable resource over the long term. There is lumber of good quality left; availability is the problem. Builders have to be concerned with a balance between conservation and use.

Albert Sidl

Hardware

Several builders had negative things to say about the use of bronze fastenings in a boat's hull. Stainless or Monel was their preference, bronze only for interiors. Two builders had a positive view of the hardware situation, the others didn't say

The tepee method of curing stock prevents the timber-splitting sun from cooking the top planks of a conventional stack.

too many printable things about suppliers or manufacturers. Around Harkers, builders were particularly dismayed over the slowness of delivery.

It will remain strong. If we can solve the lumber problem, the demand will be there. Word-of-mouth advertising is all we've ever had to have.

Alex Willis

Cooperatives

Ten said they thought coops weren't applicable to their situation. Of the six who liked the idea, five had reservations as to their feasibility.

The Market

Twelve expected a small but stable market in the future. Three saw the future as unlimited, one said it would decline.

The market is fantastic—phenomenal! We've never seen anything even approaching it. I think governmental subsidy, the 200-mile limit, and a greater demand for seafood (one of the best sources of protein) are all contributing factors.

Desco Marine

Fiberglass is hurting us, but there'll always be a few people who prefer wood, no matter what.

Edward Davis

The Labor Pool

Sixty-one percent said the situation was bad and/or declining.

I can't get anyone I'm satisfied with—most are dreamers if they are "trainees." Commercial boat owner/helpers are good, though; they get down to work without any problems.

Bryan Blake

Sure can't get the quality or the quantity we want! There's not much future for the work you have to put in, so young people are going into other fields where they used to work in Dad's shop.

Edward Davis

We tend toward local, Portuguese craftsmen. When these are all busy with other work on their own, we generally have to go north (to New England) to find the men we want.

Manuel Dos Santos

The few that can really do the job are on their own or have a good job already.

Raymond LeMay

There are *still* not enough young people interested. . . .

Gerhard Schwisow

Vocational Training

Only four builders had any awareness of programs whatsoever. Two of those referred only to the Carteret program.

Carteret's training program seems to be pretty good. I have a couple of their students who've come to work for me full-time.

James Gillikin

Miscellaneous

Because southeastern builders were dispersed, and even lacked the consistent commercial orientation I found in the South, I got no sense of a cohesive future, but rather one of isolated pockets that will sink or swim without affecting the others significantly.

SOUTHEASTERN BUILDERS

Ancient City Boatyard
Steve Sarris, General Manager
P.O. Box 3167
St. Augustine, FL 32084
(904) 829-2611

General Information

Number of builders: About 60.
Capacity: 73 feet.

Not all the yards steam bend their frames in place. Four jigs at Ancient City Boatyard do most of the work. The steel straps help to keep the frames from splitting at the turn of the bilge.

Specialties: The standard, round-bottomed shrimp trawlers.

Preferred paints and glues: Mostly traditional.

Facilities

Design and drafting: We work from three stock molds and space them differently to control shape and length.

Metal working: Welding.

History

Origin of interest: Steve Sarris has boatbuilding in his family and was on his own (in St. Augustine) for 30 years before coming in on the ground floor at Ancient City.

Recent Projects

We have two 65-footers and a 68-footer under construction, with an additional two 72-foot shrimpers almost complete.

Projects in Store

More of the above. We aim for an eight-to-10-week completion cycle for the hulls alone, with six boats underway at all times.

Lumber and Hardware

Lumber is no problem! Preservatives make boats longer-lasting than at any stage in traditional boating history. It's just that most builders don't take the time to do it.

The Market

The market is very good right now. We have two or three good years to each bad one. It's almost predictable.

The Labor Pool

I'd say there was a good supply, and it's holding. We teach two areas of the production process to each man.

Modern and Traditional Design

Traditional.

Bryan Blake
Blake Boatworks
P.O. Box 41
Gloucester, NC 28528
(919) 729-3471

In an area known exclusively for its powerboats, Bryan is "trying to get a handle on the impending swing toward sail power." Like many others elsewhere, he believes that fuel shortages and high prices will induce both commercial- and pleasure-boat users to consider power/sail combinations. He has a questioning, creative mind to go with a straightforward, open personality.

General Information

Number of builders: One, sometimes two.

Capacity: 60 feet.

Specialties: Traditional sailboats, both round- and V-bottomed.

Nontraditional modes: Yes.

Experience: Yes, strip.

Preferred paints and glues: Fifty-fifty modern and traditional.

Sail and/or power: 60 percent sail to 40 percent power.

Facilities

Design and drafting: No; *some* lofting capabilities.

Lumber storage: 3,000 to 4,000 b.f.

Metal working: Welding.

History

Origin of interest: My interest in sailing and sailboats is lifelong, going back to my childhood in Charleston.

Training: I was originally a carpenter. I worked at Original Rose Brothers before coming here.

Selection of location: I ran across this place by accident. I took one look at the little railway off the channel, the little house back in the greenery, and that was it. It was a good opportunity for work and living in general.

Recent Projects

An 18-foot powerboat of the Harkers type; a 20-foot cutter, gaff-rigged, based on a 90-foot schooner from about 1800. She carries a foresail and topsail as well.

Projects in Store

A 26-foot Presto-style cat ketch. She will draw 18 inches with the board up, 4 feet 6 inches down. There'll be laminated mahogany frames and 1⅛-inch strip juniper planking.

Lumber and Hardware

There'll be a problem getting quality juniper, cypress, and pine because there's no program to replant. We've got to get something started in this line. Hardware is highly priced, that's all. You know how it is, any item that has "marine" printed on it doubles in price automatically.

Cooperatives

I'm positive about them, but I doubt builders here would go for one.

Bryan Blake's 20-foot gaff-rigged cutter is based on a 19th century 90-foot schooner. Note the vertical staved well with its tiny outboard motor mount (left).

The Market

There'll always be a place for me in workboats, and a special market in sailing craft.

The Labor Pool

I can't get anybody I'm satisfied with—most are dreamers if they are "trainees." Commercial boat owner/helpers are good, though; they get down to work without any problems.

Open Statement

Men who used sailing craft in their work knew what they needed. I think there is a place for speed, but not at the price of lots of things like looks. Keeping that in mind, I should say that what I'm trying to do is get a handle on the impending swing toward sail power. I enjoy building more than anything else, so this allows me to combine business with pleasure.

Edward Davis
Ray Davis Boatworks
P.O. Box 51
Marshallberg, NC 28553

General Information

Number of builders: Four.
Capacity: 55 feet.
Specialties: Glued-strip, hard-chine powerboats.
Nontraditional modes: Just strip glue.
Experience: Not in other modes, no.
Preferred paints and glues: No preference; whatever's around.
Sail and/or power: Mostly power, but I have built some motorsailers.

Facilities

Design and drafting: Yes, by eye.
Lumber storage: 10,000 b.f. of juniper.
Metal working: No.

History

Origin of interest: It's all from my family—training, interest, everything.

Recent Projects

A 48-foot by 16-foot lobsterboat/potfisher to a man in Ocean City, New Jersey. It was juniper over pine, stainless-fastened.

Projects in Store

A 53-foot trawler yacht, also for someone in New Jersey; same wood but Monel-fastened.

Lumber and Hardware

The price has doubled in a year, and where I used to buy 2,000 board feet to go in a boat, I now have to buy 3,000 feet to get the same amount. I think the small mills have been bought out by big business. With hardware, shipping is just unbelievably slow.

Cooperatives

I believe that would be barking up the wrong tree. That won't change the quality of lumber.

The Market

Fiberglass is hurting us, but there'll always be a few people who prefer wood, no matter what.

The Labor Pool

Sure can't get the quality or the quantity we want! There's not much future for the work you have to put in, so young people are going into other fields where they used to work in Dad's shop.

Modern and Traditional Design

It all depends on use.

Open Statement

I'm just happy with my work—that's why I'm here.

Desco Marine, Division of Whitaker Corp.
Tom Collins, President
P.O. Box 1480
St. Augustine, FL 32084
(904) 824-4461

General Information

Number of builders: 600, 350 of whom are in wood construction.

Capacity: 73 feet.

Specialties: Large fishing vessels.

Nontraditional modes: No.

Experience: No.

Preferred paints and glues: Mostly traditional.

Facilities

Design and drafting: Yes.

Lumber storage: About 12 boats' worth.

Metal working: Welding and patterns.

History

The company was started in 1943 by L.C. Ringhaven.

Recent Projects

We complete about 10 hulls a month from our combinations of 62-foot, 68-foot, 72-foot, and 73-foot hulls and 135 cabin/house layouts. These are all fir over oak.

Projects in Store

We are working toward 12 boats a month as a production rate, or an eight-week time frame for each boat. That's eight weeks from start to finish.

Lumber and Hardware

We have two people on the road constantly looking for the best lumber. There's no problem in either for 10 years, at least. It depends on how much freight you are willing to pay.

The Market

The market is fantastic—phenomenal! We've never seen anything even approaching it. I think governmental subsidy, the 200-mile limit, and a greater demand for seafood (one of the best sources of protein) are all contributing factors.

The Labor Pool

The quality is good among local builders, but there is a shortage of skilled men. We train our own employees on the job and move them around so that we cultivate an all-around mechanic.

Open Statement

We don't try to build the cheapest boat. We stay competitive, but when it comes to a question of cost vs. quality, quality prevails.

The heavy scantlings of a Desco trawler. A nice 25′ batten has been faired in to mark the rabbet.

Manuel Dos Santos
Magus Boat Co.
2443 Lee Street
Hollywood, FL 33020
(305) 963-1430

The questionnaire was completed by Manuel's English-speaking son. Some of the answers are his, some are Manuel's comments with his son interpreting. I am sorry to say I never got the son's first name.

General Information

Number of builders: Three.
Capacity: 30 feet.
Specialties: Custom-built power craft.
Nontraditional modes: Yes.
Experience: Yes.
Preferred paints and glues: Mostly modern.
Sail and/or power: Power.

Facilities

Design and drafting: Yes, all boats built are his own designs.
Lumber storage: We buy as we go.
Metal working: Patterns.

History

Origin of interest: I emigrated from Portugal in 1964, long after I'd started building boats with some cousins. My "training" is with them, you would have to say.

Recent Projects

Our last boat in wood was a 16-foot launch for the brig *Unicorn.*

Projects in Store

A 30-foot deep-V offshore powerboat for pleasure use. The hull will be used as a plug for a fiberglass model before completion.

Lumber and Hardware

There will be less and less quality in the cheaper woods, while the more expensive ones will stabilize both in price and quality. Overall, there will always be enough wood.

The Market

It's very solid now. The future is up for grabs.

The Labor Pool

We tend toward local, Portuguese craftsmen. When these are all busy with other work on their own, we generally have to go north (to New England) to find the men we want.

Modern and Traditional Design

Traditional.

Time and Finish

Manuel builds to his own standards, but it is generally not a problem to balance that off with the owner's requirements.

Open Statement

We can build almost anything the customer wants—any size, any shape, sail or power.

SOURCE

Walter Egbert
2403 S.W. 10th Street
Fort Lauderdale, FL 33312
(305) 584-9879

In addition to being a kind and generous soul, Walter has had a hand in building, restoring, or repairing 451 boats. I can't imagine better credentials for a source of information.

History

Origin of interest: It's in the family.

Training: I served my apprenticeship on the Chesapeake Bay.

Recent Projects

I spent a year working on the reconstruction of the brig *Unicorn.* In general, these 450 (plus) boats ranged from seven-foot hydroplanes to 65-foot motor yachts.

Projects in Store

More of the same; it's where my heart is.

Lumber and Hardware

It's bad and getting worse. The lumber problem is a combination of there not being anyone out there cutting it, and there not being any wood to cut in the first place.

Cooperatives

These make sense! I've had some experience with coops of one form or another. A lot depends on personalities. Hardware coops need to stay local and concentrated to be efficient.

The Market

The market will be very small, perhaps negligible, except for one-off custom boats. These shops will be small in number, but fairly constant in number.

Who is Buying and Why

A lot of racing types have changed their emphasis to cruising, if for no other reason than savings. But, in general, I see more conspicuous spending, status seeking, than any real love of boats, particularly in power craft.

The Labor Pool

Both quantity and quality are disappearing as the older men die off.

Vocational Training

One cannot acquire the skills from books, only some basic principles. The skills come from using one's head and hands.

Two of the many classic yachts that were restored at Indian Haulover under the loving and sensible guidance of Walter Egbert and compatriot Steve Woods. Elsewhere, love and common sense are mostly at odds in the boat restoration business.

Modern and Traditional Design

They can be equally interesting and challenging. Modern hulls pose their own problems and there are no pat answers.

Restorations and Replicas

These depend entirely on common sense and its application to each individual case.

Time and Finish

This is almost solely the option of the owner. What he wants and can afford are the determining factors. It helps if he has a sense of what is in keeping with the boat in the first place, like not putting yacht finish on a tug.

Open Statement

You won't make money at boatbuilding, but if you are any good, you will always have work. It's a fine life—you'll live long and healthily. Keep it simple and the pleasures will accumulate.

Jack Ford, Foreman
Beaufort Marina
Star Route 5, Box 10
Beaufort, SC 29902
(803) 524-3949

Beaufort Marina is the focal point for much of the local boating activity. I talked with Jack Ford as he ran a trawler down the railway and expertly pulled in a 54-foot sportfisherman. This form was completed over the rumble of the winch and the whining of the cable under strain.

General Information

Number of builders: We have between seven and nine employees, three of whom we use on an individual building project.
Capacity: 45 feet.
Specialties: We are simply custom builders.
Nontraditional modes: Yes.
Experience: Yes, particularly Ashcroft and glass-over-wood.
Preferred paints and glues: Mostly modern.
Sail and/or power: Power.

Facilities

Design and drafting: No (can loft).
Lumber storage: 3,000 to 4,000 b.f.
Metal working: We handle welding and have a machine shop.

History

Origin of interest: My interest comes from my family, likewise my training.
Selection of location: We're from here.

Recent Projects

Two 32-foot twin-screw recreational powerboats for day fishing; a Jerry Gallup-designed trimaran; and everything from rowboats to yachts. We've opened a marine hardware outlet, too.

Projects in Store

We have nothing lined up in new construction, just repair.

Unusual Tools

Beaufort Marina uses an adjustable cradle for its railway. While I have seen many variations on this concept, theirs is perhaps the simplest to build and use.

Lumber and Hardware

The situation is getting worse. The good timber has all been cut in the U.S. The only worthy materials are coming from foreign sources.

Cooperatives

In places where builders are closer together and closer to the supply, it could work. Around here, the freight would kill it.

The Market

There'll always be a limited market supplying the wood buffs.

The Labor Pool

Right now we are having a hard time, but it seems to be getting better in quantity and quality overall.

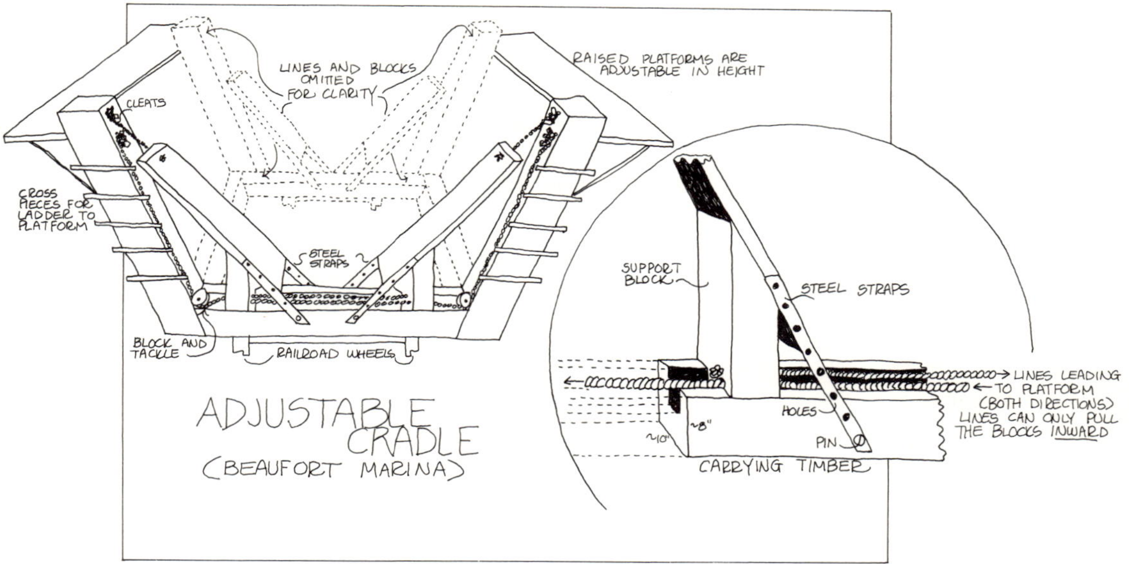

The bottom of each support block is a tenon that fits smoothly into the channel cut into the carrying timber. With the channels well greased, the blocks can be pulled inward with the lines running to the platforms. This increases the pitch of each support plank until it rests firmly against the hull. (Rebecca Wheeler illustration)

Modern and Traditional Design

Traditional is definitely our preference.

Time and Finish

There's only one way to go, and that's a dead fit.

Open Statement

Within the year we may have a Herreshoff 42-footer underway, possibly all teak.

James T. Gillikin
Gillikin Craft
P.O. Box 533
Beaufort, NC 28516
(919) 726-7284

The big shed on Radio Island, between Beaufort and Morehead City, covered a 75-foot V-bottomed shrimper and a 46-foot hard-chine run boat with room to spare. Mr. Gillikin's pleasure with boatbuilding is most evident in his "Open Statement," when he remarks, ". . . people tell me I can't quit." He smiles and laughs at the thought of retiring. A vigorous man, I can't imagine his retirement lasting for long, in any case.

General Information

Number of builders: Twelve.

Capacity: 80 feet.

Specialties: Round-bottomed shrimpers; sportfishermen; and deep- and shallow-V Harkers Island types.

Nontraditional modes: Yes, strip-planking.

Experience: Yes.

Preferred paints and glues: Traditional, for the most part.

Sail and/or power: Power.

Facilities

Design and drafting: Yes.

Lumber and storage: Anywhere from 5,000 to 20,000 b.f. We are also Gillikin Lumber Sales, specializing in heart pine and juniper.

Metal working: Yes, welding.

History

Training: I worked in boatyards and my own business grew naturally out of that.

Selection of location: I'm from near here, the town of Otway.

Recent Projects

A 75-foot by 22-foot sawn-frame shrimper, all pine except for the glass-over-plywood wheelhouse. A 46-foot by 14-foot pine-over-juniper run boat. Most of our boats are galvanized fastened; the headboats are bronze- or Monel-fastened.

Projects in Store

Another shrimper built to the specifications above.

Lumber and Hardware

I'm finding heart pine increasingly hard to get. We may have to go to fir.

Cooperatives

I don't know if it could work around here, but I would definitely be interested in one.

The Market

I think wooden boats will hang in there.

The Labor Pool

There are not too many boatbuilders; it's tough. Maybe too many small operations are keeping the good men busy (on their own).

Vocational Training

Carteret's training program seems to be pretty good. I have a couple of their students who've come to work for me full-time.

Modern and Traditional Design

Traditional.

Open Statement

I like to work with people, and for people. Every time I talk about quitting, people tell me I can't. Part of this is because I'm the only one around here building these shrimpers, but that's not all of it. We do the job *right* here.

Vance Gillikin and Mervin Rose
East Bay Boat Works
P.O. Box 301
Harkers Island, NC 28531
(919) 728-2004

General Information

Number of builders: Six.
Capacity: 70 feet.
Specialties: The Harkers model.
Nontraditional modes: Just strip.
Experience: Yes, glued-strip is our normal way of doing it.
Preferred paints and glues: Fifty-fifty modern and traditional.
Sail and/or power: Power.

Facilities

Design and drafting: No.
Lumber storage: Anywhere from 4,000 to 15,000 b.f.
Metal working: Welding only.

History

Origin of interest: My interest and training came through my brother and a life on Harkers Island, where boats are a matter of course.

Recent Projects

A 45½-foot by 16-foot by 4-foot sportfisherman, juniper-over-heart-pine. Fastenings are bronze along the topsides, stainless below the waterline, and galvanized in just the frames themselves.

Projects in Store

Possible 50-foot and/or 65-foot headboats.

A Harkers-type boat. Although most of the professionals in the Harkers area work indoors, they are often forced to work outside when they are building many boats at once.

Lumber and Hardware

Lumber quality has not changed a lot in the last six years, but the price has doubled. My brother (James Gillikin) is in the business. I remember him saying that a lot of juniper is going into vertical-batten house construction. Hardware comes from anywhere we can get it, delivery being so bad. Otherwise, it's holding strong.

Cooperatives

Most builders are too independent. I can think of maybe four builders in the whole county we could go in on a cooperative with. In any case, small mills would have trouble supplying large orders, and the big ones are too big to bother.

The Market

The cost of a boat is rising with the increased costs in labor and materials, but a lot of people *want* a wooden boat. The future is open to question—I would have to say I don't know what's going to happen. We've sold boats as far away as New Jersey by word of mouth.

The Labor Pool

Good labor is limited. The men that are good have jobs. Carteret's program may help the situation somewhat.

Modern and Traditional Design

Traditional.

Time and Finish

There is a balance determined by what you pay. We try to work with each boat owner to his satisfaction. We could go back and build more boats for most any of our clients.

SOURCE

Elias "Skip" Gunnell
Derecktor Gunnell, Inc.
775 Taylor Lane
Dania, FL 33004
(305) 920-5756

Mr. Gunnell runs a full-service yacht yard. As the key man, his time is valuable. He agreed to be in the book if readers were made aware of this. As with any big yard, there's a great deal of activity on Taylor Lane. Skip and his 70-man crew are happy to help, but please respect their busy schedule.

Union Guthrie
Hi Tide Boat Works
Box 74
Williston, NC 28589
(919) 729-3832

General Information

Number of builders: Four.
Capacity: 65 feet.
Specialties: Harkers-type sportfishermen.
Nontraditional modes: Glued-strip only.
Experience: Yes.
Preferred paints and glues: No strong preferences.
Sail and/or power: Power 90 percent, motorsailers 10 percent.

Facilities

Design and drafting: Yes; lofting too.
Lumber storage: 8,000 b.f., or enough for a boat ahead at all times.
Metal working: Welding.

History

Origin of interest: I took an early interest and built some sailboats on my own.
Selection of location: I'm from Harkers, but I've had this shop at Williston for 25 years.

Recent Projects

A 50-foot by 15-foot by 3-foot run boat, juniper-over-heart-pine. This boat will run catches from fishermen to wholesalers.

Lumber and Hardware

It's all right on both counts. The cost is high, but quality is holding and will continue to—as far as we can tell.

Cooperatives

We don't have enough capital to stock a lot in at any one time. I doubt other builders are much different.

The Market

Fiberglass is taking over. Still, a few people who want wood can keep *some* yards going.

The Labor Pool

It's pretty good and holding steady.

Modern and Traditional Design

Traditional.

Time and Finish

The boats we build today are better than those of 20 years ago.

Open Statement

All I can say is we're always looking for more work.

Willard Guthrie
Harkers Island, NC 28531
(919) 728-4984

I build boats to 65 feet; that's all they have to know.

Raymond LeMay
LeMay's Custom Boat Works
Box 74
Davis, NC 28524
(919) 729-3816

We sat in Mr. LeMay's cramped little office on a cold, raw, wet afternoon with our feet propped up against the heater. I recall his remark that I'd chosen a good day to come, "It's too lousy to work in this open shed, I sent two of the crew home already. The work will have to wait."

General Information

Number of builders: Four.

Capacity: 60 feet.

Specialties: I only build one design, a shallow-V sportfishing model, usually about 54 feet in length.

Nontraditional modes: Yes. Many of my boats are carvel below the chine, strip-planked above.

Experience: Yes.

Preferred paints and glues: Mostly traditional.

Sail and/or power: Power.

Facilities

Design and drafting: No. All the people in Florida buying my boats wouldn't want this hull if it weren't a good design. I don't see any reason to change it.

Lumber storage: 5,000 to 6,000 b.f., but only after a boat is on order.

Metal working: Welding.

History

Training: Working in yards at Marshallberg.

Selection of location: I'm from this area. I got started through the G.I. bill.

Recent Projects

A 60-foot by 17½-foot sportfisherman, juniper-on-cypress, and a 57-foot hull of the same design for charter use.

Projects in Store

A 65-foot by 18-foot charter boat with Coast Guard certification.

Lumber and Hardware

Lumber is getting scarce, and the price is getting high. It may hold up for five or 10 years and then it will price itself right out. We'll have to go to mahogany or cypress. Hardware is no problem; it's the price that's really outrageous!

Cooperatives

No chance. Builders wouldn't do it because they'd be too afraid of the other guy getting the better part of a shipment. I'd be for one, though.

The Market

It'll always hold up. It's like cars—not everyone drives a Ford or a Chevy. A wooden boat will outmaneuver a glass one.

The Labor Pool

The few that can really do the job are on their own or have a good job already.

Open Statement

As long as you're able, you build them. What more can I say? If it means anything, I have all the work I can handle, and then some.

Andy Mortensen
Andy Mortensen Boatyard
3007 N.W. South River Drive
Miami, FL 33142
(305) 634-2778

Mortensen is well known as one of the best builders of custom sportfishermen. As such, he is very busy. Below is what he had time for and chose to say.

General Information

Capacity: 60 feet.

Specialties: Sportfishermen of batten-seam construction, usually juniper-over-Philippine-mahogany frames.

Preferred paints and glues: Modern.

Calvin Rose
Rosecraft Boat Works, Inc.
P.O. Box 98
Harkers Island, NC 28531
(919) 728-5333

Calvin's big, airy shed had three boats under construction. Just how busy can four men get?

General Information

Number of builders: Four.
Capacity: 50 feet.
Specialties: Hard-chine powerboats of the Harkers design.
Nontraditional modes: Yes, strip.
Experience: Yes.
Preferred paints and glues: Mostly modern.
Sail and/or power: Power.

Facilities

Design and drafting: Yes.
Lumber storage: 15,000 b.f.
Metal working: No.

History

Origin of interest: It's all from my family, from living here.

Recent Projects

A 59-foot by 16½-foot charter sportfisherman, juniper-over-pine with stainless fastenings. There are some bronze fastenings in the interior only; they just don't stand up outside.

Projects in Store

Just keep going as we are.

Lumber and Hardware

Right now it looks bad. Lumber is there, but nobody's cutting much of it. Hardware is unbelievably slow in coming, and high priced.

Cooperatives

I don't know if they'd work. I'd probably be interested.

The Market

It's good and will only get better if materials can be found.

The Labor Pool

It's hard to get good men. We're basically family because the men in general are on the water where the money is.

Modern and Traditional Design

Traditional.

Earle and James Rose
The Original Rose Brothers Boat Yard
P.O. Box 181
Harkers Island, NC 28531

There were compressors chuffing in the background as Earl and James chatted amiably with two Coast Guard inspectors. Many Harkers boats go to the New York/ New Jersey charter fleet, so inspection for certification is a familiar process.

General Information

Number of builders: Ten.
Capacity: 70 feet.
Specialties: The Harkers Island sportfishing hull.
Nontraditional modes: Strip, yes.
Experience: Yes.
Preferred paints and glues: No preference, whatever is available. We use 5200.
Sail and/or power: Power.

Facilities

Design and drafting: Yes.
Lumber storage: 5,000 b.f.
Metal working: Welding.

History

Origin of interest: It's in the family.
Training: I started on my own in 1927.
Selection of location: It's home.

A white cedar and heart pine sportfisherman. Note the heavy knuckles at the chines.

Recent Projects

We've built over 350 hulls in 50 years. These last two in the shop are 50-foot by 18-foot and 48-foot by 18-foot sportfishermen—juniper-over-yellow-pine, stainless- or bronze-fastened.

Projects in Store

We have a couple of possible 50-footers.

Lumber and Hardware

Lumber is no problem. *Hardware is!*

Cooperatives

I don't think so; too hard to get supplies in quantity.

The Market

Good! I don't think glass, steel, or aluminum will ever replace wood. It's got life and buoyancy like none of the others.

The Labor Pool

It's a problem. Young people just aren't interested in boatbuilding.

Open Statement

We don't need any advertising because we have all the work that we need. The work speaks for itself.

St. Augustine Trawlers, Inc.
P.O. Box 40
St. Augustine, FL 32084
Telex: 56-8404, Cable: Tosco
(904) 824-4394

General Information

Number of builders: 490 total, 260 in wood construction.

Capacity: 85 feet.

Specialties: Shrimpers, scallopers, etc.; 75 percent new construction, 10 percent supply, 15 percent repair. We work off seven different-size hulls, the 73-foot by 20-foot is the most popular.

Preferred paints and glues: Modern.

Sail and/or power: Power only.

Facilities

Design and drafting: Yes.

Lumber storage: Yes.

Metal working: Fabrication, patterns.

Recent Projects

In 1978 alone we completed 70 vessels; eight weeks to finish a hull.

Projects in Store

More of the same—at a faster rate.

Unusual Methods

Lots of air tools.

Lumber and Hardware

No problem. We use fir, oak, cypress, and pressure-treated pine.

The Market

Very strong.

The Labor Pool

It's hard to get people to learn the skills.

Vocational Training

We train on-the-job for a specific aspect of construction, or perhaps two phases. We try to move people around as little as possible.

Open Statement

St. Augustine Trawlers, after only six years in the business, is a yard that has built its reputation on top-quality work and extra value; they're determined to keep it that way.

SOURCE

Albert Sidl and Gerhard Schwisow
S and S Boatbuilders
P.O. Box 2032
Savannah, GA 31401
(912) 233-8555

General Information

Number of builders: Two.

Specialties: We are specialty shipwrights and operators of larger vessels.

Nontraditional modes: Sure!

Experience: Yes.

Preferred paints and glues: Natural fibers—when properly treated—work best.

Sail and/or power: Sail.

Facilities

Design and drafting: Yes, we have a good deal of experience in these.

Metal working: We will set up a shop for this when we get moving on the S.S. *Savannah* (see below).

History

Origin of interest: A family of ship people.

Training: Out of the merchant marine and sailing/restoration projects in the Caribbean.

Recent Projects

The restoration of the *Barba Negra*. The top-to-bottom rebuilding project took 18 months.

Projects in Store

A 10-foot mahogany-and-oak dinghy and 12-foot and 16-foot Bank dories. We are presently working on the financing for a replica of the S.S. *Savannah*, the first steam ship to cross the Atlantic—98 feet on deck, 151 feet overall. She will be built entirely on our own initiative (with mostly private funds) and with a volunteer-trainee program as well.

Lumber and Hardware

Let's not forget about the quality of lumber as a renewable resource over the long term. There is lumber of good quality left; availability is the problem. Builders have to be concerned with a balance between conservation and use. In hardware, demand will create supply. For instance, low-carbon steel will come into greater use as more people realize its potential.

Cooperatives

They're excellent and appropriate to boatbuilding. We've had some experience with them in Vancouver, British Columbia.

The Market

Wooden boats are coming back, particularly with young people. This is not because they are more practical, but because people want and like them.

The Labor Pool

There are very few men who can build a traditional hull as they used to. The number of men who can do this is diminishing too, as the old-timers depart. I would say there are *still* not enough young people interested if this is to change.

Vocational Training

I feel there are good programs.

Modern and Traditional Design

You can see from the *Barba Negra* that our preference is traditional.

Restorations and Replicas

Both have their points. There is a problem with the question of *using* boats vs. the older museum concept of storage and preservation. We feel that using them has educational value, as well as risks. But even risks have their good points in that they build character.

Open Statement

As a basically happy person, I like to see more and more happy people. Boats are good places to do this. It is our responsibility to the world to give a damn.

G.C. Whiticar
Whiticar Boat Works, Inc.
3636 S.E. Old St. Lucie Boulevard
Stuart, FL 33494
(305) 287-2883

I drove into Whiticar's on a Sunday in hopes of finding someone in by chance. The place was so neat, so clean, and so quiet I was sure it was permanently shut down. The immaculate white buildings on the edge of a canal in a residential neighborhood hardly conformed to the usual clutter I had come to expect. The yard was anything but shut down. I must say, though, that it's the only one I know that has a well-kept lawn!

General Information

Number of builders: 20.
Capacity: 62 feet.

Specialties: We build custom, deep-V sportfishermen.
Nontraditional modes: Just Ashcroft.
Experience: Yes.
Preferred paints and glues: Mostly modern.
Sail and/or power: Power.

Facilities

Design and drafting: Yes.
Lumber storage: 18,000 to 20,000 b.f. on hand at most times.
Metal working: Patterns.

History

Origin of interest: My family is in the charter-boat business.
Training: I apprenticed in yards but am basically self-taught.
Selection of location: I'm from here.
Financing: Through charter work and selling our off-season projects.

Recent Projects

Three 46-foot twin-screw (diesel) sportfishing cruisers with all the customary accessories. These range from a Raritan icemaker to automatic fire extinguishers. The boats are finished with AwlGrip.

Projects in Store

We have a 48-footer to be named *Sun Times* on order, also a 40-footer in progress.

Unusual Tools

We use a shortened saw that cuts on the pull stroke to scribe in waterlines. We've found it both faster and more accurate.

Lumber and Hardware

It's getting to the point where extra-extra effort is needed to get either quality or quantity in lumber. We plan to simply continue to shop around as we always have. Hardware is out of sight in price, even though the yard has a chandlery, which helps.

Cooperatives

I doubt it. There's too much work necessary for the return. In any case, the mills cannot handle the large amounts that would be necessary.

The Market

Personally, I think there'll always be some demand. A *good* fiberglass boat is so heavy that one might as well go with wood for better performance and economy, all other needs being equal. A *well-built* wooden boat has a future; forget the rest.

The Labor Pool

It's not too good. It takes a good many years to acquire the diversity needed, and then the good men tend to go off on their own. We have tried to stabilize things with a profit-sharing plan and other inducements.

Modern and Traditional Design

It's a case of *good* design, whether you classify a boat one way or the other.

Time and Finish

We try to build a quality boat, uniformly fitted throughout. What our selective clients are looking for is quality, thorough integrity, and performance.

Alex Willis
Lloyd Willis and Son Boat Works
Harkers Island, NC 28531
(919) 728-5977

General Information

Number of builders: Four.

Capacity: 50 feet.

Specialties: Any kind of hard-chine power craft that fits the Harkers style.

Nontraditional modes: Yes, glued-strip.

Experience: Yes.

Preferred paints and glues: Fifty-fifty modern and traditional.

Sail and/or power: Power.

Facilities

Design and drafting: No.

Lumber storage: 2,000 b.f.

Metal working: No.

History

Origin of interest: Family.

Training: In this yard under my father, Lloyd.

Selection of location: Harkers is home to me.

Recent Projects

A 50-foot by 17½-foot juniper-and-heart-pine workboat. This one had a 12-foot stem. We build two 50-foot boats and about a dozen 20+ -foot ones each year.

Projects in Store

A 32-foot shrimper and a 55-foot sportfisherman, both juniper-over-heart-pine.

Lumber and Hardware

Quantity and quality are down, cost is up. Recently delivery has also been very slow. Over the long term we may not be able to get cedar at all. Hardware has been fine.

Cooperatives

There's a chance it might work. I'd be interested.

The Market

It will remain strong. If we can solve the lumber problem, the demand will be there. Word-of-mouth advertising is all we've ever had to have.

The Labor Pool

The cost of labor is high, but like lumber, the quantity and quality are down. A man can make more money out on the Sound shrimping, scalloping, and/or clamming.

Modern and Traditional Design

Traditional.

Open Statement

I think that wooden boats are the best when built right. I'd run a wooden boat against another of *any* other material (same design) *anytime.*

INTRODUCTION TO THE CHESAPEAKE BAY

Turning north from Harkers Island, my plans to explore wreck-strewn Cape Hatteras were thwarted when the bridge over Oregon Inlet suddenly settled. I was poking around Manteo and Wanchese when I heard the news. Somebody crossing the bridge on foot had felt the shift, and within an hour, the Army Corps of Engineers had closed the span to traffic. Much of the underpinning had apparently washed away.

So instead, I made a return visit to Kitty Hawk and the Wright Brothers Museum. Each time I have been there I have been more awed. The Wrights' most astonishing feats were not those first brief flights we all know so well. They went back to Dayton, Ohio, and developed a plane they could launch and steer at will. Few people know that they managed this in total secrecy. They found a field that was both big enough to fly over and shielded from view, and there they experimented, designed the launching tower, perfected the plane, and practiced. It is difficult to imagine designing, building, and flying the world's first plane; having the skies opened to you as they had never been before; and then for three and a half years resisting the temptation to fly beyond one small field, to shout your accomplishment to the world. The finished plane sat in a shed outside of Dayton for 3½ years while the Wrights negotiated with skeptical governments both here and abroad. When I saw films of a replica in flight, I understood immediately why so many wooden boat buffs are also devotees of antique airplanes. With a head full of dynamic images of wood, metal, and cloth (both in the air and on the water) I skirted the Dismal Swamp and tackled the Chesapeake Bay.

Late spring on the Bay; the temperature had been into the eighties already,

A handsome deadrise is almost ready for her first season. Her sleek, clean appearance gives her an air of speed even as she sits at the dock.

Chesapeake workboats. Oyster tongers gather on opening day of the season. Long tongs are worked over the side to lift the oysters from the bottom. (John Frye photo)

and 102 degrees with 87 percent humidity was on the way. Everybody could feel it. Even the B-52-size mosquitoes seemed to slow down in anticipation of the leaden warmth. As dusk fell and the bats skipped between the fireflies, there was laughter coming from a park by the shore. The season's first hot peppered crab feast was underway.

Each layer of crab is sprinkled liberally with a spicy concoction of celery salt, pepper, mustard, pimiento, cloves, laurel, mace, cardamom, ginger, cassia, and paprika—then steamed over an equal mixture of water and vinegar. The crabs are served cold, with a keg of beer, on picnic tables covered with many layers of newspaper. The only utensils are wooden mallets for breaking open the claws. Empty broken shells are tossed into a pile at the center of the table. Every so often they simply roll up the carcasses in half a dozen layers of newsprint and start with a clean slate. It undoubtedly sounds crude, but the approach is as much a part of the tradition as the dish. Crab without newspaper and beer could never be called a feast.

Afterward, the feasters polished off the barrel and took up those bottomless topics of fishing, crabbing, and boats.

"Hey, now, you hear that Jimmy's closed his shop? Says he'd rather bust his you-know-what for $350 a week on the water than do the same thing in the shop for half that. I think he made up his mind when that last keel timber came in at $185 for freight alone. Whew, what a price!"

"I heard him say that he can't see how he can face his customers when the whole boat's totaled up. It don't seem reasonable."

"Well it ain't reasonable. But nothing is these days. Sam said the reason he closed is that OSHA came around, and Jimmy figured it'd cost him all the profits for two years' work to do all the things they wanted. For %$# sake, they wanted him to pour a concrete floor.

"You can call me a doomsdayer, but I don't see how fishing is gonna be much of a solution come 10 years from now. I read in the paper that they're gonna put in an oil refinery down Portsmouth way; just one more thing to mess up the fishing. The other day in the diner, someone stared into the soup that had all the chunks and stuff in it and said, 'Look, it's the Bay!' It's no joke, though, somehow."

"Some days it seems all right to me, and others. . . . Well, I just have second thoughts."

Second thoughts—that is the Chesapeake Bay situation in a nutshell. Nothing is in balance and everything is in question. Like Jimmy, a lot of men have closed their shops in favor of working on the water. The Eastern Shore has always been economically depressed; a remote, backwoods corner in the megalopolis stretching from Norfolk, Virginia, to Portland, Maine. With tougher times on the Bay, the area is changing, if slowly. It is difficult to imagine, but some have predicted that it will become a summer refuge from the heat of the nation's capital, Baltimore, and Annapolis. Of three dozen names I had collected for the areas in and around Cambridge and Saint Michaels, almost 30 were either retiring, quitting early, or "gone fishin'."

General Information

Number of builders: Fourteen builders and two sources, 5.5 men per shop.

Capacity: The average shop capacity was 62 feet.

Specialties: Nine shops worked regularly in traditional Bay sailing and power craft: the "deadrise" workboats, skipjacks, and/or log canoes; four worked mainly in custom sail or power.

Nontraditional modes: Eleven builders had worked with nontraditional modes and continue to do so, especially in glued-strip; two had and wouldn't again; one hadn't and would.

Preferred paints and glues: Six used a combination of the traditional and modern; four used traditional only; four leaned toward the modern.

Sail and/or power: Seven were strictly in power; four had a majority of their experience in sail; three had equal experience with both.

Facilities

Design and drafting: Twelve builders had design and drafting capabilities, but four of the twelve said they were limited to certain types. Two neither designed nor drafted boats.

Lumber storage: The average amount of lumber stored was 3,820 board feet, excluding the two builders (Miller and Dean) who sell lumber as part of their business.

Metal working: Seven had welding capabilities; six did their own patterns; three did neither.

Recent Projects

Four skipjacks from 24 feet to 50 feet have been built by as many builders in the last year or so. At least a dozen powerboats for commercial and recreational use have been launched, the largest being a 56-foot headboat built by Virgil Sibley of Deltaville. Sibley and Virgil Miller are just two of that town's 10 full-time professionals. Richard Saunders of Deltaville is gearing up to build a 70-foot (106 feet overall) Chesapeake Bay schooner to be donated upon completion to the Hunger Project. From his base in Annapolis, Melbourne Smith is reportedly talking to the City of New York about a replica of the clipper *Sea Witch*. On a more modest scale, Fred Ajootian and Tiffany Cockrell have built a 34-foot Presto ketch and a 52-foot sportfisherman, respectively.

Projects in Store

More skipjacks, tong boats, and deadrise sportfishermen. A 36-foot Herreshoff *Diddikai* is in the works at Zahniser's yard at Solomons, Maryland. Gentleman Jim Richardson is again trying to find the time to build himself a 48-foot bugeye now that he's completed the 64-foot *Maryland Dove*. Every time he's tried to retire, somebody has come up with a project for which he is indispensable.

Unusual Tools and Methods

There is Sam McQuay's plane, a somewhat unusual brass-bound model. Maynard Lowery has a meat cleaver of substantial age and dimension that he occasionally makes use of in the shop. He told me it had to be tried to be appreciated.

Lumber and Hardware

As mentioned earlier, builders were pretty discouraged about the materials situation.

The availability of lumber leaves something to be desired. We'll always be able to get *something*, but the quality may deteriorate significantly. There is a worldwide money problem, and until that's solved, the above won't improve.

Maynard Lowery

Lumber, as it has been used, is hard to find; pressure treatment is going to have to be considered a lot more if we are going to open up the field. For instance, pine takes 100 percent penetration.

Carl Pederson

Lumber availability will outlast hardware. The latter is getting to be impossible. In the back countries, lumber will be available for a while yet.

James Richardson

There's plenty of white oak locally, but spruce is getting scarce, so we'll have to go to mahogany there.

Tiffany Cockrell

Cooperatives

Eleven of the 12 builders responding had negative reactions to the idea, fewer considered it a realistic possibility.

The Market

Pollution, governmental regulations, and declining oyster beds were the chief reasons behind the significant skepticism shown by 32 percent of the builders. There is an oil refinery being proposed at Portsmouth. Bill Hall reports that the parent company of the power company involved is based in Atlanta, Georgia, and that there is a cabinet-level fight in progress over approval. In Bill's words, "We wonder if the present occupant of 1600 Pennsylvania Avenue will tumble to this one." Maryland Sea Grant just predicted a 28 percent drop in the oyster catch from the Maryland portions of the Bay over the next three years. The picture is pretty grim if you add it all up. On the other hand, the builders who are more involved with the recreational market were generally more optimistic.

A man who does good work is always busy and always will be. Youngsters can make more money on the Bay, as long as it is clean.

Neal Dean

The market is declining and will continue to do so.

Maynard Lowery

There's plenty of demand . . . the cost of materials is skyrocketing. The working waterman may not be able to afford a wooden boat pretty soon.

Robert Meekins

There'll always be a market for good wooden boats. I think it will be relatively stable, as good as it ever was. We'll see a return to more working sailboats due to the cost of gas and oil.

James Richardson

The Labor Pool

It's very poor and there appears to be no future. It takes a lifetime . . . to know what you are doing. The young people don't have the eye, the aptitude.

John Belvin

I am by myself because you can't keep the good men, and the bad ones you don't want to keep.

Maynard Lowery

There are *some* good men, both young and old. You've got to love boats and be someone who can be content with good work. You can't come to work thinking about your lunch box. There'll be a greater problem here with molded materials. Men will come to work hating every moment of the job.

Virgil Miller

Seventy-five percent of the builders saw the labor situation as declining.

Vocational Training

Virtually all the builders responding had a suggestion to make about time, productivity, or a lack of realism.

The ones I have seen do not have a cost-effective, get-the-job-done approach.

Albert Zahniser

The programs should be geared to learning by *doing;* working on boats with market value, not Indian canoes or guide-boats.

James Richardson

If you know drafting and hand-tool skills, you are better off learning in the yard.

Fred Ajootian

It must be noted here that the Norfolk School of Boatbuilding had not yet opened its doors when I came through the area. These comments cannot then be construed as reflecting on NSB. It remains to be seen just how much effect the school can have on the labor shortage and builder/trainee relations in general.

Miscellaneous

As a result of a catastrophe in the darkroom, I owe an apology to builders on the Chesapeake Bay and to readers for the paucity of photographs pertinent to the region.

CHESAPEAKE BAY BUILDERS

Fred Ajootian
Ocran Boat Shop
White Stone, VA 22578
(804) 435-6305

Fred Ajootian's shop is well laid out and equipped. With his sharp mind and the shop's good facilities, he runs a small, efficient operation.

General Information

Number of builders: Four sets of hands: a mechanic, two carpenters, and a general helper.

Capacity: 50 feet.

Specialties: Custom sail and power, both round- and V-bottomed.

Nontraditional modes: Under certain circumstances only, like starvation. Seriously, our interest here is limited.

Experience: No, I think carvel construction is simplest and best.

Preferred paints and glues: Mostly traditional.

Sail and/or power: 50 percent sail, 50 percent power.

Facilities

Design and drafting: Yes.

Lumber storage: 3,000 to 4,000 b.f.

Metal working: Patterns and welding.

History

Origin of interest: Boatbuilding is a bad habit I acquired at an early age.

Training: On my own.

Selection of location: There were available on-the-water sites.

Financing: Through earlier business as a machinist farther north of here.

Recent Projects

A 34-foot Presto ketch of juniper, fastened with bronze to oak. Two V-bottomed tong boats (for tonging clams), one 34 feet and one 32 feet in length.

Projects in Store

Four 16-foot skiffs; a 25-foot bass boat; a pound-net skiff; a 25-foot deadrise sportfisherman; and a 34-foot Presto ketch.

Unusual Methods

For things like the tonging boats, I often loft to a more convenient scale, say three inches to the foot. I can then loft a 30-footer on one sheet of plywood, and since the lines are compressed, get a more accurate boat.

Lumber and Hardware

There'll always be lumber of reasonable quality, as far as I can tell. My biggest problem is hardware. Distributors don't carry stock and even when they do, they are unreliable in delivery. I can never tell when it will get here. In general, anything useful is getting hard to find. We *can* get water skis, cocktail glasses, and cleats with sharp edges—this last always chrome-plated.

Cooperatives

No. Everyone has their own needs, ideas, and sources. Anyway, there's a lot of barter and trade between shops; people are very cooperative already.

The Market

As long as there is somebody dumb enough to build a wooden boat, there'll be somebody dumb enough to buy one. [Fred can't keep the grin off his face as he says this—P.L.]

The Labor Pool

Decent labor is a major problem nationwide, not just in boatbuilding. A man can make better money elsewhere. People are watching television and riding mopeds instead of rowing or what-have-you. And who can blame them for not wanting to work in a yard where the conditions are often rough and the work hard?

Vocational Training

If you know drafting and hand-tool skills, you're better off learning in the yard.

Modern and Traditional Design

I like good designs, old *and* new. At the risk of repeating myself, a good design is a good design, period.

Time and Finish

I have been exposed to some of the fine builders—Nevins, Minneford, Herreshoff, etc.—and they cut perfect fits quickly and accurately faster than any clown can cut a two-by-four. I don't think there are too many like that, but everyone has to produce the best they can toward that standard.

John Belvin
269 Dandy Road
Yorktown, VA 23692
(804) 898-8820

General Information

Number of builders: Three employees and myself.
Capacity: 60 feet.
Specialties: Custom Chesapeake Bay sailing craft.
Nontraditional modes: Yes.
Experience: No.
Preferred paints and glues: Mostly modern.
Sail and/or power: Equal experience with both.

Facilities

Design and drafting: Yes, I design many of the boats we build.
Lumber storage: 10,000 b.f.
Metal working: No.

History

Origin of interest: I'm the third generation of boatbuilders in my family.
Selection of location: I'm from here.

Recent Projects

A 50-foot skipjack of white-cedar-over-heart-pine, Monel-fastened, and a 46-foot sportfishing boat. We have built a good many trunk-cabin boats and open workboats, but this may decline a little.

Projects in Store

A 46-foot skipjack, a 42-foot sportfisherman, and some more small, open powerboats. Our primary goal for the near future is to really push the skipjacks; we'd like to specialize in them.

Lumber and Hardware

The lumber is there in the timberland; limited availability is really what makes it hard to get and the quality hard to keep up. Over the long term I think it will become and stay more solid. We have found hardwood to be plentiful and of good quality.

Cooperatives

No, too independent.

As John Belvin takes photographs and directs the action, his latest skipjack is launched.

The Market

The market will never be as big for wood as it is for fiberglass, or even close. It's strong for us because we build a few boats at a time on a custom basis.

The Labor Pool

It's very poor and there appears to be no future. It takes a lifetime to become a boat carpenter—'til you are 50 years old—to know what you are doing. The younger people don't have the eye, the aptitude. I'd say you practically have to be born into it. This is why I believe that cold-molding is the wave of the future on the big-business scene. It requires less skill due to the nature of the method.

Vocational Training

I think it's great for keeping interest going, but I doubt it will produce competent boatbuilders.

Modern and Traditional Design

Traditional.

Time and Finish

That all boils down to who is paying the bill. I believe in doing the best work, but not at the risk of losing my shirt.

Open Statement

We are trying to build the finest skipjack available on the Chesapeake Bay. I think we've accomplished this already.

Tiffany Cockrell
Glebe Point Boat Co., Inc.
Glebe Point Box 133
Burgess, VA 22432
(804) 453-3464

General Information

Number of builders: We have 32 employees but rarely have more than a dozen working on one boat.
Capacity: 30 feet to 65 feet.
Specialties: Sportfishermen of sandwich construction.
Nontraditional modes: Yes, strip.
Experience: Yes, and Ashcroft also.
Preferred paints and glues: Mostly modern.
Sail and/or power: Power.

Facilities

Design and drafting: Yes.
Lumber storage: 2,500 b.f.
Metal working: Patterns.

History

Origin of interest: My family has lived for over 200 years in this part of Virginia, and my father had a shop right here before I did.

Recent Projects

We've built 156 sportfishermen in 23 years. The last one was 52 feet and double-diagonal planked. Before that there was a 65-foot schooner. She's Philippine-mahogany strip over marine plywood, on white-oak frames. We built the hard-chine hull alone; the owner is handling the interior. We pushed some, but we got our share of the work completed in four months. (See *National Fisherman*, July 1978.)

Projects in Store

We are going to build a third railway and double our docking capabilities to 20 boats. We are still streamlining the system we use to build the sportfishermen, and are planning to reach our three-large-ones-a-year goal fairly soon. We are making every effort to keep the cost of these boats down.

Unusual Methods

We have developed a foredeck combination of a fiberglass-over-plywood center area with a teak walkway around the rail. Apart from its appearance, owners like the savings in cost and the better footing on the teak.

Lumber and Hardware

Hardware is no problem. I *do* see greater use of stainless as a possibility. There's plenty of white oak locally, but spruce is getting scarce so we'll go to mahogany there. No problem with mahogany even in the future, but teak *will* be difficult to find, since we're only getting it from one country, Thailand.

Cooperatives

Builders are too divided and too different for a coop to work here; where needs are similar, they have a chance.

The Market

There will always be a market for wooden boats. We do have to watch out that we don't price ourselves out of the middle class. (The yard has developed a 36-foot deadrise boat they can sell for $26,000.)

Who is Buying and Why

Sportsmen, because we custom-build a boat to their needs. They don't have to accept a boat just like all the others. Among these men, there are no particular "types."

The Labor Pool

We know that 68 percent of the cost of a new boat is labor. The quality and quantity of the pool is going down. We don't train men in more than one or two areas because the boats are so complex you need specialists. There are miles of wiring in some of those things! Also, we aren't near any big industries offering $6 an hour, so it's easier to get and keep good help.

Vocational Training

No contact.

Modern and Traditional Design

This is a different tack, but we've found that a hard-chine hull is easy to drive and not necessarily any worse as a sea boat than a round-bottomed hull.

Time and Finish

We try to maintain a high-quality level throughout. If you allow X in the hull, you'll find X in the finish work. You'll never compromise without taking a beating one way or another.

Open Statement

If every boat I build isn't better than the last, I won't survive in this business. I want our boats to have pride and individuality—you'll be able to spot our boat a mile away. Our boats have to be worth a 12-month wait.

Miscellaneous

We concentrate our efforts on the bridge, it being the most-used part of the boat. It should be quiet, spacious, etc.

F.O. "Neal" Dean
F.O. Dean Boatyard
Box 8
Wingate, MD 21675
(301) 847-8158

General Information

Number of builders: Three.

Capacity: 48 feet.

Specialties: We build only strip-planked, Chesapeake Bay deadrise workboats, fishing partyboats, or yachts.

Preferred paints and glues: 50 percent modern.

Sail and/or power: Power.

Facilities

Lumber storage: 27,000 b.f.—10,000 cedar, 10,000 pine, 5,000 oak, and 2,000 mahogany.

Metal working: Welding and machining.

History

Training: I worked for another yard.

Selection of location: I'm from here.

Recent Projects

A 43-foot by 13-foot workboat of old-growth pine and cedar-on-oak. Fastenings are 316 stainless, Monel, and bronze. Before that, a 48-foot fishing boat (Coast Guard approved for 26 persons), powered with a 555 Cummins diesel.

Projects in Store

Two local machinists are retiring, so we are going to develop our machine shop some more. We'll start a 40-foot boat on speculation and work on it as we can spare the time from developing the machine shop. We will remain essentially boatbuilders, for sure.

Lumber and Hardware

A lot of North Carolina cedar was bought up by some big firms and is getting depleted. We can get mahogany as a rule, but you have to hunt around for the right price.

The Market

A man who does good work is always busy, and always will be. The market is real good.

The Labor Pool

The youngsters are watermen, not boatbuilders. They can make more money on the Bay, as long as it's clean.

Modern and Traditional Design

Traditional.

Open Statement

I feel somebody ought to be regulating the backyard fiberglass builders; that person will have to know what he's doing, obviously.

SOURCE **William H. Hall, Jr.**
Staff Naval Architect and Boat Captain
Calvert Marine Museum
Solomons, MD 20688

In addition to his duties at Calvert Marine Museum, Bill produces a gutsy little newsletter called *The Professional Waterman*. It is a monthly, no-holds-barred assessment of, and advocacy for, the fisheries of the Chesapeake and the Carolinas. Here's a sampling:

> Some months ago we said that if the various states couldn't come up with suitable plans and work together to manage their inshore fisheries, then the Feds would do it. *So don't believe us*—but do read on. Now the GAO wants the

The log-and-frame bugeye William B. Tennison.

Secretary of Commerce to use preemptive powers or seek legislation TO EXTEND FEDERAL FISHERIES MANAGEMENT OVER THE TERRITORIAL SEA. This means from the beach to three miles out and includes inland tidal waters. *You think it can't happen in your state?* Like Hell it can't, and it *certainly will if you keep your mouth shut and do nothing about it.*

P & I INSURANCE: One of the companies that writes insurance for the Massachusetts Inshore Draggers Association has proposed that they give a 20% reduction in rates if your boat is equipped with C.G.-approved survival suits. *Excellent!* That is a step in the right direction. Hopefully other writers will follow suit.

Bill's experience is as varied as his style is forceful. He worked with the Navy as a naval architect from 1948 to 1963, had a hand in some of the early fiberglass-boat experiments, and is now Captain of the Museum's recently acquired 1899 log-and-frame bugeye, *William B. Tennison* (page 229). She is in good enough condition to be licensed by the Coast Guard for 49 passengers! Bill will be at the wheel for a variety of trips, including educational estuarine programs on the Patuxent River.

Dave Judson
Box 395
Grimstead, VA 23064
(804) 725-2654

General Information

Number of builders: One.
Capacity: 35 feet.
Specialties: Custom boatbuilding.
Nontraditional modes: Yes.
Experience: I've done some strip-planking and built a few boats out of plywood.
Preferred paints and glues: I prefer working with traditional materials, but I like epoxy glues. I use modern materials where I feel they will do a better job.
Sail and/or power: 80 percent sail, 20 percent power.

Facilities

Design and drafting: I have limited design capabilities. Most boats I have built have been designed off the top of my head. These range from a 14-foot skiff to a 24-foot skipjack sloop.
Lumber storage: 2,000 b.f.
Metal working: No.

History

Origin of interest: I became seriously interested in boatbuilding after completing high school. I bought an Alden sloop that was all but shot. I started rebuilding her and ended up working for the yard where she was hauled. This got me hooked. I had been interested in boats since my childhood around the

Chesapeake Bay. I spent the next six years working in yards at repair and new construction. The last two years I've been on my own. In addition to some repair and new construction, I have built a shop and a home in this time.

Selection of location: I chose this area because I'd spent time here when I was growing up and had always liked it. We are pretty rural but still have access to most suppliers in Norfolk and Baltimore.

Financing: From the sale of a 32-foot Alden cutter I'd owned.

Recent Projects

A 24-foot skipjack of cypress-over-fir-and-oak; a 24-foot Chapelle sharpie of plywood-over-fir; a 19-foot Carolina dory of plywood-over-fir. As above, I set up a new home and shop.

Projects in Store

The interior of a 30-foot Bolger aluminum yawl, a 25-footer on speculation (design not yet determined). I would like to stick to traditional designs and new construction, but when you are just starting out, you have to be realistic.

Lumber and Hardware

Lumber will be available, but it will be hard to get good quality and long lengths. It's a matter of being in the right place at the right time. I buy lumber in the woods from whoever is cutting it at the time.

Cooperatives

I think they would be an effective means to lower material costs.

The Market

There will be a limited market, but I haven't been around long enough to predict the future. We still have plenty of commercial construction in our area.

Modern and Traditional Design

I like traditional designs because they are often simpler and much more pleasing to the eye.

Restorations and Replicas

I think skills preservation should have higher priority. The City of Baltimore's project with the *Pride of Baltimore* [see Melbourne Smith interview—P.L.] was worthwhile because it exposed people to the skills involved in building her *and* produced a working exhibit.

Time and Finish

In a boat, all work should be done to the limits of the craftsman's abilities.

Open Statement

I believe I have the facilities and ability to build anything to 35 feet. The experience is there.

Maynard Lowery
Box 266
Tilghman, MD 21671
(301) 886-2268

I first heard of Maynard while visiting the Chesapeake Bay Maritime Museum in Saint Michaels, Maryland. I heard good word of him again at Wittman, Cambridge, and

Church Creek. When I finally got to his shop on Chicken Neck Road, I was not disappointed.

General Information

Number of builders: One.

Capacity: 53 feet.

Specialties: V-bottomed planing hulls, which is not to say I can't build in roundbottom. I'm a custom builder.

Nontraditional modes: Yes, glued-strip.

Experience: Yes.

Preferred paints and glues: Half traditional, half modern.

Sail and/or power: Power.

Facilities

Design and drafting: Yes.

Lumber storage: 2,000 to 3,000 b.f.

Metal working: Patterns.

History

Origin of interest: My father and uncles were boatbuilders. I learned from them before I went into the Coast Guard and later studied naval architecture.

Selection of location: I was born and raised here.

Recent Projects

A 32-foot pleasure fishing boat of yellow-pine-on-oak, Monel-fastened. That was followed by a 39-foot pleasure boat of cedar-strip-on-oak and Everdur bronze. This boat in the shop is 35 feet and for commercial use; she's yellow-pine-on-sawn-oak frames. Yes, the finish is nice; I tend to carry things over from the yachts a little bit, without taking too much more time, of course.

Projects in Store

I have a 36-foot pleasure boat to build. I'll just keep on; I like it!

Unusual Tools

Well, it's not the least bit unusual as a tool itself, but it *is* unusual in a boat shop. I've got an old, heavy meat cleaver that's very useful at times. It has to be tried to be appreciated.

Lumber and Hardware

The availability of lumber leaves something to be desired. We'll always be able to get *something* but the quality may deteriorate significantly. There is a worldwide money problem, and until that's solved, the above won't improve.

Cooperatives

I doubt it—as a business. Occasionally two "friends" will get together when their projects coincide.

The Market

The market is declining and will continue to do so. There are easier ways to make a buck, on the builder's end. It takes a long time to build a reputation and a young man can't afford that time.

The Labor Pool

This is another area to get uptight in. I am by myself because you can't keep the good men, and the bad ones you don't want to keep.

Vocational Training

It's a good thing. Interested young men with that background will carry on the profession. Without the schools it will die quickly. The ex-students I've met seem to have good basics, at any rate.

Modern and Traditional Design

Traditional.

Time and Finish

I studied naval architecture so that I could become more efficient *and* improve the construction and design methods in my boats. It's a competitive thing. You've got to expedite a boat to keep in the market while also pleasing the customer. A boat has to be well made, regardless.

Open Statement

I get satisfaction out of producing a nice boat. It will have character and live on after I'm gone. Boatbuilding also promotes an integral part of our heritage. Our nation was built on, and remains, a maritime nation.

David McQuay
Sam'l T. McQuay and Son
Sewell Point Road
Wittman, MD
or P.O. Box 126
Tilghman, MD 21671

I recently received word that Sam McQuay had died less than a year after we talked. My sadness at the news was lightened a little by word that his son, David, is continuing the family tradition. Furthermore, he has decided to keep the original name.

General Information

Number of builders: One.

Capacity: 45 feet.

Specialties: We have worked on log canoes and round-bottomed boats in general, but most of our work is with hard chines.

Nontraditional modes: Yes, glued-strip.

Experience: Yes.

Preferred paints and glues: Mostly modern.

Sail and/or power: Mostly, but not exclusively, power.

Facilities

Design and drafting: Yes.

Metal working: No.

History

Origin of interest: Sam worked with his father-in-law, also a builder. David followed that course with his father, Sam.

Selection of location: This is home.

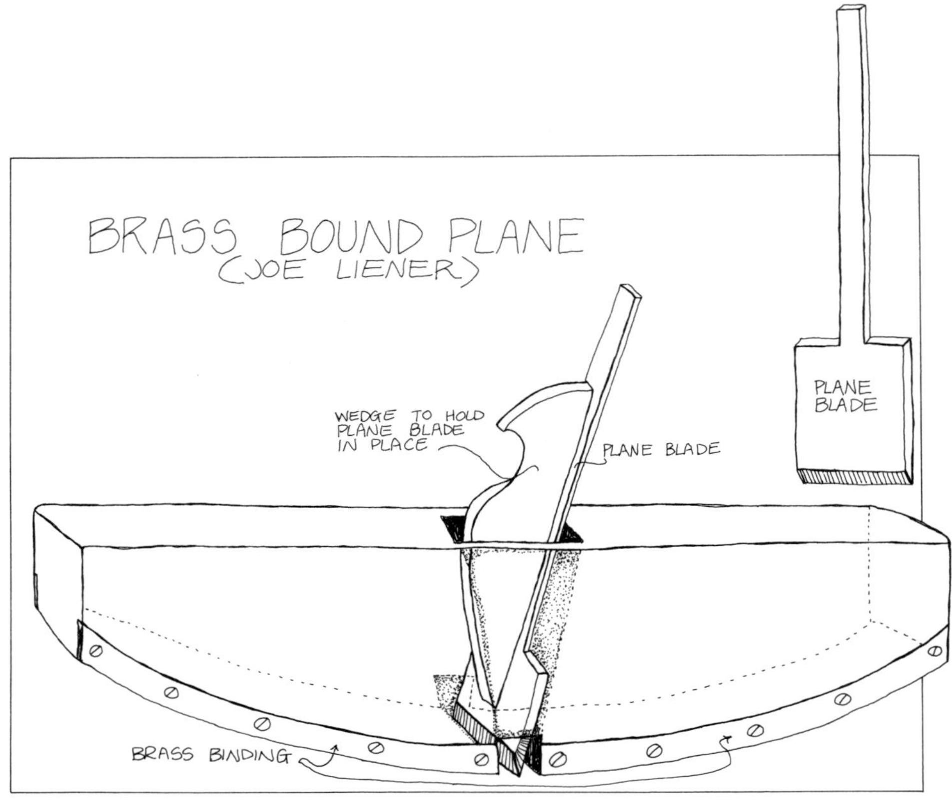

The last time Sam McQuay used this brass-bound plane was to fair off the inner face of the stem to a 16′ Whitehall. (Rebecca Wheeler illustration)

Recent Projects

A 16-foot Whitehall; a 44-foot by 13-foot powerboat of mahogany-and-fir-over-oak; and a 42-foot workboat of cedar-and-fir-over-oak.

Projects in Store

A 42-foot deadrise for fishing, crabbing, oystering, and clamming.

Unusual Tools

We have a plane that our local genius, Joe Liener, is responsible for; I think it's different enough to be more than just *another* modified plane.

Lumber and Hardware

Lumber is both expensive and hard to get if you want decent quality. We may have to go to woods (like mahogany) that are not local, or at least standard practice.

Cooperatives

I'm doubtful.

The Market

There'll be no professionals at all, just the amateurs and hobbyists to build the boats.

The Labor Pool

Just forget the quality and then you have to hunt for quantity. If you find a man, his salary is going to be a problem. How can you keep him when you can't afford to pay him more than three or four dollars an hour?

Modern and Traditional Design

Traditional.

Time and Finish

With workboats, you don't build it any better than it has to be.

Open Statement

I spent 17 years with my father-in-law, and I must have learned something, because we've built 57 boats since 1957. We've done everything from Whitehalls to a Japanese bathtub.

Robert Meekins
Robert Meekins Custom Built Boats
P.O. Box 602
Church Creek, MD 21622
(301) 228-8952

General Information

Number of builders: One.

Capacity: 45 feet.

Specialties: Hard-chine, Chesapeake Bay, deadrise boats to suit any purpose.

Nontraditional modes: Glued-strip only.

Experience: Yes.

Preferred paints and glues: We use oil-base paints and 5200, so you'd have to call it a mix.

Sail and/or power: Power.

Facilities

Design and drafting: No.

Lumber storage: 4,000 b.f. We like to stay a year ahead.

Metal working: Welding and patterns.

History

Origin of interest: I'm a professional waterman.

Training: I've worked in yards ever since high school, right here in Church Creek.

Recent Projects

Forty-foot and 44-foot workboats of North Carolina cedar-and-pine-on-oak.

Projects in Store

Another 40-foot workboat.

Lumber and Hardware

Over the long term, it is hard to say; quality is all right but availability is tough.

Cooperatives

No.

The Market

There's plenty of demand.

The Labor Pool

It's better now than it ever has been.

Open Statement

The cost of materials is skyrocketing. The working waterman may not be able to afford a wooden boat pretty soon.

Virgil Miller
Miller's Marine Railway, Inc.
Deltaville, VA 23043
(804) 776-4162

Virgil Miller is perhaps the best known of the more than half-dozen boatbuilders in Deltaville. In addition to the railway and repair business, he sells lumber and builds in steel and aluminum. He has been able to get fir keel stock from Oregon in lengths over 60 feet and in dimensions of 12 inches by 14 inches.

General Information

Number of builders: We have about 18 men on the crew.

Capacity: 100 feet.

Specialties: Custom, deep- or shallow-V boats, including multichines.

Nontraditional modes: Glued-strip.

Experience: Yes.

Preferred paints and glues: Mostly modern.

Sail and/or power: Power, as much as 95 percent.

Facilities

Design and drafting: Yes.

Lumber storage: Yes, a whole lumberyard full of fir, oak, Virginia spruce, and longleaf pine.

Metal working: We have a machine shop with our steel/aluminum capabilities, of course.

History

Origin of interest: I married into the business.

Training: In the Navy Yard, among other places.

Selection of location: I'm from here.

Recent Projects

A 51-foot by 16-foot deep-V sportfisherman of juniper-over-juniper, with Monel fastenings. Before that, a 55-footer in aluminum.

Projects in Store

A 51-foot houseboat/sportfishing combination of juniper and oak, it will have a cross-planked pine bottom. We may have two trawlers, 60 feet and 72 feet, respectively, but that's not firm yet.

Lumber and Hardware

Wood is getting scarce. Tremendous demand for it in other industries is using up local sources. We have little clout because it's easier for the mills to use and handle the short logs that other industries need.

Cooperatives

Builders are too independent and don't want to lay out that much cash and/or labor.

The Market

The market is going to molded materials due to the shortage of craftsmen and the ease of the molded materials' application. Lots of people *want* wood, but the problem of finding craftsmen to maintain the boat later is turning some away.

The Labor Pool

There are *some* good men, both young and old. You've got to love boats and be someone who can be content with good work. You can't come to work thinking about your lunch box. There'll be a greater problem here with molded materials. Men will come to work hating every moment of the job, like on an assembly line. I never did know a man who liked assembly line work.

Vocational Training

I like the idea, but it's hard to get students to stay with it and learn over the long term.

Open Statement

We will be continuing in wood as long as we can, as long as we have qualified men who can do the work. We will do this while continuing to expand into new fields.

C.V. Pederson
Virginia Boatshop
Shirley Road, Box 277
Seaford, VA 23696
(804) 898-7450

General Information

Number of builders: One.
Capacity: 50 feet.
Specialties: Chesapeake Bay sailing craft, custom construction in general.
Nontraditional modes: Yes, strip.
Experience: Some.
Preferred paints and glues: Mostly traditional.
Sail and/or power: About half of each, but I'm sail-oriented.

Facilities

Design and drafting: Yes, limited.
Lumber storage: 2,000 to 3,000 b.f.
Metal working: No.

History

Origin of interest: I was in the lumber business for 17 years before I bought a shop in Deltaville.

Training: From years of using boats, and learning from good employees in the Deltaville shop.

Selection of location: It's a good spot with a deep creek.

Recent Projects

Reconstruction of a 45-foot bugeye, new construction of a 30-foot hard-chine schooner with outside ballast and juniper planking over pine frames.

Projects in Store

A new shed and railway. Eventually, we want to specialize in traditional sailing watercraft. For now, we have a 25-foot Chincoteague deadrise scow and a conventional deadrise fishing launch of 22 feet on line.

Lumber and Hardware

Lumber as it has been used is hard to find; pressure treatment is going to have to be considered a lot more if we are going to open up the field. For instance, pine takes 100 percent penetration of preservatives under the right conditions.

Cooperatives

Not enough builders. I may get into stocking boat lumber for the other builders locally, though.

The Market

It's weak. Over the long term, perhaps 20 years, it will pick up. Right now, I don't see all that much renewal at the market place.

The Labor Pool

The quantity is low. Lots of young people are getting into it, but *it takes time*. Lots of old-timers have dropped out and there is a lag between them and the new men. The young men will make just as good builders in the end.

Modern and Traditional Design

Traditional.

Time and Finish

It depends on the client. Some people cannot afford the best finish work, but *structural* standards have to be basically the same. It has to be right.

Open Statement

In this country, we have some of the finest wood in the world for boatbuilding. It's not being used or understood properly even by many builders. We need to know more about the wood we have in *this* country, the most reasonable stuff available. People don't fully understand grades, coloration, etc. I include myself in that statement. I do have a background in southern lumber—I know a lot more than most, but you never know enough.

SOURCE

James Richardson
Richardson Boat Yard
RFD 1, Box 20 A
Cambridge, MD 21613
(301) 228-3036

Mr. Jim, age 72, is well known for his work with historian and naval architect William Baker on museum replicas such as the *Mayflower II* and, more recently, the *Maryland*

Dove (see *WoodenBoat,* No. 24 and No. 26). He has tried to retire on a number of occasions so that he might complete his own 48-foot bugeye, but each time, the soft-spoken, even-tempered gentleman has been cajoled into building "just one more."

General Information

Number of builders: For *Dove*, we have eight.

Capacity: 65 feet.

Specialties: Custom construction and traditional Chesapeake types have always been our bread and butter.

Nontraditional modes: Just glued-strip.

Experience: Yes.

Preferred paints and glues: Traditional. I'm one of those who isn't too excited by "miracle whips."

Sail and/or power: Fifty-fifty.

Facilities

Design and drafting: I've done my own boats, but as a rule, we don't loft boats here. It's usually an unnecessary expense to the customer.

Lumber storage: 4,000 to 5,000 b.f.

Metal working: Welding and patterns.

History

Origin of interest: I come by it honestly through my father's family. I learned from them, too.

Selection of location: My family's been here for generations.

Recent Projects

These would be the 65-foot *Dove* we're finishing now for the St. Marys City Commission. She's a replica of the first vessel to bring settlers to Maryland in 1634. She's oak-on-oak frames, with pine decks and galvanized fastenings. There was a 42-foot skipjack before, yellow-pine-and-cypress-on-oak.

Projects in Store

I'm still trying to finish a 48-foot bugeye for myself. I think now I'll be able to *really* retire. I never could remember how many boats I've worked on, and these days I don't always like to think about it. It's been a long time.

Lumber and Hardware

Lumber availability will outlast hardware. The latter is getting to be impossible. In the back countries, lumber will be available for a while yet.

Cooperatives

Not in this area.

The Market

There'll always be a market for good wooden boats. I think it will be relatively stable, as good as it ever was. We'll see a return to more working sailboats due to the cost of gas and oil.

Who is Buying and Why

Most of the people I know are past middle age and have some money; tax writeoffs are not uncommon as a reason to have a boat built. I think the young people are out rebuilding older boats, not buying new ones.

The Labor Pool

The future is looking up. Young people have stepped in in the last four or five years. They are returning to skills in lieu of professions.

Vocational Training

The programs should be geared to learning by *doing*; working on boats with market value, not Indian canoes or guide-boats.

Open Statement

Do the very best you can and be sure to meet the payroll.

Richard Saunders
Fishing Bay Boat Yard
Deltaville, VA 23043
(804) 776-6803

General Information

Number of builders: Minimum of two, maximum of six.

Capacity: 70 feet.

Specialties: Traditional small craft and the repair and restoration of Lawley, Herreshoff, and other quality boats.

Nontraditional modes: I have experience in all forms of construction but will do only plank-on-frame.

Preferred paints and glues: Traditional. With the exception of epoxy glue, I find modern chemicals don't hold up.

Sail and/or power: Sail, 100 percent.

Facilities

Design and drafting: No.

Lumber storage: I can keep enough on hand for my own use only.

Metal working: We can make patterns.

History

Origin of interest: Always have been interested in boatbuilding.

Training: School of hard knocks.

Selection of location: This is paradise on earth.

Financing: Credit, bull, and a small bank loan.

Recent Projects

An 11-foot LOA lapstrake mahogany yacht tender by Bolger; a 13-foot 6-inch Pete Culler Good Little Skiff; rebuilt a 1904 57-foot Herreshoff (gorgeous boat); and rebuilt a 1931 Danish 30 square-meter.

Projects in Store

A 70-foot (106 feet LOA) authentic Chesapeake Bay schooner. She will be loblolly pine on white oak, the former of which will be treated quite thoroughly with copper salts. When complete, she will be donated to the Hunger Project. I have always wanted to build a large boat that I didn't have to be so particular with—not to have to worry about every scratch under seven coats of varnish.

Unusual Tools

Nothing that isn't in the books.

Lumber and Hardware

I can get any lumber I want except close-grain, quarter-sawn, heart Georgia pine, which is the best planking material on earth. Lumber isn't cheap and it isn't easy to get. I cut a lot of my needs with an Alaskan mill. You have to travel and haul it, but there is plenty of it. Most hardware for sale today is junk. I buy used or make my own.

The Market

With welfare paying good money to just sit, you can't get anyone to be crew any more. So large traditional wooden craft are for the rich only. Trouble is, nowadays the rich have no taste. *There is no market for beauty—witness modern houses, cars, and buildings!* I won't sell to someone who I feel won't care for the boat.

The Labor Pool

Improving. The young people of the U.S. seem to be getting tired of nine-to-five jobs in the office. I can get some good people willing and capable of learning quickly.

Modern and Traditional Design

Traditional. My favorite is Herreshoff's *Queen*, or maybe Phil Rhodes' *Escapade*, or John Alden's *Malabar X*. Modern boats are *ugly, ugly, ugly*. I don't like to be seen with ugly boats or ugly women.

Time and Finish

We operate doing the best work we can. If the owner doesn't like it he can either learn to, or go elsewhere. We make some mistakes, but I won't make them on purpose, as a cheapskate.

Open Statement

I love the beautiful old yachts—long, graceful sheers; long counter sterns; low freeboard. Satisfaction and beauty are the only things we can get from this; there is certainly no money in it. My employees and I only work on boats we love.

Virgil A. Sibley
Sibley's Marina
P.O. Box 302b
Deltaville, VA 23043
(804) 776-6625

General Information

Number of builders: One, I'm self-employed. The others here are all subcontractors.
Capacity: 55 feet.
Specialties: Headboats, deadrise workboats, and sportfishermen.
Nontraditional modes: Yes.

Preferred paints and glues: We use some 5200 and epoxy glues, but we use oil-base paints also; call it half-and-half, traditional and modern.

Sail and/or power: Power.

Facilities

Design and drafting: Just in my head.

Lumber storage: 5,000 to 6,000 b.f.

Metal working: Welding.

History

Origin of interest: It's in the family.

Training: I worked for my father-in-law.

Selection of location: I'm from here.

Recent Projects

A 56-foot by 17-foot headboat, all cypress; a 51-foot by 16-foot passenger boat of spruce-pine bottom, white-oak ribs, and a fir keelson.

Projects in Store

We have a number of possible contracts for sportfishermen and headboats, but none are solid yet.

Lumber and Hardware

The boats are getting better because we are selecting materials more carefully. Using certain woods in certain areas is extending the life of boats. The quality of materials is better than before, just like marine engines are better than they used to be.

Cooperatives

I don't know if we can get together or not. We'd still want to hand-pick our own lumber anyway.

The Market

There's plenty of work once you've built your reputation. I've never had any problems getting work.

The Labor Pool

Good mechanics are hard to find. This is one reason why we stay small, to get the better work force.

Vocational Training

I've not had contact before, but I've got a couple of young men coming in from Richmond for two or three weeks as part of their summer school program. We'll have to see what happens.

Melbourne Smith
International Historical Watercraft Society
P.O. Box 54
Annapolis, MD 21404
(301) 268-0847

Last heard, Mr. Smith was talking to the City of New York about the possibilities of building a replica of the famed clipper ship *Sea Witch.*

General Information

Number of builders: Three, between jobs.

Capacity: 90 feet.

Specialties: Historically accurate, custom, traditional sailboats.

Nontraditional modes: No.

Experience: Yes.

Preferred paints and glues: Traditional.

Sail and/or power: Sail.

Facilities

Design and drafting: Yes.

Lumber storage: We gear up for each job, as needed.

Metal working: Yes, we make patterns, do welding and machining. We work in wrought iron only.

History

Origin of interest: I left home and went to sea.

Training: On our own in Central America. My partner is a professional builder there.

Selection of location: I had a contract here.

Recent Projects

The *Pride of Baltimore*, 90 feet on deck, built for that city, used as a good-will vessel. In her first year she logged 13,000 sea miles! She was built in nine months for $1.25 per pound. (See *WoodenBoat,* No. 14, for more.) Our last project before the *Pride* was five 33-foot gaff-rigged cutters.

Projects in Store

Possible *Sea Witch*; possible 110-ton brig for the City of Newport News.

Lumber and Hardware

We are running out of good hardwoods even in Central America, where we cut and ship our own. As far as large vessels are concerned, there is no decent lumber in the United States anymore.

The Market

The market is improving all the time. There's more interest now than ever.

The Labor Pool

There are lots of young guys who are good and have the capability to learn fast. The future of the pool is all right as long as there is one man to teach people how it's done.

Vocational Training

At some schools, speed doesn't get enough emphasis. Time is the big factor. The secret of wooden boatbuilding is speed. After all, it's only another boat. Let's get it sailing. Look at all the miles under *Pride* after a year!

Modern and Traditional Design

I think modern designs are fine, particularly applied to modern situations. I'm not hidebound.

Restorations and Replicas

I think replicas are cheaper, easier to "build" than restorations, and in the end, a better-built boat gets on the water faster.

Time and Finish

It depends on who wants to pay what. There's nothing wrong with beauty, but function comes first. Boats are for sailing, not scraping and sanding. If your hobby is boat maintenance, fine. If you want to go sailing, replace that varnish with paint.

Albert W. Zahniser III
Zahniser's Marina and Boat Yard
Solomons, MD 20688
(301) 326-3311

General Information

Capacity: 45 feet.
Specialties: Custom cruising sail, power, workboats, and traditional small craft.
Nontraditional modes: Yes.
Experience: Yes.
Preferred paints and glues: Mostly modern.
Sail and/or power: Sail.

Facilities

Design and drafting: Yes.
Lumber storage: 5,000 b.f.
Metal working: Patterns only.

History

Training: 20 years of owning and operating a repair yard.
Selection of location: Home.

Recent Projects

A 30-foot by 10-foot A. Mason (1948) cruising sailboat; an 18-foot by 5-foot Gardner launch; and a 36-foot by 9-foot Herreshoff *Diddikai* cruising sailboat.

Projects in Store

A 36-foot by 9-foot *Diddikai.*

Unusual Tools

All the time, there is no one else to depend on.

Lumber and Hardware

Expensive. The worst problem is large pieces of oak for keel, frame, and frame stock.

The Labor Pool

There is a general lack of experience.

Vocational Training

The ones I have seen think of themselves as artists. They do not have a cost-effective, get-the-job-done approach.

Modern and Traditional Design

Traditional.

Restorations and Replicas

The fact is, the knowledge and skill are dying.

Time and Finish

We are not dependent on new-boat construction financially. Actually it is a burden. We are building for the enjoyment of it, to feel creative. I am tired of repair. Our standards are not compromised, they are only the highest.

Open Statement

Financially, the building operation can be a loser. I use it as an incentive to keep good carpenters, to enhance our reputation, and because I enjoy it.

The Norfolk School of Boatbuilding
Nick Benton, Interim Chief Instructor
Box 371
Norfolk, VA 23510
(Located at the foot of Brooke Ave., Pier B.)
(804) 627-7266

Instructor Nick Benton is best known for his work with his rigging business, The Rigging Gang. He is on leave of absence from the Gang in order to assist in the development of the broad-based program at NSB. The school is part of a waterfront redevelopment program and teaches standard carpentry as well as boatbuilding, repair, and joinerwork. Students are drawn from federal manpower programs, as well as from the private sector.

General Information

Number of builders: Up to 60 students, and five instructors.

Capacity: 40 feet.

Specialties: We attempt to produce as large a variety of craft as possible, giving the student the widest possible range in experience.

Nontraditional modes: Yes. We are constructing both cold-molded and strip-planked boats right now, as a matter of fact.

Preferred paints and glues: We stick principally to modern paints, glues, and adhesives.

Sail and/or power: Most of our boats are pulling or sailing craft.

Facilities

Design and drafting: Yes.

Lumber and storage: 3,000+ b.f. Much of our lumber comes through a student/professional lumberman who buys from many small and deliberately obscure sawyers.

History

As readers may recall, NSB is just in its second year. The school has renovated a huge waterfront warehouse to include industrial shops, classrooms, drafting rooms, lofting floor, reference library, offices, and a ship's store. The school is open to the public during regular class hours.

Recent Projects

A 16-foot box-keel, V-bottomed sloop, oak and pine; a 17-foot Newfoundland skiff of mahogany-on-oak; a 12-foot lapstrake dinghy, also of mahogany-on-oak.

Unusual Tools and Methods

We try to teach our students to keep their spontaneity in problem-solving and use lots of human engineering—wedges, jigs, patterns, molds, wire gizmos, etc. Working with students, you find they do not rely on habit, and frequently we learn from their green insight, instead of just relying on "the way Uncle Buck does it."

Lumber and Hardware

Our supplier seems to have no shortage of good, cheap lumber.

Cooperatives

Most of the local cabinetmaking shops are most cooperative in their efforts to find cedar, oak, and so forth.

The Market

All involved here function as adults on a very realistic level. We love traditional vessels and tend to be partial, but as a school directed at providing the current industry with journeymen, we must turn out people capable of repair, maintenance, and construction in any medium. To stay alive one must consider production. Before the Industrial Revolution, quality was assumed and productivity measured how well someone did at his trade. Things have gotten switched around. How often do we hear someone bray about how long it takes to make a quality product. I have deliberately turned the students away from an artsy-craftsy view of the industry. Reality is what will feed them. Compromise is the name of the game even though quality is infringed upon at times. We attempt to have the students hone their skills here, but they understand that they are doing just that and that they are compromising money and time to learn here. On the outside, it will be totally their decision, and they know all the consequences.

Vocational Training

Students are included in the entire decision-making process as full participants. I encourage decisions being made upon an advantage-vs.-disadvantage basis.

We provide a basic knowledge of essential principles and concepts in an academic course for 12 to 15 weeks at 80 minutes a day. We have 12 to 15 weeks of conventional wood-shop class for 45 minutes in the afternoon. Students' products, such as tool boxes, mallets, sea chests, etc., help to generate exposure to and confidence in woodworking and problem-solving. They are slowly broken into full participation in boat construction. With essential principles and basic skills, they go after specific knowledge; 37 to 40 weeks of building every kind of boat we can cram into the program. They make the decisions regarding materials, method, procedure, etc., as we attempt to de-emphasize replication of others' work in favor of student self-sufficiency.

Restorations and Replicas

Reproductions teach skills geared toward production, and production is the ultimate measure of craftsmanship. A quality product is assumed.

Time and Finish

We teach compromise on an advantage-vs.-disadvantage basis. No morality. No perfection. It is between the individual and the customer. For professionals it is an all-economic decision.

IV.
The Northeast and the Great Lakes

When I thought of New Jersey, it was as the bedroom communities of New York City. I thought of fast food and highways spewing thousands of account executives and stockbrokers into the city every morning and receiving the returning hordes every evening. But in the southern and inland parts of the state, I discovered the Pine Barrens and small towns that had retained some of their colonial grandeur.

In its heyday, coastal New Jersey was a busy area. There were boat shops in every town; dozens, perhaps hundreds, of skiff builders, repairers, and larger operations turning out craft for fishing and the coastal trade. I saw a couple of shops that probably began as settlers' home sites in the early 1700s. Though they've been rebuilt again and again, the heritage is apparent in floors laid with 16-inch-wide pine boards. Hackmatack knees are let into the hewn carrying beams with hooked scarfs. One builder pointed to the extreme shallowness of the well where he built his boats, "My great, great uncle built small hauling barges and shoal fishing sloops here, so he didn't give the floor much pitch."

In Barnegat, New Jersey, my odometer crossed the 100,000-mile mark. I'd started at 74,480 and logged an additional 10,000 miles of hitchhiking. The builders' names were becoming familiar. I was spending fewer nights camping and more evenings with friends. I was going to have to put off my brief trip to the Great Lakes until I had replenished my energy and finances. This, then, was the home stretch. Touring up and down the Jersey Coast, I could find only two active builders where once there had been so many. Charles Hankins is taking up some of the slack, building over a thousand powerboats since 1945. I visited his shop in the late spring of 1978, and he had completed a dozen sea skiffs since the first of that year. Warren Nau is still building the boats that the lifesaving teams race in the surf every summer.

Around New York City, northern New Jersey, Long Island, and southwestern Connecticut, in the web of thruways and identical marinas, there was little to suggest a traditional watercraft survival. Among the "teeming millions" I had expected to find one builder, perhaps even someone using part of an old Manhattan warehouse. The only contacts I located were the handful of people who had just started a New York chapter of the Traditional Small Craft Association. Dick Janda of City Island, Ken Steinmetz of Long Island, Jay Rothbaum, and Amé Hall began their membership drive with a small craft meet. Business seemed to be picking up for the few Connecticut builders I found, though the lack of public access to local waterways can be a problem for their clients.

Although the laws differ from state to state, many have rules that promote private ownership of access roads. This means that while the beach from high tide to low water is (as always) open to the public, that public has no way of getting there. Connecticut has only a handful of open sections for several hundred miles of ocean frontage. Boat owners, particularly those with trailerable small craft, face the same crunch. Even where public landings exist, confusion, displeasure, anger, and/or injury can result when you mix traditional small craft with the high-powered outboard set. This is an issue of increasing magnitude throughout the U.S., and one of those that won't go away without action. Connecticut and Cape Cod builders are likely to be embroiled in this before anybody else, since the problems are most acute in these areas.

Cape Cod shops have increased in number over the last three or four years, as have the number of small craft meets. Bud McIntosh of Dover, New Hampshire, has trained many men in his day, and three or four of these are still in that area. They are a closely allied conclave—a tribute to Bud's inspiration.

In Maine, the grapevine worked faster than I could drive. For the first time, I found that builders had not only heard of my project but were aware of my presence in the area. "Oh, yes, Walter said you'd been by his shop." I would meet people in Kittery on Wednesday and run into them again in South Bristol on Saturday.

Maine is still the traditional heart of traditional watercraft. Since it is the home of two major trade journals, it is also the best-known region. To many outsiders, it is typified by that most tradition-laden word, "Downeast." The word triggers images of a lobsterboat at work along the rocky shore and a terse, gruff character who is more complex than any of his many caricatures. Perhaps the strongest image is that of a people with certain set ways of doing things and a Yankee will that knows no bending. Those who live in Portland say that Downeast begins at Cape Elizabeth. In Rockland, the St. George River marks its beginnings. There is no doubt about Penobscot Bay and its towns such as Deer Isle, however, where Arno Day, fourth-generation boatbuilder

The Downeast scene from Beals Island. The Willis Beal-built Glenda Glenace *is getting some engine repairs on a stormy November afternoon.*

and Downeaster, has a shop. Arno Day's doors are never closed; he commands so much respect in the community that he doesn't need locks. Sitting quietly, speaking in a low, soft, sure voice, Arno had this to say:

> We have a lot of new people here who've gotten into building a quality boat above making money. I think they'll do fine, although they may well end up having to supplement their income with other kinds of work in order to be free to build boats for part of each year. In my shop, a lot of men I have trained leave eventually for better-paying jobs. But I don't blame them, because I believe that we have to return the things that are given us. When I think of all the time that people spent with me, I feel it's only fair that I pass on what I've learned. I don't claim to be perfect; when in a rush to finish a boat, or tired and overworked, I may snap at some guy who didn't do a job a hundred percent as I would like it. But I always feel bad about it in retrospect 'cause I know all the mistakes I've made in my days.
>
> I've been at it a long time and don't have any great claim to fame save being a flexible builder, willing to work with customers. I've had a good time doing it! At the same time, I've come to believe that I'm not infallible, nor capable of doing less than what I believe is right and the best I can do within reasonable time spent on a job. Five years ago, I built a 29-foot pleasure boat for a couple from Boston, retirees. On the shakedown run, while I was talking with the wife in the dinette below, she asked me how many boats like theirs I had built. When she understood that theirs was the only one in the world just like it, that I had spent a good part of a year working with their best needs and interests in mind, this lady who'd spent so much of her life having to fight for every little thing just

stopped cold. Tears came down her cheeks. That moment meant more to me than the biggest check I've ever received.

Piercing gray eyes lit up Arno's face as he dismantled the downeast caricature, piece by piece. He is what a friend once called, "a graduate human being."

My tour of the Great Lakes region (American side) was very brief. In short, I had run out of steam. There is no regional assessment because I feel unqualified to make one. Also, with just five builders listed, it seemed unnecessary. I would like to quote Chip Stulen of Sutton's Bay, Michigan, however.

Compared to the East and West Coasts, the revival is lagging behind here, but it *is* [emphasis mine—P.L.] coming along.

General Information

Number of builders: Forty-nine and two sources, 2.63 men per shop.

Capacity: 22 feet average, and a high of 100 feet.

Specialties: Twenty builders specialize in traditional small craft; 22 are in custom sail or power; seven are in commercial power.

Nontraditional modes: Eleven used nontraditional modes regularly; two would do so, but had no experience at the time of the interview; nine have used them and wouldn't do so again; 24 had not and would not.

Preferred paints and glues: Twenty-five use a mixture of traditional and modern paint, glues, etc.; seven were strictly traditional; and two leaned toward the modern.

Sail and/or power: Twenty-two had experience predominantly in sail or oar power, with minimal experience in power craft; five worked strictly in sail; nine strictly in power; nine had equal experience with both; two had done most of their work with power, but had some sail experience.

Facilities

Design and drafting: Thirty-three have capabilities with both; six more have "limited" capabilities; eight do not design or draft at all.

Lumber storage: The average amount of lumber storage was 3,330 board feet, excluding the Concordia Company's high of 50,000 board feet.

Metal working: Twenty-nine make their own patterns; five have welding facilities; four specified that they cast their own lead keels (I suspect many more do but didn't say); two said they were developing foundry capabilities.

History

Training: Forty builders were self-taught through working on their own, apprenticing in yards, or in a family tradition. Eight had received their primary training from boatbuilding schools.

Recent Projects

The builders listed have produced in recent months some 28 powerboats, from 18-foot weekenders to 65-foot oak draggers. Also among these are 50-foot O. Lie-Nielsen power yachts, simple 21-foot Casco Bay Hampton boats, a dozen lobsterboats, and half again as many pleasure boats with similar hull shapes. Seventy small craft have hit the water, from the usual Whitehalls and wherries to 7-foot 9-inch Murray Peterson tenders. There are double-paddle canoes and a Bolger-designed catboat that has to be seen to be believed. (See the interview with John Wisner.) There are 25 cruising sailboats to 65 feet, the names of Bolger, McIntosh, Atkin, Alden, Herreshoff, Gillmer, Williams, and Winthrop Warner being the most common.

Projects in Store

More of the above; 18 powerboats, 23 small craft, and 11 cruising-sail contracts have been nailed down, with an additional half-dozen "possibles" in each category.

Unusual Tools and Methods

The dory bed and dory timber plate; a combination workbench-tablesaw and shaper; a planking ladder; bottom bevel gauge; rabbet cutting rig for a router; a shop that fits on the back of a truck; finger rings; "keyhole clasps"; spar-sander attachment for an electric drill; vertical-grain fir flooring for oar material; and special wires for holding frames to ribbands.

Lumber and Hardware

Twenty-one said the situation was improving, 22 said it was declining. My personal impression was that builders were beginning to use materials they would have rejected five years ago.

We've got to change our ways from talking of cedar on oak to spruce on whatever. Perhaps preservatives are the answer. I'm willing to learn.

Bob Baker

Lumber is no problem because I can always take the horse to it and get my own.

Douglas Dodge

Lumber hasn't been a problem; I just have to think ahead. I can see a problem in that we're not reseeding it, but when or how severe it will be, I don't know. You have to have capital to jump when it *is* there.

Michael Porter

Lumber quality is down; forests are diminishing due to overdevelopment and housing. I'd like to have my own woodlot some day.

Bill Shuman

Cooperatives

Nineteen were in favor, 23 opposed the idea or thought they were unworkable. I foresee a shift in favor of coops as the younger builders increase in number. Most of those in favor were the more recent entries into the field.

The Market

Eighty-five percent were optimistic; 34 expected a small but stable market; seven saw the future as more or less unlimited.

I pick up the paper and see all these builders I've never heard of—all the potters are building boats now! I wonder how many will be here in five or ten years' time.

Roy Blaney

There have *always* been (and *always* will be) people with money, common sense, and good taste—potential buyers.

Art Brendze

People require more comfort and more electronics.

William Pinney (Concordia Co.)

The wooden lobsterboat is a thing of the past, and I can't blame them either. If I were going into the fisheries I'd think twice before investing in a wooden boat. There *will* always be a market for wooden yachts, though.

Eric Dow

The market has hit bottom and will improve. The individual is turning away from the cookie-cutters to custom work. He's being specific—I want this, and that, and *that* is it.

Bruce Farrin

I would have to say that John Gardner's articles in *National Fisherman* started the ball rolling, and now *WoodenBoat*, by Jon Wilson, is keeping it going. There is no question about it in my mind. From here there may be some slight increase, and then a stable plateau. Probably only two out of a hundred people interested in wooden boats are willing to spend the money to have one built, but that's an improvement.

John Little

The Labor Pool

Eighteen thought the labor situation was good and/or improving, 12 were negative in their outlook. One said there were already too many builders.

There will be fewer and fewer good builders because you can't afford to pay an apprentice a living wage while he learns.

Bunker and Ellis

Quantity is no problem. Many young people just have a dream of working on wooden boats—but not working hard. This is the problem with the romantics. Those from the schools are just great. They have skills and a definite idea of what they are after.

William Pinney

Much enthusiasm among the young may be the saving grace as far as skilled men go.

Seth Persson

I would say that competency is high in small shops.

Bill Shuman

Vocational Training

While only 4.1 percent were negative or thought there were no jobs available for graduates, 27 percent still had serious criticism in the area of time productivity.

It seems to be the thing to do to start a school. I think there's always going to be a need for boatyard workers, but people seem to be putting boatbuilding into the arts-and-crafts category. I think the Eastport School (as opposed to Bath) is a little more realistic.

Roy Blaney

With the question of in-yard vs. school training, it depends on the individual's motivation.

Bill Cannell

There's a need for balance between the "romantics" and the "manufacturers." Schools need to develop in students a sense of speed and efficiency while emphasizing the beauty and quality of wooden boats as well. Some schools are placing too little emphasis on the *whole* of boatbuilding and too much on slathering on more resin.

Sam Guild

After you've learned a few basics at school, you'll come to find that you are then just ready to start learning. I've been at it 41 years and *I'm* still learning.

Sonny Hodgdon

I think they'll make good boat carpenters, but small shops will be fewer and fewer because it takes too long to get into the black ink.

Ronald Rich

Boatbuilding's rewards are in personal pride and satisfaction, not financial, and this must change to some extent.

Jim Odell (Lowell's Boat Shop)

NORTHEASTERN BUILDERS

Luke Allen
Rockport Marine, Inc.
Town Landing
Rockport, ME 04856
(207) 236-2330

General Information

Number of builders: Five.
Capacity: 45 feet.

Specialties: Power pleasure boats.
Nontraditional modes: Only as a last resort.
Experience: Yes.
Preferred paints and glues: Fifty-fifty, oil paints and epoxy glues.
Sail and/or power: Power.

Facilities

Design and drafting: No.
Lumber storage: As needed.
Metal working: Yes.

History

Origin of interest: From childhood.
Training: Self-educated.
Selection of location: Availability of space.

Recent Projects

A 43-foot Eldredge-McInnis powerboat of cedar-on-oak and bronze; a 25-foot Ray Hunt of diagonal mahogany-over-spruce—both of these on speculation.

Projects in Store

Not yet determined.

Lumber and Hardware

Lumber of course is getting snugger and more expensive; hardware is harder to get, but that's it.

Cooperatives

No.

The Market

Always be some.

The Labor Pool

Scarcer and scarcer. The quality of the few is holding up.

Vocational Training

No contact.

Modern and Traditional Design

Traditional.

Time and Finish

We build to suit ourselves and apply our own set of standards.

Bob Baker
Baker Boat Works
29 Drift Road
Westport, MA 02790
(617) 636-3272 (evenings)

The accompanying photograph says it all about Bob's standards. The 28-foot schooner was built by Sam Guild to Bob's design about eight years ago.

General Information

Number of builders: One.

Capacity: 18 feet.

Specialties: Restoration and new, custom, traditional small craft.

Nontraditional modes: No.

Experience: No.

Preferred paints and glues: Like epoxy, but otherwise traditional.

Sail and/or power: Sail.

Facilities

Design and drafting: Yes, as illustrated above.

Lumber storage: 1,000 b.f.

Metal working: Patterns.

History

Origin of interest: I grew up haunting boatyards.

Training: With Fred Tripp and Son, in boatyards.

Selection of location: I'm from here, and better sailing water you can't find.

Recent Projects

A 14-foot 11-inch California Whitehall of cedar and oak, copper-fastened; built a replica of a Newport fishboat (circa 1850). She's 17½ feet by 9 feet by 22 inches.

Projects in Store

I may build a horse-drawn omnibus for the Fall River Historical Society.

Lumber and Hardware

We've got to change our ways from talking of cedar-on-oak to spruce-on-whatever. Perhaps preservatives are the answer. I'm willing to learn.

Bob Baker's well-organized shop and the beginnings of a Whitehall speak well for simplicity. The use of a blackboard for taking notes, doodling, and roughing out ideas is a unique and appealing concept.

Cooperatives

I wouldn't be surprised if *buying* coops had a future. They can go direct to the mill.

The Market

Expanding. As the world runs out of petroleum and energy-intensive materials in general, wood will be more and more viable—perhaps even as a medium in mass production.

Who is Buying and Why

I suspect it may be those who grew up in wooden boats and are fed up to the teeth with fiberglass.

The Labor Pool

High quality/low quantity, and vice versa. I don't believe some of the vocational programs are turning out quality workmen.

Vocational Training

I'm generally positive about the programs—somebody has to be brought along, but perhaps more emphasis ought to be placed on working with hand tools. People don't understand that learning the basics (for example, hand tools and sail training) provides the proper perspective and balance to make working with power tools or steam power sensible.

Modern and Traditional Design

There's not much that's new. It's really old stuff reworked or modern ideas that don't work (designed without environment or medium in mind). Eventually people will return to what *does* work, like traditional small craft.

If you think technology is ugly and destroys the simple pleasures of life, look at Bob's bandsaw and think again. Much of the pleasure of woodworking is in the unadorned design and strength of a given tool.

Time and Finish

It depends on what you are building. Workboats get workboat finish. Structural integrity is the same, regardless of whether it's yachts or working watercraft.

Open Statement

I'm not trying to prove a point or set the world on fire. I like and enjoy working with wood and *sailing*. I have a finite number of days on this earth and I have to enjoy them. I don't get a second chance.

Steve Ballentine
Ballentine's Boat Shop, Inc.
1104 Route 28A
Cataumet, MA 02534
(617) 563-2800

General Information

Number of builders: Four.
Capacity: 40 feet.

Specialties: A Herreshoff 12½, older wooden sail, wooden tenders.
Nontraditional modes: I expect 95 percent will always be traditional.
Preferred paints and glues: I'm inclined toward the product that does the best long-term job.
Sail and/or power: 90 percent sail, 10 percent power.

Facilities

Design and drafting: Yes.
Lumber storage: I keep at least 5,000 b.f. under roof and will be expanding this.
Metal working: Patterns only.

Recent Projects

A Herreshoff 12½, *complete* rebuild; 30 new frames and a floor for an 18-foot Bigelow catboat (1930); a 10-foot Lawley tender (new) of cedar, oak, mahogany, and locust. Restored a 20-foot catboat (1920): stem, deck, moldings, and cockpit floor, along with refastening.

Projects in Store

Another 10-foot Lawley tender and a 22-foot canoe yawl of cedar-on-oak.

Lumber and Hardware

Hardware can always be fabricated—lumber can't! Good supplies of lumber are still available but are becoming *very* expensive. Much is used as cordwood and is buried as housing development expands.

Who is Buying and Why

People who want a possession to be proud of and to take care of. They want to pass on either that boat or that feeling, or both, to their children.

Open Statement

I build and repair wooden boats in the best way possible so that in 25 years, when they may need a major repair, it can be done with the same integrity and longevity that I had in mind when we did our work. I try to keep professionals working here who have the same standards. We store and maintain boats with this in mind, also. We try to maintain the standards of old for people who appreciate them.

Walter Baron
Old Wharf Dory Co.
Box 518
So. Wellfleet, MA 02663
Shop: Bank Street, Wellfleet

In turning out his first 20 prams, Walter nailed down his system. With these prams and repair work as his mainstays, his goal of building "boats people can use, enjoy, and *pay* for . . ." is in sight. Set up on Cape Cod, he is well situated to tap the summer market that strolls by his door.

General Information

Number of builders: One.
Capacity: 25 feet.

Walter Baron blends plywood garboards, cedar, oak, and nice workmanship into a Swampscott dory. A plywood subfloor gives him something to fasten molds to and saves his feet from the tiring effects of an inflexible concrete surface.

Specialties: 7-foot 10-inch flat-bottomed prams; 17-foot Swampscott dories; traditional small craft; and workboats.

Nontraditional modes: No.

Experience: No.

Preferred paints and glues: What works best is what I use. It's about fifty-fifty each way, modern and traditional.

Sail and/or power: Power and rowing.

Facilities

Design and drafting: Limited.

Lumber storage: 800 b.f., not counting plywood.

Metal working: No.

History

Origin of interest: I wanted a boat, built one, and liked it enough to continue.

Training: Mystic's accelerated boatbuilding course and experience.

Selection of location: I was here.

Financing: Working on boats and some loans.

Recent Projects

About 20 prams a year; one 15-foot and one 19-foot skiff of pine, oak, and plywood; and three Swampscotts—two rowing and one rowing/sailing, all with plywood garboards, cedar and oak.

Projects in Store

Develop an 18-foot to 20-foot working skiff and jig it up. Eventually I'd like to get into things like catboats and the local surf boat.

Lumber and Hardware

If the demand increases, the supply will come along. Look at Skookum Fastenings. The trees *are* there; all you have to do is make it profitable for someone to cut it. If they can make a dollar, they'll do it. Hardware is the same way.

Cooperatives

In general, buying works only on a small scale—two or three people in an area going in on an order. These are not real cooperatives but rather cooperation. As for cooperative shops, personalities are often a source of trouble.

The Market

Wooden boats are certainly not getting *less* popular. As people become more aware of wood as a competitive, biodegradable, renewable resource, things will improve. The personal touches will make for greater support for the small businesses in general. A guy can say, "There's the guy that built my boat."

Who is Buying and Why

Whoever needs a pram (or whatever), because they are very competitive in price, lightweight, well built, simple, and easy to maintain.

The Labor Pool

I doubt there are prime woodworking opportunities (jobs) for the products of the boatbuilding schools. The jobs are in repairing—replacing floor timbers, sistering frames, hanging upside down in a bilge with rain dripping down your neck and oil down your arm—*not* in varnish and Whitehalls.

Vocational Training

There aren't any in-yard apprenticeships, and you have to learn somewhere. While building traditional small craft trains people in fits and construction, it might lead people to believe that that is what they are going to be doing. More emphasis on productivity is needed, too.

Modern and Traditional Design

Traditional.

Time and Finish

I try for the best fit I can for the intended purpose; good strong fits for workboats and/or perfect fits for brightwork. *I won't do anything unsound!*

Open Statement

I'm trying to get to the point where I'm building boats people can use, enjoy, and *pay* for—good simple boats that last. With that in mind, I should always be able to make a living.

Willis Beal
Beals Island, ME 04661
(207) 497-5630

The strength in Willis' grip leading me down the dock to view one of his 38-footers was one part genuine excitement and one part muscle. The freshness of his pleasure after a lifetime in the business was an eloquent, silent statement.

General Information

Number of builders: Two.
Capacity: 42 feet.

Specialties: Lobsterboats and pleasure boats.
Nontraditional modes: No.
Experience: No.
Preferred paints and glues: Traditional.
Sail and/or power: Power.

Facilities

Design and drafting: Yes.
Lumber storage: 8,000 b.f.
Metal working: No.

History

Training: With the other local builders.

Recent Projects

A 40-foot by 13-foot cedar-on-oak, galvanized lobsterboat with a 455 Buick engine and one 35½-foot by 11-foot of the same specs.

Projects in Store

One 38½-foot by 11½-foot and one 40-foot by 13-foot.

Lumber and Hardware

I've been getting pretty good lumber; I've only sent one load back in 14 years. Sometimes you have to send the hardware back or get it reworked locally, but we've almost come to expect that.

Cooperatives

Builders are too independent, have different schedules, etc.

The Market

Lots of interest! If I had a yard full of them ready to go, I could sell them all.

The Labor Pool

We work alone, fewer headaches.

Vocational Training

Positive. Students seem to be interested in working with wood and their hands, and in working *hard*.

Modern and Traditional Design

Traditional.

Open Statement

I don't like to brag, but there's no better than these.

Myron "Mike" Bigelow
R. Bigelow and Company, Inc.
140 MacArthur Boulevard
Bourne, MA 02532
(617) 759-5531

This is the home of the Wenaumet Kitten and many classic catboats. On my way to and from Martha's Vineyard I had passed this shop beside Route 28 many times but had never been in. The storage shed under the big shop held more than a dozen Kittens. Though they are down to building just two new ones a year, Mike likes to "keep an eye on our children," as one crew member put it.

General Information

Number of builders: Two.

Capacity: 50 feet.

Specialties: The 13-foot 6-inch by 6-foot by 17-inch (board up) Kitten with a marconi catboat rig. Custom sail and power.

Nontraditional modes: No.

Sail and/or power: Sail.

Facilities

Design and drafting: Yes.

History

Origin of interest: I'm the fifth generation of boatbuilders in my family.

Recent Projects

Two Kittens a year, southern cedar-on-oak with bronze fastenings.

Projects in Store

More of the same.

Lumber and Hardware

Plenty of wood around—it's a matter of not enough demand.

Cooperatives

Not enough demand to bother.

The Market

There is more interest now than in the past few years. I think it will increase slightly and then pretty much stay at that level.

Who is Buying and Why

We sell all over, but it's mostly locals of all ages. Everybody loves this boat.

The Labor Pool

Only if you train your own can you get the men you want.

Open Statement

We expect to be active in repair and just build a boat or two a winter. On that level, we'll be busy for quite a while yet.

Roy Blaney
101 Atlantic Avenue
Boothbay, ME 04537
(207) 633-4247 (home)

Nothing can quite capture the sense of the beamy 37-foot Gillmer ketch under construction in Roy's 38-foot shop. To say it fills the space would be misleading. The building seems to stretch to contain it. The shop door sits amidships, and as you enter, a wall of cedar and oak curves away in every direction.

General Information

Number of builders: Self.

Capacity: 38 feet.

Specialties: Catboats and custom sail.

Nontraditional modes: No.

Experience: No.

Preferred paints and glues: Traditional.

Sail and/or power: 99 percent sail.

Facilities

Design and drafting: No.

Lumber storage: As I go, one boat at a time. No real average.

Metal working: Keels and patterns.

History

Origin of interest: I've been a nut about boats since I was five.

Training: I spent four years at Flyer's in Provincetown.

Selection of location: I set up here in 1953, primarily because there were good support industries: mills, foundries, and so forth.

Recent Projects

A 37-foot Thomas Gillmer ketch drawing 5 feet 2 inches; she's number 23 in 26 years. A 34-foot Stadel ketch. I've built eight Stadels since 1953. A number of Fenwick Williams catboats, around 18 feet. I've occasionally let owners work with me on their boats.

Projects in Store

A 25-foot Williams catboat.

Lumber and Hardware

The quality of local woods has held up—no better or worse than it ever was. Hardware is a terrible problem. Stuff you counted on as standard is now being discontinued. I've even had to try Canada and England for some stuff.

Cooperatives

I don't know. It wouldn't interest me. Builders are pretty independent.

The Market

I pick up the paper and see all these builders I've never heard of—all the potters are building boats now! I wonder how many will be here in five or ten years' time.

Copper rivets poke through the butt blocks of Roy Blaney's well-built ketch; there's little doubt this boat will survive longer than many small boat shops.

Vocational Training

It seems to be the thing to do to start a school. I think there's always going to be a need for boatyard workers, but people seem to be putting boatbuilding in the arts-and-crafts category. I think the Eastport School (as opposed to Bath) is a little more realistic.

Modern and Traditional Design

Traditional.

Time and Finish

I see myself putting more time into a boat than I'm paid for, more time than I should. I usually take on boats I *like*, meaning that I care enough to put my own standards into it—I make a boat I would go sailing in.

Open Statement

I started back when all the boats were wood and even *then* I considered I was doing well if I could survive—put food on the table, etc. I've done it because I care; it's what I enjoy.

Arthur Brendze and Arthur Wester
Brendze and Wester
Box 434A
Kennebunkport, ME 04046
(207) 967-5550

Here are two men who have met head-on the challenge of earning a decent living by building boats, and they are coming up winners through hard work and much self-examination.

A fish-eye view of a 24-foot cedar-on-oak Fenwick Williams yawl.

General Information

Number of builders: Up to six.

Capacity: 55 feet.

Specialties: Our catch phrase, "Traditional Marine Services," means what it says. We are a classic, full-service yacht yard in addition to custom cruising sail or powerboat builders.

Nontraditional modes: No.

Experience: No.

Preferred paints and glues: The best; we go by experience.

Sail and/or power: Fifty-fifty power and sail.

Facilities

Design and drafting: Yes.

Lumber storage: 3,000 to 4,000 b.f.

Metal working: Patterns, welding, and finishing of castings.

History

Origin of interest: I was bitten early. Later, I learned the hard way that good construction would not grow into a business all by itself. After much thought about starting an alternative school centered around boat work, I opted for the common-sense choice—the full-service yard in the real business world.

Training: From a childhood in Marblehead and Swampscott, Massachusetts, I went to work in boatyards.

Selection of location: I liked the town.

Financing: From capitalized earnings.

Recent Projects

Six 21-foot Swampscott dories of pine, cedar, and/or mahogany-on-oak; two 14-footers of the same materials and model; the 24-foot Fenwick Williams double-ended yawl of cedar-on-oak we have cooking out back; and *much* sanding, scraping, hauling, launching, and repair work.

Projects in Store

The good Lord willing, after all the scraping, etc., is done, we will build a classic boat our own way, one a year eventually. We are thinking about a 35-foot Herreshoff on speculation after the yawl.

Lumber and Hardware

The longer you are at it, the easier the supply becomes; neither is a horrible barrier any more.

Cooperatives

If enough folks could make it in the business long enough to organize, it would be a help.

The Market

Let there be no mistake: if you want to build, you have got to swim against the mainstream of a ready-made, showroom-bred society all day, every day. Most boats today are built with little or no recognition of common sense or good taste. They only look like real boats in a picture or at a boat show. Imitation boats are what are hot today with those who find the truth too much work and trouble. This does not exclude other materials; occasionally we see a truthful plastic boat.

There have *always* been (and *always* will be) people with money, common sense, and good taste. I've come to the conclusion that there is a world of difference between boating and yachting, boaters and yachtsmen, and most of all, people who "go sailing" and people who are sailors. Don't confuse the two worlds or markets to which they belong. The difference between the two can be ascertained by asking if they'd consider drinking fine wine (whether they consider "fine wine" Gallo or Chateau Rothschild) out of a paper cup, or would insist on the proper-shaped glass. Cheer up, Mates! In my time the market has grown larger. We see not only the old-time sailors who have always known what's good, but also folks who are completely new to yachting, and even ex-plastic people, joining the traditional crew. And "traditional" should not be confused with tradition-bound, which allows no new information or technique.

The Labor Pool

There are the old-timers, most of whom have retired or passed on. We are extremely fortunate to have on our crew a man who was a junior member of this group. Then there are the "boatbuilders" who have done their six-month to two-year apprenticeship and are ready to play master (for which they still lack 10 years' experience). But don't tell them they have to paint a bottom. Most of this crew are scared to death that they'll find out it's hard work to "mess about with boats." Alas, if you go through enough years, and enough prospects, you may come up with a workable crew of dedicated, boat-oriented people. If we had a work force trained as our finish man was in Germany, then there would be no doubt as to the success of the traditional boatyard in today's market place.

Vocational Training

Don't confuse boatbuilding schools with other alternative education programs that use boatbuilding as a means to an educational end. There is value here, and it may result in some decent boats built, but master builders won't be turned out.

Restorations and Replicas

Without the skills, you will soon have nothing.

Time and Finish

Anyone who has a grip on what it means to be building a classic wooden boat is going to have to make only the best fits that are within his capabilities. If he does less, he will soon find that the truth dictates he can switch to plastic—an easier way to make a living. Combine money, common sense, and good taste with honest craftsmanship and you come up with a product as close to impeccable as any man can produce. This is Truth, and every line, board, and screw may be asked at some point to prove it!

Don't ask me why I possess these feelings; it's probably for the same reasons I get excited about the salmon swimming upstream to spawn or the Declaration of Independence. Some of us are just plain addicted and must pursue the truths of well-built boats. Such is apparently my fate.

Amos Brown
Amos Brown & Co.
Deep River Marina
Deep River, CT 06417
(203) 526-5560

General Information

Number of builders: Three to four.
Capacity: 30 feet.
Specialties: Traditional small craft.
Nontraditional modes: No.
Experience: No.

Preferred paints and glues: Traditional paints but modern glues (mainly epoxies).

Sail and/or power: Fifty-fifty each way.

Facilities

Design and drafting: Yes.

Lumber storage: 1,000 b.f.

Metal working: No.

History

Origin of interest: I've always owned and tinkered with boats.

Training: Apprenticing with active builders.

Selection of location: Access to activity on Long Island Sound.

Financing: Savings from repairing boats.

Recent Projects

Mostly cedar-on-oak and copper; a 16-foot Whitehall; an 11-foot Herreshoff pram; 10-foot dory tenders; 13-foot Pete Culler Good Little Skiffs.

Projects in Store

A 26-foot catboat and several dory tenders.

Lumber and Hardware

Everything is getting scarcer; quality is going down in lumber. Hardware lines are being reduced and prices are skyrocketing.

Cooperatives

No experience with any, but it sounds sensible.

The Market

It depends on what glass does. Right now, we can't effectively compete on price.

Who is Buying and Why

Traditional boat lovers who like my work and products.

The Labor Pool

A very difficult situation in this area; poor wages and an uncertain future.

Modern and Traditional Design

Traditional in the small-boat field. Modern lines and designs can't compete with Gardner, Herreshoff, Chapelle, et al.

Restorations and Replicas

Skills preservation first.

Time and Finish

Structural integrity can't be compromised; nonstructural imperfections can slip by if they "look right."

Open Statement

Our shop is set up to build three or four small boats simultaneously. We are doing this, but costs can be almost impossible to recoup. Check the price of a thickness planer these days, copper rivets, lumber, and the *time* required to do quality work. We are working to build quality wooden boats that can compete with fiberglass not only in price, but in appreciation by buyers who may believe the maintenance and repair of wood is not worth the extra pleasure of ownership.

Bunker and Ellis
Manset, ME 04656
(207) 244-3033

Bunker and Ellis, two of Maine's best-known lobsterboat builders, were "awful busy" when I dropped in. There were chips flying off a rapidly lengthening rabbet, and paper-fine, three-inch-wide shavings coming off a cabinet scraper from the stem.

General Information

Number of builders: Two.

Capacity: 46 feet.

Specialties: Lobsterboats, yachts, and outboard skiffs.

Sail and/or power: Power.

Facilities

Design and drafting: Yes.

Lumber and Hardware

It's better since Pineo Lumber Co. started cutting oak.

The Labor Pool

There will be fewer and fewer good builders 'cause you can't afford to pay an apprentice a living wage while he learns.

Bill Cannell
William Cannell Boatbuilding
P.O. Box 911
Camden, ME 04843
(207) 236-4592

I worked with Bill for 18 months during my apprenticeship in Maine, so I must admit to a certain prejudice in his favor. We need more men like him.

General Information

Number of builders: One.

Capacity: My new shop is 72 feet long, but I don't think I'll take on anything quite that big *this* week. Let us say 45 feet.

Specialties: Traditional small craft.

Nontraditional modes: No.

Experience: No.

Preferred paints and glues: Fifty-fifty modern and traditional.

Sail and/or power: Sail.

Facilities

Origin of interest: Through building surfboards.

Training: Sam E. Guild, Ted Brewer, and Walter Simmons.

Selection of location: I like it.

Financing: Savings.

Bill Cannell has become known for his work with these Virginia cedar, mahogany, and oak Murray Peterson tenders. They're 7' 9" long.

Recent Projects

Three Peterson tenders, 7 feet 9 inches, of Virginia cedar, mahogany, oak, and yellow metal. A 17-foot light, double-ended pulling boat of my own design. It's been a good success. I've just finished a lapstrake Whitehall for the *Whitehawk*.

Projects in Store

Set up this new shop and get cracking.

Lumber and Hardware

No problem in either.

Cooperatives

Definitely, but they are limited in application. For example, the heating bill of a large space is going to break you if you've warmed the whole building for two members' use.

The Market

As far as traditional methods, there is going to be growth in the market and materials, both supply and demand.

Who is Buying and Why

Bill Peterson is my broker. I build for his clients.

Bill Cannell fits the sheerstrake on a 7′ Bill Peterson skiff. (Jennifer Cannell photo)

The Labor Pool

For a small builder the quantity is there but not the quality. For a larger shop, neither is available. I see no change in the future due to good people wanting to be on their own, not working for others.

Vocational Training

In-yard training is the best, but hard to find. With the question of in-yard vs. school training, it depends on the individual's motivation.

Modern and Traditional Design

I prefer traditional yacht design as opposed to workboats. I think there will be more modern designs in traditional modes and that older designs will be dug up and dusted off to suit the new market.

Restorations and Replicas

Both are important, but more emphasis and attention should be given to replication than there is at present. The Apprenticeshop in Bath is the best example of a cost-efficient, creative operation, in my opinion.

Time and Finish

I try to do the best job possible, yacht finish, without exception.

Open Statement

It makes me mad when someone comes along and, having felt they've paid a lot for a boat, goes out and abuses and misuses it. Also, they should rely less on books, articles, and glossy photographs, and more on experience. Use it before you buy it.

William Pinney, Jr. (President)
Concordia Co., Inc.
South Dartmouth, MA 02748
(617) 999-1381

Leo Telesmanick (Manager)
Beetle Cat Division
Smith Neck Road
South Dartmouth, MA 02748
(617) 996-9971

Concordia's Beetle Cat Division is the second oldest wood-production shop in the country geared toward the recreational market. The Division sits across the inlet from Concordia's wooden-boats-only repair and storage facilities. As you look across, the yard's influence is evident in the high ratio of wood to fiberglass yachts at anchor.

General Information

Number of builders: We have 10 woodworkers and an overall crew of 60, including the yacht yard.
Capacity: 12 feet to 55 feet.
Specialties: Custom boatbuilding and 40 to 50 Beetle Cats a year.
Nontraditional modes: Yes, glued-strip.
Experience: Yes, glued-strip.
Preferred paints and glues: We're inclined toward what works.
Sail and/or power: 70 percent sail to 30 percent power.

The backbone (upper right) *is placed over the jig and the frames are bent over it* and *the form to be hooked into the one-sided cleats on the lowest ribband.*

Almost every piece is traced from one of the patterns hanging on the wall. Patterns are often replaced and/or corrected as part of the Beetle Cat production system.

Facilities

Design and drafting: Yes.

Lumber storage: 50,000 b.f.

Metal working: Welding, and patterns for casting.

History

The yard has been around 40 years; I bought the business in 1969.

Recent Projects

A 48-foot gaff-rigged schooner of cedar on oak; *re*built a 50-foot Indonesian ketch. One big boat a year for many years.

Projects in Store

Possible 40-foot gaff schooner also of cedar and oak; continue Beetle Cat production as always. The Cats are cedar, oak, and bronze, and the 1978 price is $1795, less sail, f.o.b. South Dartmouth. Price subject to change. These 12-foot 4-inch by 6-foot by 2-foot (board down) gems are an institution here!

Lumber and Hardware

Lumber is no problem; that is, cedar and oak are okay. Teak and mahogany (all the imported woods) are high-priced for declining quality. Quantity and quality of the local woods are holding up. Hardware gets worse and worse and worse.

Cooperatives

No.

The Market

Small but stable. Traditional boats are going downhill; they are poorer and poorer in quality and fewer in numbers. People require more comfort and more electronics.

Who is Buying and Why

Our customers are people who like traditional boats and realize that it's sometimes cheaper to build one-off in wood than in glass.

The Labor Pool

Quantity is no problem. Many young people just have a dream of working on wooden boats—but not working hard. This is the problem with romantics in the field. Those from the vocational training schools are just great. They have skills and a definite idea of what they are after.

Vocational Training

As long as they keep weeding out the dreamers, they'll be turning out men and women who can produce. Students should know their skills first, be wood fanatics second.

Modern and Traditional Design

Traditional.

Time and Finish

It is entirely up to what the owner wants within the limits of structural integrity. If he wants to leave panels unplaned, that's fine with us, or we can work toward the ultimate yacht.

Open Statement

It is difficult for small businesses to survive. Shops of more than five employees are forced to expand any way they can by regulations, cost, etc. We have to grow or sell out.

Arno Day
Deer Isle, ME 04627
(207) 359-8807

As I said earlier, here is a "graduate" human being and a fine boatbuilder.

General Information

Number of builders: Up to two others.
Capacity: 36 feet.
Specialties: Lobsterboats and yachts, custom sail and power to the tune of about two a year.
Nontraditional modes: Not really.
Experience: No.
Preferred paints and glues: About half each—traditional and modern.
Sail and/or power: Power.

Facilities

Design and drafting: Yes.
Lumber storage: 3,000 b.f.
Metal working: Patterns.

History

Origin of interest: It's in my blood, literally.
Training: I'm the fourth generation.
Selection of location: I'm from here.

Along the Maine coast, there are conflicting opinions regarding the wood versus fiberglass markets for lobsterboats. About half the builders shared Arno Day's opinion that lobstermen are returning to wood in large numbers, having tried fiberglass without success.

Recent Projects

A 30-foot lobsterboat, cedar-on-oak, Everdur-fastened; a 26-foot pleasure boat of the same specs.

Projects in Store

Haul and rebuild a 50-year-old, 30-foot, German-built Atlantic class sloop. A 28-foot and two 26-foot lobsterboats, to be followed by a 28-foot Lyle Hess-designed cutter (big sister to *Seraffyn*). Wood is not dead yet.

Lumber and Hardware

Manufacturers are geared toward stock, mass-ordered items. The small custom builders have to work a boat or two ahead, do their own hunting, etc. You can get the items you need; it's just slow. Retailers want to do everything by forklift, convenience; not work with their hands and brains. The average sawyer doesn't know much about what a stem is, or how to cut one to suit a builder. Fewer still are interested in slowing down production long enough to do so.

Cooperatives

Builders are too independent and too different here.

The Market

My customers are people looking for a hand-crafted wooden boat, not boats squirted out of a tube. There'll always be a small, limited custom market.

The Labor Pool

We have a lot of new people here who've gotten into building a quality boat above making money. I think they'll do fine, although they may well end up having to supplement their income with other kinds of work in order to be free to build boats for part of each year. In my shop, a lot of men I have trained leave eventually for better-paying jobs. But I don't blame them, because I believe that we have to return the things that are given to us.

Vocational Training

When I think of all the time people spent with me, I feel it's only fair that I pass

Arno Day's brother, Frank, has his own shop in Brooklin, Maine. Generally, photography in boat shops consists of shooting large objects in relatively small spaces with poor lighting, but Frank Day's was a pleasant exception.

on what I've learned. I don't claim to be perfect; when in a rush to finish a boat, or tired and overworked, I may snap at some guy who didn't do a job 100 percent as I would like it. But I always feel bad about it in retrospect, 'cause I know all the mistakes *I've* made in *my* days. The schools are turning out a pretty good supply of good, well-rounded, repair, hauling, storage, and new construction men. My advice to young people is to go to the schools. You can learn more in less time, and with fewer mistakes, than you can learn just building a boat on your own. Then get a job in a boatyard. If you have what it takes, you *will* get out on your own. It takes a long time to build a reputation. I've been at it 38 years and had a family reputation to help me out. The young people just starting today have a tougher and longer way to go to build that reputation.

Time and Finish

I've been at it a long time and don't have any great claim to fame save being a flexible builder, willing to work with customers. I've had a good time doing it! At the same time I've come to believe I'm not infallible, *nor* capable of doing less than what I believe is right. I do the best I can do within reasonable time spent on the job.

Open Statement

Five years ago, I built a 29-foot pleasure boat for a couple from Boston, retirees. On the shakedown run, while talking with the wife in the dinette below, she asked me how many boats like theirs I had built. When she understood that theirs was the only one in the world just like it—that I had spent a good part of a year working with their best interests and needs in mind—this lady who'd spent so much of her life having to fight for every little thing just stopped cold. Tears came down her cheeks. That moment meant more to me than the biggest check I've ever received.

Basil Day
Georges River Boatbuilding and Repair
Booker Street
Thomaston, ME 04861
(207) 354-2465 (home)

One of Martha's Vineyard's best-known fishermen had a boat built by Basil some 27 years ago. He thought Basil was a little slow in delivery. Nowadays, however, the crew at Georges River are known for their speed.

General Information

Number of builders: Four to five.
Capacity: 55 feet.
Specialties: Spars and custom sail and power.
Nontraditional modes: Yes.
Experience: Yes.
Preferred paints and glues: Fifty-fifty modern and traditional.
Sail and/or power: Both equal.

Facilities

Design and drafting: I work from models and do drafting. We have access to naval architects if things need to go further than that.
Lumber storage: 1,500 b.f.
Metal working: Patterns only.

History

Origin of interest: From my father.
Training: Also from my Pa.
Selection of location: I'm from here.

Recent Projects

85-foot and 115-foot spars for the 92-foot ketch *Whitehawk* (see *WoodenBoat,* No. 25); a 25-foot cedar-on-oak Friendship sloop of the Pemaquid model with a teak interior; and the interior of a 25-foot Jarvis Newman hull.

Projects in Store

Two 30-foot Hurricane Island pulling boats, strip-planked of cedar-on-oak, bronze-fastened. These are for the Outward Bound program. Following the pulling boats, we will be finishing a fiberglass patrol boat for the State of Maine, also building two sets of masts.

Lumber and Hardware

You can get the good lumber if you'll pay the price. Hardware is hard to get and the quality is going down.

Cooperatives

Don't think so. Builders up this way have limited capital; don't have much money to fool around with.

The Market

There'll always be wooden boats built, but it's probably been more down than up over the last five to 10 years.

The Labor Pool

You've got to have men with experience, that's all there is to it.

Vocational Training

I think it's a good thing. Their work habits are okay. We've had one or two from the school who worked out well.

Modern and Traditional Design

Traditional.

Restorations and Replicas

They should get equal support.

Time and Finish

It depends on the use, work or pleasure, and what the owner is willing to spend. There is a point where I'd rather not build a boat than throw one together.

Open Statement

We started from scratch 30 years ago and we're still going strong. We haven't been out a day's work since we opened our doors.

Douglas Dodge
Gower's Boat Shop
Beals, ME 04611
(207) 497-2838 (home)

General Information

Number of builders: One.
Capacity: 50 feet.
Specialties: Power and sail custom boatbuilding.
Nontraditional modes: No.
Experience: One strip-planked boat.
Preferred paints and glues: Traditional.
Sail and/or power: 99 percent power.

Facilities

Design and drafting: Powerboats only.
Lumber storage: 10,000 to 15,000 b.f.
Metal working: Welding.

History

Origin of interest: My grandfather built the first Jonesport or Beals model lobsterboat.

Training: On my own and it's in my blood.

Selection of location: I'm from Beals.

Recent Projects

I helped start and run the Washington County Vocational Technical Institute's boatbuilding course from 1970 to December 1974. A 35-foot by 11-foot cedar-on-ash powerboat and a 40-foot model of cedar-on-oak.

Projects in Store

A 50-foot lobsterboat of cedar-on-oak and two fiberglass hulls to finish.

Lumber and Hardware

Lumber is no problem, because I can always take the horse to it and get my own. No problems with hardware, either.

Cooperatives

Too much jealousy around here.

The Market

There'll always be a market for wooden boats. I don't think the glass boats are being put together well. The boat is only as good as the workman, be it glass or wood. Look at fishermen—they trust a wooden boat to last 30 years.

The Labor Pool

The good man won't work for four dollars an hour when he can make four times as much building houses or whatever. And that's easier work. The only way you'll get a good builder is if he likes it. The work is just too hard.

Vocational Training

There's a problem in *one* school with too much free money, veteran's benefits, food stamps, etc. That makes it a big ripoff. If they had the right people, the idea is fine; the problem is the teachers.

Modern and Traditional Design

I like modern designs, particularly my own. I'm prejudiced, you might say.

Time and Finish

I do the best I know how, regardless of whether it's the keel or the finish work.

Open Statement

I'm making a living doing something I enjoy. The difference between a good builder and a bad one is that the former happens to like wiring and plumbing as much as he does woodwork.

Eric Dow
Eric Dow Boatbuilder
P.O. Box 108
Brooklin, ME 04616
(207) 359-2277

General Information

Number of builders: One.

Capacity: 30 feet.

Eric Dow clamps the garboard to one of the five 13′5″ peapods he has built. The pads keep the clamps from marring the soft cedar.

Specialties: A 13-foot 5-inch peapod, 15-foot and 20-foot powerboats of my own design (see *WoodenBoat*, No. 21).
Nontraditional modes: No.
Experience: Glued-strip only.
Preferred paints and glues: Fifty-fifty each, modern and traditional.
Sail and/or power: Equal.

Facilities

Design and drafting: Yes.
Lumber storage: 3,000 to 4,000 b.f.
Metal working: No.

History

Origin of interest: I grew up with boats.
Training: Washington County Vocational Technical Institute.
Selection of location: Had a shop here.
Financing: Through the family.

Recent Projects

Five peapods, a 15-foot outboard boat, and a 22-foot Friendship sloop.

Lumber and Hardware

I don't see any problem in lumber, although we may have to work harder to get it. Quantity and quality are there. Hardware: It seems as if every so often they drop stuff off the line, particularly bronze. It's getting impossible to open a catalog and find what you want.

Cooperatives

Not around here. Boatbuilders are too much like fishermen, too independent.

The Market

The wooden lobsterboat is a thing of the past, and I can't blame them, either. If I were going into the fisheries I'd think twice before investing in a wooden boat. There *will* always be a market for wooden yachts, though.

The Labor Pool

Quantity is up, quality is down. Places are just cranking out boat people, not builders. In any case, I don't know if there will be any work for them, particularly in the future.

Vocational Training

I think they could teach a lot more in less time with more and better instructors and a better student-to-teacher ratio. Basically, the schools are a good idea.

Modern and Traditional Design

Traditional.

Restorations and Replicas

The money needed is the determining factor. Remember that even when you can afford to fix up an old boat, you will still have an old boat.

Time and Finish

I have a definite set of standards that I won't compromise, but I'm not a perfectionist. I do take pride in turning out a quality boat. On a quality scale of one to ten, I'd say I'm a seven.

Bruce Farrin
Farrin's Boatshop
Sproul Road
Walpole, ME 04573
(207) 563-5506

Early in 1978, winter storms demolished Bruce's shop and the almost-complete hull of the boat within. He has since moved inland and built a fine new shop and a 32-foot lobsterboat. Not bad work for a year.

General Information

Number of builders: One.
Capacity: 45 feet.
Specialties: Custom boatbuilding.
Nontraditional modes: No.
Experience: No.
Preferred paints and glues: Traditional.
Sail and/or power: 60 percent power, 40 percent sail.

Facilities

Design and drafting: Access.
Lumber storage: I keep a *minimum* of 1,000 b.f.
Metal working: Patterns.

History

Origin of interest: The necessity of making a living.

Training: I spent 9½ years at Gamage's yard.

Recent Projects

A 32-foot by 11-foot 5-inch by 3-foot mahogany-over-oak (bronze) powerboat; a 33-foot sportfisherman was the boat destroyed by the flood and storms (see *National Fisherman*, February 1979). A 32-foot handliner is what we have going here now.

Projects in Store

A 33-foot fisherman and a possible 45-foot dragger.

Lumber and Hardware

No problem, if you have the bucks.

Cooperatives

It has been tried here. There are not enough builders, and organization takes too much time.

The Market

The market has hit bottom and will improve. The individual is turning away from cookie-cutters to custom work. He's being specific—I want this, and that, and *that* is it.

Modern and Traditional Design

I like them both equally.

Restorations and Replicas

There are things to be learned from both.

Time and Finish

If it's worth doing, it's worth doing well.

Open Statement

I think the work speaks for itself. If it didn't, we wouldn't be here.

Jeff Fogman
Barrington Boat Shop
Swain Road
Barrington, NH 03825
(603) 664-9752

Like many young builders, Jeff built his home adjoining his shop.

General Information

Number of builders: One.

Capacity: 60 feet.

Nontraditional modes: Maybe.

Experience: Strip, yes.

Preferred paints and glues: Traditional.

Sail and/or power: Sail 60 percent, power 40 percent.

Jeff Fogman is kept busy with a 34′ cutter and a 32′ powerboat.

Facilities

Design and drafting: Drafting capabilities only.

Lumber storage: 10,000 b.f.

Metal working: Yes.

History

1968-1970: built a 40-foot ketch alone; that experience led to my working for D.C. McIntosh on a 40-foot ketch and a 48-foot schooner. McIntosh's statement to me about my skill level then (having built a 40-foot ketch on my own) was that I "probably knew enough to sweep [his] floor and hand him some tools." After leaving McIntosh's, I cruised the ketch for a year or so, sold it down south, and returned to this area to set up a shop. The proximity of McIntosh as well as the availability of native materials were the two factors that decided me on this area.

I financed this effort with the sale of my boat and the assistance of the bank.

Tom Colvin's conception of what a cruising boat is, or should be, has been a positive influence on what I, as a builder, like to see incorporated into the designs I build.

Recent Projects

A 34-foot McIntosh-designed cutter; also a 32-foot powerboat, a 40-foot schooner, and a 17-foot wherry—all designed by McIntosh.

Projects in Store

To build boats that have long lives.

Lumber and Hardware

If you can make patterns for casting and pick out wood standing, in this region you are set.

Cooperatives

Not for us, but perhaps it is viable for a group of amateur builders each hoping to own a boat.

The Market

Every builder I know can pick and choose the work he is presented with.

Who is Buying and Why

People with taste *and* money. Why from us? Because they like our work.

The Labor Pool

Quantity is great, quality is very spotty. To quote a friend of mine, "Every person who owns two copies of *WoodenBoat* seems to feel he/she is a builder."

Vocational Training

It's a beginning point, I suppose.

Modern and Traditional Design

There is something to be gained from each.

Restorations and Replicas

It seems to me that the two are mutually interdependent.

Time and Finish

Form follows function by definition; therefore, one suspects the degree of finish is dictated by the customer's pocketbook and desires.

Linwood Gamage
Gamage Shipbuilders, Inc.
South Bristol, ME 04568
(207) 644-8181

The Gamage yard is well known. This is the yard that built the topsail schooner *Shenandoah* and the schooner *Harvey Gamage*. This last was named for the yard's founder. Though working increasingly in steel, they intend to stay in wood as long as possible.

General Information

Capacity: 140 feet by 31 feet.
Specialties: Custom sail and power.
Nontraditional modes: No.
Experience: No.
Preferred paints and glues: 50 percent traditional.
Sail and/or power: Power.

Facilities

Design and drafting: No.
Lumber storage: 5,000 b.f.
Metal working: Patterns and welding.

The topsail schooner Shenandoah *under construction. (Ivan Flye photo)*

History

Origin of interest: In family; yard founded by father, Harvey, in 1925.

Training: In the family yard.

Recent Projects

A 65-foot Bud McIntosh-designed schooner for a circumnavigator, white-oak-on-oak, cedar decks, galvanized fastenings. A 36-foot lobsterboat, mahogany-on-oak, Everdur fastenings.

Projects in Store

Nothing in wood at present.

Lumber and Hardware

Lumber is getting better. Second growth is sometimes better in grade than virgin timber. Hardware is getting better, also.

Cooperatives

I don't think so, not in this business. This requires too much supply-and-demand pricing.

The Market

I think it's gradually going down, less interest in boats.

The Labor Pool

Way down and getting worse. Nobody's interested in learning the trade.

Modern and Traditional Design

Traditional.

Vocational Training

There's no light and easy way to build wooden ships, and people today seem to want only light and easy jobs.

Time and Finish

I have my own standards; I would rather work quality than quantity.

SOURCE

John Gardner
Small Craft Shop
Mystic Seaport Museum, Inc.
Mystic, CT 06355
(203) 536-2631

In 45,000 miles, I heard more compliments for, and inquiries about, John than any other person by far. This book is dedicated to him. Readers of *National Fisherman* and *WoodenBoat* are thoroughly familiar with his insight and knowledge. To say much more would be a mistake. It would fall short of the mark. I will say that his contributions to the field are equaled only by the strengths and qualities of his personality.

General Information

I head the small-craft program at Mystic, where we are now building boats for

John Gardner, the dean of traditional small craft.

The four photographs accompanying John Gardner's interview were taken in Seattle in the floating barge/shop of master shipwright Frank Prothero. Not easily impressed, Frank remarked to the author, "Now that Mr. Gardner, he *seems to have his head on straight. I'd sure like to meet* him.*"*

sale, in addition to our other activities, which include teaching, research—both historical and technical—writing and publication, collection of boats, their preservation, and their exhibition.

It should be added that in answering these questions I cannot confine myself merely to what applies to Mystic, as I do not, and cannot, draw any hard-and-fast line between what I do at Mystic and what I do as a writer and a contributor to the *National Fisherman* and other publications.

Specialties: Working small craft—oar and sail—of the North Atlantic coast before the advent of the gasoline engine. They were perfected in an area extending roughly from the Chesapeake to Newfoundland. Also the pleasure craft derived from these workboats or closely related to them. This not only defines the scope of specialization now adopted by Mystic Seaport Museum but conforms to my major personal interest as well.

History

I cannot remember when I first began to use woodworking tools and to work around boats. As a small boy, nearly 70 years ago, on the home place of Passamaquoddy Bay in Calais, Maine, I helped to build boats for our own use, and spent many fascinating hours hanging around boat shops. Later on, after college and several years as a teacher, I hired on as a boatbuilder in Marblehead, Massachusetts. I did this at the beginning of World War II and continued to work at the trade until 1969, when I came to Mystic Seaport Museum to set up its small-craft program. This program was the first of its kind in the country, and the first to provide hands-on instruction in boatbuilding for amateurs. I never attempted to set up in business for myself, preferring instead to work for wages in order to have as much free time as possible for research and writing. In 1951, I entered upon a period of close collaboration with Howard I. Chapelle. This was shortly after the publication of my first article on the Hammond dory in the *Maine Coast Fisherman*. That article began my association with that publication and its successor, *National Fisherman*. I'm still a regular contributor on boatbuilding history, design, and methods. Since coming to Mystic Seaport, I have participated in developing a diversified small-craft program that is taking an active part in the current revival of traditional small craft for recreational use. This revival is changing the American boating scene, and changing it for the better.

Recent Projects

Boats recently built at Mystic Seaport in connection with its small-craft program (some for use at the museum and some for sale) include Marblehead dory skiffs (rigged for sailing as well as for rowing), Swampscott dories, Rangeley Lake boats, a Piscataqua River wherry, yacht tenders after Herreshoff and Nevins, and small flatiron skiffs. These are all clinker-planked and range in length from 10 to 17 feet.

Projects in Store

I foresee no major changes in the small-craft program here, which I expect to continue supervising for some years yet. In addition, I shall continue researching and writing for the *National Fisherman* and other publications, with possibly an additional book or two.

Unusual Tools

Boatbuilder's specialized wooden planes are superior tools. The directions for making them, which I published in the *National Fisherman* some years ago, were the first to be printed and are still the most complete. Boatbuilder's scrapers, filed on a 45-degree bevel and turned with a burnisher, are superior to power sanders for many jobs, and they don't throw clouds of unwholesome dust.

Lumber and Hardware

Use local lumber. Search out the small mills on the back roads that don't advertise and establish working relationships with them. Let them know what you want over the long haul and arrange for them to set it aside for you when it becomes available. Put it in storage and have it available for future use when you need it. There is still plenty of lumber growing; the bottlenecks are in cutting and distribution. The best source today is the small local mill, which can still be found in most sections of the country. The situation with hardware is not good. It no longer pays to manufacture many of the items once produced in bulk, when the demand was greater. This applies to fastenings and fittings of all sorts, especially for working sail. It is here that a large cooperative might be able to exercise some leverage, but how much remains to be seen. I am afraid we shall be obliged to make do with much less in the way of hardware, fittings, and fastenings than was available a generation ago. Also, when we have items cast to order at the local foundry, we will have to pay through the nose.

This struck the author as the finest workmanship he'd seen carried out by one man on such a tremendous scale. For Frank Prothero, only the best will do. The fits on these 4" and 6" sided timbers and hanging knees are faultless.

The teak deck on this 65-foot schooner is an awe-inspiring example of the craftsman's art. Like John Gardner, Frank Prothero has had a lifelong involvement with boats. The Protheros have been boat and shipbuilders on Lake Union for over a hundred years. Frank was just 19 when he built his first 50' schooner: "I was working 12 hours a day in the family yard, so it took me a year or two to complete her in my spare time."

Cooperatives

These would appear to have great possibilities, provided they can be organized on a scale large enough to be effective, and if they are run in a businesslike manner. Besides lumber, such coops would naturally handle hardware, paint, and other materials and supplies. No sharp line need be drawn for professionals and amateurs. Both have the same interest in obtaining quality products and materials with the savings in price that a buying cooperative can provide.

The Market

The demand for wooden boats has picked up in the last few years, and this trend will continue, I believe. The price differential between boats of wood and those of reinforced plastics will shift increasingly in favor of wood as the cost of petrochemical products rises. Furthermore, emerging public awareness of serious health hazards presently existing in the manufacture of fiberglass boats will require the installation of expensive health safeguards for the work force, sending the cost of fiberglass boats much higher.

The Labor Pool

The supply of labor depends on wages. As long as the industry cannot or refuses to pay wages comparable to other skilled trades, and particularly those that are unionized, it will have a labor problem.

Vocational Training

Boatbuilding schools are new and few, and it is too soon to judge their effectiveness. Americans, however, have been oversold on schools and the academic formula in general. Up to now, most boatbuilders either picked up the trade on

One of a pair of booby hatches gleams in the light of bare bulbs in Frank Prothero's shop.

their own or learned it piecemeal on the job. It remains to be seen what impact, if any, will be made on the trade by the graduates from newly formed schools and apprentice courses.

Restorations and Replicas

This is mainly a museum question. In the past, irreparable damage was frequently done to a unique surviving example of an historic craft in the attempt to restore it to something approaching a new boat. Now, it is generally conceded that such extensive rebuilding and refinishing was a mistake. The old boat is recognized for what it is—an historic document—and for the purposes of exhibit, we build a replica.

Time and Finish

There are all kinds of boats for all kinds of people, for all kinds of uses. At Mystic Seaport we can take our time and are inclined to be fussier than is usual in most professional shops. But in building a working peapod, we are not as fussy with the finish as we would be with a varnished Herreshoff yacht tender. Both must be structurally solid and tight, of course.

Open Statement

Boatbuilding instruction at Mystic Seaport is recreational and avocational rather than vocational. There is no essential conflict, however, between the two. The two support and reinforce each other. Increased amateur boatbuilding activity cultivates and spreads interest in, and appreciation of, boats, and can only result in more business for professionals. I once knew an old boatbuilder who complained that backyard builders were taking the bread out of his mouth. He was wholly mistaken. No one can appreciate the fine points of wooden boatbuilding, as well as the effort and skill required, better than the amateur who has built, or who has attempted to build, a boat. Backyard builders of small boats frequently turn to professionals to have a larger one built. And if they insist on good work, they are generally willing to pay the price.

Sam E. Guild
S.E. Guild, Boatbuilder
Pleasant Point
Cushing, ME 04563
(207) 354-2309

Sam's solar-heated shop overlooks the St. George River. (That Andrew Wyeth chose to settle there in summers is some measure of the town's beauty.) During the first winter, with the heating system not yet complete, the shop had an average temperature in the high forties. Light and airy, the space is a boatbuilder's dream-come-true.

General Information

Number of builders: One.
Capacity: 35 feet.
Specialties: Custom cruising sail, launches, wherries, and steamboats.

Top: *The full inch-and-one-eighth cedar planking will be good insulation for the owner of Sam Guild's Friendship sloop—the buyer is a veteran rock climber who plans to explore some cold northern waters as well.* Right: *Efficiency in boat shop heating means good insulation, as the shutters on Sam's shop emphasize.*

Nontraditional modes: No.
Experience: Yes.
Preferred paints and glues: 50 percent traditional.
Sail and/or power: 80 percent sail, 20 percent power.

Facilities

Design and drafting: Yes.
Lumber storage: 1,000 b.f.
Metal working: Patterns.

History

Origin of interest: In the family.
Training: Self-taught.
Selection of location: Liked the area.

Recent Projects

A 22-foot Friendship sloop, *Demian*: cedar, oak, bronze, teak cabin and cockpit sole; a 28-foot schooner designed by Bob Baker.

Lumber and Hardware

There will always be some lumber available if you'll cut it yourself. There are a few small foundries coming along that may fill our needs, but otherwise it's bleak. Suppliers and manufacturers are phasing out everything they don't sell by the thousands.

Cooperatives

Could work with lumber, yes.

The Market

There will always be wooden boats and boatbuilders, if only as a support group for amateurs.

The Labor Pool

Quantity is high; one has to train them oneself. There's a problem with the old vicious circle of not being able to afford to pay a man who's unskilled and/or expect him to work for nothing.

Vocational Training

There's a need for balance between the "romantics" and the "manufacturers." Schools need to develop in students a sense of speed and efficiency while emphasizing the beauty and quality of wooden boats as well. Some schools are placing too little emphasis on the *whole* of boatbuilding and too much on slathering on more resin.

Restorations and Replicas

Efficiency in the use of funds, to me, is better represented by *participatory* arrangements and lower cost. Usable replicas are better than restorations of huge pieces of relics that are doomed to sit unused in museums.

Time and Finish

The use or type of boat determines the level of workmanship; that is, beyond a certain standard, I will not compromise.

Open Statement

There's a need to train more people in traditional seamanship *as well as* traditional boatbuilding. This goes hand in hand with the concepts of smaller, simpler cruising boats that people can afford to buy and maintain.

Charles Hankins
Charles Hankins Boatbuilder
504 Grand Central Avenue
Lavallette, NJ 08735
(201) 793-7443

In completing over 1,000 powerboats since 1945, Hankins' efficiency has not been hurt by his location, which in some ways is surprising. The shop is right next to the post office on Lavallette's main thoroughfare. In addition, in the corner of the shop nearest the door is a small chandlery, and during the summer the town is filled with tourists.

General Information

Number of builders: Up to five.

Capacity: 16 feet to 40 feet.

Specialties: Jersey sea skiffs, Sea Bright surfboats, and custom work. Most of the first two are stock items.

Nontraditional modes: No.

Experience: No.

Facilities

Design and drafting: Yes, but I do very little these days.

Lumber storage: 8,000 to 10,000 b.f.

Metal working: Patterns.

History

Origin of interest: My father started building pound boats in 1912.

Training: I started working full time with him in 1945.

Selection of location: This is home.

Recent Projects

A 16-foot surfboat, and a 16-foot sailing one. We've built about 13 boats in 5½ months. (See also *WoodenBoat,* No. 18.)

Projects in Store

A 35-foot diesel express cruiser; another dozen or so surfboats and sea skiffs; and a 26-foot pound sea skiff.

Unusual Tools

Just the usual shop-made ones, spar planes, skew planes, etc.

Lumber and Hardware

No problem, and quality is holding up. Sitka spruce is a little short in supply and the price is steep, but that's all.

The Market

It's slow right now, but that's a nationwide money problem. Over the next 10 to 12 years there will be a strong but small market. My customers are mostly working people, and overtime is getting scarcer for them. That'll hurt.

The Labor Pool

There's nobody really interested in learning, particularly where wages can't compete with regular jobs.

Vocational Training

I like the idea.

Modern and Traditional Design

Traditional.

Time and Finish

We try for the greatest possible durability within reasonable cost.

Open Statement

We'll always try to do the best we can for you, within the limits of the money you want to spend.

Carl Hathaway
Hathaway Boat Shop
Saranac Lake, NY 12983
(518) 891-3961

General Information

Number of builders: Two.

Capacity: 30 feet.

Specialties: Traditional rowing and Adirondack guide-boats.

Nontraditional modes: No.

Experience: No.

Preferred paints and glues: Traditional.

Sail and/or power: 60 percent rowing, 20 percent power, 20 percent sail.

Facilities

Lumber storage: 6,000 b.f.

History

Origin of interest: Worked with a builder.

Training: In his shop.

Selection of location: Took over shop upon the death of owner.

Financing: One mortgage to a bank, second mortgage with owner's wife.

Recent Projects

Repair of some sail and powerboats, and a 16-foot guide-boat.

Projects in Store

Mainly repair of canoes and guide-boats, with another new guide-boat to be built by summer.

Lumber and Hardware

Very poor, and the future is not promising.

Cooperatives

Sounds good, but we have tried it and it doesn't work up here. There aren't many boatbuilders locally that can get together. I have worked successfully with Ralph Morrow on this, and it works one-on-one.

The Market

Being in recreation, I feel it depends directly on the economy. During the last recession, about four years ago, I lost eight orders on new boats. I was lucky; there was enough repair to keep us busy 'til things picked up.

Who is Buying and Why

Middle class (and above) for fishing and rowing, also for an investment.

The Labor Pool

Men are hard to find, and in order to keep down charges to customers, we can't offer competitive wages or benefits. A man can't live on love of work in this day and age.

Vocational Training

I have used the local, on-the-job training program; it is good, but the time span is not long enough to be practical.

Modern and Traditional Design

Traditional. I have repaired many old boats and they, with their craftsmanship, have stood up well to time. Some are in the hundred-year bracket. I feel the modern designs, materials, and workmanship have a long way to go to be as good as a lot of the traditional boats.

Restorations and Replicas

Many of the old boats should be saved by restoration. In its turn, this takes skill and craftsmanship. I also feel that real craftsmen are getting fewer. Some of the young people seem to have the right idea; slow life down, and take to crafts to keep up their pride and their skills at top quality. I sure hope they will stick with it and make crafts grow again.

Time and Finish

If I can't do the work to the best of my ability, I will not take the job.

Open Statement

If you are in Saranac Lake, please stop by and compare notes.

Sonny Hodgdon
G.I. Hodgdon Co., Inc.
East Boothbay, ME 04544
(207) 633-3676

Sonny's was one of the best-equipped shops I saw.

General Information

Number of builders: Five to 10.
Capacity: 55 feet.
Specialties: Custom sail and power.
Nontraditional modes: No.
Experience: Glued-strip only.
Preferred paints and glues: Traditional, for the most part.
Sail and/or power: Equal experience with both.

Facilities

Design and drafting: I have and can, but I don't any more.
Lumber storage: 10,000 b.f.
Metal working: Patterns and lead keels.

Only a few of the machines and tools are visible, but the large adjustable roller, the "planer's hand" at left, indicates just how thorough Sonny Hodgdon is.

History

Origin of interest: It has been in the family since 1818.

Training: With the family.

Selection of location: From here.

Recent Projects

Three 50-foot and one 32-foot O. Lie-Nielsen-designed powerboats of oak, cedar, mahogany, and silicon bronze. There were three McInnis powerboats to 50 feet, a 38-foot Stadel schooner (mahogany-and-teak-on-oak) and a 35-foot Alden ketch.

Projects in Store

A 32-foot soft-chine powerboat double-planked of cedar and mahogany.

Lumber and Hardware

Lumber is no problem for us because of the many years we've been doing business. You just have to hunt and pick. Hardware: since nobody is stocking items, you have to order with about six to eight weeks' lead time. As inventory continues to drop, there will be more and more local castings from builders' shop-made patterns.

Cooperatives

No.

The Market

I think you'll see wooden boats come back again due to a fall-out effect from glass. People are starting with the cheaper glass production boats, but once they learn what they want, they switch over to a custom-built boat.

The Labor Pool

I've had no problems with a crew of old-timers. I think it will stay about the same. There's more money elsewhere, so if we take on five men to find one that will stay on in the end, that's part of it.

Vocational Training

Ex-students know just enough to be dangerous. You can't build a boat from books. It's a matter of getting out in the field after you've learned a few basics (at school). You'll come to find that you are then just ready to start learning. I've been at it 41 years and *I'm* still learning.

Modern and Traditional Design

Traditional.

Time and Finish

My training comes indirectly (through my uncle and my father) from Nat Herreshoff. The best fits are none too good. We may cost a little more than some, but in the end, the boats cost less to maintain, be it workboat or yacht. I will say it's darn hard to switch from yacht work to workboat standards and back again. It's a rare man that can do both.

Open Statement

Our shop is small, but we are better equipped than many. There's nothing that we can't make that a larger shop can.

John D. Little
R.F.D. North Union Road
Washington, ME 04574
(207) 845-2708

Over the years, soft-spoken John Little's reputation has grown. As he wrote me recently, he is now "very busy building boats, and have to turn down any repair work and also new construction unless they are willing to wait." Would that all builders had such well-deserved problems.

General Information

Number of builders: My son and myself.

Capacity: 45 feet.

Specialties: The Black Hall River skiff, a lapstrake catboat (16 feet), and custom cruising sail.

Nontraditional modes: No.

Experience: No.

Preferred paints and glues: The usual mix, some of each.

Sail and/or power: Probably 85 percent sail, but I have built bass boats.

Facilities

Design and drafting: Yes.

Lumber storage: 1,000 b.f.

Metal working: Patterns.

History

Origin of interest: From childhood.

Training: On a fishing schooner; I've been a navy carpenter and worked for Luders, among others.

Financing: I ended up buying the shop I was working in as an employee.

Recent Projects

Various small craft: a 10-foot 4-inch Chapelle dinghy; three 10-foot whitewater dories; and a 30-foot Atkin double-ended gaff sloop of cedar on oak. In 1975 we completely rebuilt the 44-foot by 12-foot fishing schooner *Alicia*.

Projects in Store

A 21-foot by 10-foot carvel catboat designed by Fenwick Williams; another Black Hall River skiff; and more coming.

Lumber and Hardware

If there's demand, the price will be high, but quality will generally hold up. There's no one at the mill level saving the high-quality oak; they place no more value in a nice white-oak log than a mediocre red one. Hardware: the new chrome stuff is simply not of use to us.

Cooperatives

Builders are too independent and have too many ideas as to what are "acceptable" materials and practice.

The Market

I would have to say that John Gardner's articles in *National Fisherman* started the ball rolling, and now *WoodenBoat*, by Jon Wilson, is keeping it going. There is no question about it in my mind. From here there may be some slight increase, and then a stable plateau. Probably only two out of one hundred people interested in wooden boats are willing to spend the money to have one built, but that's an improvement.

The Labor Pool

Sufficient for the amount of business, perhaps even *more* than is needed.

Vocational Training

I'm for the schools, but I have had no contact with them. Can't judge.

Modern and Traditional Design

Traditional.

Restorations and Replicas

I'd say, put the emphasis on skills.

Time and Finish

For pleasure boats one wants the best you can get, since pride of ownership is much of it. In workboats it's got to be structurally sound but there's a limit to the finish.

Open Statement

It's a big reward to see the boat launched, but it's a bigger one to see it still going strong years later; to see people enjoying themselves and/or making a living through one of my boats. This all ties in with a love of woodworking and the outdoors in general.

Lowell's Boat Shop, Inc.

459 Main Street
Amesbury, MA 01913
(617) 388-0162

Perched on the edge of the Merrimack River for 186 years, Lowell's is probably the oldest active boat shop in the country. For most of those years, it was in the hands of seven consecutive generations of the Lowell family. The first true dory is believed to have been developed here, along with its building bed and timber plates. Note the typically New England, cavernous appearance.

General Information

Number of builders: Fred W. Tarbox, George R. Odell, Douglas M. Scott. Designs by owner M. J. Odell, who completed this questionnaire.

Capacity: 26 feet.

Specialties: Semiproduction of dories, dory/skiffs, and small wooden boats for work or pleasure.

Nontraditional modes: To a limited extent we will use these, and have some experience with wood-epoxy systems.

Preferred paints and glues: Our business is building traditional boats, but we don't hesitate to use proven modern materials or methods. Traditional-type paints on wood we find hard to beat, however.

Sail and/or power: 65 percent rowing boats, 22 percent sailing, 13 percent power. That's out of the 58 boats we built in 1978.

Facilities

Design and drafting: Yes.

Lumber storage: 10,000 b.f.

Metal working: We design and make our own patterns and have local foundries and machine shops cast and work on oarlocks, pintles, gudgeons, cleats, etc. These are cast of silicon and manganese bronze.

A 16-foot Lowell surf dory, pine on oak. (Betsy Williams photo)

History

Origin of interest: At six years old when a carpenter showed me how to make a boat out of a shingle.

Training: At home and at school.

Selection of location: The shop was up for sale, and I'd spent summers in New England as a child.

Financing: Out of personal funds.

Recent Projects

A 16-foot sailing surf dory of mahogany; two 14-footers of the same model with pine; three 15-foot rowing skiffs of pine and epoxy; a 14-foot sport (motor well) surf dory also of pine and epoxy; one 10-foot and two 8½-foot sailing tenders, topped off with Pete Culler's wheelbarrow boat. (See *WoodenBoat,* No. 27, for more on this and Lowell's in general.)

Projects in Store

An 18-foot sport surf dory; a 20-foot sailing surf dory; a bunch of camp rowboats.

Unusual Tools and Methods

The dory bed (in 1780s) and the timber plate later on. The former is a jig on which the skillet (bottom, frames, stem, and transom) is placed for completion, and, more specifically, to give it rocker. The ends are held up by blocks and the midship sections worked downward with shores.

Lumber and Hardware

Good bronze hardware is becoming extinct, so we have gone to the local foundry for much of this. So far so good. As for lumber, good softwood and oak are increasingly hard to find and expensive. I see no improvement in prospects but expect to continue by encouraging local mills.

Cooperatives

None locally.

The Market

Very hard to say, but camps and some commercial institutions are returning to using wooden boats. In one segment of the population, there seems to be an increasing interest in owning wooden boats, partly due to dissatisfaction with other available types and partly to an awakening of interest in boatbuilding as a heritage.

The Labor Pool

We have a considerable file of applicants with a range of little to extensive experience, and lots of aspirant boatbuilders. I expect this situation will continue as long as young people find more satisfaction in creating or participating in creative work than they do in production-line work.

Vocational Training

Eastport and Whittier Vocational Technical have good fundamental training programs. So does the Apprenticeshop, but I wonder if its graduates will stay with the trade. Boatbuilding's rewards are personal pride and satisfaction, not financial, and this must change to some extent.

Modern and Traditional Design

We are traditional boatbuilders—this is our business. If we should find that public interest in this type of craft dies, we will have to depart from it to survive. However, interest seems to be increasing at present.

Restorations and Replicas

Restoration work is frustrating to the professional because it entails so much *un*doing (and is so costly to the collector). We do it both for survival and to enable the relic to survive.

Time and Finish

The basic decision is ours, with customer response being the ultimately determining factor. We insist on maintaining the basic quality of our boats and improving it as we learn more; our reputation has been built on this. Finish must be good enough to provide added quality and satisfy the owner as to appearance and cost.

Open Statement

We enjoy building our traditional boats, particularly for those who can enjoy them. We must find enough people who want what we can produce to support our efforts to do this. We are working as hard as we know how in this direction and are encouraged but not home free. We have the capabilities to continue to grow considerably (after having been very close to disappearing) and are encouraged, but we still aren't sure that a manufacturer of wooden boats, as such, can survive in the market we serve. Although all of our boats are handmade and are altered to meet the customer's needs, we *are* manufacturers, one of the few remaining.

Ralph Morrow
Morrow's Boat Shop
46½ Duprey Street
Saranac Lake, NY 12983
(518) 891-0432

Ralph prepared for the 1980 Olympics by trying to figure out a way to avoid having to cross Main Street for the duration of the Winter Games. Two years ahead of time, businesses were already gearing up. Many local people I talked to were less than overjoyed at the prospect of a town jammed way beyond capacity. Montpelier, Vermont, was the nearest town with any hotel vacancies for the winter of 1980!

General Information

Number of builders: One.
Capacity: 24 feet.
Specialties: Adirondack guide-boats and the restoration of runabouts.
Nontraditional modes: No.
Experience: No.
Preferred paints and glues: Traditional.
Sail and/or power: Power and oar.

Facilities

Design and drafting: No.
Lumber storage: 1,000 b.f.
Metal working: No.

History

Origin of interest: I've been around these waters all my life.
Training: On my own and working in other boatyards.
Selection of location: I'm from here.

Recent Projects

Restoration of a 17-foot canoe; a new 14-foot guide-boat of cedar on spruce ribs; and a 16-foot one of pine-on-spruce.

Projects in Store

Restorations of an 18-foot Hacker, a 20-foot Chris-Craft, and 21-foot Penn Yan runabouts.

Lumber and Hardware

"Piss poor and getting worse—standards are dropping." You go to the yards and pick through a whole pile for one clear board, and all the time you're at it, you can hear the cash register going. You have to get it wherever you can find it.

Devotees of classic runabouts can make wooden boat buffs seem tame. They are a breed unto themselves. This photograph taken in a shop in Minnesota is typical of the restoration and refinishing work routinely demanded by runabout enthusiasts and performed by professionals like Ralph Morrow.

Cooperatives

Our needs are too different.

The Market

If you can get the materials, you can sell the boats you build. People *want* wooden boats.

The Labor Pool

Not so good. People don't want or have to work this hard. If you don't work, the government will feed you.

Modern and Traditional Design

Traditional.

Time and Finish

If you have to eat, you can only go so far. We'd all like to put together the perfect boat, but the job is to work within the time and money that the builder and owner can afford.

Warren Nau
Nau's Boat Works
Hwy. 35 (Morgan)
South Amboy, NJ 08879
(201) 721-0116

General Information

Capacity: 38 feet.
Specialties: Traditional small craft.
Nontraditional modes: No.
Experience: No.
Preferred paints and glues: Both traditional and modern.
Sail and/or power: 75 percent power.

History

Origin of interest: Born with it.

Training: Dad started using boats in 1895 and worked as a commercial fisherman up until 1951. When he started to build boats in 1928, I tried to help, though I was only seven. In 1948, I started on my own and in 1951, Dad came in with me.

Selection of location: I was born here.

Recent Projects

We build two to four surfboats a year, only on order. We don't build the larger skiffs much anymore; with the price of materials and inexperienced help, it's not profitable. We do build the dory the North Jersey lifeguards use in their races. There have been several articles in *National Fisherman* about these. The rest of our work is repair.

Projects in Store

A couple of surfboats before spring.

Lumber and Hardware

The present supply of cedar is very poor. We have to do a *lot* of chasing around to get any. We have to travel 150 miles to get a supply of green white-oak.

Cooperatives

None around here.

The Market

Where are we going from here? That's a good question. Men won't work for boatbuilder's wages anymore. This used to be one of the busiest areas for wooden boatbuilding, but there are none beyond myself now. None that I know of, anyway.

The Labor Pool

Very bad. There's not enough money for the hours and skill. An *un*skilled factory worker gets $6 per hour, plus benefits.

Vocational Training

Nothing in this area. I was approached to be a teacher at one point, but the people couldn't get funding.

Modern and Traditional Design

We try to stay with the traditional. With the gas situation the way it is, I hope to develop the rowing dory into a sailing model. I think it's headed that way, toward taking advantage of the wind.

Open Statement

We try to be honest with a person and give him a dollar's work for his dollar.

SOURCE

North End Shipyard, Inc.
Box 482
Rockland, ME 04841
(207) 594-8007

General Information

Number of builders: Three partners: John Foss, Doug Lee, and Linda Lee.

Capacity: 100 tons and/or 8-foot draft, sailing vessels only.

Specialties: Rebuilding wooden sailing vessels, and some small-boat restoration and construction.

Nontraditional modes: No.

Experience: No.

Sail and/or power: Yawl boats are as far as we go with power.

Facilities

Design and drafting: Yes.

Lumber storage: 5,000 b.f.

Metal working: Patterns.

History

Origin of interest: In our blood.

Training: By mistake.

Selection of location: From here.

Recent Projects

Total restoration of the 64-foot *Lewis R. French,* a coasting schooner; new spars for the 65-foot *Isaac Evans,* a schooner; a new 14-foot yawl boat of cedar-on-oak; and restoration of two pulling boats for the *Isaac Evans.*

Projects in Store

Two yawl boats; two pulling boats; and we will build and/or restore at least two more 100-ton vessels. Note: we have rented space to other projects in the past on a selected basis, but any building we do is for ourselves.

Lumber and Hardware

Expensive. The same old stuff is rising in price faster than other items you buy; lumber has more than doubled.

Cooperatives

No. Once in a while we'll get an order up with some others for West Coast spars, but otherwise, it is not in the nature of builders to cooperate.

The Market

I couldn't say. It's kind of depressing at times, but we won't change, regardless.

The Labor Pool

There's a good supply of labor. The quality is okay, too, if you can get them to stay for long.

Vocational Training

They learn the methods, but not the productivity/time considerations. These things occasionally develop with time, but the schools need to emphasize them more.

Restorations and Replicas

In the effort to save the boats, you learn the skills.

Time and Finish

Structural integrity and cost considerations are the determining factors. A balance is needed, regardless of who is paying, whose boat it is.

Open Statement

This is a support yard for 100-ton and smaller wooden vessels. The yard is really a labor-intensive effort providing us with off-season work and a place to maintain the schooners. The two windjammers we operate are an example of the most economical way to rebuild and maintain, in good condition, large, wooden sailing vessels.

Miscellaneous

P.L. Note: I used to live not far from North End Shipyard and have long been most impressed with the operation. The crew at the shipyard works long hours and hard ones. Serious business only is the name of the game for visitors. I freely admit to pressuring them for an interview (and permission to publish it) because they are an inspiring example. Please respect their busy schedules, should you have good reason to contact them.

George A. Patten
George A. Patten Boatbuilder
Norton Road
Kittery, ME 03904
(207) 439-3967

George's shop is as nice as his workmanship.

General Information

Number of builders: Self.
Capacity: 40 feet.
Specialties: Custom cruising sail—cost plus.
Nontraditional modes: No.
Experience: No.
Preferred paints and glues: Fifty-fifty of each, modern and traditional.
Sail and/or power: 90 percent sail, 10 percent power.

Facilities

Design and drafting: Yes.
Lumber storage: 2,000 b.f. of what *isn't* readily available; the rest I buy as needed.
Metal working: No.

History

Origin of interest: Growing up in Newcastle, Maine.
Training: In yards—among them, Dion's yacht yard.
Selection of location: This coast is home.
Financing: A bank loan and from work in yards.

Recent Projects

A 33-foot Concordia sloop (the 27-footer scaled up) of African mahogany-over-white-oak, copper and bronze. A 36-foot Royal Lowell lobsterboat of Virginia cedar-over-oak, copper and bronze.

Projects in Store

Possible cruising sloop on speculation; too early to tell for sure.

The African mahogany garboards and first strakes are copper riveted to the frames and butt blocks of this Concordia 33-footer. The through-bolts with blocks under them will presumably be used to tie together the floors, keel, and ballast after the floors have been fitted.

Unusual Tools

A 4-foot by 8-foot plywood-topped workbench/table saw/shaper. (I run the table saw off an old 3-h.p. motor.) The shaper and saw are at diagonally opposing corners so the same fence can be used for either. As a whole, it's a great space saver having them all in one.

Lumber and Hardware

It depends on what happens in Africa. Worldwide instability makes predictions difficult. Local woods require more effort to get good quality of late. It's hard to get loggers to saw for boatbuilders, but basically the wood is there. Hardware is terrible; the quality of casting is poor, and the variety is very limited. most of it is chrome-plated plastic.

Cooperatives

Builders are too dispersed.

The Market

There'll be just enough to keep a limited number of small shops (one to three men) in business.

Who is Buying and Why

So far, mostly guys with time off and limited funds who work along with me.

The Labor Pool

It's good on both counts, quality and quantity, but there are always guys with a truck full of tools who don't know which end of the chisel to use.

Vocational Training

The idea is great and the products are good, but there aren't jobs for these guys. Furthermore, you can't make a living on three bucks an hour working in a repair yard.

Modern and Traditional Design

I prefer the traditional, but I will build what comes along.

Restorations and Replicas

Both need support.

Time and Finish

I work toward good-quality workmanship in the best possible time. But I have to do good work; sloppiness is *out.* There must be a balance.

Open Statement

I'm just trying to make a fair living and a decent reputation doing something I enjoy. I'd like to make enough so that I can go sailing in the summertime.

Seth Persson
Seth Persson Boatbuilder
Route 3, Box 90 (on Riverside Avenue)
Old Saybrook, CT 06475
(203) 388-2343

Seth Persson died in June 1980; his two sons are continuing to run the business.

General Information

Number of builders: Five.
Capacity: 45 feet.
Specialties: Custom cruising sail and some power.
Nontraditional modes: No.
Experience: No.
Preferred paints and glues: Fifty-fifty.
Sail and/or power: Fifty-fifty.

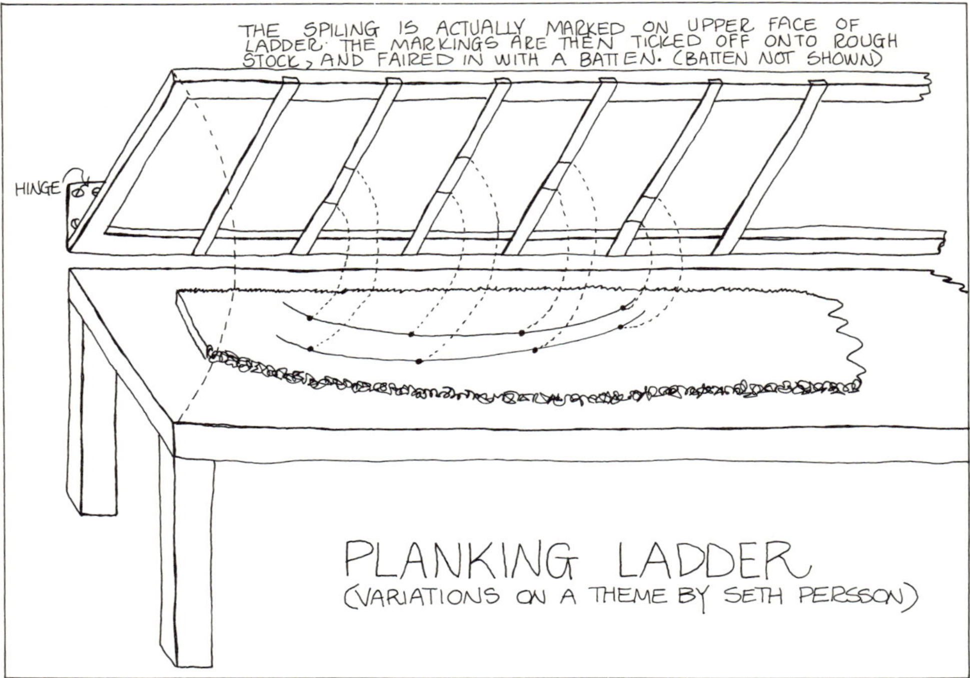

Rebecca Wheeler

Facilities

Design and drafting: Yes.

Lumber storage: 2,000 to 3,000 b.f.

Metal working: Welding and patterns.

History

Origin of interest: Family—my father was a sailing man.

Training: I worked at Consolidated and other yards.

Selection of location: I wanted to get out of New York, and land was cheaper here.

Recent Projects

A 32-foot Sparkman and Stephens double-planked-on-laminated-oak sloop, and a Herreshoff Alerion-class sloop of cedar-on-oak and bronze.

Projects in Store

A 38-foot Persson design (sloop or yawl rig) of double-planked (mahogany-over-cedar) construction and bronze. We also have on line a 29-foot Newport and a Herreshoff Bullseye.

Unusual Tools

To some it's common enough, a planking ladder. There are different kinds, but they're basically a long wooden grid (mine's hinged to the wall so it drops down over the entire length of this 40-foot bench) used for recording spilings, plank shape; it's very fast, accurate. Once a spiling is transferred, you can lift the grid and lay plank stock underneath it, move it around, even change planks and never worry about losing the spiling or its accuracy.

Lumber and Hardware

The only problem is in the price of imported lumber. Local woods are available because fewer people are using it less. Hardware? I have to get 90 percent cast special.

Cooperatives

Good idea for buying; I'd like to try it with teak.

Who is Buying and Why

People who wouldn't have anything else, who prefer wood to any other medium.

The Labor Pool

Diminishing, but much enthusiasm among the young may be the saving grace as far as skilled men go.

Vocational Training

I'd like to pass on what I know.

Modern and Traditional Design

Traditional.

Restorations and Replicas

Equal support within financial considerations.

Time and Finish

You can do a good job just as fast as you can one with poor joints.

Open Statement

I wanted this yard very much, and I still enjoy putting my energy into the creation of each boat.

Michael Porter
Chebeague Island, ME 04017
(207) 846-3146

Poor Michael and family! I dropped in on them (on an hour's notice) just days after they had literally moved their house. They hardly broke stride. Michael cheerfully stopped rebuilding his chimney long enough to do a nice job on my questionnaire and invited me to a most pleasant dinner. They were some of the nicest people of the many I met.

General Information

Number of builders: Just self.
Capacity: 30 feet.
Specialties: Dories and lapstrake construction.
Nontraditional modes: Yes, strip.
Experience: Strip only.
Preferred paints and glues: Half traditional.
Sail and/or power: Sail and small powerboats, outboards.

Facilities

Design and drafting: Yes.
Lumber storage: 500 to 1,000 b.f.
Metal working: No need for it.

History

Origin of interest: From childhood.

Training: On my own. I built one for myself when I had no money to buy one, and I kept on going from there.

Selection of location: I'm from here.

Recent Projects

Four Pete Culler 13-foot 6-inch sailing skiffs; a 16-foot outboard of pine-on-oak; a 15-foot dory; and an 18-foot Friendship sloop of pine-strip-on-oak, bronze fastened.

Projects in Store

Another Good Little Skiff; an 18-foot outboard; a 17-foot sailing Swampscott; and a regular dory. Just to get out of the dory routine, I have a possible 24-foot Hampton boat and some flatiron skiffs.

Unusual Tools

This bottom bevel gauge for flat-bottomed boats.

Lumber and Hardware

Lumber hasn't been a problem. I just have to think ahead. I can see a problem in that we are not reseeding it, but when or how severe it will be, I don't know. You have to have capital to jump when it *is* there. Hardware is a problem due to discontinuing lines—suppliers now have one item where they used to have 10. I have a Wilcox-Crittenden catalog from 1940 that would make you cry.

Cooperatives

Not for me. It would be a good idea where there's a concentration of builders.

The Market

Fishermen are coming back to wood. In small boats, fiberglass dories have never been accepted. There is a movement away from plastics toward wood as something genuine. Not a boom but a steady increase.

The Labor Pool

I have no contact with it.

Vocational Training

It depends on what you want. They are fine if you want to work in boatyards, but they don't give you any basis for starting on your own. The business side is never touched; you can play and make mistakes without the consequences of the "real" world. An apprenticeship in a working shop is much better.

Modern and Traditional Design

Traditional.

Restorations and Replicas

Of the two, skills preservation is probably more important. A little less of preserving every relic at any cost, and more toward a sane view—making them pay for themselves. A participatory program—get the people into and onto boats, not just looking at them.

Time and Finish

I don't have an inviolable standard; I *do* have a concern that I do the best work I can within reasonable time. With utility boats, anything less than what works

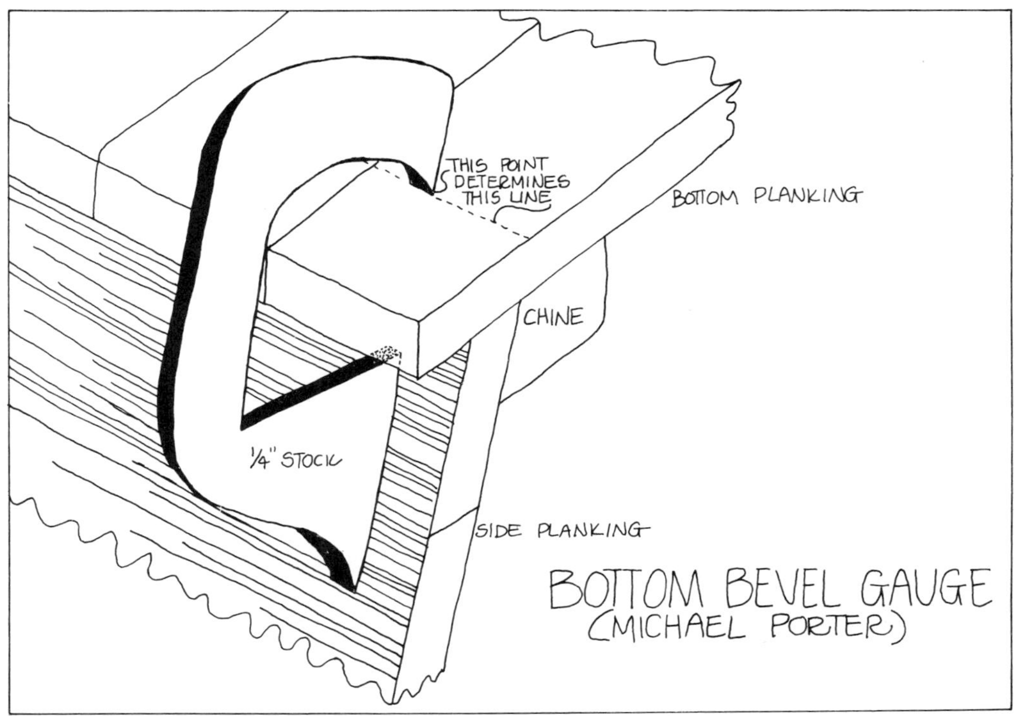

In this cutaway view of a flat-bottomed boat being built upside down, the bottom bevel gauge helps determine the bevel and line along which the overhanging cross planking will be cut so as to run fair with the first strake. (Rebecca Wheeler illustration)

and lasts is unacceptable. I don't believe in perfectionism. There are tolerances, and the question becomes what tolerance is appropriate. It's up to the prospective owner what tolerance is used. That's important to consider in choosing a builder. We may admire Rolls-Royces, but more of us drive VWs, and is the VW (*where it counts*) really less well built than the Rolls? And if you think so, you should be able and willing to pay for it *before* you ask a builder to put one together for you.

Open Statement

You have to compete with the concept of the maintenance-free boat, the fallacy of haul it and forget it. We, the revival, are a dent in that.

Miscellaneous

(From a subsequent update.) Nothing much is happening on Chebeague, except that we are frozen in, and it is always a question whether even the mail boat will make it through the ice. All I can do with finished boats is set them out in the snow and send pictures to their owners. No way to deliver them. Our house no longer looks like the warehouse of a used-furniture dealer [in moving, all the furniture had been piled in one large room—P.L.], which is good, and in a period when everyone on the island is either cold or frozen, it seems to function well. I have also enlarged the shop to 30-foot capacity.

Richard S. Pulsifer
Richard S. Pulsifer Co.
RFD 3
Brunswick, ME 04011
(207) 725-5457

General Information

Number of builders: One.

Capacity: 25 feet.

Specialties: I only build one boat, this 21-foot Casco Bay Hampton powerboat developed by Charles Gomes.

Nontraditional modes: Yes, strip.

Experience: Yes, strip.

Preferred paints and glues: Modern.

Sail and/or power: Power 100 percent.

Facilities

Design and drafting: Limited.

Lumber storage: 1,500 b.f.

Metal working: No need.

History

Origin of interest: Growing up on Casco Bay.

Training: On my own.

Selection of location: I'm from here.

Recent Projects

About one 21-footer a year for the last five years. They are all 1⅛-inch pine-on-oak, with silicon-bronze ring nails for the strip planking. Beam is 79 inches, draft forward is 13 inches, aft 28 inches, displacement about one ton. The price (subject to change) is $9,000 at my shop. That includes an automatic bilge pump, running lights, towing and mooring rings, a 14-gallon fuel tank, and a 16-h.p. Universal diesel turning a 14-inch-by-14-inch prop.

Projects in Store

To get up to about three boats a year. Construction time now is about 450 hours, and it's still coming down.

Lumber and Hardware

Availability is having the stuff on hand at a reasonable price, being a *wise* buyer. There's a time to cut your own and a time to go through the middleman. Price, speed of delivery, etc., are all concerns to be weighed. It's important to be independent. I *try* to be a primary manufacturer, not an assembler. I cut a lot of my own lumber.

Cooperatives

I think they are fine ideas; however, it's not particularly applicable to my venture. If a coop can apply greater leverage (buying power), *that* never hurts.

The Market

I think there is going to continue to be an interest in all products that have quality in their construction, not just their conception.

The Labor Pool

As far as locally developed, simple boats go, it's strong. It will always meet the demand.

Vocational Training

I worked at The Apprenticeshop for two years. I felt and still feel that keeping a valid world element on the shop floor is essential. So far, there has been a market for the shop's graduates.

Restorations and Replicas

I'm interested in preserving the skill inherent in this particular design. That speaks for my attitude about skills and boat preservation in general.

Time and Finish

I keep to structural integrity—workboat honesty. To attempt to go to any high degree of finish, beyond an occasional oiled bulkhead, is simply inappropriate for my boats.

Steve Redmond
Redmond Designs
4 Howard Street
Burlington, VT 05401
(802) 862-7435 (evenings)

There was a flurry of last-minute letters between Mr. Redmond and myself, trying to determine whether he qualified for this book. The deciding factors were the quality of his response and the lack of coverage in his area. This is perhaps the best possible (and most borderline) example of the weeding-out process, and of the grapevine's diversity.

General Information

Number of builders: Two.

Capacity: 32 feet.

Specialties: Custom-designed cruising sailboats, rowboats, canoes, and kayaks.

Nontraditional modes: Yes, regularly.

Experience: Yes.

Preferred paints and glues: Both have their place, depending on the project.

Sail and/or power: Sail 50 percent, rowing and paddling 40 percent, power 10 percent.

Facilities

Design and drafting: Yes.

Lumber storage: 1,500 b.f. at present.

History

Origin of interest: I became interested in boatbuilding in 1971, while living in Vermont, when I built a James Wharram 27-foot Tane cruising catamaran. I was a novice at the time, never having built a boat before, but I was encouraged by the advice of several well-known boating authorities that the best way to learn boatbuilding was to "dig in." Throwing caution to the winds, I did indeed dig in, and the great number of mistakes and difficulties that ensued are a tribute to the bullheaded nature of amateur boatbuilders and to, by way of contrast, the tremendous amount of acquired wisdom and skill demonstrated by boatbuilders of professional caliber. The authorities were right, though. I learned a tremendous amount from that project—also that I liked boatbuilding. Determined to learn more, I enrolled in a boatbuilding school and also the Westlawn yacht design course. Westlawn has proven valuable, but the boatbuilding school was a hoax and a ripoff, as any of its unfortunate students will tell you . . . many were discouraged from boatbuilding as a result of the many thousands of dollars taken. . . . The school is no longer in existence. I quit there after seven months of frustration, worked a short time at a boatyard in the county, designed a 26-foot skipjack, and built a 16-foot skiff and 21-foot Noank sloop of my own design before moving back to Vermont.

Selection of location: The Burlington area is Vermont's equivalent of a small coastal city, without the disadvantages of the East Coast megalopolis. Wood is available; there is good sailing activity on Lake Champlain, a decent market, and little competition in the boatbuilding field. Lake Champlain also provides an ultimate access to the sea at both its northern and southern extremities. It's a nice place to live, too.

Financing: My tools were all acquired over the last eight years individually. Financing the shop was, therefore, relatively simple, and came out of my savings.

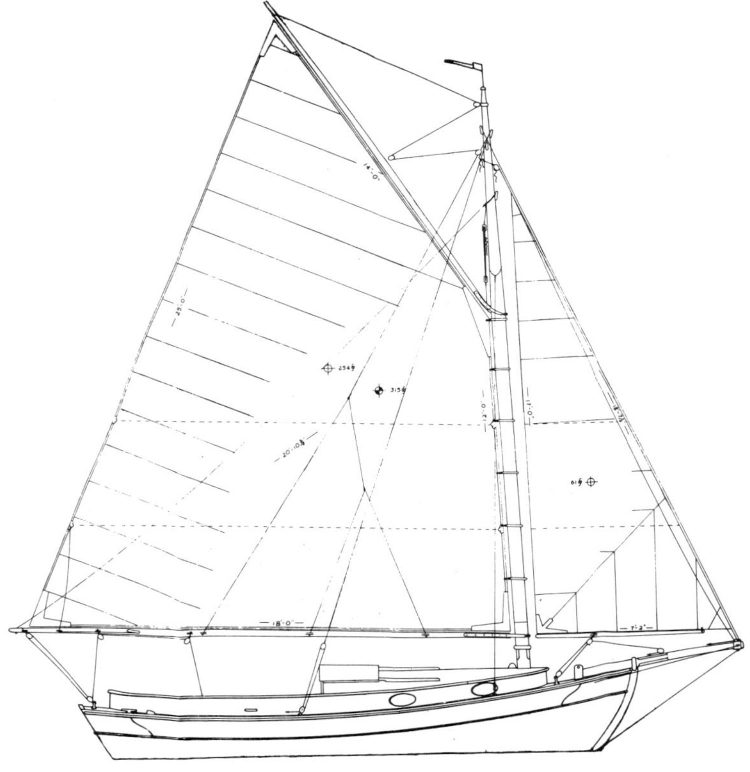

Steve Redmond's Noank sloop.

Recent Projects

A two-man decked sailing canoe; a solo flatwater sport canoe; a sailing skiff; a general-purpose canoe of various materials including the WEST system and fiberglass-reinforced plastic.

Projects in Store

A lateen-rigged 1690-type Admiralty wherry; a dugout canoe (Philippine style) for a rather wild play production of *Beowulf*; a 14-foot Bruynzeel lapped sailing skiff.

Lumber and Hardware

The present quality of lumber is okay, in light of modern glues usable for small craft and moderate-to-large boats constructed by modern methods. Without a doubt, the larger trees of the world are being destroyed in forests and jungles at a rate that will, in a few years, mean an end to large or long unlaminated timber. Dependence on glues will increase as lumber quality decreases. Local wood will remain available for some time, but at lower grades.

Cooperatives

Difficult to organize. Most builders are too dispersed; therefore, transportation of lumber becomes a problem.

The Market

Traditional wood boats will always be built, at least in smaller sizes, but we are going to have to adapt to changing lumber quality.

Who is Buying and Why

I am disturbed by cost trends that encourage only a wealthy clientele. Research in design and building economy is absolutely necessary for wooden boatbuilding to survive its current renaissance.

The Labor Pool

Improving. On-the-job training will expand. There are many novices with the willingness to learn out there.

Vocational Training

Schools, boatbuilding and otherwise, are an imperfect representation of the real world. Their pros and cons both center around the fact that the learner is undisturbed by the necessity to make a living and run a business. Also, the learning process is not amenable (in boatbuilding) to a mere year or two in school. Schools *do* teach skills and are okay if of good quality and the student has the time and money. On-the-job training is preferable, and builders should take advantage of government training aid like CETA when possible.

Modern and Traditional Design

I am prejudiced only toward a customer's unique needs and the materials and design that would best suit those needs.

Open Statement

Biases in boatbuilding are easily acquired and counterproductive. Openness to the advantages and disadvantages of particular materials or methods does not seem to be as common an attitude as it should be among wood builders. A good boat is simply a good boat, and "traditional" is a relative term, depending on when a person lived. Everything we build now will be traditional in the 21st century. I like all boats that are well designed and built. I happen to be looking for customers who need and can afford traditional wood, plank-on-frame boats, but that is not a limitation.

Robert Rich
Bass Harbor Boat Corporation
Bernard, ME 04612
(207) 244-3514

General Information

Number of builders: Average of five.
Capacity: 60 feet.
Specialties: Powerboats only, for work or pleasure.
Nontraditional modes: No.
Experience: Yes.
Preferred paints and glues: Half modern.
Sail and/or power: Power.

Facilities

Design and drafting: Yes.
Lumber storage: Limited.
Metal working: Patterns.

History

Origin of interest: It has been in the family for five generations.
Training: I worked for Southwest Boat Corporation and in Rhode Island.
Selection of location: I'm from here.

Recent Projects

Three lobsterboats of my own design, 36 feet, 37 feet, and 43 feet, of cedar, oak, and bronze. The 43-footer is for gillnetting, too.

A Robert Rich lobsterboat is getting her deck bunged as the bright afternoon sun shines through a skylight overhead. Flitch-sawn cedar planks help to hold the hull's shape until bulkheads can be built.

Projects in Store

A 48-foot offshore lobsterboat and a 43-foot gillnetter.

Lumber and Hardware

Hardware: It's getting almost impossible to find some items. Apparently the big companies are getting out of small, slow-moving items and turning to plastic, quick-sell. I think the unions are one of the big causes of high cost and delay. There's no shortage of lumber and never will be.

Cooperatives

No, too independent.

The Market

It's anybody's guess. I suppose it's getting better all the time. The only problem would be a recession; until then, it'll be no problem keeping busy. Wood is more popular than glass, but wood boats can be hard to find, so people are buying glass.

The Labor Pool

It stinks and it is getting worse all the time. The minimum wage is up so high you can't afford to pay an inexperienced man in order to teach him.

Vocational Training

The problems are in the administration, not the idea. As it is, it's a waste of the taxpayers' money. The few men who manage to get something out of the schools would be better off living off their school money and working in a regular yard for a year. Too many others are looking at how much they have in their pockets at the end of the day, not even what they have come Saturday. They'd rather make $12,000 on and off than $10,000 steady.

Time and Finish

I claim we are one of the best builders; we use better materials, help, and methods than the average. I don't claim to know everything—I learn something new every day—but we have standards we won't compromise.

Ronald Rich

Herrick Road
Southwest Harbor, ME 04679
(207) 244-5489

"I'm satisfied that I've contributed to the lobster/pleasure boating industries more than financially. There's a joining between the owner and the builder born of the builder's concern that the boat do its job and last. The satisfaction lies in the continuing knowledge of how your boats are doing."

General Information

Number of builders: Self.
Capacity: 36 feet.
Specialties: Lobsterboats and pleasure boats.

Ronald Rich has cut the rabbet, drilled out and plugged the bad knots, and mastered the tricky grain of large oak timbers to get a nice, clean boxed keel.

Nontraditional modes: No.
Experience: Yes.
Preferred paints and glues: Traditional mostly.
Sail and/or power: Power.

Facilities

Design and drafting: Yes.
Lumber storage: 2,000 b.f.
Metal working: Patterns.

History

My brother Robert and I are the fifth generation.

Recent Projects

Six pulling boats for the Hurricane Island school, and two 34-foot by 11-foot lobsterboats of cedar, oak, and bronze. One of those went to Marblehead, Massachusetts.

Projects in Store

More of the same; I'll carry on.

Lumber and Hardware

I don't know. Inflation may get us, but as long as the fishermen are getting the good prices, we'll be able to keep busy.

Cooperatives

Builders are too dispersed, independent, and diverse to get them to agree on anything.

The Market

There will always be some demand for wood, but fiberglass will be the mainstream. I think wooden boatbuilding will gradually decline because the older masters won't be replaced by young builders at a one-to-one rate.

Skill and concentration in conflict with the camera caused a slight frown to break onto Ronald Rich's face. His expression, the swirling grain of the oak, sunlight, and paint-speckled floor comprise what might be called "boatyard art."

The Labor Pool

The schools are doing okay at filling the need for now.

Vocational Training

I think they'll make good boat carpenters, but small shops will be fewer and fewer because it takes too long to get into the black ink.

Time and Finish

In my experience, there's a balance between the boat's integrity and making money. If I can build a boat that lasts as long as any other man's, but puts more money in my pocket, I'm not against that.

Open Statement

[See the opening paragraph.]

Miscellaneous

I once had a guy come in here and ask me how I would do a certain thing on his boat if I were to build it for him. I told him I couldn't say, off the top of my head, because they were not regular practices and I'd have to think about it, look around, and work it out with him. That secured a contract. He told me I was the first builder of a number he'd talked with who hadn't had a quick answer, who didn't pretend he knew everything.

Paul E. Rollins
RFD Scotland Bridge Road
York, ME 03909

General Information

Number of builders: Three.
Capacity: 60 feet.
Specialties: Custom sail and power.
Nontraditional modes: Yes.
Experience: No.
Preferred paints and glues: 50 percent modern.
Sail and/or power: Equal experience.

Facilities

Design and drafting: Yes.
Lumber storage: 6,000 b.f.
Metal working: Patterns.

History

Origin of interest: From childhood.
Training: As a house carpenter, with Bud McIntosh, and with Harold Kimber at The Apprenticeshop.
Selection of location: I'm from here.

Recent Projects

A 12-foot No Man's Land boat as a tender (cedar-on-oak); a 38-foot cedar-on-oak powerboat (copper-riveted); the restoration of the 73-foot brigantine *Varua* in Samoa; and a 44-foot mahogany-on-oak dragger.

Projects in Store

A 48-foot McIntosh schooner. We had expected to be restoring a 54-year-old Alden schooner this winter. The boat was beyond repair, so we are just now setting up a new hull on the old ballast. She's 44 feet and will be planked and decked with iroko, the former being copper-riveted. We are building at least two 16-foot double-paddle canoes on speculation. Progress on these should accelerate a bit, as 1,000 board feet of cedar has just arrived. In between these I'm building a 15-foot McIntosh pulling boat—warmer weather and the spring rush of work.

Lumber and Hardware

You run in cycles; sometimes it's the end of the world, sometimes it's rosy. I'm inclined to be optimistic. Prices aren't too bad; you just have to work at least two months ahead.

Cooperatives

I suppose they'd be good for amateurs.

The Market

I don't think fishing boats are the future; pleasure is where wood is going. Logically, the market will be in varnished beauties, something that has snob appeal, something to show off. There are a few who understand wood (and will buy it) on its own merits as a structural material, but they are very few.

The Labor Pool

I'm pretty optimistic. I think I can get whomever I need.

Vocational Training

They've often no basis in economics. Bud taught me to push the project along, and with time, the skill comes. I suggest that those who start slow, working for perfection from the start, never learn the speed.

Modern and Traditional Design

It all depends on how you define them. I've built mostly Bud McIntosh's designs which, while traditional in appearance, I consider to be eminently modern.

Time and Finish

I've done all kinds of work: a $5,000 Whitehall; a 36-foot lobsterboat with labor cost at $18,000. I desire to do the better work. I cannot *afford* to build a boat that doesn't conform to the owner's and my standards of what is seaworthy. At the same time, it has to have as much the appearance of quality as the reality.

McKie "Nick" Roth
Roth Corporation
Westport, ME 04578
(207) 443-3832

Nick builds houses of classic New England styling (saltboxes, for instance) when he's not building boats. His houses and even his shops have choice locations in keeping with their appearances. When I worked for him briefly some years ago, we used to sit on the roof of his spacious, skylighted workshop and watch the osprey feeding across the river.

General Information

Number of builders: Up to three.
Capacity: 45 feet.
Specialties: Custom sail and power.
Nontraditional modes: No.
Experience: Yes.
Preferred paints and glues: Mostly traditional.
Sail and/or power: I've worked about equally with both.

History

Origin of interest: From childhood.
Training: In boatyards.
Selection of location: Favorable climate for doing business.

Recent Projects

An H-28 of cedar, oak, and bronze; a 23-foot Stone Horse of Philippine mahogany-on-oak; a Herreshoff 12½ of cedar-on-oak.

Projects in Store

Another H-28, and I'm working on plans for a portable combination-sawmill for logs, resawing, and heavy timber.

Lumber and Hardware

No problem on lumber. There are so many trees growing, to worry about it is like worrying about a shortage of potatoes. The only hitch is what the suppliers are willing to cut. The only way to get decent hardware is to make it yourself.

Cooperatives

Good idea, but for materials only, not for shops run on that basis.

The Market

Where are we going? I have no idea.

The Labor Pool

It's as good as it has ever been, perhaps better due to the influx of young people. The only problem with the youngsters is that they are not taught the standards of production—speed. This is what causes boats to be artificially high priced.

Vocational Training

I think they are doing a pretty good job. I am concerned that there is perhaps a shortage of work for them in *new* construction, but the need in repair, hauling, and storage is still strong.

Modern and Traditional Design

Traditional.

Time and Finish

I don't turn out "piano-finish" boats—they are simply not practical, since they don't stand up. On the other hand, we build boats that are as well put together as any, perhaps better than most. A well-built boat is *well built*, whether it's covered with paint or varnish. The fit is what counts.

Open Statement

There are several groups presently cashing in on the apprenticeship-type programs. These programs are teaching the mechanics of boatbuilding without the economics. The best way to learn is *in a yard*, and if there aren't many in-yard apprenticeships available, it is because the harsh reality is that the work isn't there to support them. The apprenticeship program is a good idea as an educational experience, which doesn't necessarily lead to professional boatbuilding.

Dick Shew and Cecil Burnham
Shew and Burnham
Box 131
South Bristol, ME 04568
(207) 644-8120

Dick and Cecil have been heavily involved with the Traditional Small Craft Association since its inception. They have sponsored the Christmas Cove small-craft gatherings and, until recently, raised prize-winning milk goats. It was not unusual to find a kid penned off in a corner of the shop so that they could keep an eye on it.

General Information

Number of builders: Two.

Capacity: 18 feet.

Specialties: We have been active building traditional small craft since 1968; 12-foot and 18-foot Whitehall pulling boats, the New Buzzards Bay 14 (a Herreshoff 12½ stretched), and custom construction.

Fine craftsmanship is evident in the boats of Dick Shew and Cecil Burnham.

Nontraditional modes: No.
Experience: No.
Preferred paints and glues: Mostly traditional.
Sail and/or power: Sail and oar.

Facilities

Design and drafting: Yes.
Lumber storage: 500 b.f.
Metal working: Patterns.

History

Origin of interest: From childhood.
Training: Cecil worked at Goudy and Stevens and I worked for Seth Persson.
Financing: From working at Fuller Shipbuilding.

Recent Projects

A 16-foot Whitehall; 20-foot and 23-foot wherries of Spanish-cedar-on-oak. They had sliding seats and outriggers.

Projects in Store

Four 12-footers and an 18-foot pulling boat.

Unusual Methods

We've found that Douglas fir, vertical-grain flooring makes excellent oars.

Lumber and Hardware

Quality is declining in the cedar; oak is okay. We want to get away from imports; there are too many variables such as shipping and politics to stay with them. Hardware? Lousy! The inventory changes according to computer, so there's no telling what they'll drop or pick up next. We are setting up our own gang patterns for oarlocks, etc.

Cooperatives

The future of buying cooperatives is positive.

The Market

More people want a simple boat. These, even though the price is up, are still good buys—the water is always there to enjoy, with half the problems of a larger boat.

Who is Buying and Why

White-collar workers who want a small boat they can row and take care of themselves with minimal money or time. Many enjoy the maintenance as much as the use.

The Labor Pool

It's holding its own and will improve if the problems with vocational training and such are dealt with.

Vocational Training

There may be the need for *some* kinds of standards so that the traditional wooden boat market isn't hurt by dreamers and/or shoddily built boats. There is a need for clarification in the schools on the element of speed. If you don't or can't get into that, don't go professional so that in the end, the field doesn't get hurt.

Modern and Traditional Design

Traditional.

Restorations and Replicas

If someone *has* the skill, then it is more likely that the older boats will be better maintained and reconstructed, and new boats will be both more common and finished *properly* more often.

Open Statement

We plan to expand the shop and streamline the 12-footer construction techniques so as to free us for more one-off work.

Bill Shuman
P.O. Box 86
Wells, ME 04090
(207) 646-5775

General Information

Number of builders: One.
Capacity: 45 feet.
Specialties: Custom construction and traditional small craft.
Nontraditional modes: Yes.
Experience: Strip only.
Preferred paints and glues: Half traditional, half modern.
Sail and/or power: Sail.

Facilities

Design and drafting: Yes.
Lumber storage: 2,000 b.f.
Metal working: No.

History

Origin of interest: My folks are sailing people.
Training: At Washington County Vocational Technical Institute.
Selection of location: I moved from Downeast for a better market.
Financing: Loan and personal work.

Recent Projects

A 15-foot 3-inch peapod, Virginia-cedar-on-oak; a 16-foot No Man's Land of the same materials; a 28-foot whaleboat as a gig for the *Constitution*; and a 20-foot dory skiff.

Lumber and Hardware

Lumber quality is down; forests are diminishing due to overdevelopment and housing. I'd like to have my own woodlot someday. Hardware: I never *have* been able to find most of the items I need.

Cooperatives

A cooperative sawmill has real possibilities, likewise a cooperative for fastenings.

The Market

There will always be a demand for a good boat built out of wood. The market is growing now and will continue to do so.

Who is Buying and Why

So far it has been young, working people and the U.S. Navy.

The Labor Pool

I work alone, so it's not applicable. I would say that competency is high in small shops.

Vocational Training

My attitude is basically positive. Five years ago, WCVTI had its problems, but it seems to have improved. The best way is to apprentice in a small shop with an experienced builder.

Modern and Traditional Design

Traditional.

Time and Finish

As regards traditional small craft, all work is structurally important. The best fit I can do is warranted. On the interiors of larger boats, it comes down to what people want to pay for.

Walter J. Simmons
Duck Trap Woodworking
RFD 2, Cannan Road
Lincolnville Beach, ME 04849

Walter is no stranger to readers of *WoodenBoat* issues 2 and 26, or his recent books, *Lapstrake Boatbuilding* and *Lapstrake Boatbuilding,* Volume 2. For those less familiar, his businesslike attitude is evident in his comment on how he approaches each project. "I build the boats in the order that the contracts are signed. I pick up the top one on the stack, look underneath long enough to get the information I need to order materials, and then I get to work."

General Information

Number of builders: Just myself.
Capacity: 20 feet.
Specialties: The Lincolnville Wherry, Matinicus Double-Ender, and the Newfoundland Trap Skiff.

Walt Simmons stokes up an old favorite before tackling the inwales for a Lincolnville wherry.

Nontraditional modes: No.

Preferred paints and glues: Mostly traditional.

Sail and/or power: Sail and oar.

Facilities

Design and drafting: Yes.

Metal working: Patterns; distributor for Skookum Fastenings.

History

Origin of interest: Chromosomes—raised with it.

Training: With Merrill Young.

Selection of location: I'm from here.

Recent Projects

A 9-foot yacht tender, a wherry, and a Newfoundland Trap Skiff.

Projects in Store

A Culler Staten Island Skiff; *more* wherries, tenders, and double-enders.

Unusual Tools and Methods

See *Lapstrake Boatbuilding* and *Lapstrake Boatbuilding*, Volume 2, by W. J. Simmons.

Lumber and Hardware

Except for cedar, which *is* in question, it is no worse than it was before. Builders have been complaining about lumber for 50 years. They are cutting more than before so there is more garbage, but it's the same percentage of what is cut. In hardware, there will be more of the here-and-there stuff, with Skookum, Steinmetz, etc., filling in the gap for themselves, and consequently for other traditionalists.

Cooperatives

No.

The Market

If the Kansas Coast Guard gets off our backs, we'll stand a chance. We must also realize that (pardon the pun) the screws are being put to us on fastenings; compared to labor costs, these are skyrocketing.

Who is Buying and Why

Everybody. I was flooded with orders after that last *WoodenBoat* piece. It's the vicious circle; you can't get work without experience or experience without work. We need to return to a *real* apprenticeship with a mutual agreement on who works how long, and what he will *learn* in return. Of course, this brings in regulations again, but it all has to be dealt with somehow. The labor pool is better than most people think. A lack of communication has a lot of us thinking we are one of a few. I think the Traditional Small Craft Association and active listings like this book can go a long way toward dealing with this.

Modern and Traditional Design

Traditional.

Time and Finish

If you are a boatbuilder, dead fits are not *that* time-consuming. It takes a little longer to do it right than it does to do it wrong—sometimes *less* if you have your efficiency down. There is no way to excuse what you can't do, so don't try.

Open Statement

One of our wherries parted her painter while being towed offshore in October 1976 and was presumed lost. In May 1977, we received a call from the Coast Guard station at Cape May, New Jersey, saying one of their cutters had picked her up about 70 miles off the Jersey shore. She had about three inches of water in her, and some chafed paint, but all her gear was intact—afloat alone for better than six months. Are they good sea boats? You tell us.

F. Everett Smith
The Everett Canoe and Guide-boat Works
Parishville Road
Parishville, NY 13672
(315) 265-3224

General Information

Number of builders: Myself and David Obermeyer.

Capacity: 30 feet.

Specialties: Adirondack guide-boats; Rushton reproductions; St. Lawrence skiffs; canoes; early runabouts; and launches.

Nontraditional modes: No.
Experience: No.
Preferred paints and glues: Modern adhesives, older varnishes.
Sail and/or power: 25 percent paddle; 25 percent rowing; 25 percent power; 25 percent sail.

Facilities

Design and drafting: Yes.
Lumber storage: 4,000 b.f.
Metal working: We make some small-boat hardware when necessary.

History

As a kid in the Adirondacks it was just a part of summer to use and maintain the wooden boats. A great-uncle, George Everett, made lovely canoe paddles of black cherry and encouraged my interest in craftsmanship and quiet boats. The rest of my training came from old books, the builders I could find, the museums, and experience. It's an ongoing process through the new books, publications, and the shared experience of other builders. I set up shop in the North Country because it is my *home* country, and the boats we build are native to this area. The new shop, an ex-gas station and laundromat, was financed by the sale of an old farmhouse we had completely revitalized.

Recent Projects

A 14-foot lightweight sporting boat; a 15-foot 6¾-inch reproduction of Rushton's *Vesper*; a 16-foot Adirondack guide-boat; and restoration of a 1928 hydroplane.

Projects in Store

An 18-foot St. Lawrence skiff; a 16-foot guide-boat; restoration of an early Gold Cup contender; and restoration of a small steam launch.

Lumber and Hardware

The wood is still available in our area but has to be actively searched for and selected from the smaller mills. The future is uncertain as more and more trees are cut young for pulpwood and firewood, not to mention the industrial reapers of furniture woods.

Cooperatives

Could be good but difficult to set up. We already do it on an informal basis with local woodworkers.

The Market

Interest in traditional wooden boats is growing. I think there will always be a market for a limited number of boats native to a given area or region.

Who is Buying and Why

My customers have been various types: an antique-car restorer who wanted to do some old-style cruising; the proprietor of a wooden-boat shop who wanted a boat for his mother; and a local man who wanted a small boat for fishing.

The Labor Pool

It's hard to find experienced boat carpenters here. It's easy to find someone interested, but rare that someone has the patience to do a good job while learning.

Modern and Traditional Design

I enjoy the traditional lines. They are easy to look at, easy to understand, hold some history, and just seem to belong in the water.

Anyone who has ever rowed an Adirondack guide-boat like this nearly completed one in Everett Smith's shop can only shake their head in wonder and disgust at what passes for a "row-boat" in most places to-day. There can be almost no comparison with the joyful quiet of a guide-boat as she slips along. (Everett Smith photo)

Restorations and Replicas

I prefer to build a new boat from scratch, but it can be positively exciting to find the physical evidence of a process—the tool used, the direction of the cut, or the quality of the work. There is plenty of work to be done in the preservation of historically significant boats, but I feel there should be more emphasis on the new boats and boatbuilders.

Time and Finish

This is a question I've been wrestling with. We often spend too much time on a job just to get the good fit—then don't charge enough for the time spent—and still seem expensive. I have the idea that speed and accuracy come with experience and age. When you're starting to train new fellows on the job, the tight fit can be costly, but I think it's necessary. Once accomplished, everyone is confident and more productive.

Open Statement

It is our intention to help keep wooden boats on the waterways of the Adirondacks—old boats or new boats—and to provide a viable, satisfying occupation for a few boatbuilders.

Ralph W. Stanley
Ralph W. Stanley, Inc.
Southwest Harbor, ME 04679
(207) 244-3795

General Information

Number of builders: Four to seven employees.

Capacity: 50 feet.

Specialties: Powerboats for work or pleasure; traditional sailboats; Friendship sloops.

Nontraditional modes: No.

Experience: Yes.

Preferred paints and glues: Traditional.

Sail and/or power: Both equally.

Facilities

Design and drafting: Yes.

Lumber storage: I have room for 6,000 b.f. but don't usually have that much on hand.

Metal working: Patterns.

History

I became interested in boatbuilding as a boy. During the war years, there was much building here and I had a good chance to observe firsthand. I built several small boats and when I finished school (1951), I wanted a 28-foot motorboat. The only way I could get it was to build it myself. I found it was much better to wait, watch, and think about some particular phase that I might be stuck on, rather than ask. Some builders were real jealous about their secrets and some might even intentionally tell you to do something a wrong way. Others would be helpful and tell you the best they could, but each had his own way to do the same job. I found it better to observe and draw my own conclusions. Maybe I could figure out a better way. Such was my training. After I had built my first boat I thought, "I'm glad it is done. I won't have the courage to start another." Several months later, when a man wanted me to build him a boat, I couldn't wait to get started. I've been building ever since. I set up here because it is where I had always lived, and because my parents had a barn that I could use as a shop. My business grew over the years and I set up my new shop with bank financing.

Recent Projects

Presently building a 36-foot by 12-foot passenger boat; last year, restored a 1916 R-class racing sloop; year before *that*, built a 26-foot Friendship sloop. All were bronze-fastened, mostly cedar and oak.

Projects in Store

A 46-foot pleasure cruiser and restoration of a classic antique catboat.

Lumber and Hardware

There is plenty of good lumber in the woods. The problem is to find the mill that'll do custom sawing and milling. I have to have most of my hardware custom-made.

The Market

There will be fewer builders in wood and customers will expect first-class quality construction. And they will expect to pay top dollar. Some have tried fiberglass boats and are coming back to wood.

Who is Buying and Why

People who come to me seem to have put a lot of thought into their boat and know what they want.

The Labor Pool

It's getting better. The boatbuilding school at Eastport puts out some good students.

Age has only enhanced the appearance of this tender, though good maintenance has helped. An oversized canvas-covered, rubber-cored outwale has been added to protect her from the buffeting that comes with heavy use.

Vocational Training

The trend in vocational schools is toward younger students right out of high school. In the past, most were college graduates who had good-paying jobs but decided to give it all up to study boatbuilding. It seems much easier for the younger students to acquire the necessary skills and dexterity. I'm not saying that a boatbuilder shouldn't have a college education (which could come later). One thing I think should go along with the study of boatbuilding is bookkeeping and accounting—a course in running a business.

Modern and Traditional Design

I wonder how many modern boats will be considered worth preserving when they get old.

Restorations and Replicas

I cannot restore just any old boat. It has to be a classic example of historic significance that appeals to me. That R boat was a classic example, unlike some Rs that were built to extremes; I wouldn't want to attempt to restore something extreme. Some boats are too far gone. One Friendship sloop brought in for rebuilding was so out of shape and altered that we sawed her up and built a replica. Skill is something very hard to teach. Boatbuilding is a challenge, and each boat often requires a new skill. If you accept the challenge, you will develop the skills.

Time and Finish

I do set a standard. Do the best you can and you will always do your best.

Open Statement

Many of the customers who have boats built here want us to store and take care of them also. My business is small, but I try to keep it growing slowly, not let it get too big too quickly or take on more work than I can handle. I want to take an active part in the building of my boats from start to finish, and in the maintenance after it is in use. I follow problems that might arise with its operation and keep track of how I could improve the boat or model—whether it suits the man for whom I built it, etc. The opportunity to expand is there, but I'm afraid I would spend all my time running around with a pencil and paper giving directions to the crew. I would lose my sense of satisfaction in seeing a boat that I had built (especially a workboat) out sailing and in feeling that I'm contributing to the economy and the good of the people.

James Steele
Downeast Peapods
Brooklin, ME 04616

It takes just 80 hours for Jimmy to build a "Chevy-model" peapod. With the jig and router (accompanying photos), he can cut all four stem and stern rabbets in minutes!

General Information

Number of builders: Myself and my son sometimes.

Specialties: I build only this 13-foot 6-inch by 4-foot 6-inch peapod. I have a Chevy model (paint finish), a Cadillac (varnished mahogany thwarts and sheer strake), and a Rolls (all-varnish, including cedar planking).

Preferred paints and glues: Mostly traditional.

Facilities

Lumber storage: 5,000 to 7,000 b.f.

History

Training: In yards around the Blue Hill area.

Selection of location: I'm from here.

Recent Projects

Ten years ago I was building 10 to 15 boats a year. Now I've cut back to five or six so I can work at house construction.

Projects in Store

I'm booked through 1980.

Unusual Tools

Maynard Bray helped me work up this router rig. I think it is self-explanatory, if you just think of the two spring-loaded wheels keeping the rig tight to a jig.

Lumber and Hardware

Cedar is being cut for fences and shingles. We are lucky they don't make paper from it or it would *all* be gone. I don't think hardware will ever be a problem for me.

Cooperatives

We all ought to get together and buy 1,000,000 wooded acres. Seriously, it's a fine idea, but who's going to do the work?

The Market

About the time the lumber runs out, so will the builders. If you can ever get the materials and know-how to build a wooden boat, you'll be able to sell it. There's a small, steady market.

The Labor Pool

It'll never be like it was. The market simply won't support the numbers. As for the present, I don't know whether there are more good than bad men.

Vocational Training

They ought to teach more repair, hauling, storage, and engine work. It would be nice if they could all make a living building new boats, but I don't think it is realistic to expect that to happen.

Modern and Traditional Design

Traditional.

Time and Finish

You do it one way whether it's a Cadillac or a Chevy. My best is that one way. The only difference is the finish; with the first, you might go to 200-grit paper, instead of something less fine on the Chevy.

Ken Steinmetz
Ken's Boat Shop
3710 Ocean Avenue
Seaford, NY 11783
(516) 826-8116

"I won't work below my own standards for anybody or any price. That boat is me; it's Ken's Boat Shop. It represents me after it leaves here. When someone sees the boat, it shows my workmanship and standards in general. It even has a name plaque *saying* Ken's Boat Shop!"

General Information

Number of builders: One.
Capacity: 17 feet.
Specialties: Custom, traditional small craft; power, oar, and sail.
Nontraditional modes: Strip only.
Experience: No.
Preferred paints and glues: A mixture of old and new. For instance, I use pine tar but also Thiokol.

Sail and/or power: Sail, in new construction, but some of my bread and butter is in repair of powerboats.

Facilities

Design and drafting: No.

Lumber storage: I buy when it is available. Right now I have about 600 b.f.

Metal working: Patterns; distributor for Skookum Fastenings. I sell a #1½ (2-inch inside diameter) bronze oarlock that fits a standard socket. This is from my own casting blank. With a lot of people returning to traditional longer oars, this is a great boon.

History

Origin of interest: Seeing my first Whitehall.

Training: In boatyards.

Selection of location: I'm from the area.

Recent Projects

A 16-foot John Gardner-designed peapod; a 16-foot 9-inch fancy Boston Whitehall (replica of the one in the Mystic Seaport collection); and a Culler Good Little Skiff.

Projects in Store

Possible Rushton double-paddle canoe, and I'd like to build a lighter, finer boat in general. I also finish off to order a [cringe] fiberglass 14-foot 3-inch Whitehall, and always try to keep one in stock.

Lumber and Hardware

The price will be high, but more wood will be available because we will be a market. Hardware: More people could do what I do with oarlocks: carry and/or

Ken Steinmetz has a nice eye for proportion, as can be seen in the small details such as the beaded stringer and knees of this Good Little Skiff.

produce an item needed on a small scale, since the big companies can't or won't handle it. This is particularly true of stuff for traditional small craft.

The Market

As regards traditional small craft, the market has just started; it is improving and can only get better. The key is to give the public a good boat, a quality boat.

Who is Buying and Why

People with renewed interest in rowing and sailing small, practicable boats.

The Labor Pool

I steer clear of problems by having a one-man shop. In general, as a builder of traditional small craft, I don't have the volume to hire additional help—yet.

Vocational Training

With five or six schools in the whole country, even if they *are* producing enough workmen for new construction, the quality of repair work is generally very poor. There's a place for more students in repair. I'm all for the schools.

Modern and Traditional Design

I don't scorn things modern because they are modern; it's quality I'm after. You can't beat the older designs for rowing.

Time and Finish

I think the "old ways," where joints were dependent on the quality of the fit (not on modern sealants), are the ways to learn and emulate. If all the compound squeezes out of a joint, all well and good. Use good new materials, but don't depend on them. This will produce a superior boat.

Open Statement

It all comes down to the quality of the workmanship in construction or repair. The customer must be happy and satisfied.

David and Mark Stimson
Stimson Brothers Boatworks
Box 820
N. Falmouth, MA 02556
(617) 759-5038

General Information

Number of builders: Two.

Capacity: 50 feet.

Specialties: We like to build the designs of Pete Culler and other no-nonsense craft.

Nontraditional modes: No.

Preferred paints and glues: Pine tar, pitch, red lead, Weldwood glue, etc.

Sail and/or power: 70 percent sail, 30 percent power.

Facilities

Design and drafting: Yes.

Lumber storage: 1,000 b.f.

Metal working: No.

History

Origin of interest: Grew up around boats.

Training: Learned the trade in assorted boatyards and from the late Mert Long, master catboat builder and sparmaker.

Selection of location: I grew up here and like it here.

Financing: A bit at a time—savings from working at boatyards.

Recent Projects

A 44-foot McManus schooner *Surprise* (1918): new stem, breasthook, knightheads, frames, foredeck, sternpost, horn timbers, rudder well, deadwood, transom frames, 11 futtocks, topside planking, refastening, transom, and foremast step. *That's* what you'd call a rebuild. Built new: a Pete Culler Good Little Skiff; a 15-foot quahog skiff; a Herreshoff double-paddle canoe; masts and booms for a 55-foot Newfoundland schooner.

Projects in Store

A 13-foot dory and a 20-foot St. Lawrence skiff, on speculation.

Unusual Methods

We work out of a 6-foot by 16-foot shed, which houses a 16-inch planer, 20-inch bandsaw, workbench, and so forth. The shed is designed to fit on our 26-foot flatbed trailer, so we can go where the work is.

Lumber and Hardware

Good-quality lumber and hardware will always be available—for a price.

Cooperatives

No need for one. We cooperate with other builders in our own simple, if unorganized, way.

The Market

See Open Statement below.

Modern and Traditional Design

Traditional boats are simple, easy to build; materials are less costly, time-tested, and better looking.

Restorations and Replicas

If you concentrate on boat preservation, the skills preservation is maintained automatically.

Time and Finish

Our standards vary according to the job; an old workboat should receive different treatment from a fine yacht.

Open Statement

We'd like to do more new construction, but the bread and butter seems to be in repair work. Maybe the market will improve when the oil runs out. Fiberglass boats are made out of *oil*, you know.

David Sweet
P.O. Box 178
Northeast Harbor, ME 04662
(207) 276-3272

General Information

Number of builders: One.
Capacity: 22 feet.
Specialties: Traditional small craft and cruising craft.
Nontraditional modes: No.
Experience: No.
Preferred paints and glues: Traditional—I hate epoxy.
Sail and/or power: 90 percent sail, 10 percent power.

Facilities

Design and drafting: Yes.
Lumber storage: 3,000 b.f.
Metal working: Patterns.

History

Origin of interest: The enjoyment of sailing.
Training: The Apprenticeshop and three months at Shew and Burnham's.
Selection of location: I'm from here.
Financing: By building boats.

Recent Projects

A 7-foot (¼-scale) model of a Pemaquid Friendship sloop of cedar and oak for the Penobscot Museum and two 15-foot sailing peapods of cedar and oak, copper-fastened.

Projects in Store

A 13-foot by 48-inch peapod with a little reverse curve in the frames at each end, eight planks to the side. There's a local boat to take the lines off of and build a replica for one lady, and then a companionway for a sailboat.

Unusual Tools

To hold the frames of small boats to the ribbands, I use these wire ties about 7½ inches long that I get at Agway. You just need the tightening hook to give them a twist—very fast.

Lumber and Hardware

Hardware is getting better because we now have a local foundry. Lumber is about the same. The quality would improve if they'd stop cutting up all the stumpage for shingles.

Cooperatives

There's a problem with getting past the talk to action. It's all in the individuals; there is generally a lack of "pride of ownership"—responsibility.

The Market

There's more free time and pleasure craft are an outlet for this. People are beginning to appreciate wood again—its beauty. On the whole, I don't know where it is going; I'm relatively new at this.

David Sweet's beautifully lined-off peapod fits right into Northeast Harbor, Maine, where traditional boats have been known to outnumber the usual alternatives. The problems of boat ownership were brought home to him moments after this photograph was taken, when he realized that someone had stolen her hand-made spruce oars.

Vocational Training

I think they are doing a good job. The biggest problem is to learn to "read," understand wood.

Modern and Traditional Design

My preference is for *good-looking* boats.

Restorations and Replicas

They are inseparable.

Time and Finish

If you're gonna do it, you might as well do it *right*. To spend the time to do it right the first time makes more sense than doing it over later.

Open Statement

Enjoying your work is important—banging on boats (or woodworking, in general) is just that for me. But to make a living at this is even nicer.

Gordon Swift
Swift Custom Boats
RFD 2, Shaws Hill, Kensington
Exeter, NH 03833
(603) 772-5557

General Information

Number of builders: One.
Capacity: 40 feet.
Specialties: Custom sail.
Nontraditional modes: Prefer not to.
Experience: Some.
Preferred paints and glues: Mostly traditional.
Sail and/or power: Sail.

Facilities

Design and drafting: No, just interior layout.

Lumber storage: 2,000 b.f.

Metal working: Keels only.

History

Origin of interest: Sailing my own boat.

Training: I spent 13 years with Bud McIntosh.

Selection of location: I was in this area from working at Bud's and liked it.

Recent Projects

A 34-foot 8-inch William Warner ketch, cedar-on-laminated-white-oak, copper-riveted.

Projects in Store

Another 34-foot ketch like the last one.

Unusual Methods

These finger rings for opening lockers are easy to make with hole-cutting bits. I drill the outside of the cylinder first, stop short to create the lip, then come back through, cutting out the entire inner cylinder. By cutting the largest diameter last (the outside of the lip), I free the ring from the block of wood. The collapsible engine box under the bridge-deck allows complete access to the engine, yet it is quite tight. Part of this is due to these plates with keyhole slots set at the bottom of this panel. The pin is nothing more than a round-headed screw set into

Left: *The interior of the 34' William Warner ketch that Gordon Swift built for wooden yacht broker Bill Page. Bill and Swifty put many years of experience into the design and construction of Bill's dream-come-true. It shows.*

Right: *Gordon Swift's finger rings for opening lockers. Keyhole locks for collapsible engine blocks. A unique spar sander attachment: with one hand each on the drill and rod control handle, the rough sanding of a spar is a snap—likewise furniture legs, balusters, and other turned woodwork. (Rebecca Wheeler illustrations)*

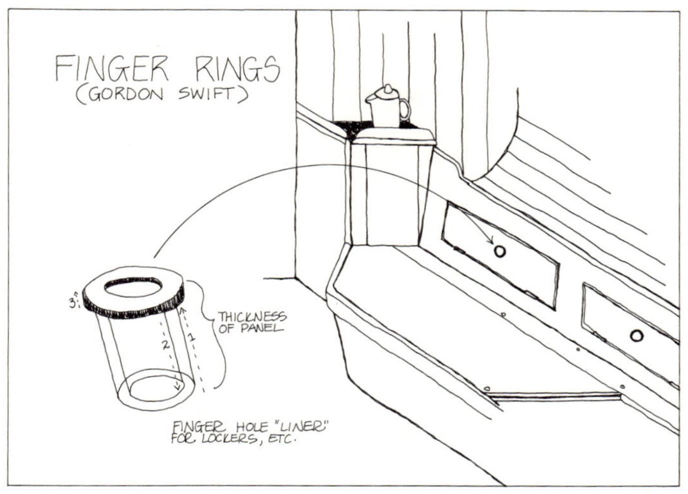
FINGER RINGS
(GORDON SWIFT)
3"
THICKNESS
OF PANEL
FINGER HOLE "LINER"
FOR LOCKERS, ETC.

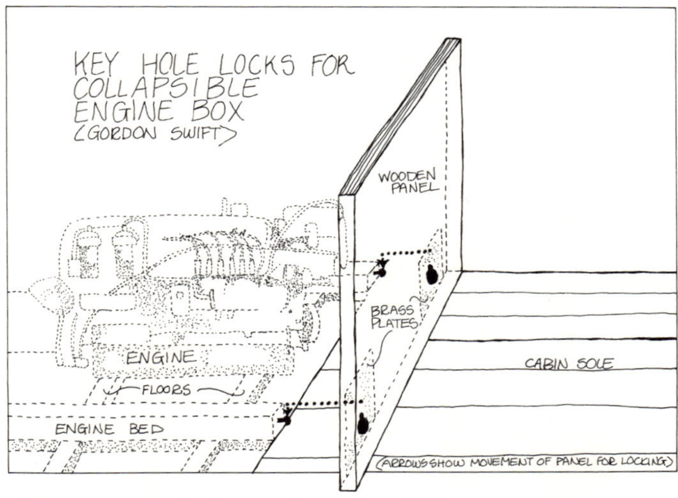
KEY HOLE LOCKS FOR
COLLAPSIBLE
ENGINE BOX
(GORDON SWIFT)
WOODEN
PANEL
BRASS
PLATES
ENGINE
FLOORS
CABIN SOLE
ENGINE BED
(ARROWS SHOW MOVEMENT OF PANEL FOR LOCKING)

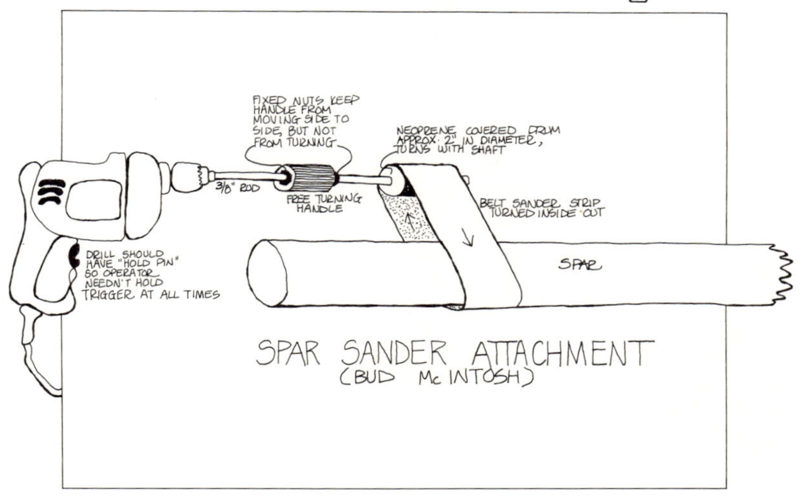
FIXED NUTS KEEP
HANDLE FROM
MOVING SIDE TO
SIDE, BUT NOT
FROM TURNING
NEOPRENE COVERED DRUM
APPROX. 2" IN DIAMETER,
TURNS WITH SHAFT
3/8" ROD
FREE TURNING
HANDLE
BELT SANDER STRIP
TURNED INSIDE OUT
DRILL SHOULD
HAVE "HOLD PIN"
SO OPERATOR
NEEDN'T HOLD
TRIGGER AT ALL TIMES
SPAR
SPAR SANDER ATTACHMENT
(BUD McINTOSH)

the engine bed. You've probably seen Bud McIntosh's spar sander, and that stuff. [I had, but this is a good time to show it.—P.L.] A three-eighths rod is fitted with a free-turning handle and a larger-diameter fixed cylinder, the latter covered with a rubber strip to prevent slippage. Belt-sander strips turned inside out loop around the fixed drum and spar, the operator controlling the tension on the strip and the direction and speed along the spar with his grip on the drill and the handle.

Lumber and Hardware

The oil crunch will raise Cain with the wood market since good-quality timber is being cut for firewood. Cutting is indiscriminate.

Cooperatives

Negative, too individualistic.

The Market

More and more people are getting into cruising sail in wood, as they become disenchanted with fiberglass.

The Labor Pool

Lots of quantity, not much quality, and no change coming. Most want to learn it all in five minutes, not take seven years building boats and another few in a marina to learn that they didn't know anything when they started.

Vocational Training

As a rule, I'm for it since it's the only chance a guy has. A yard can't afford to pay an apprentice.

Modern and Traditional Design

No preference.

Restorations and Replicas

I'd like to see more emphasis on skills.

Time and Finish

I think the criteria are in the owner's pocketbook, what he or she can afford, With the average customer, there's no such thing as a simple boat—you start with that and end with a yacht.

Open Statement

It's a good living. I like the hours, work, etc. There's a certain satisfaction in the completed work, seeing the boat on the water.

Ray Wallace
R.L. Wallace and Sons
P.O. Box 209
Thomaston, ME 04861
(207) 354-6391 (home)

When I worked next door, the *scrap* pile at the seemingly ancient Wallace boatyard and mill was 70 feet by 18 feet by 6 feet of flitch-sawn oak. The bottom of the pile disappeared in a heap of sawdust and wood chips of unknown depth. At times, taking the truck in for materials was like driving across a firm sponge.

General Information

Number of builders: Fourteen.

Capacity: 100 feet.

Specialties: Custom sail and power.

Nontraditional modes: No.

Experience: No.

Preferred paints and glues: Some of each.

Sail and/or power: 60 percent power, 40 percent sail.

Facilities

Design and drafting: No.

Lumber storage: 20,000 b.f., if you include the mill.

Metal working: Limited.

History

Origin of interest: The yard's been in the family since 1941.

Training: Right here.

Selection of location: I'm from here.

Recent Projects

A 60-foot hard-pine-on-oak, galvanized-fastened dragger; a 60-foot oak-on-oak dragger; a 92-foot centerboard cargo schooner for Ned Ackerman.

Projects in Store

A 40-foot lobsterboat; a 30-foot ketch; and possibly a 120-foot schooner for Ned.

Lumber and Hardware

Lumber is getting scarce, getting hard to get. Quality can only be upheld if you pick more selectively out of what you've got.

Cooperatives

I don't know; it might come to that.

The Market

Gaining all the time. I've seen more people talking wooden boats in the last year than ever before. I don't know why, perhaps publicity from the schooner and/or the steel yards being too booked-up.

The Labor Pool

For the most part, I've been able to get good help.

Vocational Training

The schooling helps quite a bit. It's all right as far as it goes. They don't teach much on repair or on building big stuff, but on that last, there's only going to be so much new stuff.

Modern and Traditional Design

Traditional.

Time and Finish

We work mostly within what the owner can pay, as long as the boat is seaworthy.

Joel White
Brooklin Boat Yard
Brooklin, ME 04616
(207) 359-2236

Despite a very busy schedule, Joel White made time for me. When he said he trained with Arno Day, I wasn't surprised. Here's another man with a heart of gold.

General Information

Number of builders: Ten crew, total.
Capacity: 45 feet.
Specialties: Custom sail and power.
Nontraditional modes: Yes, strip only.
Experience: Glued-strip only.
Preferred paints and glues: Mostly traditional.
Sail and/or power: Sail.

Facilities

Design and drafting: Yes.
Lumber storage: 2,000 to 3,000 b.f.
Metal working: Patterns.

History

Origin of interest: I grew up loving the water.
Training: With Arno Day.

Recent Projects

A 34-foot lobsterboat-type yacht (my own design); a Herreshoff 12½ sailing dinghy; a 14-foot peapod for sailing. (See *WoodenBoat*, No. 26 and No. 27, for a step-by-step story on building the 12½.)

Projects in Store

Another 12½-foot sailing dinghy; a peapod; and we are finishing off a 31-foot fiberglass scallop/lobsterboat.

Lumber and Hardware

Lumber is scarcer and hardware is poorer. I think the good-quality stuff is being used elsewhere, in other industries. Local wood is there; it's just hard to find someone to cut it because of low demand.

Cooperatives

You might be able to work it out with enough builders.

The Market

A lot of small wooden boats will be built, mostly by amateurs or by people who *think* they are making a living at it, but aren't. Fiberglass builders are the ones who'll do well in the next 10 years. Still, the small one- and two-man wood shops will survive.

Who is Buying and Why

Lots of people are interested, but most get scared off by the price.

The Labor Pool

I'm positive about it, but only because I just need a small number of men and I can train my own. I don't work with dozens or hundreds.

Vocational Training

Good. It works fine for some (the doers), and the dreamers are always in the yard looking for work.

Modern and Traditional Design

I think traditional craft look better and are probably better sailing boats as a whole.

Time and Finish

It's hard to do a rough job after you've done a fine one. We always try to do the best we can at the risk of doing more than we have to.

John Wisner
Daybreak Boat Shop
18 Concord Street
South Norwalk, CT 06854
(203) 866-2252

As you can see from the photographs on page 348, Wisner and clan do not hesitate to explore new territory. Theirs is a can-do attitude. Among the things they have done and will do are rebuilding antique cars and wooden airplanes.

General Information

Number of builders: Four.
Capacity: 40 feet.
Specialties: Custom pleasure boats from traditional small craft to 40 feet.
Nontraditional modes: Yes.
Experience: Yes.
Preferred paints and glues: Modern, mostly.
Sail and/or power: 90 percent sail.

Facilities

Design and drafting: Modification of existing designs only, but we have access to some fine local NAs.
Lumber storage: Limited.
Metal working: Patterns.

History

Origin of interest: I had an early interest in woodworking and eventually came to feel that boatbuilding is the ultimate form of woodworking.
Training: With Ely Boatworks for four years and on my own.
Selection of location: I'm from here.
Financing: We started on $500 with two months rent ahead and a will to work.

Recent Projects

A Phil Bolger-designed 51-foot three-piece collapsible ketch, with a gaff main and Chinese lug mizzen. She has internal water ballast and leeboards. At the same time, we've got this Bolger catboat going. We've torn the roof off the shop, enlarged our capacity, and generally updated our facilities.

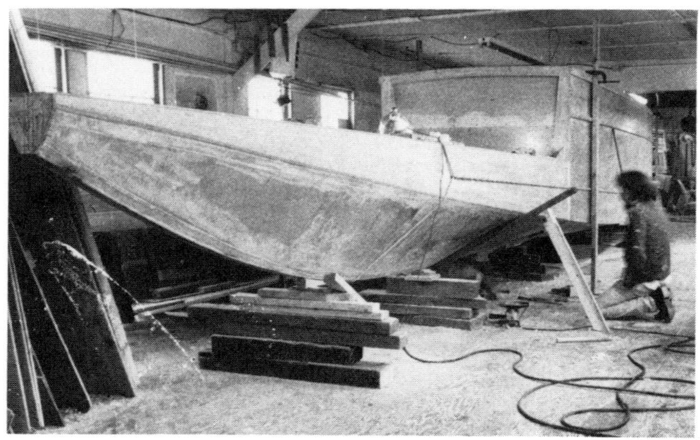

John Wisner and his crew are fitting the mounting brackets on this three-piece ketch. A Spanish windlass helps to pull the bow and midsections together. A tip made out of a large block of fir will be attached to the bow of the former as an emergency shock absorber.

Projects in Store

New canvas decks on a 42-foot Persson-built Herreshoff; some basic boatbuilding and seamanship courses during the evenings through our new "Traditional Boat Center."

Lumber and Hardware

Both are good. With modern techniques, we can make up for deficiencies in quality. Cost will go up, of course, if we have to laminate to get bigger timbers, but then the piece is that much stronger.

Cooperatives

Yes for shops run on that basis—no for buying. In general, boatbuilding is too personal an expression to buy materials in lots.

The Market

Wooden and/or steel boatbuilding is where the whole boating field is turning, due to the cost and politics inherent in fiberglass—national economics remaining as they are.

Who is Buying and Why

People of the greater New York area who want boats as luxuries.

This Bolger catboat was designed for do-it-yourself builders used to thinking in the simple planes of house construction.

The Labor Pool

Good on both quantity and quality.

Vocational Training

Great, though I don't feel that even a two-year course is more than introductory. If they don't emphasize the cut-and-dried realities of making a living at it, there is a lag between the graduating student and the 20th century. These programs are preparatory for real on-the-job apprenticeships, where being right *and* fast are essential.

Modern and Traditional Design

No preference.

Restorations and Replicas

I'm more into the functional aspects of boats than their charm. Charm is more an expression of function. Form follows function, that is the beauty.

Time and Finish

One has to have commercial awareness. Beyond function or structural integrity, the owner-to-be must pay for aesthetics. Consideration and understanding of this often determines whether or not a shop is successful.

Open Statement

Beyond cost and time invested, the answer lies in complete satisfaction and involvement with every project, the priority being that a boat must be built *right*, above how much money we are going to make.

The Apprenticeshop and Restorationshop
Lance Lee, Director
Dave Foster, Master Builder
375 Front Street
Bath, ME 04530
(207) 443-5638

The ideas evident in this interview coalesced in Lance Lee's fertile mind while he was working for Outward Bound. In 1972, the present shop was constructed almost entirely of "scrounged" materials with volunteer labor, thus setting the tone of this small-is-beautiful, labor-intensive program. The two-year apprenticeship and six-week internship spark about 35 letters of inquiry every month, underlining the fact that this is the best-known school in the country. For more on it, see the June 1974 and May 1975 issues of *Sail* magazine; *WoodenBoat*, No. 4; Volume 5, Number 2, of the American Heritage Society's *Americana*; and the September 1978 issue of U.S. Naval Institute *Proceedings*.

General Information

Number of builders: One master builder, two journeymen, 16 apprentices, and a pair of interns.

At the Apprenticeshop, an enthusiastic intern's handsome skiff shows a good starting effort. The internship program was developed "due to an incredible interest in participation at the shop," and involves "total immersion" in the Apprenticeshop and its philosophies.

Capacity: 30+ feet.

Specialties: Traditional small craft from the East Coast and, occasionally, modern adaptations of those designs. We have also had Paul Schweiss here to teach Scandinavian practices.

Nontraditional modes: No.

Preferred paints and glues: Traditional; particularly linseed, pine tar, and turpentine. We do use Deks Olje.

Sail and/or power: Sail and oars. We have rarely worked with power craft and prefer not to, though we have been known to make exceptions for the restoration of a successful older type.

Facilities

Design and drafting: Limited.

Lumber storage: We have two spaces we try to keep well stocked; they are 30 feet by 20 feet and 50 feet by 30 feet.

Metal working: We are just beginning to develop a machine shop, blacksmithing shop, and casting facility.

History

Training: Dave Foster's training comes from Flyer's Boatyard in Provincetown, Massachusetts; his own yard in Truro, Pamet River; Reed's in Boothbay, and others.

Selection of location: Availability to older builders, craft, and materials.

Financing: Monies are scrounged from all sorts of sources: boat sales, admissions to the Bath Museum, etc. Everything is volunteer-built.

Recent Projects

A 35-foot Tancook whaler; a 15-foot Washington County peapod; a 22-foot Muscongus sloop; and others too numerous to mention.

Projects in Store

A Casco Bay Hampton boat; a Gardner-designed Matinicus Island peapod; a 15-foot Whitehall; and the metal-working facilities mentioned above.

Lumber and Hardware

Smaller boats and finer craftsmanship seem a simplistic but true way to deal with wood availability, which we believe to be declining, even though wood is a renewable resource. We expect, however, that as demand rises and portable mills develop untapped sources, things will improve. With hardware, lamentable stuff abounds, providing the impetus to make our own, or to train the younger generation with the master machinists around, etc. We also believe in wood hardware—cleats, etc.

Cooperatives

Lumber buying: We have done so and will continue to. We believe it's absolutely essential. In the shop, tools seem to cry out for owner-only usage, but power, space, heat, and administrative back-up will all increase costs. Hence, I increasingly like the idea of coops.

The Market

Smaller and finer. As the market sees and learns how shoddy many boats are, the market for good wood craftsmanship will rise. We believe that that and the cost of petrochemicals—together with a discernible impatience with the quality of life as a fast-food franchise in a revolving door, Muzak process—will turn them toward us.

The Labor Pool

We must train journeymen and pair trainees with the finest older craftsmen, or lose invaluable continuity. Apprentices and candidates are increasing in numbers; this is the need in the industry. The attraction of satisfying work remains the draw that compensates (somewhat) for the wage disgraces generally felt.

Modern and Traditional Design

Our preference is flagrant—traditional. The finest moves we see are in adaptations, taking a fine old design and bringing her up to date with the application of what has been learned or is available today. Epoxies solve some of the riddles posed by imperfect lumber; rig changes boost performance of older hulls; changes from fishing to recreational purposes can be a great design exercise.

Restorations and Replicas

We are adamant about skills preservation but in no way mean to ignore boat repair as significant. Our accent is on restoration of skills and realistic types. True replicas are nearly impossible to construct due to different lumber, fastenings, etc. In the past, a mistaken sense of responsibility led some to feel they "owed" the public a restored, varnished boat. We are about to display, with blowup photos and the like, a hulk—real basket case and a half a replica. This is to show the public that if some well-intentioned soul had replaced her strange, sawn-spruce framing with steam-bent ones, she'd be useless, even as an accurate artifact. On the question of priorities, I can only say that I have watched intelligent people put graving pieces into rotten timbers, in the side of large vessels. I cannot speak too strongly against such wasteful efforts that go beyond reason.

Time and Finish

Ours is an unusual situation in that the "dead fit" is a better opportunity for an apprentice to learn thoroughly than a fit that is only structurally sound. We probably overbuild in order to set standards for incoming students and others. We believe, however, in workboat finish as the most sensible route for most future wood revival work.

Open Statement

Wooden boats and good shops appear to us to be useful and needed statements for a nation exploring some of the most awful standards and sorriest integrity of product in history. We have here a gentle reminder of how things can be done—the means and methods—of the whole centuries-old tradition of the many skills that go to make up a good boat and boat shop.

The Landing Boatshop
Cricket Tupper and John Burgess
Turbat's Creek, Box 461
Kennebunkport, ME 04046
(207) 985-7976

One wall of the shop at Turbat's Creek is made of translucent panels, which lighten considerably the former cow barn. This change was just one of the many that the crew at the Creek accomplished in a single summer. They knocked out walls and ceilings, poured floors, wired, installed plumbing, brought in machinery, set up offices. . . . When the nine apprentices arrived, they were ready. Several years of planning, fund raising, and hard work came to fruition in a single day.

General Information

Number of builders: Nine apprentices, two instructors.
Capacity: 30 feet.
Specialties: Instruction in traditional plank-on-frame construction as practiced today; lap and carvel boats from 13 feet to 30 feet, built by apprentices.
Nontraditional modes: Glued-strip only.
Experience: Instructors do not, but we have the supervision and advice of Cyrus Hamlin, an accomplished glued-strip designer/builder. His office is in the same building.
Preferred paints and glues: Modern.
Sail and/or power: Tupper and Burgess work 50 percent each way; most of the apprentices are more experienced with sail.

Facilities

Design and drafting: Yes, as well as close connections with Cyrus Hamlin, as mentioned earlier.

Lumber storage: 3,000 b.f.

Metal working: We are considering establishing a small foundry.

History

Training: John Burgess started boatbuilding straight out of college, on the then-state-sponsored apprenticeship program. He worked for Earl Rummery in Biddeford, among others. He has also worked as a draftsman for Cyrus Hamlin. Cricket Tupper was one of John's first apprentices when he became the resident instructor at Project Seal—a small, multipurpose apprentice program in Marion, Massachusetts. She studied yacht design at Brown University the following year.

Selection of location: We set up in this area because John and Linda Burgess come from Kennebunkport, own a house here, and were homesick in Massachusetts. It proved to be an excellent choice, since we are accessible to both Maine and Massachusetts; many of our suppliers are in Boston.

Financing: Our school is privately financed and nonprofit. We have accepted donations and raised funds to buy the major shop machinery. Students pay tuition and the boats are sold by the school to defray expenses. We hope to be financially independent within the next few years, so as not to rely on fund-raising.

Recent Projects

So far the apprentices have built a 13-foot Chamberlain dory skiff and a 17-foot 3-inch Swampscott dory—that was in their first three months or so. At the same time they pushed along the construction of a 30-foot Sparkman and Stephens auxiliary sloop.

Projects in Store

To become a respected and recognized part of the wooden boatbuilding scene and develop a reputation for quality in both our apprentices and their work.

Lumber and Hardware

We hope that the resurgence of interest in traditional small boats will make it worthwhile for someone to hire more people to go into the woods and get it out. Like everyone else, we see the quality going down and the prices going up. So far, it hasn't done us much harm. Hardware is expensive and we can't see that this will get better!

Cooperatives

We approve of *any form* of cooperative buying/shipping that will reduce costs, and we hope that this can be arranged by us and/or others in the not-too-distant future.

The Market

We've noticed a new kind of boating hobbyist in the traditional watercraft enthusiast. They aren't necessarily previous boat owners. We wonder if it is a fad or people who really enjoy wooden boats and wooden boatbuilding.

Who is Buying and Why

Our apprentices' work is of "yacht" grade. Our boats are sold at respectable prices in yachting centers such as Cape Cod, Marblehead, Long Island Sound, etc.

The Labor Pool

Since we are a school, we work on quantity and quality. We give our apprentices work habits that will make them *useful* to professional builders and yards, rather than just good, but unemployable, trained craftsmen.

Vocational Training

This is our purpose. We do not expect that each of our apprentices will become a professional boatbuilder, but our program is essentially vocational. We require that work slips be filed and we try to develop a balance between speed and accuracy in each apprentice.

Modern and Traditional Design

We approve of both but build more of the traditional designs at present because they seem to be in greater demand.

Open Statement

We are enjoying ourselves and we know that the apprentices enjoy the work also. While we concentrate on having everyone do the best possible job of building and instructing, we are careful not to lose contact with the professional builders in our area. We will consider ourselves a success when we hear that our apprentices are doing good, solid, professional work on a career basis. This goes hand in hand with striving for high-grade work (of all types) in ourselves and the apprentices.

GREAT LAKES BUILDERS

Dean Haynes
D.E. Haynes
Box 262
Stillwater, MN 55082
(612) 439-6489

General Information

Number of builders: One employer, one subcontractor.
Capacity: 14 to 18 feet.
Specialties: Traditional small craft, the Whitehall skiff.
Nontraditional modes: No.
Experience: Yes.
Preferred paints and glues: Modern.
Sail and/or power: Rowing.

Facilities

Design and drafting: Yes.

Dick Wagner of Seattle's Old Boathouse was an early client of Dean Haynes. Dick's schooner Sinbad *and a Haynes Whitehall are shown here at the Port Townsend Festival, where they received a lot of attention from passersby.*

Lumber storage: Presently, 1,000 b.f. of white cedar, 200 feet of red cedar, 400 feet of white oak.

History

Origin of interest: Growing up on a lake.

Training: In boat shops—Johnson's Boatyard, White Bear Boat Yard, Lewis Yacht Co.

Selection of location: Job and marriage.

Financing: Small bank loans.

Recent Projects

14-foot, 16-foot, and 18-foot Whitehall skiffs of white cedar, white oak, teak, mahogany, cherry, copper, brass, and T-88 adhesive. (See *WoodenBoat*, No. 16.)

Projects in Store

More of the same.

Lumber and Hardware

Very little *good*-quality cedar. Hardware is no problem.

Cooperatives

There are none that I know of.

The Market

With a full-time employee I hope to be able to build more boats.

Who is Buying and Why

Customers are looking for hand-crafted and seaworthy boats with good rowing qualities.

The Labor Situation

I have tried training my own, but they don't last. I've spent a lot of time on apprentices with no return.

Modern and Traditional Design

My interests are in traditional.

Restorations and Replicas

Both are equally important.

Time and Finish

Only the best quality is the finished product. If it takes additional time, we spend the *time*!

Open Statement

I would like to see something in Minnesota in regard to a traditional boat society.

Ted McCutcheon
McCutcheon Boat Works
Charlevoix, MI 49720
(616) 547-9714

General Information

Number of builders: Six.
Capacity: Unlimited.
Specialties: Custom cruising sail.
Nontraditional modes: Yes.
Experience: Yes.
Preferred paints and glues: Fifty-fifty.
Sail and/or power: Sail.

Facilities

Design and drafting: Yes.
Lumber storage: 3,000 to 4,000 b.f.
Metal working: Patterns.

Recent Projects

The 55-foot by 16-foot, 45-ton *Welcome*, a working replica of the armed sloop the British had at Mackinac in the 1870s. She's white-cedar-on-fir. (See *WoodenBoat*, No. 10.) We also have going a 20-foot Flicka of cedar and oak, my design.

Projects in Store

A 24-foot Flicka.

Lumber and Hardware

Quality has been going down steadily for the last 20 years, and there's no end in sight. They are cutting smaller and smaller trees. The simpler the hardware, the harder it is to get.

Cooperatives

No. Somebody always ends up trying to make a buck off it.

The Market

I think the market is coming back. If you want a high-quality boat, you almost have to be in wood. Look at the number of fiberglass builders that have come and gone.

The Labor Pool

Very poor on both quantity and quality. The schools are a possibility, but it takes years to become a craftsman. It's not all that glamorous; it is hard work, difficult, even monotonous at times. You must be able to take pride in your work, in every shaving.

Vocational Training

There are a lot of dreamers and fanatics in them, but I think it's a fine idea, and they are doing a lot of good.

Modern and Traditional Design

Traditional! I think the modern racing hulls are some of the ugliest I've ever seen. I couldn't even enjoy looking at them, let alone building them.

Restorations and Replicas

Both. Old boats should be restored because we need the real thing as well as replicas whenever feasible.

Time and Finish

Up to a point, it depends on the owner's wallet. Some can't afford the best (which lasts longest) and since we tend to do the best we can, regardless, we lose a lot of money.

Open Statement

The trend in the modern world toward functional but ugly boats is dreadful. Much of the pleasure in sailing is the beauty of the craft. I'd rather look at a pretty woman all day than an ugly one. Besides, I find these modern, complicated, gadget-ridden boats are *not* all that fast, or as good as the older, prettier boats.

Ferdinand "Red" Nimphius
Nimphius Boat Co.
Neshkoro, WI 54960
(414) 293-4465

There are builders by the score who don't work within sight of water, but Red is more than 80 miles from the Great Lakes! Delivery of large boats often requires a house-moving crew and much ingenuity, but Red and his crew of young people thrive on it. (See *WoodenBoat*, No. 25, for an excellent interview.)

General Information

Number of builders: 17.
Capacity: 50 feet.
Specialties: Custom sail and power.
Nontraditional modes: Yes.
Experience: Yes.
Preferred paints and glues: We use a mixture, what works best. We use different glues with different woods, too.
Sail and/or power: 90 percent sail.

A lifetime of boatbuilding has brought Red Nimphius a well-deserved reputation for being able to build almost anything, including this 50′ Dutch frigate, Red Lion, *which weighs 38 tons.*

Facilities

Design and drafting: Yes.

Lumber storage: 50,000 b.f.

Metal working: Patterns and welding, including heliarc.

History

Origin of interest: Building boats for myself.

Training: From books, common sense, and old-timers.

Selection of location: I moved out of the city (Milwaukee) after the business got started.

Recent Projects

Whoa, all of them? Let's hit the biggies: the 50-foot Dutch frigate *Red Lion*—38 tons, three-masted, of pine and oak on 2½-inch by 3-inch oak frames; the Nimphius-designed 60-foot *Yellowbird* (private yacht) of 2-inch yellow cedar on oak, a ketch; and hull number 101 (over 25 feet); a 34-foot Atkin cutter of cedar-on-oak; a 30-foot Tahiti ketch; and a 25-foot Nimphius-designed racer.

Projects in Store

Two schooners, a 34-foot William Garden and a 47-foot Banks-type of my own design; an Al Mason 39-foot cutter; and a Ted Brewer 32-foot sharpie.

Lumber and Hardware

It's getting harder; I used to be able to order almost *anything*! I wish they weren't selling it all overseas. They are careless in what and how they are cutting; after the fast buck. They will wake up soon enough to their mistakes. They'll have to replant two for every one they cut—hardwoods, too. As to hardware, we're considering setting up our own foundry.

The workmanship of Red Nimphius' young crew is quite impressive, as evidenced by this companionway. Plastic dropcloths and paper protected the deck and superstructure of this 60′ private yacht during the spray painting.

Cooperatives

On a small scale it will work, builders splitting truck loads—shops too, if the men are honest. Lumber buyers for the coop would really have to know their stuff.

The Market

I think it's coming back, but not to its former peak. Better preservatives will make 50-year-old boats more common. People having more money helps too.

The Labor Pool

These young guys are dedicated as hell. My present trainees are *better* than those I had 30 years ago. Quantity is no problem either.

Vocational Training

I train my own, taking about three years with no set program. Some of them are damn good. I don't have any contact with the schools, but I'd have to say I'm for them in that they get people started.

Modern and Traditional Design

My preference is for the traditional, but I build both. We built the first Airex-foam boat in the U.S.; had to import the foam. I've built modern hulls but find the reverse-sheer, high-sided jobs ungraceful.

Restorations and Replicas

Boat preservation is expensive and too much work in most cases. Replicas last longer and are generally cheaper.

The Red Lion*'s poop deck and transom had to be constructed separately—in different buildings. The size of the project spurred Red Nimphius and his crew to create distinctive details like these circular patterns on the poop.*

Time and Finish

A good fit is essential, wood to wood, but you have to produce it in less than 99 years. That's the hard part, to get things done in reasonable time.

Open Statement

Don't sell wood short, even for spars. I once made a spar for the Smithsonian Institution that had to be lighter than aluminum and as strong.

Bruce W. Sodervick
Sodervick Studio
78 Main Street
Scottsville, NY 14546
(716) 889-4012

General Information

Number of builders: Three.
Capacity: 40 feet.
Specialties: Gaff rigs.
Nontraditional modes: Yes.
Experience: Yes, fiberglass and the WEST System.
Preferred paints and glues: Doesn't matter, as long as you keep them separate.
Sail and/or power: Fifty-fifty.

Facilities

Design and drafting: Yes.
Lumber storage: 1,000 b.f.
Metal working: Welding and forging.

History

Well, when I was about six I plugged the holes in my brother's discarded push-pole long boat, sawed some planks for the tongue-and-groove cross-planked floor, pounded them in, tarred everything, and had her all set to go. But when you are six you can't drive the truck, so I just sat in that boat on barrels in a field and never could get it to the water—a trike couldn't tow it. I reckon that sort of sets your teeth for the next boat. It was an eight-foot beat-up wherry. I converted it to a sailboat with a lightning jib for a mainsail and a plowshare for a keel. I worked it on with fiberglass and polyester resin (this was about 1954), even faired it off with the stuff, and damned if it didn't sail so well that some s.o.b. stole it. Then came working in, on, and behind all those 1940–1960 wooden-hulled Chris-Craft, Century, Hacker Craft, and Gar Wood runabouts. All this was in a place called Culver, Indiana. Of course we all got excited about building and designing water skis, and just "water inventions" in general. I nearly drowned twice. Been playing with sailboats only for the last 10 years or so. I'm in Scottsville, New York, because some financial support comes from teaching and commissions—allowing me to work on boats the way I wish.

Recent Projects

A 19-foot Swampscott sailing dory (Pete Culler's two-master); restored a 1924 plumb-stem 39-foot by 9-foot 6-inch gaff ketch of mahogany-on-oak; and restored a 1938 16-foot Comet, hull number 1119.

Projects in Store

Cold-molded lapstrake dinghies.

Unusual Methods

I loft on photographic backdrop paper—it comes in rolls 9 feet by 50 inches, has a perfect surface, is extremely durable; but alas, it expands when humid.

Lumber and Hardware

Farmers are increasingly my best source for lumber, and hardware is a toss-up between what you have to buy and what you can make. I stay simple.

Cooperatives

These don't seem to have much to do with me and my little operation.

The Market

First of all, this whole business isn't about *most* people. So the market, what little there is, will always be not worth it in dollars and cents, and always worth it as a life.

Who is Buying and Why

When they are taking pictures and staring, they often ask the price.

The Labor Pool

All the kids who are sick of college want to work on boatbuilding for a while; they are in abundance. Quality of temperament and skills are rare, and training usually costs more time and tools than they are worth, since they invariably move on.

Vocational Training

As with any school, I believe there are a few people teaching here and there doing a good job.

Modern and Traditional Design

Traditional. Actually, this question should ask, "Racing-rules designed or free-designed?" to which I would answer *free-designed*.

Restorations and Replicas

From what I have seen of replicas, I'd go with restoration. The subtle differences make all the difference in the world.

Time and Finish

Never having had a dead fit. . . .

Open Statement

Good boats carry spirit, they are important to be around—repairing, building, and sometimes touching that spirit.

Chip Stulen
Faering Design
Route 1, Box 223
Suttons Bay, MI 49682
(616) 271-6729

Working with Einar Eilefsen in Bjørkedal, Norway, Chip came to "appreciate the aesthetic and functional qualities inherent in these craft."

General Information

Number of builders: One.
Capacity: 25 feet.
Specialties: Traditional Norwegian lapstrake design and construction.
Nontraditional modes: No.
Experience: No.
Preferred paints and glues: Traditional to about 80 percent; I do use Deks Olje.
Sail and/or power: Sail 80 percent.

Facilities

Design and drafting: In the conventional sense, no. In the faering sense, yes.
Lumber storage: 1,000 b.f.
Metal working: No.

History

Origin of interest: I was in Scandinavia for cultural experience and schooling and ended up with Einar Eilefsen in Bjørkedal. This is the same man Paul Schweiss apprenticed with. The town is situated around a high lake in western Norway, and the people of Bjørkedal have been working at farming and boatbuilding since the Viking age.
Selection of location: From here.
Financing: From the gradual accumulation of tools and labor-intensive work.

Recent Projects

An 18-foot motor faering (6-h.p. Sabb diesel) cedar-and-copper-on-oak; a 14½-foot Bjørkedal faering; several 16-foot faerings; and a 24-foot cutter, Atlantic-white-cedar-on-white-oak, spars of Sitka spruce.

Open Statement

Perhaps I should explain the building process a little bit. Take the 16-footer; it has been evolving for over a thousand years. There seems to be nothing oversize,

One of Chip Stulen's elegant faerings.

nothing in the construction, that is not a necessary part of the whole. The stems are sawn to shape and then tapered in both cross and longitudinal sections, the latter being accomplished by roughing out with an axe and then fairing with a plane. I even use the axe for roughing out plank scarfs. [I have seen Chip and Paul Schweiss do this with great speed and extraordinarily fine results.—P.L.] The keel, stem, and stern are 1½ inches by 3½ inches, with the keel being somewhat rockered. The fineness of scantling on this particular model is possible due to the omission of the rabbet, the planks being beveled to fit the backbone. After the stems are scarfed and riveted to the keel, the assembly is plumbed on a jig and secured to a beam directly over the keel (right side up). As each strake is added, it is first clamped at its hood end and then to the preceding strake or keel. At the same time, shores are wedged between the top edge of the strake and the overhead beam, bending the plank out to the proper angle. This gives the hull its proper shape. At three predetermined stations, you check this angle with a batlodd, literally "boat plumb bob." This is basically a protractor with a plumb bob attached to its extra-long arm. The other factor that must be known for this moldless construction is the width of the strake at each point. It is lofting as you build, in 3-D, bending and shaping these planks to follow the points in space. [Paul Schweiss calls it "lofting in air."—P.L.] In just the same way, the spiling board is clamped to, and overlaps, the previous strake. It is bent outward to the proper angle and then scribed off the top edge of the preceding strake. After the new plank is fitted and secured, its top edge can be easily planed and faired by eye to its final shape—there being no molds in the way. As planking proceeds, many of the shores on the lower strakes can be removed.

*This photograph and the one opposite were taken in Paul Schweiss' shop (*see page 118*) almost a year before the interview with Chip Stulen. By sheer coincidence, the photographs are tailored to Chip's description, which only underscores the closeness of their styles and workmanship.*

Only five sawn frames are fitted after the faering is planked. Due to the resulting flexibility, Norwegians ask not how the faering rides in the seas, but rather how it "swims."

This system lends itself very well to modifications in the hull lines for rowing, sailing, row/sail, or even to accommodate a small diesel. It helps me to be much more in tune with the lines of the hull, and gives me insight into the particular shape and lay of each strake for the development of those lines. (See also *The Mariner's Catalog*, Volume 7.)

Projects in Store

An 8-foot round-bottomed pram of cedar and oak; a 12-foot rowing faering; and, tentatively, two others slightly larger, both for oar and sail.

Unusual Tools and Methods

Just the batlodd mentioned before, and the small axe. Oh, this plane might qualify, it's for rounding the outside edges of the planks.

Lumber and Hardware

Lumber quality is declining and the resource is *not* being properly managed. My basic attitude is one of striving for self-sufficiency—my own woodlot. It's merely a matter of access. Lumber I don't supply myself is basically a source of uneasiness. Hardware: I feel optimistic. As long as demand is there, supply will hold up. Witness the Skookum-type home industries.

Cooperatives

I think they'll work for buying lumber. I prefer to work alone, but cooperative shops for both professionals and amateurs can provide financial and *emotional* support.

The Market

Compared to the East and West Coasts, the revival is lagging behind, but it *is* [emphasis mine—P.L.] coming along. Wood boats are coming across as a new

Some of Paul Schweiss' tools, the same as those used by Chip Stulen. From the top: a Norwegian riveting hammer with holes for the rivets countersunk to fit the cupped rove Paul uses; the fairing hatchet made famous by the half-a-minute plank scarf; the batlodd; a riveting tool kit and Paul's flat-headed nippers (the blades can be removed for sharpening by loosening the screws just visible on their tops).

alternative to the umpteen-million glass hulls that people have seen and thought to themselves, "They are all the same."

The Labor Pool

Nationally, it is good and getting better; a revival of younger craftsmen. Locally, I am virtually alone as the only *professional* builder, so I can't compare.

Vocational Training

My only exposure is to Bath and Lubec [now Eastport]. One is a vocational institution, the other a living/learning experience. Neither is right for everybody, so I am positive about them within their respective purposes. I feel I had the ideal; one-on-one in a professional shop, surrounded by other professional shops. I would say Bath is the next best thing.

Modern and Traditional Design

Traditional.

Restorations and Replicas

I'd rather build a close replica of a fine piece than restore an original. That way I can learn all the steps of the original craftsman.

Time and Finish

As a craftsman, I like striving for the dead fit throughout a piece—perfection. There's a place for *both* high-finish work and good, honest, unfancy boats to fit the individual's pocketbook. I prefer the former, as it allows me the maximum opportunity for personal growth. The more you strive for a dead fit, the *faster* and more economical it becomes, as opposed to compromising from the beginning.

V. How to Use This Book

A YEAR ON THE ROAD

Traveling alone for most of a year in a Volkswagen bug convertible is not without its pleasures. A cheap, unobtrusive car (unlike the van, recreational vehicle, or camper), the bug allowed me the freedom of anonymity and surprise. It is so unlikely to be used as a roving home that people often assumed I was a local—at least until they saw my (rear only) license plate. The advantages of this are obvious. I didn't have the disadvantages inherent in driving into a backwoods shop in "a van like some of them weirdo hippies from California . . ." or in "a wreck-vac destructo-vehicle suitable only for tearing up the countryside." I didn't fit into a political category, or any category.

And the conditions under which I traveled helped to prove the seriousness of my endeavor. Only someone who was totally committed to such a project would put up with the inconveniences of sleeping, eating, working, even cooking out of a bug. "This guy's committed, all right. He ought to *be* committed—to an asylum."

In answering the usual questions about who I worked for, and what the survey was about, I intentionally tried to destroy any preconceptions people had. The first question usually thrown at me was: "Who do you work for—*National Fisherman, WoodenBoat,* or the government?" The second was: "For what school is this a thesis?" Traveling alone in a VW, the survey's unique purposes, my boatbuilding experience, my nondescript clothes, the fact that I'd never gone to college . . . all led people to accept me for what I was because they couldn't find a label that fit. Any connection to an organization or grant would have been a liability. I was free to travel and say what I liked, to be taken for who and what I was. My independence was my good-as-gold trump card. People opened up in incredible ways as a direct result of the respect it earned me. "You may be crazy . . . no, you are *undoubtedly* crazy. But I bet you're for real, and what a grand time you must be having! Stay over this evening and tell me about it." That was how one builder put it.

It was just that sort of reaction that made it possible to keep going. Total strangers offered a place to sleep, a hot shower, and so forth. It isn't enough that builders' housemates have to put up with their boat mania; they sometimes have to put up with unannounced guests. "Why didn't you let me know? He warned you *this morning* that he was a lifelong vegetarian and you couldn't have called? I ought to run your head through that old thickness planer." In return for these kindnesses and/or information about their boatbuilding, I paid them with a choice tip, exposure in the survey, an evening away from the television set in good conversation, or whatever seemed appropriate. The point is, I paid people back in unusual and affordable ways. I'm not sure I would have experienced anywhere near the same level of acceptance if I had done the survey in a conventional way.

I found the first names for the survey by going through two years of back issues of *WoodenBoat* and *National Fisherman*. In the Northwest, Bob Chapel of the Traditional Wooden Boat Society provided me with a list of members who were active as professionals or amateurs. That made it easy. On the Gulf Coast, I worked the grapevine. In Brownsville, Texas, I called on the marine hardware dealer and asked him whom he knew. When he came up blank, I asked him who *would* know. "Let's see noooowwww. Old so-and-so, he's a retired Navy man. You'll find him down at Mary's Coffee Shop—he almost lives there. There isn't much around here that he doesn't get the dope on. If he can't help you, nobody can." If a town seemed to be coming up blank, I'd ask what I would find farther up the coast.

I rarely knew where I would be more than 24 hours in advance. That had its advantages, too. I saw people, places, and things I might never have found the time for otherwise. For example, I fell into judging an incredibly creative pumpkin carving contest in which many of the contestants were art majors. I recall spending four or five hours one afternoon working my way back and forth within a 15-mile radius of Hansville, Washington, trying to find a newly relocated and reclusive builder. Everyone I talked with had heard of him, but nobody knew just where he lived. I was frustrated and angry at my research methods. I felt worse as I, and the day, faded. I never did find him, but as I drove down one last road I came upon the high and superstructure of a merchant vessel. It sat amid a collection of split-level, suburban houses overlooking Puget Sound. Right next door to the Joneses, so to speak, this white, well-tended home rose out of a gravel lawn. A life preserver hung at the ready on the observation deck's rail. Out front near the road, planted on a boxed-in

10-by-15-foot plot of grass, was the ship's anchor. At that moment, my only regret was that I had no film in my camera.

On some days I'd do as many as four interviews between dawn and dusk. On others, I'd do nothing but strike out. There was the time I asked for directions to reach "Harry's place." The old-timer I was speaking with started off on a long list of directions that ended, "When you get there, you'll see a cemetery on your left, and a dirt road just beyond. You take that road down about a hundred feet, turn left again and you'll find Harry and his place, such as it is, about six feet down." Of course, all that time I'd been scribbling furiously. Less funny but more common, I'd get to a shop only to hear, "Oh sure I build boats. I'm now in cold-molding. Oh yeah, it's a pain being 15 miles from town without a phone, but I like the quiet."

Even if Mr. Cold-Mold had had a phone, I probably wouldn't have called before going out. There were several advantages to arriving unannounced. Skeptical builders didn't have a chance to say automatically, "I'm too busy" to a disembodied voice. They had to say it to my face, in their shops, where it would be perfectly obvious how busy they were. If I called, they often seemed to spend my intervening travel time getting anxious (and forming preconceived ideas) about what I was up to. In person, it took less than three minutes for me to explain just that, and *then* if they were uninterested, I'd give them not the slightest hassle. In fact, the first 30 seconds were the crucial moments.

As I drove or walked up, I would have my radar going. Any clues were valuable. Anything anybody else had told me about the shop was compared to what I saw and heard. A large operation meant an older man, usually. What kind of car or truck was out front? Did the place look newly rearranged? Had it changed hands? Stepping through the door and/or into view was a moment suspended in time. The surprise and amazement that many visitors unfamiliar with boat shops show often counts against them. I made a concerted effort to be unfazed, unhurried, unassuming, and businesslike in my manner and appearance. I'd try to take in the whole shop in a quick glance, locate the builder, and then zero in.

A long pause usually helped to get things going on a respectful footing. There would be a firm handshake, my name, if possible a name of some other builder who sent greetings, all accompanied by a look in the eyes. The handshake, the tone of voice, and the eyes were all that really mattered. Some wanted to challenge me, to make me prove myself. If they were immediately curious about my project, I'd give them a quick sketch. On a good day, I could "sell" the interview in five minutes to the nastiest curmudgeon.

"What do you want, a job so you can build a boat to sail to Tahiti? No freeloaders here, so get out."

I'd noticed him looking at my (then) long hair, so I looked him in the eye and smiled. "No, I'm gonna *weave* one out of this stuff. Seriously, I want to do you and me a favor."

A tough night on the town has caught up with the shop mascot at Portsmouth, New Hampshire's Strawbery Banke museum.

"What's it gonna cost me?"

"Two minutes for me to explain and however long you wish to take with this questionnaire—two minutes to two hours. I can see you're busy; can you spare the first two minutes? Then if you want to put my project through the mill or tell me to get lost, I'll be only too happy to oblige."

He turned to his partner, "The guy's got spunk for a longhair. Ok, what's your business . . .?"

It was easy to tell if I was getting the here-comes-the-IRS-or-insurance-salesman look. I almost always met it head on and turned it into a joke: "Hi, I'm from the IRS and I've come [waving the little black notebook] to do an audit." Often the fact that I'd recognized their thoughts and turned them back broke the ice.

I don't wish to give the impression that reaching builders amounted to a sparring match. The reception was usually tremendous.

"This is quite the service you are doing here. Just let me send the clan to lunch. How many shops did you say? The West Coast, too? Oh yeah, the Gulf; we do tend to forget it. What's happening down there? Anything much? Say, you didn't meet a builder by the name of . . . when you were in . . .?"

Rule: the wooden boat world is so involved and interconnected that not a whisper is heard to which somebody doesn't take exception. If rumor doesn't get you, distortion will. I forgot this axiom one morning in Florida. I was gamming with some waterfront pundits when one allowed as how there wasn't a builder "anywhere, anyway, no-how who could hold a candle to" a certain famous southern Florida yacht builder. "Oh," I quipped, "I've seen as good, even bett . . ." and stopped too late. Silence. Then they started taking me down to size.

I worked around the questionnaire to fit the situation. Interviews took anywhere from 10 minutes to five hours. The 10-minute version was applied in situations where the builder would be very busy for the foreseeable future and unlikely to fill out the form if I left it with him. I would run through the categories of general information, facilities, and recent projects as quickly as possible and finish with two or three from the second page: the market, materials, and perhaps the open statement. Even with longer interviews, I made every attempt to let the builder get back to work. If I took photographs, I worked as quickly and as unobtrusively as possible. Hunching over a tripod on a 14-inch-wide scaffolding, making minute adjustments, while a yard hand carrying 25 pounds of oak waited to get by me, was not likely to endear me to him, or his boss.

I believe that there were two reasons for the generosity shown me by builders and their families. First, I was sensitive to their situations. Second, builders felt that with all the enthusiasm and hoopla about a revival, many enthusiasts had left reality—"there's a lag between them and the 20th century"—and I was tapping into that uneasiness directly, particularly with the questions on labor and the market. Here also was the reason why many saw themselves as separate from the mainstream enthusiast. Only one builder looked to the traditional boating public for activist help with *any* of the relevant issues. Yet there were ample indications from both builders and enthusiasts that the energy for, and commitment to, problem-solving were there.

The Traditional Small Craft Association has been gearing up to work on such problems and pleasures as governmental regulations and sponsoring small craft meets. There has been some talk of a national information center to coordinate and make available pertinent data. This last idea has fired many imaginations. Getting hooked up with lumber sources, for example, would be greatly facilitated by such a system. Work continues on these and other ideas, but they take time to set up. All face the usual funding and manpower shortages. And there are the myriad personal complications that would severely limit their effectiveness with certain low-level problems. I think the grapevine can go a long way toward filling these gaps. Take that single irreplaceable part that breaks or is lost. Boatbuilders (and boat people in general) are wonderful packrats. What they have salted away in their barns, basements, and lockers has to be seen to be believed. The longer they've been at it, the better. The grapevine can locate the best boatyards and backyards in which to begin the search. If the time for such meandering is not available, it can quickly locate the retired builder or amateur who could make the part, or at least make a pattern.

Almost every bit of information contained in this book came to me through the grapevine. It could easily provide 10 times as much data. I spoke of the nature of this network as omnipresent, and I use the term advisedly. The grapevine is just that: a huge, sprawling, unruly, many-branched tree through which you can invariably climb from here to there, if not always in a straight line. Yet, it will also surprise you with its directness. I was three weeks west of the Louisiana bayous when I heard from Dick Jagels, then of the Louisiana Cooperative Extension Service in Baton Rouge. Dick responded to a plea for information in *WoodenBoat.* We met and went south to see Francis Robichaux, the lumberman, who in turn provided me with the name of Gerard Ledet. Gerard proved invaluable in putting the Gulf Coast boatbuilding situation into perspective. The grapevine is virtually without beginning or end. We are confined only by the limits of our own willingness to pursue the information we need.

The grapevine is (to me) the perfect means to problem-solving, information gathering, and so forth, because it requires quality effort to make it work. The user must be responsible in the way he/she treats others, both in pursuing information and in the use of information received. Very simply, participants must give of themselves. Thus the grapevine has its own means of protecting itself from those who wish to be spoon-fed information, and who consequently don't value what they learn.

In the previous pages I have attempted to give some demonstration of the practical applications of the grapevine's operating principles.

1. The field is large, but not so big that its members can't be treated as unique individuals. Avoid stereotyping yourself and others. If you drive a phosphorescent Caddy, leave it down the block.
2. Set your own standards. Unless you have somebody smarter around, use your own judgment as to what is appropriate to the matter at hand. Turn on that radar.
3. Do your homework. Use the appropriate periodicals, books, individuals, etc., before bringing your project to a builder or *any* source. Libraries, trade publications, and government services are there to be used, often cheaply or free of charge. The Picketts' excellent fact sheets on West Coast lumber and air drying cost a whopping 40 cents in total. *The Mariner's Catalog, Volume 7,* lists 150 boat-related periodicals.
4. Consider the relevance of your query to the source beforehand. Is 200 board feet too much or too little for this builder or sawmill to sell to me? *Be specific.* I have heard the staffs of *WoodenBoat* and *National Fisherman* talk about people who write (or call) them saying, "I'd like to have whatever you've got available on plans for cruising boats between 30 and 50 feet."
5. No matter where you go, the builders are the best. On Beals Island, Maine, they build the best lobsterboats anywhere; the same is true of Mount

Desert Island. In the same vein, if you ask for advice, at least listen carefully. There's always more than one way.

> So I was telling this guy how we would replace his carlins, since he asked me about it, and he starts to contradict me! I don't mean he suggested this change or that, this guy was telling me I didn't know my business. Tell me, why'd he come here?

6. Be determined, even tenacious, in your pursuit of information, but remember that the nicest builder in the world is likely to turn you away with a grunt if he's framing up. Consider timing and remuneration. Builders are highly skilled, knowledgeable craftsmen; pay them in some way for that knowledge. They can always refuse, but at least it will be at their discretion.

7. A severe warning. If you follow these procedures, you are likely to find yourself heavily involved. I have rediscovered in the course of this project that you can always be more heavily involved than you are at present. You may be walking into a bottomless cavern if this book has held your interest this far. If you use the grapevine much, you are sure to find information gaps. One of these may interest you enough to try to make a business of filling it. If so, you have my support and sympathy; the bug you've been bitten by is probably incurable.

8. As amazing as boatbuilders are, they are also just people trying to do a job and get along. They don't want adulation, just consideration. Much of what I've said seems fundamental to life, not just boats and boat people. I spelled it out here because I was amazed at some of the insensitivity I encountered among otherwise brainy, nice individuals. On the coast of Maine, I was preceded (by about six months) by a couple of surveys connected with universities and such. The bad taste these left in the mouths of builders made my job much harder. If you know by reputation that your style is likely to rub a builder the wrong way, it seems fundamental (to me) to tone it down during a visit.

Speaking of approach and consideration, I'd like to go back to the early dissection of boat people and examine how they fit into the grapevine and problem-solving:

repairers
cold-molders
fishermen and fishermen-builders
itinerants
serious sailors
sailmakers
harbormasters
personnel of related organizations
retired builders
amateur builders
semipro builders
wooden boat owners
marine hardware dealers
marina foremen
museum personnel
apprentice builders

Ask an established marina foreman about working with governmental regulations. A marine hardware dealer should know the local builders (professional and amateur); a harbormaster will know the best owner-maintained boats. (I met a man who prepared himself for wooden boat ownership by talking to three experienced top-notch owners for a total of about 12 hours. He said it "saved his neck.") There is usually an obvious type whose expertise relates more or less directly to the problem at hand. "Personnel of related organizations" is an intentionally vague term. These can be the crews of Tall Ships or people at the Cruising Information Center.

The Cruising Information Center is a fine example of just how far the grapevine has gone.

> . . . incorporated in 1974 . . . . The major objective was to provide data for long cruises, foreign ports . . . long shore cruises.
>
> We frequently unearth obscure data that otherwise would never come to light. We try to keep abreast of political problems of concern to yachtsmen . . . where sensitive situations exist. Charges are based on the expense of running the non-profit operation.
>
> *Frederick Johnson, Director*

One more comment is relevant to the whole question of using sources and approach: inflexibility gets nowhere. The case of the itinerant builder/mechanic is illustrative. Boat people often picture the itinerant as a lazy, unreliable sort because he is not always "credit card normal" in his appearance or lifestyle. Above and beyond the fact that the itinerants I know work more hours for less pay than many others, they tie into the grapevine as an unparalleled source of information and assistance. No one can tell you what is going on in town faster than an itinerant, because it is his business to know.

FOR BUILDERS ONLY

Or, What do I get in return for putting up with all the raving boat nuts at my door?

If successful, this book should cause some increase in business for boatbuilders. The grapevine is advertised here, and the grapevine will carry their names. If readers make use of the grapevine, it will grow larger and more interconnected to include more builders in a comparatively short time. Still, it is unlikely that this book is going to improve their business *radically*.

A more balanced, informed, and aware clientele certainly can't do them any harm, and it may even have some small effect on the manners and attitudes of visitors. The only value in recognition is in increased business—understanding from the public can help with this. I don't expect that the marathon chats that are so common will be any fewer in number as a result of this book, but it is possible that builders can now exert a little more control over "chatters" during shop time. They can always threaten to beat disrupters over the head with this book . . . .

The philosophies of alternativists and capital-oriented shops are not as divergent as it would seem. I know of few builders in either camp who do not share some of the others' aspirations. Alternativists aren't anti-money any more than the others are against personal satisfaction. If the following ideas stem largely from the capitalist mode, it is because I believe that in some cases the pendulum has swung too far the other way.

The validity of reasonable and honest promotion—as opposed to all-out, degrading hype—has too often been learned through bankruptcy. When I began the survey, I thought, "I don't want to make money, just let me build boats . . . ." As the survey progressed, it became evident that this approach was inadequate. Many new shops were offering to lose their shirts for a chance to lay a keel. There is nothing wrong with this if you are financially and emotionally prepared for it. Few seemed to be. They drove themselves to open a shop any way they could, as soon as they could. If jobs didn't materialize quickly and consistently, two or three years brought the end, or at least a semipermanent switch to house carpentry. Marginal profit from good-selling underpriced craftsmanship, or poorly selling, overpriced, pretentious work has been evident in too many shops.

A man from the Internal Revenue Service enters a boat shop one afternoon requesting to see the builder's books. Eddie (not his real name) has to think about that one. He sits down and turns to his apprentice, "Hey, Jerry, what do you suppose we did with that board?"

"Board?" the revenue agent asks in confusion.

Jerry has begun to sort through the huge pile of scrap lumber they have amassed over the year. After a prolonged search, he turns back and says with a straight face, "I'm fairly certain we used that piece in the transom of the last boat."

Eddie turns back to the increasingly befuddled revenuer, "If you want to see them, you sure are welcome. I'll give you the name and address of the owner. He lives and keeps the boat just down the river. I'm sure he'd be only too happy to let you crawl under that transom and take a look. I do believe the figures are on the inside."

The young man leaves in a huff. He doesn't come back and he doesn't instigate an audit.

It's a good story that happens to be more or less true. (My thanks to Gordon Swift for permission to use it.) It also serves to point out that this time the builder was lucky—a reputation doesn't mean much to the IRS. An audit would probably have meant the end of the business, no matter how long it had been around.

It is nothing new that boatbuilders are terrible businessmen. What may be a surprise is that many are proud of the fact. I know of an instance where a builder was criticized because he made it a point to beef up his reputation by talking modestly, if often, about how many good boats he had built in a short time. What is it that makes a builder proud of the haphazardness of his business, or jealous of another who openly pushes his? I call it the badge-of-honor syndrome. In its extreme manifestation, builders wear their condition on their sleeve. It becomes part of the *proof* of their validity as a builder. In milder form, the syndrome is noticeable in such comments as, "I've been broke for years, but I'm happy," or "I don't like to demean my workmanship by hyping it." While being happy in one's work is the pinnacle of true success, it shouldn't be considered against the rules to do so *and* bring home a decent paycheck. For some, insurance, capital and liability are dirty words.

There is everything right with an alternative business except that, as a rule, it doesn't provide much working capital. And there are "life needs" to consider that do require substantial capital—catastrophic illness, old age, or simply a trip to Europe. There are no pension plans.

Of the hundreds of boat shops I've seen, the most likely to succeed are those willing to blend alternativism with the other factors necessary to a properly capitalized business. One semiprofessional with a high-paying job in another field put it this way: "I like the opera, which costs 22 bucks a show now, and I like my Volvo. Everything else I could do without, and *did* at one time." Metaphysically and metaphorically speaking, these builders have found a balance between canning their own food and carrying insurance. They attend all the boat festivals and boat shows, no matter how bored they feel, keep proper books, and run a businesslike operation.

How much the builder can take home out of the hourly rate is directly connected to just how fast the mind and body can deal with the everyday operations of the shop—from red tape to red oak. An ability to assess the situation and decide whether it makes more sense to pay somebody else to do the job is crucial. To balance this tendency toward high cash flow, builders make extraordinary efforts to learn to do as much as they can, as fast as they can.

Time vs. finish is perhaps the most important factor. We have a responsibility not to drive the price of traditional boats out of sight. Tiffany Cockrell has put his action where his words are. Speaking of the market's future, he said, "We have to watch out that we don't price ourselves out of the middle class." So saying, he showed me a well-built, handsome, 36-foot deadrise fishing boat that he was marketing for $26,000, ready to go. Thirty feet away, his crew was putting the extensive electronics in a new 52-foot sportfisherman. Though the two boats are a world and hundreds of thousands of dollars apart, the yard seems to have no difficulty in switching back and forth between these two distinct markets. Can a fine yacht builder afford to build a plain and simple boat? For Glebe Point Boat Company, the answer is "yes."

It seems silly to have to say it, but traditional small craft needn't be all varnish and bronze. With a price-and-maintenance-conscious public, this is all the more true. A light touch of spit-and-polish is really all that is needed to accentuate the aesthetic qualities of wood, and won't add discouraging amounts of labor. Only a wooden boat fanatic enjoys all those hours of preparation and protection. "Boats are for sailing, not scraping and sanding. If your hobby [or the owner-to-be's hobby] is boat maintenance, fine. If you want to go sailing, replace that varnish with paint." (Melbourne Smith)

Or, as Paul Glassen put it, "They are not monuments, just boats." Those who are looking forward to a return of working sail surely don't expect to see it happen in perfectionists' No Man's Land boats or coastal schooners with bright decks. It is (at least in part) the builder's responsibility to educate the prospective client and the boating public at large to this—an admittedly long-term process.

It could be pointed out that people don't walk into a car dealer's showroom and specify what kind of handles to put on the doors. Clients should pay not only for the additional cost in a part, but for some portion (if not all) of the builder's time spent getting, making, or modifying it. More and more builders are making it the owner's responsibility to locate obscure hardware. Like Bent Jesperson, they recommend sources and prices, while the owner does the legwork.

The boatbuilder is building something on which people's lives depend—he should charge accordingly. A neatly lettered sign could total the number of years the builder spent perfecting his skills and a simple line-by-line comparison of the cost of a particular craft at a doctor's rates, an auto mechanic's, etc.

In most highly skilled professions, people are paid well for dispensing their knowledge. It is routine for builders to spend shop and home hours consulting at no charge. Builders ought to be more businesslike. There is a reasonable medium somewhere between the present exploitation and: "Take two fungicides and a sealant and call me in the morning. That'll be $25."

I met one builder who dealt with the problem of talkative visitors by posting hours. A sign on his door reads:

> I talk shop from noon to one (when I'm here). Otherwise interrupt me for the most serious business only, or call me at home, evenings.

There is the well-known office joke, "Our rates are $17 an hour; if you watch, $26.50 an hour; if you comment, $34 an hour; if you help, $52.75 an hour." A visitor's proper response may be to bring coffee and doughnuts for the crew; it may actually be to pay a consultant's fee. I can't help thinking that this shouldn't sound anywhere near as revolutionary as it does.

The builder should post a list of boats he's built, with prices and photographs so that inquirers can not only see his work but have the opportunity to save him time and themselves money by picking a boat already lofted and familiar to the builder. For distant inquiries, a brochure is almost a must.

Regional differences in construction methods are often based upon special regional needs. But there are certainly some regional methods that could be more widely applied: for example, the western method of inside-and-out framing, the southern sprung and/or shapeless planking, and most particularly, the Scandinavian method of "lofting in air." Ray Speck of Sausalito, California, uses the British variation on this method in building his own designs. It is reasonable to assume that a conversion system from standard offsets and lines plans to this faster method could be developed. The benefits would be substantial. Some of the deeper deadrise hulls of the Chesapeake Bay and Deep South (and V-bottoms in general) have been neglected as cheaper and fully seaworthy possibilities for other areas.

I have heard it suggested that while the standards of excellence in construction and design are better than those in other fields, they have declined considerably from the days before the market's collapse. Jon Wilson of *WoodenBoat,* among others, has repeatedly called for more experimentation. Legitimate innovations in wood usage, both structural and chemical, are too rare. There is cold-molding, of course, but there is also room for more creative ideas in plank-on-frame construction. The professional must be constantly reviving the good designs and methods almost forgotten, and developing new ones to make wooden boatbuilding more feasible economically and more *enjoyable* for everyone.

More emphasis should be placed on organizing, which is considered by many to be a dirtier word than insurance. Individuality has been the last great bastion in the battle against fiberglass, boredom, and poverty. Now, however, there are issues requiring visible and concerted action. Yet it is doubtful that there would be much support for any organization that didn't choose its issues very carefully.

> Somebody ought to regulate the Coast Guard so they don't hurt themselves or anyone else. The Coast Guard may guard the coast, but who will guard us from the Coast Guard?
>
> *Paul Glassen*

> If the Kansas Coast Guard gets off our backs, we'll stand a chance.
>
> *Walter Simmons*

Winter storage awaits this Friendship sloop at Ralph Stanley's crowded and busy yard in Southwest Harbor, Maine.

While Paul and Walter would be the first to applaud the Coast Guard in its lifesaving and navigational responsibilities, they and others feel that discrimination against traditional watercraft is another matter. Coast Guard regulations geared toward the mass-produced boat and its users need to be rewritten to accommodate boats that do not fall within those criteria. This is only common sense.

> Regulations need to be changed, not loopholes exploited, because the next inspector may not let your shop slip by.
>
> *Gardner Grice*

It has been suggested by some private citizens that a certification system be established to approve boatbuilders. Some participants at the National Trust for Historic Preservation's 1978 conference spoke strongly in favor of this. From the builders' view (and mine), a good organization would work actively with the Coast Guard to show them the difficulties they are creating where few exist. On the other hand, the same organization would realize that builders are too diverse, and their circumstances too different, to fit into the rigid categories necessary to establish a certification system. I admit to being completely biased on this issue. The boats and the workmanship in them speak for themselves. The field is small enough so that a good builder is never out of work, and the con man doesn't last long at any job he lands. With the tightness of the field, he soon runs out of areas where his shenanigans aren't known. As long as individuals continue to get a decent product for the time, energy, and money spent, they can't complain. Irresponsible behavior is not in building a cheap boat, it is in the misleading pretension to the contrary. The libertarian cry goes up, "Let reputation police the field!" The average level of what is considered acceptable workmanship and materials is substantially higher than that found in the U.S. as a whole. By comparison, wooden boatbuilding is a model of responsible manufacturing. All this is not to deny that there is always room for improvement. Participants can decide on an issue-by-issue basis whether or not they wish to sacrifice a degree of the security of anonymity. Public access to waterways is a good case in point. I expect that another dozen years will see some major battles over this issue.

The grapevine, as presented here, could be the basis for organization on either a formal or informal basis—locally, regionally, or nationally. It is hoped that some ongoing dialog on the pros and cons of organization may be initiated here. It may even be that the Traditional Small Craft Association will come to fill this role. Speaking as a nonvoting member of its National Council, I can say we welcome input on this and other matters, particularly from members. Please join! Write to Membership Secretary, Traditional Small Craft Association, Post Office Box 350, Mystic, Connecticut 06355.

Those in the forefront of wooden boatbuilding have gone beyond wooden boat faddism, alternative lifestyles, or conservative backlash to a blend of these concepts. These people are not automatically trying to gross $50,000 a year, carry insurance, or follow Coast Guard regulations. They *are* making very sure that they understand and accept the ramifications of their decisions one way or the other. As the Coast Guard rules change, they update their assessment of them. When taking on a project with particular hazards (such as having the boat's owner helping in the shop), they are careful to get a waiver of responsibility in writing, so as not to increase their risks unnecessarily.

I know of only a couple of builders who will not go beyond the rudimentary preliminary talks with a potential customer until they have a deposit. Yet few people would expect an architect to draw up a conceptual floor plan without one. Builders often design whole boats and build models on the basis of some pretty skimpy correspondence. The deposit need not be large, perhaps in the tens of dollars, but it seems to do the trick. Not only does it weed out the dreamers, but the more serious inquirers seem to value the service accordingly. Some builders have said, "If you don't want to get into this sort of thing, don't go professional."

There are always special circumstances. The builder who lives on an island, operates a portable mill, and so forth, can throw much of this out the window, gross $10,000 a year, and bank a third of it. That is certainly his choice. Most people live farther from the basics of life and must generate proportionally more capital. Somewhere between a paranoiac obsession with goods and security and denying oneself all luxuries or desires lies a happy sanity.

I find more and more people are pursuing just that. It is as if wooden boatbuilding has gone beyond its rebirth to approach a coming of age.

LOOKING TO THE FUTURE

The combination of new blood and older diehards finding new focuses for their energy has resulted in the resurgence of interest in traditional watercraft. This resurgence is an expression of joy at the fact that wooden boats are not dead, as much simple celebration as advocacy for wooden boats. There are tens of thousands of interested and active wooden boat enthusiasts overflowing with free human energy. If you doubt the figures, look at the rapidly rising subscription levels of small craft societies and trade publications. But, as David Eastman rightly pointed out in the pilot issue of *The Small Boat Journal* in March 1979, the biggest-selling recreational boat is a trailerable fiberglass outboard—with sales of over 56,000 units per year.

Today's wooden boat builder is often attempting what has heretofore been impossible—making a living entirely from new construction. Ninety percent of the future traditional wooden boats will be fine craft built by part-time builders or amateurs. Of the remaining 10 percent, perhaps eight percent will be built by yards combining new construction with strong repair, hauling, and/or storage facilities. That leaves only two percent of the market for full-time, new-construction-only professionals. The number of shops out of this last group that generate better than what most Americans would call a subsistence level income is probably under 20. A long, hard row is ahead for builders who wish to join those few. These builders will continue to establish themselves by turning out as many good boats as they can realistically afford, while building up experience, speed, and so on, until they gradually find themselves "making it." I know several young people with this goal in mind. They grit their teeth and say that life begins anew at 50—the age at which they expect to be established.

The future of wooden boatbuilding for commercial use is in question—if only because the state of the American fisheries is so much in question. Some would say, "in such a mess." In the Southeast and Gulf, regulation, pollution, overfishing, and foreign competition all threaten the fisheries. In Maine, Ronald Rich said, "Inflation may get us, but as long as the fishermen are getting these good prices, we'll be able to keep busy." Yet, recent reports indicate that that state's lobster stocks are in trouble. Keeping up with the fisheries is a full-time occupation, but the *National Fisherman* and other publications can help those who wish to keep score.

The labor situation is improving. Builders are beginning to use their heads and such strategies as profit-sharing plans to hold good workers. Those headed

Above: *Dennis Holland has built this 122′ replica of the famed* Pilgrim, *Richard Henry Dana's vessel in* Two Years Before the Mast. *Smack in the middle of Costa Mesa, California, she's quite a shock to the eyes.* Below: *Dennis takes his ease in* Pilgrim*'s main cabin. Already he is talking about a true iron ship to follow* Pilgrim.

into the boatyards for work/training might ask for a written agreement between the "apprentice" and "master," wherein the builder agrees to teach XYZ of the related skills and techniques and the employee agrees to work for a specific period. Even if not legally binding or successfully negotiated, such an agreement could clear up differing expectations and/or help each party to keep his promise in the face of difficulties. We need not return to a rigid, indentured servitude; the agreement can be as flexible as the individuals feel is necessary.

Amateur builders provide additional support for the wooden boatbuilding industry:

> Increased amateur boatbuilding activity cultivates and spreads interest in, and appreciation of, boats, and can only result in more business for professionals. I once knew an old boatbuilder who complained that backyard builders were taking the bread out of his mouth. He was wholly mistaken. No one can appreciate the fine points of wooden boatbuilding, as well as the effort and skill required, better than the amateur who has built, or who has attempted to build, a boat. Backyard builders of small boats frequently turn to professionals to have a larger one built. And if they insist on good work, they are generally willing to pay the price.
>
> *John Gardner*

I can only add to that by saying that a new wave of family-operated shops may be developing in the children of amateurs.

Given a few more years, women may finally get the chance to break into the field in significant numbers. As the younger, hopefully less sexist, builders come into their own, they will be able to hire women. Right now, these builders aren't always paying themselves. The roots of prejudice against women around ships are deep. One theory espoused at my kitchen table by a (female) carpenter suggests that having a woman on board during long voyages constituted competition for the crew's love of the ship. Such a woman would supposedly awaken jealousy in the ship, which then took care of her (and the fickle crew) by foundering. That says nothing of the distractions caused by having any women aboard for the duration of a three-year whaling voyage. Whatever the reasons, when women break into yard crews today, they are employed as riggers or varnishers, but not carpenters. One woman I talked with said people have asked her incredulously, "You mean *you* work with power tools?"

In crowded summer harbors, marinas and repair facilities often have to keep boat owners waiting weeks for repairs. A small percentage of these jobs are relatively minor and constitute more trouble than profit for a high-overhead firm. Couldn't qualified itinerant repairers, semiprofessionals and amateurs, work out agreements to handle this kind of overflow on a referral basis? This arrangement could mean better money for the itinerant, less hassle for the yard, and savings in time and money for the boat owner.

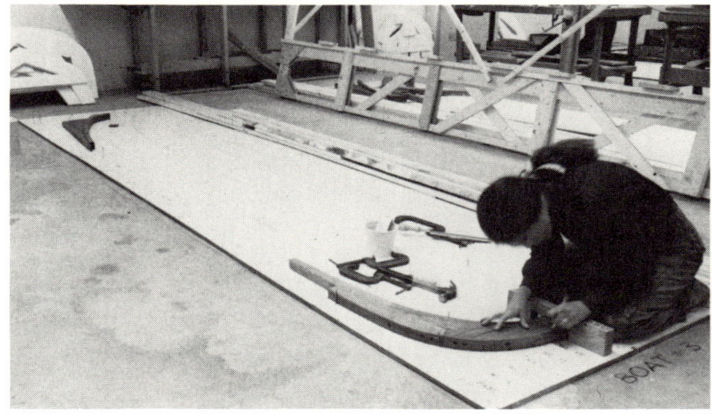

One of the first women to enroll in the boat-building course at the Washington County Vocational Technical Institute in Maine takes care in marking the rabbet for just one more Whitehall.

According to the builders, trainees, students, and schools have a clear mandate to bring romance vs. business into greater consideration. Closely tied to this is the appalling shortage of good boat carpenters in the boat maintenance/repair industry. Few newcomers are willing to work for somebody else, and this shows limited judgment. While Joe Rigger has to work in the rain, he is also at the movies while Joe Boss is at home doing books. Take your pick.

In hardware, there seem to be signs of improvement. Small businesses such as Flounder Bay Lumber and Skookum Fastenings, and buying coops such as Boatbuilders and Sailors of Costa Mesa, are beginning to gather widespread support. Skookum's 1978 sales were up 150 percent from 1977. There is an increasing number of small foundries specializing in boat-related piecework. Small-scale manufacturing of traditional hardware may someday become a reality. Already, builders are having casting blanks made of common fittings and carrying the items as a sideline. For hardware and tools, flea markets, junkyards, and scrapped boats are all fair sources. For some pieces, nonmarine hardware can be located and exploited. One builder used European brake lining rivets he got from an automotive supply house. To carry it one step further:

> I think the wooden boating world needs to get together on all kinds of things like insurance, collection of payment for work done, lumber and hardware purchasing, etc.
>
> *John Swain*

Opinion is sharply divided on the present lumber situation. I feel that declining quality will be a critical problem, regardless of quantity, on the Gulf, Southeastern, and North Atlantic Coasts. In the Northwest, the question is arguable—but it won't be arguable for long at the present logging rate. Regardless of which side you are on, there can be no question that high lumber prices are going to hurt all builders where it counts most.

In considering the lumber problem on a large scale, there are a number of questions.

1. Will laminations and/or preservatives make the use of lesser grades truly viable; and assuming so, how significant an effect will it have on the overall, long-term situation?

2. How can we deal with the problems of "availability" when the standards of what constitutes quality and availability are so diverse?

3. If we advocate the importation of woods from other countries, should we, and *how* should we, present a case for reforestation to the exporting nations?

Putting aside clear-cutting, the reseeding of hardwood forests into pulpwood tree farms and the planting of hemlock where Douglas fir once grew has the public hoodwinked. Advertising campaigns have dispelled concern for the nation's timber resources but ignore the entire question of the quality of harvestable timber.

It is some indication of the public's awareness that everyone has seen commercials promoting "the tree-growing company," but almost no one has heard of or understands RARE II.

RARE II is the acronym for the Second National Forest and National Grassland Roadless Area Review and Evaluation. A roadless area is one that does not yet show "significant marks of human development—roads, buildings, evidence of tree culture."* Still in progress at this writing, RARE II will determine the future use of some 1,920 areas totaling 65.7 million acres of public lands (an area about the size of Arizona). Review and evaluation will be made on the basis of major land forms, representation of ecosystems, presence of certain wildlife, distribution of wilderness area for better accessibility to the nation's population, the effect of wilderness and nonwilderness designations on timber resources, energy resources, mineral resources, recreational resources, and wildlife management.

While this sounds terribly thorough, RARE II is anything but. Though it professes great dedication to a "balance," the program has enough coincidental prejudices to raise serious doubts that any real balance can be achieved. For instance, the range of proposed alternatives covers both extremes *(all* areas to be designated wilderness, *all* areas to be designated nonwilderness), although by the Forest Service's own admission, ". . . most of the alternatives displayed suggest that most of the inventory be allocated for nonwilderness uses."** The Service goes on to say that the Review "is definitely not restricted to possible outcomes from these displayed alternatives." But it must also be pointed out that while one moderate wilderness-oriented alternative was added at the last minute under citizen pressure, this addition was not in the Draft Environmental Impact Statement that thousands of people used for review in preparing

---

*U.S.D.A. Forest Service pamphlet FS-320.

**John R. McGuire, Press Conference given by the Forest Service, June 15, 1978.

their comments. The Sierra Club's *National News Report* of June 1978 pointed out that many people ". . . will simply pick a favorite from among those [alternatives] presented, as though 'professional judgment' had determined these to be the reasonable, superior possibilities."

M. Rupert Cutler, RARE II's chief architect, said in *American Forests* in May 1978 that RARE II takes a "comprehensive, rather than piecemeal approach . . . that could keep most areas in limbo for years." Forest Service brochure FS-320 says that "RARE II is designed to help settle . . . debate as quickly as possible. You can help. However, a little background is necessary before we go into that." "A little background" is an understatement. The time allotted for public input in the first phase is 3½ months. The Environmental Impact Statement needed to formulate your personal recommendations runs over a hundred pages of complex jargon, charts, and graphs. That's just the national section. Specific objections and recommendations must be made on specific areas, for which you need the regional supplement covering the areas you wish to address. The process assumes a degree of public dedication and education far in excess of realistic standards.

All these points aside, Cutler called RARE II "a town meeting on a grand scale." In fact, we now know that during the first phase only 50,000 people and organizations responded. This seems like a small group for determining the future of some 300 million board feet of timber on 15 million acres, let alone for deciding the broader ecological questions. Critical forest industry needs have been pitted against conservationist ideals in a battle in which there is no room for those who aren't a part of some special-interest group, those who aren't ready to enter the fray on short notice, or those who still have a relatively open mind. Though the final disposition has not yet been made, the outlook is pretty grim.

Let us assume for the sake of argument that a balanced RARE II process has been achieved, and that proper forest management can significantly increase forest yield *and* quality of timber while preserving much of the ecological balance. As always, such programs would be extraordinarily expensive, particularly over the short term. When you consider that we are talking about the reseeding of many species that grow very slowly, it is easy to see why large numbers of boatbuilders had their doubts. Corporations don't plan hundred-year growth/profit cycles.

On the positive side, fast-growing hybrids destined for pulp and specially manufactured 2 x 4's can help the quality wood user by relieving some of the pressure on first-grade timber. (For more, see Dick Jagels' excellent articles in *WoodenBoat,* Nos. 24 and 25.) Tree farms and more selective milling operations may also help ease the demand. One of the chief problems has been that when growth is speeded up by hybridization, sapwood increases proportionately. Recent reports indicate some headway is being made in this area.

We have to take full advantage of what little clout we have. The commercial builders and fisheries, as economic powers, may be especially important. We (the enthusiasts) must have solid economic arguments as to why they (the professionals) should stick their necks out. Appeals based on "our great maritime heritage" will not move them. We need to define our goals with figures based on cost-per-thousand-board-feet; length, clearness, and quality of grain; and the energy (either as direct dollars or human effort) necessary to get this lumber stacked, cured, and ready for shop use.

This does not preclude small-scale solutions. Careful, selective logging of normally closed timberland by forest industry trainees could be arranged and the resulting material made available to museums, restoration projects, and other high-quality users.

For builders who cannot afford to own and operate a woodlot and/or who do not care to organize with others to do so, there's another way. Private landowners don't usually understand the value of selective cutting. Builders can demonstrate this by buying a landowner's trees and handling his land as if working on their own woodlot. Any extra timber cut could be sold at a profit to be split between the owner and the builder.

I recommend that boatbuilders intensify their cooperative efforts. The list of lumber sources in this book is pretty slim in light of the number of inquiries I made. If builders keep sources a secret, then those sources will have fewer and fewer reasons to supply boat lumber as pressure to do otherwise increases. Spreads the wealth around. If an operation threatens to close down due to insufficient demand, a pool of amateur and professional builders should take action, even if only to place one large final order. Better still would be for the group to guarantee the mill or logger annual orders, in hopes of reversing the decision to shut down. Builders can continue to split truckloads, the closest thing to a cooperative commonly seen. Where sources of lumber are hard to find, remember that the Department of Forestry in each state frequently publishes a list of even the smallest lumber mills.

The would-be professional boatbuilder might look into setting up a boat-lumber-oriented mill. It would probably be profitable, would help "the cause," could allow the individual to pursue building as a hobby, and would generally keep him/her heavily involved in "messing about with boats."

What about all those cheaper non-boat woods? There are many species that deserve more attention, particularly from people who build open, less rot-prone boats. Marvel Blix told me of building a boat of vulcanized local spruce! He even got it pressure-treated for nothing because the plant operators were interested in knowing how the spruce would react. After several decades of working on the Columbia River, the boat is still rot-free.

To ignore the lumber situation or to complain without doing anything is to stick one's proverbial head in the proverbial sand. It is to speak only of independence and long traditions (stand around the wharf and cuss like the fisherman) while organized lobbies and local, state, and federal authorities run roughshod. If they don't hear from you, you don't exist. The first step is to sensitize the issue. This means not falling in line with conservationists or loggers, but rather advocating a balance between recreational, conservationist, and economic forces. The prospects are admittedly poor, but it is one of the few areas where others in the general public are more or less on our side; witness some editorials in *Forest Industries* and Allan May's book, *A Voice in the Wilderness.*

In another area entirely, we have an immense human bank of knowledge being ignored and neglected. Virtually every town with a usable waterway had *at least* one boat shop. Just by asking the marine hardware dealer, harbormaster, or fisherman, one can locate the retired builders who ran them. In a few short years these sources will be gone, and we deserve the worst if we allow these experienced individuals to go untapped and unappreciated. We ought to keep them in active circulation—along with the information they have to share.

Skills preservation, efforts toward increasing good public access to the water, developing support industries, and so forth, deserve brainstorming. Without ideas there are no solutions. Let us get serious discussion and action underway. Whatever the issue, boatbuilders (or any other group) should not be expected to face it alone. Builders don't wish to have their shops filled with wildly cheering or patronizing boat nuts. Yet I think they would welcome considerate, active support, assessed on an issue-by-issue basis. In a sense, professional builders are the only full-time representatives of the wooden boat enthusiasts. They have taken on (knowingly or otherwise) much of the burden of an enormous maritime tradition. They deserve our recognition and assistance in carrying that load.

In a number of shops from Anacortes, Washington, to Oxford, Maryland, I saw this sign.

> We, the Willing, have been doing the impossible for the Ungrateful. We have done so much, with so little, for so long, we are now qualified to do anything with nothing.

A call for greater amateur involvement will not be welcomed by some builders. Similarly, purists will have a difficult time if they cannot bear the sight of, or assistance from, those who *consciously* choose a *well-built* trihedral hull. We come back to the question of standards of quality. This is the inescapable outcome of what has been presented.

It is my opinion that the importance of Quality, both as an issue and as a force for change, deserves much greater recognition and understanding. Without such an understanding, it is too easy to find in a busy schedule, apathy, or fear reasons for never acting. There is a fine line between patience and laziness.

In reflecting upon this call for inquiry into the Quality of our lives, it is appropriate to consider Robert Pirsig's classic book, *Zen and the Art of Motorcycle Maintenance, An Inquiry into Values.* It is too important to encapsulate here—I can only touch on a few of Pirsig's more salient points and strongly recommend that those who are interested in a broader perspective read this vital work.

To paraphrase Pirsig, the standards we call Quality, Excellence, Goodness, etc., are not standards we set but the continuing stimuli that our environment exerts upon us to create, order, "civilize," change, etc., the world in which we live—"All of it. Every last bit of it." "Art," for example, "is high-quality endeavor"—specifically, our attempt to represent the godhead or Quality, call it what you will. Quality is not defined by man; it is the inspirer of man. The importance of this can only be fully understood when we realize that by showing Quality to be not just a part of, but rather the origin of, the hierarchy, Pirsig was able to show a practical way

> . . . by which reason may be *expanded* to include elements that have previously been considered irrational. I think it is the overwhelming presence of these irrational elements crying for assimilation that creates the present bad quality, the chaotic, disconnected spirit of the twentieth century.

The expansion of reason to include the irrational, instinctive, and mystical elements of Quality is the core of the traditional watercraft revival. Professional boatbuilding and other crafts are no-nonsense lessons in turning these rational and irrational elements into useful action and quality goods. Perhaps the best "rational" definition is that craftsmanship or quality effort is the integration of the mind's finest intent with the senses' perceptions and the body's movements. In the work of the Masters of any craft we can literally see the near-perfection and unity of this process. Though "science" has not *yet* gathered the empirical data to prove this, it is no less plain that the mind of the Master is clearer, the workmanship tighter, and the speed faster than is "logically" possible. The sum is greater than its parts.

The importance of wooden boatbuilding in a society-wide context lies in the breadth and force of its appeal. Any field of endeavor will have some power, but only rarely do we find that symbol that appeals to almost the entire public. Only rarely do we find something that relates well to almost every level of understanding. Wooden boats are simply better than average vehicles for increasing sensitivity. The depth and diversity of skills required, the significant amount of time and effort involved in the simplest of projects, and the function and beauty of the craft, all combine to make wooden boatbuilding a broad avenue to the expansion of reason and the unity of quality work.

In a society where specialization is increasingly the rule, it is easy to lose sight of the interrelationship of *all* quality effort. Granted, the situations are unbelievably diverse and few problems have generally applicable solutions.

But this is all the more reason to ask: "What can I do *here?*" Small, intense catalysts for change can be very effective—this form of guerrilla warfare needn't be profitless, either. Lance Lee nailed it down:

> Wooden boats and good shops appear to us to be useful and needed statements for a nation exploring some of the most awful standards and sorriest integrity of product in history. We have here a gentle reminder of how things can be done—the means and methods—of the whole centuries-old tradition of the many skills that go to make up a good boat and boat shop.

A LAST NOTE

It has been my goal to present a practical view of traditional watercraft and put wooden boatbuilding in perspective. If this in turn opens the door to greater appreciation and *enjoyment,* so much the better. The information I have presented is subject to interpretation and is rapidly becoming out of date. Still, it is valid as a sampling and as an example of what can be done. If it generates more scientific, more detailed, more controlled regional studies, all the better.

As with most work for which there is no precedent, this survey has been a case of, "Now that it's over, I know how to do it." Those who may be considering a related project and/or have comments and criticisms are most welcome to write to me. I believe strongly in the adage, "Take the time to learn from others' mistakes—you won't live long enough to make them all yourself."

Index of Boatbuilders and Boat Shops

Appendix

BOOKS AND PERIODICALS

Chapelle, Howard I. *American Small Sailing Craft: Their Design, Development, and Construction.* New York: W.W. Norton & Co., 1951.

Chapelle, Howard I. *Boatbuilding: A Complete Handbook of Wooden Boat Construction.* New York: W.W. Norton & Co., 1941.

Muir, John. *How To Keep Your Volkswagen Alive: A Manual of Step By Step Procedures for the Compleat Idiot.* Santa Fe: John Muir Publications, 1969.

Pirsig, Robert M. *Zen and The Art of Motorcycle Maintenance: An Inquiry Into Values.* New York: William Morrow & Co., 1974.

Getchell, David R., Putz, George, and Spectre, Peter H., eds. *The Mariner's Catalog,* Volumes One through Seven. Camden, Maine: International Marine Publishing Co., 1973 through 1979.

Tazelaar, James, ed. *The Articulate Sailor.* Tuckahoe, N.Y.: John de Graff, 1973.

Sears, Leslie R., Jr., et al., *The Future of Pleasure Boating: A Report to the Industry.* Cambridge, Mass.: Boating Associates, 1960.

Lines & Offsets: Journal of the Traditional Wooden Boat Society. Box 10190, Bainbridge Island, Wa. 98110. Published irregularly, but often.

National Fisherman. Journal Publications, 21 Elm Street, Camden, Me. 04843. Published monthly.

The Professional Waterman. B & G Investments, Box 142, St. Leonard, Md. 20685. Published monthly.

The Small Boat Journal. Camden, Me. 04843. Published bimonthly.

The Telltale Compass. 18418 S. Old River Drive, Lake Oswego, Or. 97034. Published monthly.

WoodenBoat. WoodenBoat Publications, Box 78, Brooklin, Me. 04616. Published bimonthly.

The Ash Breeze. Newsletter of the Traditional Small Craft Association, Box 350, Mystic, Ct. 06355. Published quarterly.

MARITIME MUSEUMS

Twenty-four maritime museums worth visiting, and two educationally oriented boatbuilding programs not detailed earlier.

The Adirondack Museum
Blue Mountain Lake, NY 12812
(518) 352-7311

Bath Marine Museum
(including the Apprenticeshop).
See Maine Maritime Museum

Calvert Marine Museum
Solomons, MD 20688
(301) 326-3719

The Center for Wooden Boats
2770 Westlake Avenue North
Seattle, WA 98109
(206) 283-9166

Chandler's Wharf
2 Ann Street
Wilmington, NC 28401

Chesapeake Bay Maritime Museum
St. Michaels, MD 21663
(301) 745-2916

Columbia River Maritime Museum
16th & Exchange Streets
Astoria, OR 97103
(503) 325-2323

Down Jersey Marine Historical Society
Box 1031
Delran, NJ 08075

East Hampton Historical Society
Bluff Road
Amagansett, NY 11930
(516) 267-6544

Hampton Mariners Museum
Charles McNeill, Curator
120 Turner Street
Beaufort, NC 28516
(919) 728-7317

Hart Nautical Museum
William A. Baker, Director
55 Massachusetts Avenue
Cambridge, MA 02139
(617) 253-5942
(Tuesday, Thursday)

Herreshoff Marine Museum
18 Burnside Street
Bristol, RI 02809
(401) 253-6660

Mackinac Maritime Park
Mackinaw City, MI 49701
(616) 436-5563

Maine Maritime Museum
963 Washington Street
Bath, ME 04530
(207) 443-6311

The Mariners Museum
Newport News, VA 23606
(804) 595-0368

Mystic Seaport Museum
Mystic, CT 06355
(203) 536-2631

National Maritime Museum
at San Francisco
Hyde Street Pier
San Francisco, CA 94109
(415) 556-6345

Peabody Museum of Salem
& The Cruising Information Center
161 Essex Street
Salem, MA 01970
(617) 745-9500

Penobscot Marine Museum
Searsport, ME 04974
(207) 548-6634

Smithsonian Institution
Nautical Museum
Washington, DC 20560
(202) 381-6277

South Street Seaport Museum
16 Fulton Street
New York, NY 10038
(212) 766-9020

Strawbery Banke Boat Shop
Ed McClave, Builder
Strawbery Banke Museum
Portsmouth, NH 03801

Suffolk Marine Museum
West Sayville, NY 11796
(516) 567-1733

Thousand Islands Shipyard Museum
Clayton, NY 13524
(315) 686-4104

Whaling Museum
18 Johnny Cake Hill
New Bedford, MA 02740
(617) 997-0046

New England Apprentice Cooperative
Old Head of Bay Road
Buzzards Bay, MA 02532
(617) 759-3650

Washington County Vocational
Technical Institute
Marine Vocational Center
Eastport, ME 04631
(207) 853-2518

LUMBER AND HARDWARE SUPPLIERS

The following lists of lumber and hardware suppliers are by no means complete or representative. Many builders who were willing to divulge names were intentionally inaccurate with addresses, particularly for sawyers and small logging firms. As a result, the information here is quite serviceable, but there may be some inaccuracies. Remember that since few builders will tell a stranger (such as yours truly) who his best suppliers are, you may well have better luck doing your own research on a local level.

Lumber

Allen & Allen
1621 North Comal
San Antonio, TX 78201
(512) 733-9191

All Woods-Schroeder Inc.
5401 Lawndale
Houston, TX 77023
(713) 921-6131

Blackstock Lumber
545 Elliot West
Seattle, WA 98119
(206) 284-1313

Brady Lumber Co.
1910 Fairview East
Seattle, WA 98102
(206) 329-6200

Brooks Mills Edgewood Tree Farm
East Holden, ME 04429
(207) 843-5531

Century Hardwood
8022 South 212
Kent, WA 98031
(206) 682-2710

M.L. Condon Co., Inc.
260 Ferris Avenue
White Plains, NY 10603
(914) 946-4111

Dalziel Box & Boat Lumber
2800 Bridge Street
Victoria, B.C., Canada
(604) 384-1422

Dean Hardwoods Inc.
3701 Elm Avenue
Portsmouth, VA 23704

J. Delano, Sawyer
157 Cross Road
North Dartmouth, MA 02747
(617) 994-8752

Disdero Lumber Co.
1504 Southeast Woodward
Portland, OR 97202
(503) 235-8383

John Donaldson
Dresden, ME 04342
(207) 737-2709

Dorchester Lumber Co.
Linkwood, MD 21835
(301) 228-1575

East Teak Trading Co.
5207 Lake Washington
Boulevard Northeast
Kirkland, WA 98033
(206) 827-3039

Emerson Hardwood Co.
2279 Northwest Front Avenue
Portland, OR 97209
(503) 227-6414

Evergreen Lumber Co.
9654 Southeast State Highway 160
Port Orchard, WA 98366
(206) 682-1664

F & K Lumber Corporation
Route 1
Callao, VA 22435
(804) 529-6522

Forsythe Lumber
255 Bay Shore Boulevard
San Francisco, CA 94124
(415) 282-0151

Fowler Lumber
1262 North Commercial
Aransas Pass, TX 78336
(512) 758-5345

Frost Hardwood Lumber
347 West Market
San Diego, CA 92101
(714) 233-7224

Fyfe-Smith Co.
424 Drake
Vancouver, B.C., Canada
(604) 683-5621

General Hardwoods
1420 Port of Tacoma Road
Tacoma, WA 98421

Gueydon Lumber Co.
4300 Airline Highway
Metairie, LA 70001
(504) 833-2828

Norman Guidoboni
Willow Lane
Wiscasset, ME 04578
(207) 882-5275

Handloggers Hardwood Lumber
1702 Bridgeway
Sausalito, CA 94965
(415) 332-0506

The Harbor Sales Co., Inc.
1401 Russel Street
Baltimore, MD 21230
(301) 727-0106

Hardwoods Inc.
760 Northwest 72nd Street
Miami, FL 33150
(305) 836-3381

Hardwoods Inc.
751 North Northlake Way
Seattle, WA 98103
(206) 632-1384

R.W. Heaps
3819 West 30th
Vancouver, B.C., Canada
(604) 228-1015

J.E. Higgins Lumber Co.
101 Barneveld Avenue
San Francisco, CA 94124
(415) 824-8744

J.E. Higgins Lumber Co.
600 Dagget Avenue
Union City, CA 94587

M.M. Hinton
Route 2
Heathsville, VA 22473
(804) 580-7110

Holt & Bugbee Co.
1600 Shawsheen
Tewksbury, MA 01876
(617) 242-0230

Hunt Brothers
Main Street
Damariscotta, ME 04543
(207) 563-3181

Hunteley's Lumber
Harkers Island, NC 28531
(919) 728-3111

Johnson Logging Co.
Longwood
Easton, MD 21601
(301) 261-2964 or 822-5476

Johnson Lumber Co.
South Mills, NC 27976
(919) 771-2480

Kiever-Willard Lumber Co.
11-13 Graf Road
Newburyport, MA 01950
(617) 462-7193

Liberty Lumber
Hosford, FL 32334
(904) 379-8675

Logan Lumber Co.
301 North Rome Avenue
Tampa, FL 33610

Lumber Sales Warehouse Inc.
9310 Northwest 36th Avenue
Miami, FL 33147
(305) 836-1221

Jim Maharun, Sawyer
Grand Ronde, OR 97347
(503) 879-5254

Mariner Lumber
Church Road
Brunswick, ME 04011
(207) 729-3901

McEwen Lumber Co.
36th Street & Columbus Drive
Tampa, FL 33610

Joe Melvin Lumber Co.
251 West Wilkes
Milton, FL 32570

John Morse
Star Route 3
Bath, ME 04530
(207) 443-3948

New England Wood Buying Cooperative
271 Western Avenue
Lynn, MA 01904
(617) 581-7264

Oriole Lumber Ltd.
7181 Woodbine Avenue
Markham, Ont., Canada
(416) 495-6242

Pacific Hardwoods Sales Co.
1918 Park Street
Alameda, CA 94501
(415) 521-4702

Palmer & Parker Co.
910 East Street
Tewksbury, MA 01876
(617) 729-5550

Paxton Lumber Co.
2900 Bryan Avenue
Fort Worth, TX 76104
(817) 492-2228

Penberthy Lumber Co.
5800 South Boyle Avenue
Los Angeles, CA 90058
(213) 583-4511

Picketts Flounder Bay Boat Shop
& Lumber Sales
Third & 'O' Streets
Anacortes, WA 98221
(206) 293-2369

Pineo Lumber
Columbia Falls, ME 04623
(207) 483-2377

Powell & McClellan Lumber Co.
3200 Lafayette Boulevard
Norfolk, VA 23509
(804) 855-4752

F. Scott Jay & Co., Inc.
Box 146
8174 Ritchie Highway
Pasadena, MD 21122
(301) 544-1122

Sheldon Lumber Co.
Toano, VA 23168
(804) 564-3311

Alton Smith
Blue Hill, ME 04614
(207) 374-5344

Spar Lumber
1325 Harbor Avenue
Long Beach, CA 90813
(213) 775-1541

Spicer's Inc.
Church Creek, MD 21622
(301) 397-3131

Swift Lumber Co.
Atmore, AL 36502
(205) 368-2138

Fred Tebb & Sons
1906 Marc
Tacoma, WA 98421
(206) 272-4107

James Thompson
Box 85
Hopkinton, RI 02833

R.D. Tucker
Box 101
Langlois, OR 97450

Umphlett Lumber Co.
Box 547
Monck's Corner, SC 29461
(803) 899-3781

Van Arsdale-Harris Lumber
& Supply Co.
595 Tunnel Avenue
Brisbane, CA 94005
(415) 467-8711

Robert Walls
Blue Hill, ME 04614
(207) 374-2442

L. Warninick & Son
32 Louise Street
St. Augustine, FL 32084
(904) 829-6422

C.D. White & Son
Hertford, NC 27944
(919) 426-7872 or 426-7637

White Brothers
4801 Tidewater Avenue
Oakland, CA 94601

ZuWallick Lumber Mill
ZuWallick Lane
Branford, CT 06405
(203) 488-3821

Hardware

Alaska Copper & Brass Co.
3223 Sixth South
Seattle, WA 98101
(206) 623-5800

Anchorage Marine
295 Harbor Drive
Sausalito, CA 94965
(415) 332-2320

Balboa Marine Hardware Co., Inc.
2700B West Coast Highway
Newport Beach, CA 92663
(714) 548-3407

Beacon Supply
701 South Peters
New Orleans, LA
(504) 523-1043

C.E. Beckman Co.
11-35 Commercial Street
New Bedford, MA 02740
(617) 994-9674

James Bliss Marine
82 Sommer Street
Boston, MA
(617) 482-1668

Boatbuilders & Sailors
Box 2445
Costa Mesa, CA 92626

Briggs Marine Products
U.S. Distributor
Sterling Hardware, Marine Division
1605 East Kalamazoo Street
Lansing, MI 48912
(517) 482-6237

Buck-Algonquin
Second Street & Columbia Avenue
Philadelphia, PA 19122

Clendenin Brothers
4301 Erdman Avenue
Baltimore, MD 21213
(fastenings)

Conklin Brass and Copper
322 West 23rd Street
New York, NY 10011

Conover Woodcraft Specialties
18125 Madison Road
Parkman, OH 44080
(tools)

East End Supply Co.
203 Front Street
Greenport, NY 11944

C.G. Edwards Co., Inc.
272 Dorchester Avenue
Boston, MA 02127
(617) 268-4111

The Flood Co.
Hudson, OH 44236
(Deks Olje)

Doc Freeman's
999 Northlake Way
Seattle, WA 98009
(206) 633-1500

Freeport Marine Supply
47 West Merrick Road
Freeport, NY 11520

Glenn-Mar Marine Supply
6870 142nd Avenue North
Largo, FL 33540

Gundy Bilmack Marine Supply, Ltd.
969 Powell
Vancouver, B.C., Canada
(604) 255-3511

J.S. Haft Co.
8925 North Tennyson Drive
Milwaukee, WI 53217
(414) 352-7551

Hardie's Wagner Marine Supply
2739 Earhart Boulevard
New Orleans, LA 70113
(504) 522-2331

Harris Co.
188 Commercial Street
Portland, ME 04101
(207) 775-5601

Kettenburg Marine
2810 Carleton
San Diego, CA 92106
(714) 224-8211

Kirby Paint Co.
163 Mount Vernon Street
New Bedford, MA 02740
(617) 997-9008

Kolstrand Supply Co.
4714 Ballard Northwest
Seattle, WA 98107
(206) 789-1500

Lewis Marine
220 Southwest 32nd Street
Fort Lauderdale, FL 33310
(305) 523-4371

Majestic Fasteners
Box 193
Morris Plains, NJ 07950
(201) 386-1616

Malkin & Pinton
325 East Fifth
Vancouver, B.C., Canada
(604) 879-4211

Manhattan Marine
116 Chambers Street
New York, NY 10007

Manhattan Tool Manufacturing Co.
38 Van Buren Street
Newark, NJ 07105
(forged tools)

Manset Hardware
New County Road
Rockland, ME 04841
(207) 596-6464

McClean Brothers Inc.
7142 Furnace Branch Road
Baltimore, MD
(301) 761-9200

Minney's Ship Chandlery
2537 West Coast Highway
Newport Beach, CA 92663

Edgar Murray Supply Co., Inc.
901 Howard Avenue
New Orleans, LA 70140
(504) 524-0481

National Builders Hardware
1215 Southeast Eighth
Portland, OR 97214
(tools also)

Norfolk Marine Distributing Co.
1340 Azalea Garden Road
Norfolk, VA 23502
(804) 853-7658

C.S. Osborne Co.
125 Jersey Street
Harrison, NJ 07029
(tools)

Peck Clamp & Tool Co.
1170 Broadway
New York, NY 10001

Pettit Paint Co., Inc.
Rockaway, NJ 07866
or, San Leandro, CA 94577

Pitalos Hardware & Boat Supply
200 Cedar Street
Biloxi, MS 39530
(601) 432-0381

Rostand Manufacturing Co.
33 Railroad Avenue
Milford, CT 06460
(203) 876-2547

Grant Sarver, Tool-maker
3030 17th West
Seattle, WA 98119
(206) 743-4780

Seattle Marine & Fishing Supply Co.
2121 West Commodore Way
Seattle, WA 98199
(206) 285-5010

Seattle Ship Supply Co.
Fishermen's Terminal
Seattle, WA 98119
(206) 283-7000

Skookum Fastenings
805 Sixth Street
Anacortes, WA 98221
(206) 293-7469
(copper nails)

South Marine Supply
2894 Palm Beach Boulevard
Fort Myers, FL 33901

Standard Fastenings, Inc.
2 Pequod Road
Fairhaven, MA 02719
(617) 993-1791

Strawbery Banke, Inc.
Box 300
Portsmouth, NH 03801
(copper nails)

Svein Madson, Ltd.
705 Northeast Northlake Way
Seattle, WA 98105
(206) 632-7726

Tampa Marine Supply Co., Inc.
202 North 13th
Tampa, FL 33602
(813) 229-2734

Tremont Nail Co.
Box 111
Wareham, MA 02571
(617) 295-0038

Western Marine Supply Co., Ltd.
528 Powell
Vancouver, B.C., Canada
(604) 253-7721

Wetzler Clamp Co.
43-17 11th Street
Long Island City, NY 11101
(516) 784-2874

Whitehead Marine
5978 Peachtree Road Northeast
Atlanta, GA 30341
(404) 451-8181

W.H. Whiting Co.
6701 Moravia Park Drive
Baltimore, MD 21237
(301) 488-3200